SHADES OF NOIR

SHADES OF NOIR

A Reader

Edited by

JOAN COPJEC

VERSO

London · New York

To Michael

First published by Verso 1993
© Verso 1993
Individual chapters © individual contributors
Second impression 1995
Third impression 1996

Photographic stills from: *The Maltese Falcon*: courtesy of La Cinémathèque Française; *Phantom Lady*, *Double Indemnity*, *Dark Passage*: all courtesy of Photofest; *Blue Velvet*: courtesy of *Movie Star News*; *Deep Cover*, *Boyz N the Hood*, *A Rage in Harlem*, *Juice*: all courtesy of *Black Film Review*.

Verso
UK: 6 Meard Street, London W1V 3HR
USA: 180 Varick Street, New York, NY 10014–4606

Verso is the imprint of New Left Books

ISBN 0–86091–460–7
ISBN 0–86091–625–1 (pbk)

British Library Cataloguing in Publication Data
A catalogue record for this book is available from the British Library

Library of Congress Cataloguing-in-Publication Data
A catalogue record for this book is available from the Library of Congress

Typeset by York House Typographic Ltd, London W13
Printed in Great Britain by The Bath Press

CONTENTS

v

CONTENTS

INTRODUCTION

Joan Copjec

After the only witness to his innocence plunges to her death, Vincent Parry (Humphrey Bogart), the escaped prisoner of Delmer Daves's 1947 film *Dark Passage*, no longer stands any chance of exonerating himself of the murder charges on which he was convicted. His only remaining option is to flee the scene and then the country, to continue to try to elude the police as he has throughout the film. Looking about frantically for a way out, he spots a door leading to the roof and quickly decides to take it. Where to go from there? Again, only one option presents itself: the fire escape that runs down the side of the building. In four successive shots from varying angles, the camera remains trained on him; we watch as he climbs down the entire façade of the building, step by step, landing by landing. At each shot change we half expect the camera to cut away to the police as they make their way toward this scene of the crime; but it does not. Parry's escape is not paralleled by a police chase. The effect is somewhat odd. Against the static and monotonous building façade, Parry, the sole moving object in the frame, is more than visible, he is fully exposed. But to whom?

Not to the police, of course, since the narrative point is that Parry escapes detection by them. But if the shots of him descending the fire escape had been intercut with shots of the police, his visibility would have indicated that even if he is not now visible, even if for this moment at least he has successfully avoided detection, in another moment, perhaps the next, he might be caught. The parallel or alternating montage that is so often used to create sequences of cinematic suspense works by inserting pursuer and pursued into a structure that makes our reading of each radically dependent on our reading of the other. Suspense is produced to the extent that the structure manages to suspend psychology; that is: to the extent that what we know of the characters and abilities of pursuer and pursued is superseded by the technical assumption that the next image has the power to reverse all our expectations and render any psychological profile of the characters irrelevant.

A similar structure of suspense supports the novels and short stories of classical detective fiction, not through alternating images, but through the central relation between the detective and his criminal adversary. Whether or not an arch criminal ever enters the space of representation (usually he does not), the supposition of his existence is necessary to this fiction, whose initial premiss is that the detective's knowledge is forcefully challenged not by some physical conundrum, but by an act of deception – that is, by another subject, or 'mastermind'. As in the alternating syntagm, here, too, psychology is suspended by a structure that invalidates it. Even as the 'psychological-realist', or 'character' novel was coming into its own, detective fiction emerged to contest its conviction that narrative action was best coaxed out of psychological portraits. In the 'whodunits', such portraits are never fully drawn; the category 'deception' destroys their possibility. Once the clues that litter the scenes begin to be taken as attempts to mislead the detective, they no longer betray the criminal who left them there and we can no longer read them as details of a portrait.

Despite the common designation 'logic and deduction', these novels and short stories arrive at their conclusions through paths that are only apparently deductive. When anything can mean its opposite, we are no longer able to proceed from assured principles. Thus the detective cannot and does not solve the crime by drawing from his observations a continuous sequence of arguments, each supported by the one before and supporting the one that follows. Instead, the investigation moves forward in fits and starts, through reversals and false solutions in which the detective must show or appear to show his hand in order to get the criminal to show his. At each step the detective's knowledge is placed at risk, and at each step some aspect of the situation, not previously known, actualizes itself. The world of classical detective fiction always materializes in bits and pieces, it never appears as a fully constituted world, visible in the simultaneity of its parts, except at the end – and retroactively. This is because detective fiction takes place in a dialecticized space, constituted by messages that acquire meaning only when and where they are received.

This dialecticized or oscillating structure is absent from *Dark Passage*, and not only from the scene where Parry escapes from Madge's apartment. As Parry jumps to the ground and rushes out into the street to board a trolley car, the camera continues to keep him fully in view. The absence of an answering look is now marked not only by the continued refusal of a reverse shot, but additionally by the disturbing depopulation of the field we are given to see. The street and the trolley car are inexplicably empty. Our disquiet continues throughout the bus sequence that follows. Narratively this sequence is set up for suspense: the bus will not leave until two more tickets are sold. We are therefore led to expect a tense countdown as the selling of the tickets is measured against the arrival of the police. But this is not what we get. The sequence is cut to disperse rather than to build suspense. A policeman does arrive, nonclimactically, at the station and, as we watch the four other passengers board the bus one by one, we wonder if Parry will make it on before he is spotted. As the last of the other passengers walks toward her seat, the camera pans slightly forward to reveal Parry, *already seated*. Not only does his sudden appearance here not answer to the diegetic look of the police, it also fails to respond to the extradiegetic look of the spectator; that is, Parry's appearance neither meets nor surprises our expectations, it simply disregards them. To whom, then, is Parry visible?

It can be argued that he is visible to no one; not articulated within a dialecticized structure, his visibility is *for no other subject*. If he is seen, nevertheless, it is by something more 'rigid' than a subject, something incapable of being deceived, the way a subject is deceived. But if the dialectic of desire – hence suspense – and the possibility of deceit are both eliminated from the world of *Dark Passage*, then we have not only left the world of detective fiction far behind, we have also left behind many of the common-places of *film noir* criticism. As an example of *film noir*, the film would be described by this criticism as a dark sort of 'thriller', filled with deceptions, false leads and sudden reversals. Would we deny these basic descriptions of the genre? Yes. What is taken for deception is, in fact, something much more sinister: the emergence of a split between power and those whom power subjects such that the very world of these subjects appears incomprehensible to them. The world no longer unfolds in nonsimultaneous parts, as in detective fiction; in *film noir* it breaks up into inconsistent and always alien fragments. As a consequence of this, nothing can remain hidden in the *noir* universe only to become visible in a future moment. The *noir* hero is embarrassed by a visibility that he carries around like an excess body for which he can find no proper place. Already encumbered by his own overexposed being, the *noir* hero has no desire to seek his being through another. The links of intersubjectivity, invisible yet essential to detective fiction, are here dissolved. A different kind of struggle with a different, unyielding adversary remains.

You will not find in these essays a point-by-point consensus about what constitutes *film noir*. While some of the essays seem to find support in the arguments of others, contrary claims are also sometimes advanced. Each essay takes up the issue from a different perspective. What unites all the essays, however, is a strong sense of the importance of the genre and of the necessity of retheorizing it. This agreement is prompted by two major factors. The first is the re-emergence of *film noir* in recent years. Once thought to be historically limited to the years immediately preceding and following World War Two, *film noir* now appears, fifty years after the first films were produced, to be a much less local phenomenon. We are obliged to ask, then, what is the significance of *noir*'s return in the sometimes lazy, sometimes inventive, occasionally obsessive (think of Wade Williams's painstakingly accurate remake of *Detour* [1992]) reworkings of the classic films; or of its merging with sci-fi and horror in films such as *Blade Runner* (Ridley Scott, 1982), *Angel Heart* (Alan Parker, 1987), *Terminator 2* (James Cameron, 1990)? And what is the significance of novels, such as Walter Mosley's *Devil in a Blue Dress* (1990), by black writers, or films by new black directors – *Straight Out of Brooklyn* (Matty Rich, 1991), *Boyz N the Hood* (John Singleton, 1991), *A Rage in Harlem* (Bill Duke, 1991), for example – where a non-nostalgic focus on real situations dramatized in the present employs methods that we know as *noir*? These questions necessarily send us back to the original films of the genre and reopen an investigation no one ever considered closed. The second factor urging a retheorization of *film noir* is the uneasy sense that we never adequately defined it in the first place. This unease is not new, but has bothered criticism of *film noir* from the beginning. Even the fundamental question regarding the status of *film noir* – is it a genre or not, does it exist as a coherent body of films or not? – remains, in many critics' minds, unsettled.

This question of genre – how is it that we can take a series of different texts as examples of one and the same textual category? – is not, of course, peculiar to *film noir*. Doubts about the existence of the category itself or about whether or not an individual text belongs to it fuel the critical discourse surrounding all genres. Within *film noir* criticism, however, these doubts nag more persistently than usual, and cannot be simply accounted for by the fact that the term *film noir* was not of Hollywood's devising and thus does not have the sanction of intention on its side. The persistence of questions of genre has also and primarily to do with the fact that *film noir* is often viewed as a political critique of American society, as a warning about the disastrous social issue of a felt mutation in the structures of power. If criticism exhibits more than an ordinary wariness with respect to this category of film, we must suppose that it fears being duped about a message whose import goes well beyond criticism's more narrowly defined professional concerns.

And yet the problems of film theorists are in some significant ways no different from those that beleaguer political theorists; in each case, in thrall to positivist fictions, analysis keeps running aground in the course of endless battles over sterile definitions. In this light, the following statement made by Claude Lefort and directed toward political theorists contains a lesson from which film criticism can benefit as well:

> The space called society cannot in itself be conceived as a system of relations, no matter how complex we imagine that system to be. On the contrary, it is its overall schema, the particular mode of its institution that makes it possible to conceptualize . . . the articulation of its dimensions, and the relations established within it between classes, groups and individuals, between practices, beliefs and representations. If we fail to grasp this primordial reference to the mode of the institution of the social, to generative principles or to an overall schema governing both the temporal and spatial configuration of society, we lapse into a positivist fiction; we inevitably adopt the notion of a pre-social society, and posit as elements aspects that can only be grasped on the basis of an experience that is already social.[1]

Film theory still operates largely according to the structuralist assumption Lefort indicts. We conceive a film as a system of relations among 'minimal significant units', at various levels of articulation. Anyone familiar with the study of *film noir*, for example, can recite a list of such units or elements thought to be necessary to the definition of the genre: a femme fatale, a morally compromised detective, an urban setting, voice-over narration, convoluted plot structure, chiaroscuro lighting, skewed framing, and so on. Lefort's implied argument that any such list, along with a specification of the relations among its individual terms, is bound to remain a mere heap of traits with no real coherency is borne out by the continued suspicion regarding the very status of *film noir*. We pay too much attention to the established terms and their relations without ever inquiring into the principle by which they are established. In virtue of what, we neglect to ask, is this particular organization instituted?

Sometimes, however, we are fooled into believing that we have asked this question, and are able to answer it, by making reference to a film's historic context. *Film noir* criticism correlates filmic elements with historical 'sources' – World War Two, an increase in crime, mounting paranoia regarding the working woman's place in society, and so on – thinking that it has thereby located the 'generative principle' of the films. But this reference to external sources in no way resolves the question of the internal logic of the films; the question is merely deferred. Raymond Borde and Étienne Chaumeton, authors of the first (1955) book-length study of *film noir*, acknoweldge this point even as they examine what they take to be the sources of the films. After discussing the rising incidence of crime during the period of the production of *films noirs*, they comment:

> The question remains: why did crime suddenly assume such importance in Hollywood productions during these last ten years? For the existence of a phenomenon does not itself explain its artistic exploitation: artists and the public could misrecognize it, intentionally reject it, or consider it unaesthetic. Why were American spectators so sensible to films of violence and murder?[2]

Unfortunately, Borde and Chaumeton quickly cover over the very profundity of their question by bemoaning the unavailability of empirical studies to answer it; but, too late: a question has been posed that no empirical study can ever answer. For however exhaustively we search, we will never be able to find in the structures of a film or of a society the principle in accordance with which these structures become intelligible. This principle can only be discovered by an investigation of another order.

Beginning with the analysis above of one scene from *Dark Passage*, this collection is aimed at seizing *film noir* from the perspective of the old unanswered question of the genre's 'absent cause', that is, of a principle that does not appear in the field of its effects. Whether by challenging certain fundamental assumptions regarding the nature of *film noir*, or by speculating on the workings of its absent cause, the essays that follow are concerted in their efforts to affirm or deny this second-order principle of *film noir*. For all the charm and all the appropriateness of its hard-boiled style, the French film historian Georges Sadoul's description of *film noir* as a 'nightmare narrated by a drunk' will no longer suffice. We now want to know why we have become sensible to these nightmares and why these drunks submit to the frustrations of their incomprehension.

NOTES

1. Claude Lefort, *Democracy and Political Theory* (Minneapolis: University of Minnesota Press, 1988), pp. 217–18.

2. Raymond Borde and Étienne Chaumeton, *Panorama du film noir amércain* (Paris: Flammarion, 1955), p. 32.

FILM NOIR ON THE EDGE OF DOOM*

Marc Vernet

As it has come down to us through the decades, it is an object of beauty, one of the last remaining to us in this domain, situated as it is between neo-realism and the New Wave, after which rounded objects like these will no longer be made. It is an object of beauty because Humphrey Bogart and Lauren Bacall are to be found there, because it is neatly contained in a perfect decade (1945–55), because it is simultaneously defined by its matter (black and white) and by its content (the crime story), because it is strange (see its relation to German expressionism and to psychoanalysis), because one cannot but love it (in contrast to its companion-objects, it is the only one that makes a place for affect and that functions as both a rallying cry and a point of exclusion), because it assures the triumph of European artists even as it presents American actors, because it is a severe critique of faceless capitalism, because it prolongs the reading of detective novels while feeding comparatism, because there is always an unknown film to be added to the list, because the stories it tells are both shocking and sentimental, because it is a great example of cooperation – the Americans made it and then the French invented it – and because a book can be made of all these reasons, in which one would finally have the feeling of having it all. On the whole, *film noir* is like a Harley-Davidson: you know right away what it is, the object being only the synecdoche of a continent, a history and a civilization, or more precisely of their representation for non-natives.

At least it is an object of beauty as long as one restricts oneself, without looking more closely, to the classics and to the presumed knowledge of one's predecessors. A first, slightly disquieting remark: speaking about *film noir* consists, from the beginning, in being installed in repetition, in taking up the unanalysed discourse of those predecessors, with pre-established definitions (*film noir* is a cinephilic ready-made) that are impossible to criticize (who has seen and studied all the films listed by Silver and Ward, Foster Hirsch or Robert Ottoson?).[1] *Film noir* is, then, an affair of heirs disinclined to look too closely at their inheritance, who take pleasure in regularly putting back into circulation topoi like the femme fatale, the shining pavement of the deserted street,[2] unexpected violence, the private detective . . . Doubtless there is something true there, but what that truth relates to remains a question: American society, the world history of cinema (German expressionism, French poetic realism and Italian neo-realism),[3] the directors, the actors, the spectators? Complacent repetition is more or less general,[4] rare being those who venture to say that *film noir* has no clothes: Paul Schrader, James Damico, Paul Kerr and occasionally Foster Hirsch[5] have had courage to cry out in the desert that the classical list of criteria defining *film noir* is totally heterogeneous and without any foundation but a rhetorical one. Moreover they cry out in vain, for it does not in the least disturb the publication of learned books on *film noir* in which one always finds the same arguments of which Paul Kerr has drawn up a highly amusing, bric-à-brac list. Some of these arguments are even to be found in the founding book by Borde and Chaumeton:[6] this book has not been superseded since 1955 because it cannot be so long as the uncriticized list of heterogeneous criteria upon which it was built is retained.[7] Its successors have only lengthened the list of films to be included, adding photographs and more extensive technical documentation: a look at these works' general presentations shows that the argumentation has remained fundamentally the same, without innovation. It is only in a few articles, here and there, that renewed arguments can be seen to appear (role of B-film production and post-war technique for Paul Kerr, a distinction between two periods for Paul Schrader, a definition of a basic plot structure for James Damico). Schrader's and Damico's essays have the additional interest of emphasizing the importance in *film noir* of the sentimental plot structure, of the melodramatic weight of the spectator's appreciation of this sort of film:[8] let us recall that, by those in charge of publicity at the time of its release, *Gilda* and films like it were presented as 'romantic melodrama'.[9]

One of the most striking points about the critical discourse on *film noir* is that the starting dates of the films are no more challenged than are the other criteria of definition, even by those (Paul Kerr for example) who contest the latter. Certainly they

The Big Gamble (Fred Noble, RKO, 1931)

are stretched back a bit (to 1941 for the father, *The Maltese Falcon*,[10] or even 1940 if *Stranger on the Third Floor* is recalled) and forward a bit (to 1958 if *Touch of Evil* is to be included). A few ancestors such as *Scarface* or *Marked Woman* (on account of the final shot and of Bogart) can be found, but the charm of the genre must be respected and no one goes any further back than these few forerunners. My purpose here is to show that this way of breaking up time has no real validity whatsoever. 1945 marks the end of World War Two, which is not a cinematographic event, and 1955 marks either the appearance of the book by Borde and Chaumeton or the year that the RKO studio sold its stock of films to television, events that are totally incommensurable with the historical weight of the first date. To put it another way, what is completely strange in discourse on *film noir* is that the more elements of definition are advanced, the more objections and counter-examples are raised, the more precision is desired, the fuzzier the results become; the closer the object is approached, the more diluted it becomes. The result is that the energy deployed passes entirely into refuting or circumventing objections and not into searching for a more solid foundation. The cause of this situation seems to me to be a triple lack, historical, aesthetic, and theoretical: a historical lack concerning the American production of the detective film and the appearance in France of the notion of *film noir*; an aesthetic lack concerning the image and *mise en scène* (film stock and lighting, but also composition of the image and stock scenes); finally, a theoretical lack concerning the plot structure and characters of these detective fictions, including those found in the detective novel.

THE CIRCUMSTANCES OF *FILM NOIR*'S FRENCH INVENTION

In fact, discourse on or around *film noir* is always and necessarily a discourse of consolidation (I could even say, of consolation) that allows us to forget what the founders Borde and Chaumeton had none the less taken the trouble to pinpoint with a great deal of intellectual honesty. The notion of *film noir*, for them, was meaningful only for French spectators cut off from the American cinema during the war years and discovering in Paris during the summer of 1946, under the impetus of the Blum–Byrnes accords,[11] a few detective films that would form the core of the genre. From 1946 to 1955, the critical work on *film noir* is effectively that of consolidation intended to justify the first impression, this initial astonishment that leads to the discovery in the post-war American cinema, coming from a nation whose military power and economic well-being were so striking, of films with an appearance of poverty in which the optimistic and moral lesson could not always be easily discerned by non-natives. The dates that have been agreed upon are thus ones that concern French critical reception and not American production.

What is forgotten in the wake of this is the French climate that allows *film noir* to be erected as an historical object. The French have a paradoxical image of the United States: on the one hand, it permitted victory in the struggle against Nazism and offers the image of a people whose standard of living is sharply superior to that of the French, who until at least 1955 were caught in an economy of scarcity inherited from the war and even from the pre-war period. But, on the other hand, the United States is an imperialist menace that threatens to impose upon France values and a culture that are not its own: if the Americans are superior and even saviours in the military and economic domains, they are judged to be inferior and dangerous in the domain of culture, for they threaten to replace red wine with whiskey, Marcel Proust with the dime detective novel, and 'Le Temps des cerises' with jazz. In this climate, the position of the Communist Party is particularly interesting, at a time when it commands 25 per cent of the vote, that is, when it is in equal measure with the Gaullists the party of the Resistance, and when it plays a considerable cultural role through intellectuals. It is ferociously opposed to everything American, and things will obviously get progressively worse after 1950, but at the same time it cannot but emphasize everything in American production that bears witness to the faultiness of capitalism. The tone is neither tender nor light. Thus the film historian Georges Sadoul could write the following in the 28 January 1954 issue of *Les Lettres françaises*, on the controversy over *Le Blé en herbe*:[12]

> The French branches of the Legion of Decency are pursuing in Paris the same goals as their American patrons: to demonstrate that the moral fibre of French cinema is disintegrating, in order to replace on our screens the loves of Phil and Vinca with the fetishism of black kid gloves, the flagellations, the disturbed perversions of a whore and a homosexual that the Hollywood Code of Decency guarantees in *Gilda*.

Sadoul equally attacks for their Americanism the existentialists, believers in psychoanalysis, and everything having to do with Saint-Germain-des-Prés.[13] The position of the Communist Party, in the name of a French identity that it advances all the more strongly to the extent that it participates in the Cold War, is paradoxical: while wanting to shine the spotlight, even in American films, on the signs of the unhealthy character of capitalism, it helps to give greater value to these same films, notably by indicating that they are a critique of the American system.

Film noir then comes to occupy a bizarre position: it can be the rallying cry of those who do not want to be caught up in the Communist Party and the moralism with which it was associated after the war,[14] as it can be the love-object of those who want to hate the United States but love its cinema. By affirming that *film noir* is a harsh critique of American capitalism, by explaining the importance of European directors and cinematographers,[15] by emphasizing the membership of Dashiell Hammett, presented as the father of the hard-boiled novel and thus of the genre, in the American Communist Party, film critics (that is, those cinephiles to whom writing is necessary) gave themselves the means to justify a love that was forbidden – whether it was the war (the impossibility of seeing the films), the Communist Party (whether one was a member or an opponent of it), or the supporters of a morality of hardship (often the same), if not all three, that forbade it. Finally, the invention of a new genre, at a few years' distance from the New Wave, is one way among others for a generation coming onto the labour market, forgetful or ignorant of pre-war production, to force recognition of its own signature. *Film noir* thus finds itself to be literally (but also in all senses of the term) a critical object: invented by French criticism, it allows one to love the United States while criticizing it, or more exactly to criticize it in order to be able to love it, in a relation that is not without connection with, on the one hand, the conflicts inherent in the Oedipal relation and, on the other (by the split that such an attitude implies), a fetishistic economy.

This much having been said, it should still not be forgotten that, if French criticism finds an advantage in inventing *film noir*, Anglo-American criticism, by taking up without any contestation its basic arguments, gives American cinema a cultural label and a critical force validated by Europe, all the while sparing itself the labour of historical research that would have to be all the more fastidious in that it would put into question, as it would for the Europeans, the love-object. This valorizing and unexamined adoption can also be found in the way that, even in Anglo-American feminist discourse, another French expression, 'femme fatale',[16] is taken up, an expression that is to the American detective film what Chanel No. 5 is to Marilyn Monroe.

I would here like to concentrate on only two arguments: that connecting *film noir* with expressionism and that linking it to the hard-boiled novel, which, between the two of them, have the advantage of seeming to cover the totality of the field: expressionism the image and the hard-boiled novel the fiction.

THE ARGUMENT OVER EXPRESSIONISM

We will not interrogate this strange coupling associating Germany and the United States at the end of the war, even though we have already noted the contradiction that exists in putting expressionism together with the realism of the décors or situations that supposedly define *film noir*. The argument according to which expressionism was part of the baggage brought along with them by emigrés holds up for no more than an instant once a bit of attention is paid to it. A good number of the directors and cinematographers in question have origins that have nothing to do with Germany or even Austria, and a good number of the directors and cinematographers of German or related origin who are often invoked have nothing in common with expressionism.[17] What is more, emigrés fleeing Nazism did not wait for 1939 to escape Hitler: they fled beginning in 1933, a fact that once again opens up the gap between their arrival and the advent of *film noir*. Finally, the historico-aesthetical argument disappears behind a very simple fact: from the start, Hollywood has always attracted and welcomed emigrés, among them Germans. It has been less frequently noted that the notion of expressionism itself, in the German domain alone, has served to prove everything and its opposite, and that the fashion for it is more a matter of the 1960s, following the appearance of Lotte Eisner's book *The Haunted Screen*, than it is of the 1920s.[18]

Expressionism is officially convoked in the name of the strong opposition between black and white (the coal-like aspect of the image) – an opposition which is valid not only in terms of light contrasts but also in terms of the relation between the expanse of dark areas and the scarcity of strongly lit areas – in the name of the disproportionate shadows accompanying the characters, and in the name of the oblique lines that dominate the composition (the famous impossible camera angles of *film noir*). Before any further examination of these ideas, it must be emphasized that this idea of expressionism is often supported, in both articles and books, by photographs of the set or even publicity photographs without any relation to the set, photographs which may very well not correspond to any image in the actual film. It often happened that the publicity department or the set photographer would reorganize and relight the *mise en scène* of an action or of an actor, adding a gigantic or strongly marked shadow to increase the dramatic effect, to visualize in a single image the idea of menacing mystery. It is also true that such photographs often constituted the only iconographical material available to anyone not in a position to make photographs directly from a print of the film.

As far as the films themselves are concerned, two facts cannot escape notice: first, the

'expressionist' image is relatively rare in the period 1941–45 (it is represented only by a few isolated scenes in an otherwise 'normally' lit film) and, second, it can also be found, and at least as frequently, in the films of the preceding decades. What is more, it is even rarer in *film noir* than is usually thought, for it is often confused with the décor, notably real exteriors. The latter appear infrequently in the 1940s before 1948, and when they do it is most frequently for daytime scenes, as in the final car chase of *High Sierra* (Raoul Walsh, 1941), or for scenes shot in day-for-night: the opposite of what is usually meant by 'expressionist' as far as lighting is concerned. In the case of real daytime décors, the 'expressionism' consists in the monumental aspect, crushing, isolating or imprisoning the human figure. The monument can be a building, a deserted spot or even a stairway, the last of which allows space and light to be played on simultaneously. After 1948, as we will see shortly, what had previously belonged to the plot structure passed into the representation, in the form of a monument, of a monumental space or landscape. On the whole

One year after the release in Germany of *M* (Lang), Edward G. Robinson in a final trial scene pleads, like Peter Lorre, that his crimes were directed by an uncontrollable force. (*Two Seconds*, Melvy LeRoy, RKO, 1932)

it is only after 1950 that night lighting and real urban exteriors came to be associated again.

'Expressionist' lighting thus is at first used in the studio (for interiors and for fictive exteriors) or in exteriors but without any visible buildings (only the characters are lit in the night). It can take many forms, among which two kinds of consistency can be found: consistency of situation and consistency of technique. The situation is that of the moonless night, with a few typical scenes like interrogations, nocturnal apartment visits and paybacks for interiors, tailings and chases for exteriors. From a technical point of view, here I can mention only the placing of light sources. 'Expressionist' lighting is placed low on the set (often on a horizontal axis), sets off a dark space in the upper part of the frame (absence of sun or moon), is partial (it lights only a part of the space and of the human figure) and apparently monodirectional. Placed to the side of the camera, it isolates the human figure in white against a black background. Placed opposite it, it isolates a silhouette against a white background. Laterally, it creates a delineation of the silhouette by maintaining zones of shadow upon it, as if only Appelles's touch had been left.[19] Three other traits can be determined. First of all, this lighting is characterized by the absence or weakness of fill lighting: the light seems to come from only one side, and it creates dense, saturated shadows. Moreover it is often these shadows, however small they may be, that indicate – that are sufficient to indicate – the nocturnal aspect of the scene, which can in the rest of the image be laterally lit *a giorno*, so to speak, in a simple but violent fashion.[20] Next, and in a seemingly paradoxical way, there is a constant attempt to diegeticize this light as a function of the situation (night) and of the light sources (streetlights, lamps), although the light is also exhibited, since the spectator's attention is drawn by its violence, its apparent rarity and the deformations it provokes. But this exhibition is diegeticized in its turn, since the light can be what pursues and threatens the character (it is a persecutory force).

Are these techniques, in 1955, 1945, or 1940, new to American cinema? Absolutely not. Beginning in at least 1915, the team formed by Cecil B. De Mille and Alvin Wickoff seems to take up some of the experiments carried out by the team of Griffith and Bitzer (see in particular the last shot of their 1909 film *A Drunkard's Reformation*), and develop them in a fairly systematic manner.[21] The campfire (*Carmen*, 1915) and fireplace (*The Golden Chance*, 1915) which light only a restricted circle, and from the side, are of course to be found, but so too is the sordid street corner (the first shot of *Kindling*, 1915). Here it is still only a matter of isolated, often very short shots, but the dramatic exploitation of such techniques is immediately followed by long scenes of nocturnal apartment visits during which a flashlight dances on the darkened walls (*The*

Golden Chance), or by sudden changes of lighting created by the turning on or off of lamps, or (the example is better known) in the most dramatic moments of *The Cheat*. In *The Heart of Nora Flynn* (1916), a number of scenes are involved: a car driving into the heart of the night, with only its headlights and the part of the road they illuminate visible, a room lit and then plunged into darkness, a final confrontation in a totally black garden, the only light coming laterally from a window. Thus several topoi emerge that can be found again and again: the secret, nocturnal apartment visit, the violent confrontation, and the car chase. Thus are constituted clichés that will recur throughout the history of American cinema. For example, in *The Big Gamble* (1931), Fred Noble shoots a '*noir*' interior scene for a dramatic card game and a remarkable chase between a train and two cars, using a real exterior at night, with light sources placed on the lower side of the street and on a mobile platform accompanying the camera during its tracking movements. In 1933, in films as little '*noir*' as *Lady for a Day* (Frank Capra) or *Footlight Parade* (Lloyd Bacon), tracking shots can be found using real streets, in the middle of the night, with the only light coming from shop windows, signs, streetlights and car headlights.[22]

The first thing that must be recognized is that, first of all, the expressionism at work here was present in the United States and in Russia from at least 1915, if not in Denmark from 1911 or France from 1913, and that, moreover, a certain continuity exists through the 1920s and 1930s, but with the use of real night-time exteriors suffering a massive disappearance after 1934.[23] The second thing that must be recognized is that '*noir*' lighting also owes its perpetuation to the gothic film, whose ambiance and décor (an old house or mansion without electricity) allows effects of darkness to be played upon. Thus, before singing the (deserved) praises of Val Lewton and Jacques Tourneur at the beginning of the 1940s (see *Cat People*, 1942), it would be necessary to recognize, after the role of Alvin Wyckoff in the 1910s, that of Tod Browning in the 1920s, notably with respect to the films he made with Lon Chaney,[24] as well as the influence of Lee Garmes (notably for his work in *Shanghai Express* [von Sternberg, 1932], or in *City Streets* [Rouben Mamoulian, 1931]). We should in fact recall that the cinematographers used in *films noirs* are not callow youths seeking to impose a new style: on the contrary, they are usually veterans who got their start in the 1910s and 20s. Tony Gaudio (*High Sierra*) began working in 1911, John F. Seitz (*The Big Clock, Double Indemnity, This Gun for Hire*) in 1916, Sol Polito (*Sorry, Wrong Number*) in 1918, Musuraca (*Stranger on the Third Floor, Out of the Past* and *Where Danger Lives*) in 1923, Joseph LaShelle (*Laura, Fallen Angel, Where the Sidewalk Ends*) in 1925, John Alton (*The Big Combo, He Walked by Night, The People Against O'Hara, The Crooked Way*), in 1928.[25]

In order to account for the aesthetics of *film noir*, Paul Kerr advances the hypothesis that production was trying to align itself with the technical norms of television in order to facilitate the sale of films to the medium then spreading through American households. I am unaware of any verification or attestation of this thesis, but one can add to it one that is internal to the cinematographic institution. The years following World War Two are not only the years of the development of television and of the break-up of the studio system as a result of the government's anti-trust suit against Hollywood, they are also the years of rapid expansion of colour filming.[26] For those films that continued to be shot in black and white, it was necessary to find, with respect to the colour film, both a diegetic justification (types of films whose action 'normally' involves numerous night scenes were shot in black and white) and an aesthetic supplement that would allow the films to hold up their end of a comparison with colour films and differentiate them from pre-war black and white production, in which competition with colour was not yet fully established for production as a whole.

What is important to us here is that the American cinema had, ever since the

A typical scene since 1915: the night-time search of an apartment. (*The Big Gamble*, Fred Noble, 1931)

Another typical scene, at least since 1931: the car chase and the train, but here in real exteriors. (*The Big Gamble*, Fred Noble, 1931)

1910s, a long and important tradition of 'noir' lighting, whether in gothic or detective films, or simply in order to give greater pathos to scenes set at night.[27] In order to account for this tradition and to cease torturing the chronology, it would be sufficient to envisage Hollywood cinema as both submitting to evolution (the appearance and development of colour production, for example) and possessing a technical know-how that is not as quickly renewed as one would like to believe. Hollywood production, in fact, for anyone willing to study a certain kind of film in depth, shows a great deal of consistency, running the gamut from typical scenes (the night-time apartment visit, the car chase . . .) to the overall organization of the script.[28]. This having been said, one still should not think of the *noir* style simply as an opposition to colour, for the renewal of the highly contrasted black and white image could very well be in part a result of experiments with colour. For example, it is well known that *Gone with the Wind* repeatedly uses foregrounded black silhouettes of unlit persons or objects, set off against a coloured background, thus putting back into play an interest in black and white figures within the heart of colour itself.

THE LITERARY ARGUMENT:
THE HARD-BOILED SCHOOL OF FICTION

If the reference to expressionism as explanation of the aesthetic quality of *film noir* does not hold up under examination, the same is true for the explanation of the narrative and emotional quality of the story by reference to the hard-boiled school of detective

The femme fatale, as she will never be shown in the 1940s and 1950s: in the detective's bed.
(*The Maltese Falcon*, Roy del Ruth, Warner Bros, 1931)

fiction. Here too we find a chronological gap between the artistic source and its being put into action: at least ten years between Dashiell Hammett's first novels and the 'first *film noir*', which, as if by chance, would be Huston's version of Hammett's *The Maltese Falcon* (1941).[29] The usual retort to recalling the existence of such a large gap is that during the 1930s the public was too affected by the Depression to be able to bear seeing the hard realities of existence recalled too strongly, and that it was necessary to wait for the post-war economic recovery in order finally to be able to make sinister films.[30] This line of defence is no sooner adopted than it must be abandoned, for it does nothing to explain why hard-boiled novels were written nor why they met with such success at the very moment that the public was supposedly fleeing this kind of story. All the more so in that adaptations of them are not lacking during the 1930s, beginning with *The Maltese Falcon*, the rights to which were purchased by Warner Brothers before its serial publication was even finished.[31] The adaptations of hard-boiled novels made during the 1930s have thus been occulted (for reasons we will have to consider shortly), just as other detective films that could easily enter into the frame of the definition of *film noir* have been. Why is the first version of *The Glass Key*, directed in 1935 by Frank Tuttle, not given the status of *film noir*, when the novel is by Hammett and the action fits all the criteria of the *film noir*? In what way is the first adaptation of Chandler's *The High Window*, directed by Herbert I. Leeds in 1942 under the title *Time to Kill*, unworthy of being taken into account? Why could not the first version of Chandler's *Farewell, My Lovely*, also directed in 1942 under the title *The Falcon Takes Over* by Irving Reis, be part of the set? What is more, one finds throughout the 1930s crime films whose hero is a private detective, about which there is nothing that allows us to differentiate them from what are ordinarily taken to be *films noirs*. Thus, the argument concerning the hard-boiled novel, as it is usually envisaged in the frame of traditional explanations of *film noir*, inevitably gives rise to a series of difficulties: (1) the creation of a gap of more than ten years between the detective novels and *film noir* invalidates its basic argument; (2) Dashiell Hammett and Raymond Chandler are mixed up (there is a ten-year gap too between their respective first novels); (3) the place of someone like William R. Burnett as both a novelist and screenwriter is obscured; (4) there is a refusal to look at the history of the cinema from the Depression to World War Two; (5) numerous films are swept under the rug in order to attempt to maintain an artificial purity and isolation of *film noir*, going against simple common sense, whereas the examination of anterior novels and films could be enlightening. The partiality of arguments, the multiplication of justifications and their heterogeneity clearly show that the problem is poorly posed, and that history strongly resists the definitions that have hitherto been imposed on it.

In order to demonstrate the extent to which the dates of 1945 (end of World War Two), 1941 (Huston's version of *The Maltese Falcon*), or 1940 (*Stranger on the Third Floor* with Peter Lorre, who serves as a tie with expressionism) are arbitrary, I will take only one example: *Private Detective 62*.

This film, dating from 1933, was directed by Michael Curtiz,[32] with William Powell and Margaret Lindsay in the main roles, and is an adaptation of a story by Raoul Whitfield, a colleague and friend of Dashiell Hammett. The hero, emblematically, is an American named Free. Like Samuel Spade or Philip Marlowe, he is a private detective, obliged to be in contact with corruption, fighting alone against all for the re-establishment of right. Like them, he got his training in the institution: an intelligence officer in Paris, he is unmasked by the French police. Abandoned by his bosses, he is deported to New York where he suddenly finds himself in the middle of the Depression. His first employers refuse to recognize him, and he is forced to seek work on his own. He finds a position with a shady and spineless detective who survives by kidnapping dogs and returning them to their owners for ransom. Free brings real, honest clients to the agency, but his boss finds it easier to be paid by a gangster in whose service he puts his knowledge of the law. It is in this framework that Free is obliged to carry out surveillance on a young woman who hangs out in chic clubs and fancy restaurants (she is a gambler) and is apparently connected with gangsters, but who quickly becomes an ally in his struggle against corruption. After some friction and bitter-sweet relations, they end up recognizing their mutual love once they have gained victory over evil. The film itself is not lacking in *noir* scenes, for example the first scenes in the shabby rooms of the detective agency or the incident in which the heroine is the victim of an attempted assassination in an apartment entirely plunged into darkness except for the windows lit from the street. What interests me in this film is the connection established between the private detective and the Depression: Free is dropped by the national institutions that were supposed to protect him and obliged to make do for himself.[33] Tempted by fast and easy money, he none the less remains faithful to an ideal of justice, with a rigour tempered only by love. *Private Detective 62* has one of the most classic of *noir* scripts, as much in its pessimistic tendencies (the solitary struggle of the individual in a universe overrun by evil) as those that are sentimental (pure love surviving in evil's midst). Above all, it makes evident the fact that this sort of script treats the question of the relations between the individual and institutions dialectically. As for the urban décors, they set forth an opposition between poverty and luxury every bit the equal of *The Big Sleep* (Howard Hawks, 1946) and its followers.

The point is not to say that the private detective is the character who defines this type

The shabby office of an obviously failed business.

This frame is strikingly similar to the beginning of the Huston version of *The Maltese Falcon*: setting, camera angle, position on the partner's desk.

Another femme fatale, but here she is defending her honour and virtue.

Five frames from *Private Detective 62* (also known as *Man Killer*, Michael Curtiz, Warner Bros, 1933)

In 1933, lighting technique that will be praised ten to twenty years later.

of crime film: the private detective is only the practical denomination that has been found, because it corresponds to a supposedly American profession, to a visual cliché (sexed male), and to a character's situation, in order to designate a type of film, but in reality it is much more likely that a rational history of the American cinema would forge a link between films of the 'fallen woman' genre, those of the 'forgotten man' genre, and detective films of the '*noir*' type. In each case, it is a question of the failure of institutions to defend the Good, of the unequal struggle of an innocent individual against evil combinations, and the general response that seems to reside in the love of a being of the opposite sex. In all these cases ('fallen woman', 'forgotten man' and '*noir*'), what astonishes the European spectator is the fact that Hollywood should produce films with a sombre ending, or at least apparently so, since in the majority of cases, even if the main character fails in his enterprise, he nevertheless keeps his pride in having remained faithful to his ideal and having refused compromise. This type of film invites us to rethink the function of Hollywood as a machine that produces dreams or fairytale spectacles, when its function was doubtless to work out in detail the ideological contradictions of a simultaneously democratic and individualist society. *Film noir* must thus lead to a double opening-up: the chronology must be opened up by moving back in time, and the genre must be opened up by making more permeable the boundaries not only with the types of films that I have just mentioned, but also with the western, in which the sheriff occupies a place very close to that of the hero of the detective film.

POPULISM AND JEREMIAD

As is shown very well by Dennis Porter in *The Pursuit of Crime*,[34] the redefinition of the private detective by Hammett, distancing him from the European gentleman master-mind, is strongly connected with the cultural and moral values of American national-ism and individualism.[35] Thus the wisecrack is at once a sign of independence (the detective does not let himself be intimidated by social or professional hierarchy), a refusal of the rules of propriety (he acts with contempt for the most normally expected politeness when it serves to cover a lie), and a mark of experience (he is not going to get fooled). In the middle of an economic crisis, Hammett invents a character who, through storms and high seas, bears the moral law within himself, takes the enemy's weapons only the better to reveal their corruption and destroy them, and fights against institutions because their anonymity, expanse, complexity and the weight of their hierarchy render them inefficient and inhuman. It has often been noted that gangsterism in film was the other face of capitalism, and this is particularly true in the climate of the Depression during which the rich tended to be assimilated to monopolists and do-nothings. Thus, in *Bullets or Ballots* (William Keighley, 1936), Edward G. Robinson plays the role of a policeman acting alone to bring down a gang run by bankers. It has less often been noted that the gangster, as a character whose social ascension is 'too' fast, is the dark image of individualism subjected to religious condemnation ('whosoever shall exalt himself shall be abased'),[36] from which the sin of pride is by no means absent. But the gangster is also a social condemnation to the extent that he re-establishes a class difference within society by placing a trench between poor and rich, between isolated individuals and those who enter into a system of organized understandings. Whether one is confronted in these fictions with rich bourgeois, the mafia, unions, or nazi or communist networks (depending on the period), the fundamental question is always that of the struggle between freedom and individual happiness on one side and, on the other, the understandings and systems that secretly are spreading or threatening to spread their ramifications through the whole country by forbidding the sacrosanct operation of free enterprise and free competition.[37] The private detective is a petty-bourgeois jealous of his independence, convinced of his moral worth and concerned with protecting what is, in his eyes, the exemplary value of American democracy. That in the process he conquers the young woman, who has all the attributes of the upper middle class, is only the necessary tribute to be paid to social ascension (but here by a love that glorifies the petty bourgeoisie) and a defeat inflicted upon the other camp.[38] From this point of view, the detective film cannot be considered to be a critique of the system; on the contrary, it functions as a necessary denial of capitalism's tendency towards concentration, by constantly reaffirming the virtues of the petty bourgeoisie and of free enterprise, so long as the latter keeps a human scale.[39]

At least two things were brought up to date through the detective film and the character of the private detective. The first was the repetition of the citizen's allegiance to national principles, but through a constant pact according to which national institutions can only maintain their power through the individual, through the simple citizen apparently lost in the masses and in the immensity of the country. The hard-boiled detective novel thus participates in a populist ideology, as is correctly emphasized by Dennis Porter.[40] This populist ideology can, moreover, largely explain the success in France of films drawn from these novels: in the first half of the 1950s, France slowly takes on the rhythm of the post-war boom years, leaving behind small businessmen and small shopkeepers along with a large part of the petty bourgeoisie, so that in 1954–55 there emerges the political movement representative of this discontent of the small, known as Poujadism. The difference between French Poujadism and American populism is not as great as might be thought: in both cases it is a matter of a conservative reaction on the part of the petty bourgeoisie.[41] The second thing (but intimately tied to the first) that was brought up to date by *film noir* was the renewal of the jeremiad, that half-political, half-religious discourse operative from the very foundation of the United States, which allows the fundamental values of the nation to be recalled by accentuating all the deviations in the nation's history that followed their not being respected.[42] Personally, I consider the American detective film to be entirely within the province of the jeremiad, of this repeated moral denunciation in the name of basic values among which one finds the privilege accorded to relations of proximity and respect for ideal virtues to the detriment of material values. There is thus in *film noir* something that Europe can only grasp with difficulty and that falls within the province of 'civil religion':[43] proof of this could be found in the unions of man and woman that end so many detective films and whose setting is not a church but a courtroom or police station. To take only two examples, there is the end of *The Cheat* (Cecil B. De Mille, 1915) where the husband and wife, reconciled, form a couple once again with the benediction of the judge, and leave arm-in-arm through the honour guard formed for them by the public, and the last shot of *The Big Sleep* where Philip Marlowe and Vivian Rutledge kiss to the wailing of police sirens.

If the thesis of populism and the jeremiad is accepted for the hard-boiled novel and *film noir*, a great consistency in themes treated from the end of the 1920s through to the Cold War can be noted.[44] The overly vast systems reacted against include the justice system and the police as well as the mafia, unions, nazi networks within the country and, later, communists: all of them are felt to threaten free enterprise and free competition. A film like *Racket Busters* (Lloyd Bacon, 1938) is symptomatic in this respect: Bogart plays a racketeer who organizes strikes whilst George Brent plays a small shopkeeper who wants to keep his independence.[45] The essential point here is not whether it is a question of detective films, gangster films, or propaganda films: the point in common must be that it is always a question of a fight to the death between an individual and a network that threatens fundamental freedoms (among which that of commerce is not, in this system, the least important). Thenceforth it is no longer necessary to isolate the private detective from his immediate cousins, whose position and function he shares. He is no different from the lawyer of the 1930s who, tempted by the easy money held out by a gangster in need of his services, ends up turning against his employer in the name of morality in order to bring about the triumph of the law: the best example is doubtless *The Mouthpiece* (Elliot Nugent and James Flood,

1932), with Warren William in the main role (an actor who, by the internal logic of events, is to be found in the second version of *The Maltese Falcon*). Nor is he different from the journalist who exposes a conspiracy or an abuse of power (*The Big Clock*, John Farrow, 1948), the isolated policeman who fights alone against all (*The Big Heat*, Fritz Lang, 1953), or the victim who has to make his own way out of the trap in which he has got himself caught (*Double Indemnity*, Billy Wilder, 1944). On a small or on a grand scale, the idea is that of the 'combo' dominating and exerting its influence, it being understood that the combo is undemocratic and (it is the same thing) un-American. It can, then, be seen that paranoia is not an American malediction consequent upon some unspecified spell cast over the whole country, that would then allow a magical explanation of *film noir*:[46] on the contrary, it is a matter of a contradiction inherent in the economic and political system of the United States, in which the citizen must constantly be reassured of his rights in the face of economic concentrations and federal power, the inhabitant of the small town in the face of the big city, the wage-earner in the face of the rich.[47] The advent of the private detective in its modern American form at the moment of the Depression indicates the urgency with which these contradictions pressed at that time. In the films of the 1950s, traces of these contradictions can still be found in the form of the grotesque[48] and the poor (often they are one and the same, as in *The Enforcer*, Windust-Walsh, 1950), who help to situate the hero at an equal distance from the proletarians and those living in misery, on the one hand, and, on the other, from the rich bourgeoisie, these two extremes being presented as two symmetrical traps into which he risks falling. We may then understand that film criticism repeats the gesture of the *films noirs* themselves, for in granting them the status of a Hollywood genre, it sees the films as playing the same role in the Hollywood system as the private detective plays in American society.

A RETURN TO THE PARIS OF THE SUMMER OF 1946

Even if the arguments advanced to define *film noir* in cinematographic terms today appear to be without foundation, it nevertheless remains the case that spectators perceived a difference between the films made after the end of World War Two and their predecessors. It seems to me that there are four important differences that must be taken into consideration: a transition towards a more serious tone, a shrinking of the frame, a change of style in the physical appearance of the actors and décor, and finally the weakening of censorship.

Production between the two wars, much like the novels of Hammett or Chandler, involved a significant amount of pure comedy or even parody, as can still be felt in *The Big Sleep*. Huston's version of *The Maltese Falcon* is no more faithful to the novel than the other two were. It is simply in greater conformity with the idea that we have formed of *film noir* as a serious or even solemn genre, because Huston, to as great an extent as possible, eliminated all comic elements and kept only the dramatic or serious ones, even in the love relationship. This tendency became more and more accentuated beginning in 1949, a date after which the detective film began to take itself seriously, to the point that it occasionally became pompous. The comedy that was allowed in the 1930s disappeared and survived only in the verbal form of the wisecrack, which is grating rather than funny, and in the visual form of the grotesque, which is more repulsive than laughable. Doubtless it is this late

A forerunner to *The Big Sleep*: The hero and the heroine practise shooting in the living room

. . . while the villain perfects his scheme. (*Muss 'Em Up*, Charles Vidor, RKO, 1936)

domination of serious tone, more than he actual plot structure or photography of the films, that contributed to the term '*film noir*'.[49] Everything seems to happen as if the detective plots that had been used since the 1920s were no longer good enough and that, now that economic pressure had been lifted and the properly sentimental framework had been removed, an 'idea' or explicitly symbolic motif had to be added (the plague in *Panic in the Streets*, the atomic device in *Kiss Me Deadly*), that supposedly had something profound to say about the human condition. In fact, this can be seen as the vein running dry, in that this 'thoughtful' dimension was already present in the detective films of the preceding decades, but diffused, encrypted in the enigma of the crime and in the opposition between the individual and the secret network. After 1948, the threat either becomes metaphorical or is visually represented in real exterior

The Big Gamble (Fred Noble, RKO, 1931)

The Penguin Pool Murder (George Archainbaud, RKO, 1932)

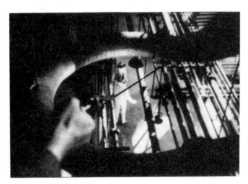

Follow Me Quietly (Richard O. Fleischer, RKO, 1949)

The exhaustion of a visual motif: from night shadows to daylight pipes.

décors by a 'grandiosely inhuman' architecture. It is at this point that the bridges of *Naked City* and *Night and the City* (Jules Dassin, 1948 and 1950) or the gasometer of *Follow Me Quietly* (Richard Fleischer, 1949) appear, monuments that form a sort of architectural 'combo' that catches the unhappy orphans in its web.

The second difference, at least during the first half of the 1940s, is that the frame shrinks. A striking feature of films of the 1930s, particularly during the first half of the decade, is the importance given to the décor, to the atmosphere surrounding the characters (this is coherent with the presence of real exteriors, subsequently eliminated to the advantage of a sort of claustrophobic space [*huis-clos*]).[50] The temporary evolution towards a more restricted framing occurs in step with the tendency towards a serious tone, but it is not specific to the detective film. No doubt implicated in this evolution is the double constraint of budget restrictions (the cinema too is subjected to a wartime economy during hostilities) and enclosure within the studio, which would indicate as an indirect consequence that the breadth of space at the beginning of the 1930s is a remnant of the silent film in the sound era.

There is a third difference that is easily noted, even if it is not entirely specific to the cinema: the difference of style. I mean by this that one can, beginning in 1941–42, observe a difference in the decoration of apartments, in clothing, but also in buildings and cars that seem to be the signature of a new epoch, all the more so in that this style will remain practically unchanged until the 1960s. In a rather odd and yet indisputable way, this change of style can also be seen in the faces of the actors. The physical appearance of actors such as Ricardo Cortez, William Powell, Warren William, George Raft or Brian Donlevy suddenly seems to belong to another era, a far-off time not connected to our own, even though they played the same roles in the same stories. The case is the same for women: Lauren Bacall is not Margaret Lindsay, Gloria Grahame is not Joan Blondel . . . In short, until today or nearly so the actors of the 1940s and 1950s have looked natural to us, because their visual form belongs to the modernity to which we still think that we belong, whereas those of the 1930s derive for us from another aesthetic that makes them look too stereotypical, overdone and thus ridiculous. Moreover there can be no doubt that the actor Bogart, in the second half of his career, did much to effect this change, and we must not try to hide from ourselves the fact that the definition of *film noir* owes a great deal to him, to the extent that it was clearly organized around him, around his new stardom. It could moreover be argued that Humphrey Bogart, Robert Montgomery or Dick Powell succeeded in doing in images what Dashiell Hammett tried to do in words: Americanize the detective.[51] Actors like William Powell, Warren William and Basil Rathbone had too 'English' a look, associating them with the mastermind detective. Our attachment to *film noir* thus has a great deal to do with the actors and actresses who succeeded in crystallizing around their persons our pleasure in the detective film. The personnel of *film noir* appears to us to be a sort of tribe, an extended family all of whose members we know and in the midst of which we are pleased to find ourselves from time to time. Like all families, it is both encompassing (it has many members) and exclusive (it thinks of itself as endowed with a particular quality that radically excludes all non-members).[52] For example, Bogart formed a troika with Peter Lorre and Sydney Greenstreet that was found together in various forms for several years, imposing a sort of canon that eliminates certain actors who were already in place. Thus Eduardo Cianelli, who had succeeded in making the role of a refined, perverse and sadistic gang leader (notably in *Marked Woman*) entirely convincing in detective films made between 1937 and 1940, was eclipsed. In *The Mask of Dimitrios* (Jean Negulesco, 1944), he appears well behind Lorre and Greenstreet. The genre can, then, be defined for the spectator by the familiarity he has with actors and characters, by the particular link there is between a type of actor and a type of character, a link that will thenceforth be enough to exclude other actors or, in a lesser form of exclusion, to classify them with respect to the actor who has become the central point of reference.

Finally (fourth difference), it must not be forgotten that French cinephiles were stunned by the erotic daring of Gilda's glove, a fact to which Sadoul's scandalized tone still bears witness in 1954[53] – as they were stunned by Phyllis Dietrichson's ankle bracelet (*Double Indemnity*) and the chorus girl's outfit that Lana Turner sports in the middle of her restaurant (*The Postman Always Rings Twice*). World War Two and the newsreels had delivered a decisive blow to the system of censorship in operation since 1933, reality having taken upon itself to extend the list of crimes and horrors that could be looked at. Acts of violence as well as bodies gained access to a more direct representation: one can only be struck by the fact that, from 1944 on, the female body is redrawn and exhibited, particularly through the quasi-obligatory sequence of singing in a nightclub, whether chic or not. If Borde and Chaumeton frequently sang the praises of this erotic aspect of *film noir*,[54] the point must be relativized today: so far as the female body is concerned there is in fact a return to the *status quo ante*, to the state of censorship prior to 1933. Directors did not have much to do with this development and their daring was negligible in that they were content to return to the codes in vigour before 1933. But the fact remains that French cinephiles experienced this as a liberation, a feeling that doubtless had more to do with the state of French cinema than with an actual comparison with pre-war American production.

FILM NOIR, MEMORY OF A MYTHIC STATE OF THE CINEMA

Having come to the end of this partial journey, one question remains to be posed. If the term *film noir* allows us to believe we can contain a certain form of detective fiction within the pages of a book written to describe it, we must ask ourselves what American detective films of the 1940s and 1950s are excluded from the proposed surveys? One can only be struck by the enlargement of the notion of *film noir* in the course of the years. When Borde and Chaumeton drew up their list of *films noirs*, they counted only twenty-two, all the rest falling into sub-categories of the traditional detective film. When Ward and Silver established an encyclopaedia of *films noirs*, their list included several hundred films. It would be an interesting experiment to try to make an encyclopaedia of detective films not included in the encyclopaedias of *films noirs*. This would engage us in a veritable archaeology of the American detective film, and no longer in a compilation attached to arbitrarily chosen dates. Still, if the context of

1946–55 in France can explain the creation of the term '*film noir*', it is astonishing that it has lasted and that it has regularly been revived and renewed by succeeding generations, until now and the present volume.

Beyond the questions examined in the preceding paragraphs, what specifically cinematographic elements have we found in American detective films of the 1940s and 1950s? The response may reside precisely in the conjunction of black and white with the studio production system. The detective film of those years represents the last moment of what for generations was *the* American cinema: black and white films produced by studios. *Film noir* began to be loved when this state of affairs began to disappear. Colour films gained the upper hand and left to black and white only films for the simpleminded or the declaredly intellectual fringe of the public; the studios were dismembered; fifty years of the history of cinema collapsed. Paradoxically, *film noir* is loved for representing a past that it in fact occults, a past that the enthusiast hardly knows, if at all, a bit of the pre-war in the post-war period. *Film noir* is, then, an eminently lost object: lost for never having been given a satisfactory definition, lost for having ended in 1955, lost for representing the 1930s in a modern form. At the beginning of this chapter I claimed that *film noir* was the Europeanized form of American cinema: black and white also militates in favour of this thesis, the European cinema of the 1950s having still not really obtained the means to produce colour films. It is thus not surprising that Italian and French cinema at the end of the 1950s (I am thinking, for example, of Fellini's *Il Bidone*[55] and Godard's *A Bout de souffle*) borrowed massively from the American detective cinema of the beginning of the 1950s, by a continuity that no longer seems extraordinary.

Film noir is thus possible only under several conditions: the break caused by the war for the European public, particularly in Paris, which allowed pre-war American production to be forgotten [56] even as it emphasized the real differences between pre- and post-war visual elements (style of the décor, objects and actors); a misunderstanding of the import of the social critique presented by the fictions and the character of the private detective; both attraction to and repulsion from American culture; a Poujadist climate in France; the formal link of black and white (a survival in the American system whereas it continues to be the general rule in Europe); Bogart's becoming a star; and, in return, on the part of Anglo-American film criticism, over-valuation of French film criticism at the very moment when a reappropriation of this cinema was attempted. *Film noir* presents a fine example of cinema history and aesthetic reflection that is founded on distribution (in France at a certain point in time) and critical discourse, and not on production (in the United States during several decades), in a complete ignorance of the larger cultural context. This is not only because the history of cinema that already exists works with very short periods (neo-realism, the Soviet school of the 1920s, etc.), but also because no one has sufficiently reflected on the ideological conditions that could have presided over the advent of a kind of fiction. The result is a sort of imaginary enclosure in which what appeared to be evident to spectators becomes a venerable concept for feminists and historians, and in which the resulting critical work ends up occulting the films themselves and their production.

As an object or corpus of films, *film noir* does not belong to the history of cinema; it belongs as a notion to the history of film criticism, or, if one prefers, to the history of those who wanted to love the American cinema even in its middling production and to form an image of it. *Film noir* is a collector's idea that, for the moment, can only be found in books.

Translated by J. SWENSON

NOTES

* For Christian Metz.

1. Alan Silver and Elizabeth Ward, eds., *Film Noir* (London: Secker and Warburg, 1980); Foster Hirsch, *Film Noir: The Dark Side of the Screen* (San Diego: A. S. Barnes, 1981); Robert Ottoson, *A Reference Guide to the American Film Noir: 1940–1958* (Metuchen, NJ and London: Scarecrow Press, 1981). Foster Hirsch's book is certainly the most open and the one that takes the greatest critical distance from traditional definitions.

2. Hitchcock, as is well known, constructed the aerial attack of *North by Northwest* as a counter-example, but without being able to avoid the deserted character of the site.

3. Only the Soviet school of the 1920s is missing to bring together all the classics.

4. The author of these lines, it should be understood, must be encompassed by the Borgesian category of the 'more or less general'.

5. Paul Schrader, 'Notes on Film Noir', *Film Comment*, vol. 8, no. 1 (Spring 1972), pp. 8–13; James Damico, 'Film Noir: A Modest Proposal', *Film Reader* no. 3 (February 1978), pp. 48–57; Paul Kerr, 'Out of What Past? Notes on the B Film Noir', in Paul Kerr, ed., *The Hollywood Film Industry* (London: Routledge and Kegan Paul, 1986), pp. 220–44, originally published in *Screen Education* (Autumn/Winter 1979–1980), pp. 32–3.

6. Raymond Borde and Étienne Chaumeton, *Panorama du film noir américain* (Paris: Les Editions de Minuit, 1955).

7. A good example of this is given by Patrick Brion's *Le Film Noir* (Paris: Editions Fernand Nathan, 1991). The introduction repeats the classical elements supposed to define the 'genre'. The thrills are produced by including, among the eighty-two films personally chosen by the author, *Rebecca* and other Hitchcock films (which marks a double boldness: 1939 instead of 1941 or 1940, and Hitchcock, who was considered as a subgenre himself), *Leave Her to Heaven* and *Slightly Scarlet* (second boldness: colour!), and even a Tex Avery

cartoon. The novelty seems to be the reduced number of films. Unfortunately, this reduction is due not to theoretical or historical precision, but to the constraints imposed by the publisher.

8. On this point, see also Jean-Paul Simon's study of *Lady in the Lake*, 'Enonciation et narration', *Communications*, no. 38 (1983), pp. 155–91.

9. Paul Schrader, in 'Notes on Film Noir', strongly emphasizes the romantic or even sentimental aspect of *film noir*.

10. This article is derived from work in progress on the detective film, working from the production of Warner Brothers and RKO, which is why so many of the examples cited in the following pages were produced by one or the other of these studios. One of the other sources of this work was the Rockefeller Grant I was given in1987 to do research at the Wisconsin Center for Film and Theater Research in Madison.

11. These accords, which reopened the French market to American cinema, were sharply attacked by the communists, particularly because their French signatory was a socialist, although they dared not over-emphasize that he was also Jewish. I will above all draw attention to the fact that *film noir* is a product of the Blum-Byrnes accords, and thus placed under the sign of the American invasion.

12. *Le Blé en herbe*, a film by Claude Autan-Lara adapted from a novel by Colette, recounts the love affairs of two adolescents, Phil and Vinca; Phil is sexually initiated by an older woman. This deliberately provocative film was the object of a local censorship campaign by Catholic groups; Georges Sadoul here is defending Autan-Lara.

13. The discourse of Sadoul and the Communist Party, as will have been understood, is motivated by an extreme and virulent puritanism.

14. For example, *La Revue du cinéma*, reborn from the party's ashes, consecrates a number of important articles to the *film noir*, notably those written by Chartier and Doniol-Valcroze.

15. It must be kept in mind that the seminal article by Jean-Pierre Chartier bore the revelatory title 'The Americans Too Make Films Noirs' (Jean-Pierre Chartier, 'Les Américains aussi font des films noirs', *La Revue de cinéma*, no. 2 [November 1946]), pp. 66–70, indicating that after World War Two the United States took up where France had left off.

16. In French this is pronounced '*la vamp*'.

17. Ward and Silver, as well as Ottoson, enlist Losey's *M* (1951) in the ranks of *films noirs*, but remain supremely unaware of the fact that, in 1932, Edward G. Robinson, in the course of his trial at the end of *Two Seconds*, under the direction of Mervyn LeRoy, gives himself over, by his cries and grimaces, to a copy of the trial scene in the original *M*.

18. On these points see Jacques Aumont, *L'Oeil interminable* (Paris: Editions Séguier, 1989), particularly pp. 198–205 and 210–12.

19. See E. H. Gombrich, 'Lights and Highlights', in *The Heritage of Apelles: Studies in the Art of the Renaissance* (Oxford: Phaidon Press, 1976), pp. 3–35.

20. This type of lighting can also be found in real nocturnal exteriors in Italian films of the 1950s and 1960s.

21. In Camille Morlhon's *La Calomnie*, made in France in 1913, there is a scene in a photographic laboratory with a bulb placed beneath the character's face as its only light source. A similar scene can be found in Yevgeni Bauer's 1915 film *After Death*. Barry Salt has cited examples of this sort of experimentation in Denmark in 1911. On the lighting of De Mille's films of around 1915, see Lea Jacobs, 'Lasky Lighting', in *The De Mille Legacy*, Paolo Cherchi Usai and Lorenzo Codelli, eds. (*Le Giornate del Cinema Muto*, 1991, Edizioni Biblioteca dell'Imagine),

pp. 250–58. Noël Burch reports that the little-known director John G. Adolfi adopted in the 1914 film *The Bank Burglar's Fate* a visual style that he claims is characteristic of the detective films of the 1940s and 1950s; see his book *Life to those Shadows* (Berkeley: University of California Press, 1990), p. 136.

22. In the case of *Footlight Parade*, the interiors of the vehicles are also strongly lit so that the action going on there can be followed, but the exterior is without secondary lighting. If it seems that the second half of the 1930s is less prodigal in such scenes, from 1939 on the cliché of the nocturnal apartment visit reappears in the Wong, Saint and Falcon series.

23. This affirmation is obviously made under reservation of a more complete inventory of films, but everything occurs as if, when it came to the *films noirs* of the 1940s, both producers and critics saw a great advantage in shooting in the studio, whereas the technique of shooting in real exteriors had existed for at least twenty-five years: to put it another way, it is not until the end of the 1940s that *film noir* gives a position of honour to a technique that was actually well known. This belated return to an old technique seems to confirm the hypothesis of a thematic exhaustion privileging an intensification of formal elaboration. Doubtless this is what made Paul Schrader say that before the *film noir* of the 1950s there was the *film gris* of the 1940s.

24. One could also cite, still with Lon Chaney, Victor Sjöstrom's film *He Who Gets Slapped* (1924), with numerous and beautiful oppositions between a highly lit zone and dense black, notably in the circus ring.

25. These cinematographers are taken more or less by chance, but however aleatory the choice may be the same conclusions will impose themselves: see, for example, the choice made by Bruce Crowther in his chapter 'Technique: The Look of Noir', in his book *Film Noir: Reflections in a Dark Mirror*

(London: Columbus Books, 1988), pp. 61–8. Crowther is to my knowledge the only writer who puts the accent on the anteriority of lighting techniques with respect to the dates habitually retained for *film noir*.

26. The available figures are not all particularly clear on the relation between production in colour and production in black and white. In 1954–55, more than half the films produced were in colour, though between 1955 and 1960 this proportion declined slightly. It is still the case that the general tendency is marked, beginning from the end of World War Two, and it is not in favour of black and white.

27. Here I am taking up the argument of Jacques Aumont in preferring the better-adapted and more accurate notion of expressivity to the hackneyed term 'expressionism'.

28. David Bordwell, Janet Staiger and Kristin Thompson, in their fine book *The Classical Hollywood Cinema: Film Style and Mode of Production to 1960* (London: Routledge and Kegan Paul, 1985), present the seductive hypothesis that there was no major change in the history of Hollywood between 1917 and 1960. I believe that this idea is also correct for the detective film.

29. It is not necessary to recall here that the invention of *film noir* in France is equally bound up with the discovery, during this same period, of American detective fiction, notably through the creation of Marcel Duhamel's famous Série noire collection at the prestigious Gallimard publishing house. One can moreover only be surprised by the place accorded to Cornell Woolrich, who would only be translated into French later and in another collection (the Série blême), whereas the titles of his novels form a tremendous litany of black: *The Bride Wore Black, Rendezvous in Black, Black Alibi, The Black Path of Fear, The Black Angel, The Black Curtain*. This novelist is largely under-

estimated in work on *film noir*, notably by A. M. Karini in his very traditional *Toward a Definition of the American Film Noir (1941–1949)* (New York: Arno Press, 1976).

30. This argument has been presented by Raymond Durgnat in particular; his articles, as is emphasized by James Damico and Foster Hirsch, did much to paralyse reflection on *film noir*.

31. To my knowledge, only William K. Everson, in *The Detective Film* (New York: Citadel Press, 1972), and Jacques Segond, in 'Sur le piste de Dashiell Hammett: Les trois versions du *Faucon maltais*', *Positif* (July–August 1975), pp. 171–2, recall that the novel was adapted three times by Warner Brothers, the first adaptation being every bit as good as the third, which moreover owes a great deal to it.

32. Tony Gaudio was the cinematographer.

33. This idea could not be better illustrated than by *The Window* (Ted Tetzlaff, 1949), which tells the story of a little boy, witness to a murder, whom no one wants to believe and who is obliged to get out of trouble himself: in *film noir*, the hero is an orphan.

34. Dennis Porter, *The Pursuit of Crime: Art and Ideology in Detective Fiction* (New Haven: Yale University Press, 1981).

35. It may be recalled that the American Communist Party was against the United States's participation in the struggle against fascism in Europe, defending the idea that priority should be given to the reinforcement of democracy on the national territory.

36. See Jack Shadoian, *Dreams and Dead Ends: The American Gangster Crime Film* (Cambridge, MA: MIT Press, 1977).

37. The conjunction of the network and the secret is very important in American ideology, the secret referring to the negation of the fundamental right to know, of each citizen's right to immediate access to information. A film like *Lady in the Lake* justifies its plot and its narrative technique by claiming that the spectator will thus have direct, unmediated access to information.

38. From the Continental Op to Columbo, by way of Philip Marlowe and Mike Hammer, indulgence in description of the splendours of power and money, or of the refinements of well-educated people, functions only as a preparation for their condemnation in the name both of humble, ordinary folk, and of an egalitarian morality. Detective novels and films thus offer the reader or spectator the double pleasure not only of contemplating the spectacle of luxury – see, for instance, the beginning of *The Big Sleep* – but also of despising the rich; the end brings catastrophe to them and moral triumph to the detective, who is poor by choice – as is the sheriff of the western.

39. On the petty bourgeoisie in *film noir*, see Hirsch, p. 182.

40. See Porter, particularly pp. 173–81. See also Peter Roffman and Jim Purdy, *The Hollywood Social Problem Film: Madness, Despair and Politics from the Depression to the Fifties* (Bloomington: Indiana University Press, 1981). I would not, however, follow these authors when, at the beginning of their book, they oppose 'shysters' and 'populists', who, for me, are part of the same scenario.

41. I do not mean here that the inventors of *film noir* (Nino Frank, Jean-Pierre Chartier, Borde and Chaumeton) were Poujadists: I simply want to remark the elements of resemblance between American populism and French Poujadism to the extent that their social motivations at the moment of the post-war economic recovery are comparable. There would also be much to say about the parallel between contempt for the crowd and misanthropy – that is, a certain rightist anarchism of directors – in French films of the 1930s (the famous poetic realism, supposed to be the French father of *film noir*)

and reactionary individualism in American films of the same period: there are elements of comparison, which do not found a similarity, but which could lead to confusion.

42. On this point, see Sacvan Bercovitch, *The American Jeremiad* (Madison: University of Wisconsin Press, 1978).

43. See Elise Marienstras, *Nous, le peuple: Les origines du nationalisme américain* (Paris: Editions du Seuil, 1988).

44. In reality, to judge by a character like Dirty Harry, as played with self-satisfaction by Clint Eastwood, the period would have to be stretched all the way to the present.

45. We may note with amused astonishment that Warner Brothers and RKO began producing films against racketeering in 1935, the year in which the studios reached an agreement with racketeers to prevent strikes. On these points, see Denise Hartsough, 'Crime Pays: The Studio's Labor Deals in the 1930s', *Velvet Light Trap*, no. 23 (Spring 1989), pp. 49–63.

46. See, for example, Paul Jensen, 'The Return of Dr Caligari: Paranoia in Hollywood', *Film Comment*, vol. 7, no. 4 (Winter 1971–72), pp. 36–45; George Wead, 'Toward a Defintion of Filmnoia', *Velvet Light Trap*, no. 13 (1974), pp. 2–6. In a more serious and developed fashion, see also Dana Polan, *Power and Paranoia: History, Narrative and the American Cinema, 1940–1950* (New York: Columbia University Press, 1986), particularly 'Blind Insights and Dark Passages: The Problem of Placement', pp. 193–249.

47. That Hollywood, from 1935 on, found it necessary to make films glorifying the FBI can only confirm this point.

48. I am here using the term 'grotesque' in its pictorial meaning: an ugly disfiguration of the face, as it is seen in Dürer's work, for example.

49. It still must be noted that among the novelist–fathers, someone like Raymond Chandler is placed on the same level as Cornell Woolrich,

the latter having a much more sinister manner than the former, which goes to show that the hard-boiled school is as much a catch-all notion as is expressionism.

50. Tom Conley has presented an interesting thesis which tries to show the influence of existentialism and its theatre on *film noir*: see his article, 'State of Film Noir', *Theatre Journal* (1987), pp. 347–63. See also Robert G. Porfirio, 'No Way Out: Existential Motifs in the Film Noir', *Sight and Sound*, vol. 45, no. 4 (Autumn 1976), pp. 212–17.

51. This Americanism, strongly marked in opposition to English canons, can be found extensively used in the case of Robert Montgomery in *The Earl of Chicago* (Richard Thorpe, 1939), in which the actor plays the role of a choirboyish gangster, who, when he is not chewing gum or shoving aside protocol and politeness, multiplies his 'yeahs' without end.

52. I am well aware of the fact that this sort of argument – identification with an actor – has nothing decisive about it and that in the end it explains nothing at all since logic would dictate that I establish what allowed this identification to occur in the first place. The argument still retains its validity here in that it draws our attention to this basic phenomenon, which has been obscured by the attempts at rationalization that I evoked at the beginning of the article.

53. In the second half of the 1980s, Huston's version of *The Maltese Falcon* was re-released in Paris with a new translation of the subtitles, and the spectators were given a fortuitous start by the reference, at the beginning of the film, to the still-warm slip of one of the characters. This shows to what extent the metaphorization of the striptease in the detective's inquiry is a good defence which, for the spectator's comfort, it is better not to touch. More exactly, it points out the extent to which the detective film instals a code of

censorship that the spectator has already agreed to and which is part of his pleasure.

54. This argument, of course, has been inscribed in the thesis of *film noir*'s victorious resistance to the Hollywood system, film criticism having seen these bagatelles as an act of defiance thrown in the face of the system of censorship by certain directors in the name of art.

55. The film uses Broderick Crawford, but in addition its ending seems to me to be very close to that of Losey's *The Prowler* (a lost character trying to climb up a mound of rocks), even while recalling the end of certain of Rossellini's films, such as *Il miracolo* and *Stromboli*. If post-war Italian cinema borrows heavily from American cinema, there is no doubt that the American detective film borrows from Italian neo-realism, particularly in the shooting of real exterior daytime scenes after 1949.

56. In France the break also allowed French production during the war to be forgotten. Nor should we forget that someone like John Huston, the better to establish his career, did not hesitate to occult this past.

PHOTOGRAPHIC CREDITS

The Big Gamble: photographer Hal Mohr; *Two Seconds*: photographer Sol Polito; *The Maltese Falcon*: photographer William Rees; *Private Detective 62*: photographer Tony Gaudio; *Muss 'Em Up*: photographers J. Roy Hunt and Joseph August; *The Penguin Pool Murder*: photographer Henry Gerrard; *Follow Me Quietly*: photographer Robert de Grasse.

2

THE SYNOPTIC CHANDLER

Fredric Jameson

Inveterate readers of Chandler will know that it is no longer for the solution to the mystery that they reread him, if indeed the solutions ever solved anything in the first place. (The story of Bogart's argument with Hawks is well known; very late at night, after much drinking, during the filming of *The Big Sleep* the two men argue about the status of the dead body in the Buick in the ocean off the Lido pier: murder, suicide or some third thing? They finally phone Chandler himself, still awake and drinking at that hour; he admits he can't remember either.) Sometimes he aggressively foregrounds the more improbable plot mechanisms, daring us to throw the book away in disbelief: '"And at that point," I said, "you run into a real basic coincidence, the only one I'm willing to admit in the whole picture. For this Mildred Haviland met a man named Bill Chess in a Riverside beer parlor and for reasons of her own married him and went to live with him at Little Fawn Lake,"' etc. (*The Lady in the Lake*, XXVII, p. 578).[1] At other times it is presumably the speed of the plot's rotation that can be counted on to distract us from everything that is unmotivated or gratuitous about certain episodes: that of Amthor and the marijuana cigarettes in *Farewell, My Lovely*, for example (triumphantly refashioned into a whorehouse with a lesbian madame in Dick Richards's 1975 film version). Finally it is for the episodes themselves that one rereads: in this, as in a few other features, Chandler participates in the logic of modernism generally, which tends towards an autonomization of ever smaller segments (the formally independent chapters of *Ulysses* are only the most dramatic emblem of the process). But since Chandler's project-units remain subgeneric, we can, as an unexpected bonus, compare successive versions of the same form in their published variants, which have not, as in the 'great moderns', been welded together in some single 'book of the world' whose repetitions would be stylistic rather than narrative. So it is that little by little we begin to collect these episode types (at least in the first four, canonical novels; Chandlerians will have their weakness for this or that feature of the later two, but we are here already beyond the naïve or natural operations of the original form). We juxtapose Harry Jones and George Anson Phillips (inept private detectives); or Laird Burnette and Eddie Mars or Alex Morny (likeable mobsters); or Vannier, Marriott, or Lavery (quintessential gigolos) – and a new kind of stereoscopic reading emerges in which each scene retains its sharpness while designating at the same time a well-nigh Platonic (yet social-typological) ultimate unit behind it that the reading eye does not so much see as intuit.

So it is that the ideal reader of these detective stories begins to dream of a synoptic Chandler which, like the equivalent edition of the four Gospels, would run the equivalent episodes side by side for our inspection, and for the exercise of those ultimate mental faculties that govern the dialectic of identity and difference. Unfortunately for this illusion of the ultimate mythical ur-text and, like the atom itself, the form of the autonomous episode is not itself ultimately indivisible. For when the would-be compiler of such synoptic columns works his way back to the pulp-magazine short stories that are predictably the episodes' first versions (and that in hindsight lend the mature Chandler novel that truly 'modern' sense of patches sewn together, in which the seams and transitions constitute the truest locus of aesthetic production), he discovers – as with electrons and quarks within the seeming unity of the atom as such – that the 'original' episodes have themselves already been contaminated by the autonomization process and thereby dissociated or uncoupled into so many micro-episodes in their own right. The alternate interpretation is plausible enough: that Chandler 'lacked imagination' and, reduced to these few episodes and character types, found himself obliged to repeat them over and over again under different guises. Those who feel this way will probably not wish to read any further in the present pages, whose thesis is rather that it was his society that lacked imagination and that such undoubted limits are those of the narrativity of Chandler's socio-historical raw material.

Still, the discovery of this micro-episodic dimension of the text beneath the larger official and ostensible plot mysteries and solutions of the Chandler novel suggests two new and complementary lines of inquiry. The first lies in supposing a system whose intelligibility could be expected to displace and replace that causal explanation in terms of the interrelationships of intrigue and action that we have already found to be somewhat less than reliable: this would presumably be a synchronic system in which the various episode or character types entertained formalizable semiotic relationships and oppositions with each other.

Alongside the project of disengaging that system, and in direct proportion to the success in doing so, there then emerges a second kind of analytic interest, bearing on the peculiar nature of Chandler's plot construction. Here the older logic of cause and effect (or deduction) will evidently be replaced by some new criterion for dealing out a hand of episodes, and an aesthetic whereby the rhythm of their succession or alternation is governed. I've suggested that at some higher level of historical or periodizing abstraction, this operation probably rejoins the modernist form problem par excellence, which is the invention and production of transitions: but Chandler's version of it is specific and has its own logic.

Meanwhile, both these lines of inquiry converge on the ultimate matter of narrative closure, which, whatever its fate in the modern and postmodern novel, continues to reign supreme in the mass culture of this period, and is if anything exacerbated by the peculiar nature of the detective story. (It could be argued that even the serial – the fundamental exhibit in any case for the openness or indeterminacy of the new mass culture[2] – reconfirms the value of closure over and over again by its intent to thwart and frustrate it.) Yet Chandler liked to argue that in matters of style he tricked his audience by giving them something other (and better) than what they wanted, thereby satisfying them in spite of themselves.[3] Perhaps in the matter of closure something similar is going on, so that the satisfaction of the detective-story puzzle has in reality been assuaged by something else: in the event something doubly spatial, as we shall see later.

I

The first source of closure is, however, the narrative content itself, whose deeper finitude is reflected in something more temporal than its capacity to be wrapped up neatly and tied into a well-made plot: it is a temporal closure more strongly marked in French than in English, and there theorized (by Gide and others) under the distinction between *récit* and narrative. The untranslatable generic word *récit* designates the classic tale-telling of events that are over and done with before the story begins or the narrator lifts his voice; this is signalled in French by that language's more elaborate system of tenses and in particular by the use of the preterite, whose presence is generally invisible in English, being indistinguishable from our generalized past tense. But this – rather than the distinctions in social content or in gentility or violence – is the mark of the more fundamental generic shift from English to American (hard-boiled) detective story, namely that where the classic tradition (continued in the former) maintained a structural discontinuity and differentiation between open narrative (the detective's quest) and the closed *récit* of the crime to be reconstructed, the newer American form, as it began to emerge in the pulps, redoubled the closure of the crime with that of the surface quest itself, which it also staged, after the fact, as a completed adventure.

What we witness here, I think – what is now difficult to perceive from the hindsight of a future from which the originary medium has itself virtually disappeared – is the omnipresence of a radio culture as it resonates out into other genres and media. Both pulp or hard-boiled detective stories and *film noir* are indeed structurally distinguished by the fundamental fact of the *voice-over*, which signals in advance the closure of the events to be narrated just as surely as it marks the operative presence of an essentially radio aesthetic which has no equivalent in the earlier novel or silent cinema. Allusions in the classical art story to oral narrative or traditional yarn-spinning (as in Conrad) are regressive and have virtually nothing in common with this new reproducible oral aesthetic (which found its supreme embodiment in Orson Welles). One may meanwhile pursue its structural specificity by way of physiology and psychology (provided these are appropriately historicized): the visual is presumably always incomplete while the auditory determines a synchronous recognition that can be drawn on for the construction of the new forms of a radio age. The thirties aesthetic – which has stereotypically been grasped as a kind of return to realism, a reaction against the modernist impulse, and a renewed politicization in the period of depression, fascism, and left-wing movements alike – needs to be reconsidered in the light of this most modern of the media, whose possibilities fascinated Brecht and Benjamin and not much later generated the lugubrious Adorno–Horkheimer vision of the 'culture industry'. The triumph of Hollywood seems to have fused many of these aesthetic developments into an undifferentiated mass, which it might be desirable to disentangle by thinking of the 'talkie', for example, as being, initially, a kind of radio film.

It is at any rate clear that the voice-over of the hard-boiled detective in general, and of Marlowe in particular, offers a specifically radio pleasure which must be paid for by a kind of closure that allows the novel's past tenses to resonate with doom and foreboding and marks the detective's daily life with the promise of adventure.[4] This temporal set toward language also seems to play a significant enabling role in what one may call the Flaubertian side of Chandler's stylistic production, which paradoxically marks one final unexpected development in the aesthetic of the *mot juste*. For it is precisely as the ultimate somersault of Flaubert's belief in the existence of one unique combination of words that Chandler's most outrageous effects are to be grasped. 'About as inconspicuous as a tarantula on a slice of angel food' (*FML*, I, 143): this simile conveys Moose Malloy – already overdetermined by his gigantic frame and his outlandish clothes – not least because he is a white man in an all-black neighbourhood and thus allows all of Chandler's most racist caricatural instincts to begin to come into play. (The least politically correct of all our modern writers, Chandler faithfully gives vent to everything racist, sexist, homophobic, and otherwise socially resentful and reactionary in the American collective unconscious, enhancing these unlovely feelings – which are however almost exclusively mobilized for striking and essentially visual purposes, that is to say, for aesthetic rather than political ones – by a homoerotic and male-bonding sentimentalism that is aroused by honest cops and gangsters with hearts of gold, but finds its most open expression in the plot of *The Long Goodbye*.) The practice of the outrageous simile, whose relations to radio might also be investigated, shares with Flaubert's quite unmetaphoric handicraft of the sentence a commitment to sense perception as that which is ultimately to be rendered and set down in indelible letters: those accustomed to frequent Chandler know how many ephemeral experiences of the southern California landscape are in his pages eternally retained in passing.[5]

At the other extreme of this production, we find the problem of closure posed in terms of the system of Chandler's characters, who manage in some of the novels to project a kind of Lukacsean 'effect of totality', without necessarily touching all the sociological bases. But this is something we can only reconstruct in retrospect by testing the completed novels for missing categories. Here are the quintessential American middle classes, for example:

> The Graysons were on the fifth floor in front, in the north wing. They were sitting together in a room which seemed to be deliberately twenty years out of date. It had fat over-stuffed furniture and brass doorknobs, shaped like eggs, a huge wall mirror in a gilt frame, a marble-topped table in the window and dark red plush side drapes by the windows. It smelled of tobacco smoke and behind that the air was telling me they had had lamb chops and broccoli for dinner. (*LL*, XXIII, 561)

But the Graysons ('he was a C.P.A. and looked it every inch') are virtually the only middle-class characters in all of Chandler; and they are there to show that in matters of wealth and power (their daughter has been murdered) the police cannot be counted on to protect even these most solid and respectable average citizens. As for the working class, Bill Chess in the same novel can be thought to stand as their 'representational representative', but he is a cripple and an alcoholic and a wife-beater and makes Chandler's problem even clearer: how to convey the average and the everyday in the course of pursuing the 'memorable' and the exceptional, of registering what breaks the routine, challenges the serene reproduction of the social order, counts as crime and adventure. In fact, the 'lower' classes in Chandler are either impoverished petty-bourgeois or lumpens, and have their lack of money stamped on them as catastrophe. Yet the rich (with the exception of the Kingsley figure in this novel, a business executive) are in Chandler not altogether normal specimens of a conventional ruling class either . . .

But at this point I propose to combine the now obligatory sociological survey with a somewhat different inquiry, which touches on the relationship between aesthetic value and closure of the Lukacsean 'totality-effect'. What makes this particular inquiry exceptionally verifiable, for Chandler, is the presence, among the first four novels, of a book not normally thought to be one of his best, which however turns out, in our synoptic perspective, to contain some of the all-time best and most memorable episodes in Chandler. This is *The High Window*, whose astonishing parts (Elisha Morningstar's office, George Anson Phillips's apartment in Bunker Hill, the Vannier house) oddly do not seem to add up to the imperfect whole. It may therefore be worth trying to determine why the novel fails to cohere, even in a formal situation in which the episodic is the law rather than the exception.

Mrs Murdock's house, for example, may be a good deal less dramatic than the Sternwood estate, in opening pages that clearly attempt to reproduce the remarkable effects of *The Big Sleep*'s entry into the narrative (something the Grayle house only distantly tried to approximate in *Farewell, My Lovely*) but Mrs Murdock's cantankerous port-drinking only imperfectly approximates General Sternwood's hothouse, and in any case a sumptuous house in Pasadena (with a fairly prosaic fortune) is not a match for the Sternwood oil rigs and the Sternwood military ancestors (nor, perhaps, in Chandler's unconscious, is an authoritarian female any match for an authoritative male). Meanwhile, the Brasher Doubloon would seem to be a regression from the nude photographs of *The Big Sleep*, replacing the technological image with older forms of minted value and thereby threatening a slippage back into the more romantic formulas of the older Hammett narrative, with its falcons and curses. Yet in the synoptic view the episodes remain equivalents and suggest a conception of the more interesting rich that is akin to sequestration – they are withdrawn inside their expensive dwellings like injured creatures, seeking shelter and protection (a characterization that also holds for Grayle himself, with his twin collections, of Fei Tsui jade and the legendary 'Velma'). What is crucial to retain of this micro-structure is the relative gap and distance between the character and the setting or, rather, the way in which the character type is itself predicated on that gap or tension. Unlike Balzac, for example, Chandler does not make the dwelling immediately express the truth of the character who dwells in it. Dwelling is here not a semiotic or expressive category,[6] or perhaps it might be better to say that it is questionable whether these supremely privileged Chandler characters are, despite their immense fortunes, able to *dwell*, in any traditional strong sense of the verb. They are within their rooms in a rather different way, which has, for the other end of the social spectrum, its equivalency in fear and vulnerability (and which is for General Sternwood and Mrs Murdock merely motivated and rationalized away as impotent old age and guilt, respectively).

To grasp the manner of this dwelling it is not sufficient simply to glance down the line, at those wealthy homes of gangsters and gigolos that come next (in this novel the houses of Morny's wife and Vannier), or at the utterly rundown houses of Chandler's impoverished petty-bourgeoisie, of which Jesse Florian's house on 1644 West 54th Place is the archetype (*FML*, V, 156), and which is epitomized in this particular novel by Bunker Hill and the unhappy George Anson Phillips's seedy apartment. We must turn also to the other dominant spatial category of the Chandlerian cityscape: the office as such.

I am tempted to say that in Chandler the office is – if not a well-nigh ontological category – then at least one that subsumes a much wider variety of social activity than it is normally understood to do. Indeed, the very notion that work is somehow funda-mentally related to the space of an office is itself a sociologically revealing marker of class. Here, to be sure, Elisha Morningstar's office and office building are among the quintessential evocations:

> The inner office was just as small but had a lot more stuff in it. A green safe almost blocked off the front half. Beyond this a heavy old mahogany table against the entrance door held some dark books, some flabby old magazines, and a lot of dust. In the back wall a window was open a few inches, without effect on the musty smell. There was a hatrack with a greasy black felt hat on it. There were three long-legged tables with glass tops and more coins

under the glass tops. There was a heavy dark leather-topped desk midway of the room. It had the usual desk stuff on it, and in addition a jeweller's scales under a glass dome and two large nickel-framed magnifying glasses and a jeweller's eyepiece lying on a buff scratch pad, beside a cracked yellow silk handerchief spotted with ink. (*HW*, VII, 351–2)

It would be a mistake to assume that these empirical details, which document age and neglect on the one hand (the dust) and a specific professionalism (the jeweller's scales, etc.) on the other, exemplify that 'reality-effect' that Barthes attributed to a realism (that, unlike his anti-representational colleagues on *Tel quel*, he himself read with relish) that he can be said to have demystified into a realism-effect per se.[7] If in Balzac the object-world was meant to give a metonymic signal (like a wild animal's den or an exoskeleton), in the Barthesian view of Flaubert's descriptions, these last were simply meant to emit the signal 'we are the real, we are reality' – by virtue of their very contingency: it was because such details (the ornate clock, the barometer) played no part in the action and, unlike their Balzacian equivalent, did not mean or express anything, that they were able to stand in for the sheer massive contingency of reality itself.

But in Chandler – however often aspects of both these descriptive logics seems to function – something else is also at work, which I can only characterize as the construction of a vacancy, an empty space. Whatever the objects mean (the twenty-year-old superannuated furniture of the Graysons, the undusted junk of Morningstar or Jessie Florian, but also the elegance of the Grayle mansion: 'A nice room with large chesterfields and lounging chairs done in pale yellow leather arranged around a fireplace in front of which, on the glossy but not slippery floor, lay a rug as thin as silk and as old as Aesop's aunt' [*FML*, XVIII, 214]), they also outline a space of a specific type which can be empty or contain a presence. For example, the description of Morningstar's office quoted above at some length is followed by the appearance of the 'elderly party' himself in the inevitable swivel chair. But what is operative in Chandler's description of this particular office cannot be discovered empirically by an inspection of any of these enumerated details: it is, on the contrary, only ratified by Marlowe's second visit, which discloses the office's essential emptiness as well as the demise of its inhabitant, now just another object on the floor.

The second visit in Chandler, indeed the return at night, under modified conditions, suggests that it is not particularly the criminal who needs this reassurance, but the detective and the novelist who pass their specific realities in review, and by rotating them throughout a variety of situations (as Monet did with his haystacks) cause them to emerge ever more strongly as formal entities. One thinks, for example, of the date with the ill-fated Harry Jones in *his* dilapidated office:

> The lighted oblong of an uncurtained window faced me, cut by the angle of a desk. On the desk a hooded typewriter took form, then the metal knob of a communicating door. This was unlocked. I passed into the second of the three offices. Rain rattled suddenly against the closed window. Under its noise I crossed the room. A tight fan of light spread from an inch opening of the door into the lighted office. Everything very convenient. I walked like a cat on a mantel and reached the hinged side of the door, put an eye to the crack and saw nothing but light against the angle of the wood. (*BS*, XXVI, 104)

Even more strikingly, there is the return to the cabin at Fawn Lake, which presents the psychically or psychoanalytically interesting structure of the repetition of a repetition (the first return is surprised by the local sheriff, lying in wait for Marlowe in the dark). But then, stubbornly:

> Three hundred yards from the gate a narrow track, sifted over with brown oak leaves from last fall, curved around a granite boulder and disappeared. I followed it around and bumped along the stones of the outcrop for fifty or sixty feet, then swung the car around a tree and set it pointing back the way it had come. I cut the lights and switched off the motor and sat there waiting. (*LL*, XII, 519)

I want to use this particular synoptic equivalence to make a structural deduction that may well seem an outrageous leap: it will involve the proposition that for Chandler's narrative economy the vacant murder cabin functions less as a dwelling place, even a former dwelling place, than as a kind of figurative office in its own right – the 'office' of those in flight, of the pseudonymous Muriel Chess for example before the novel opens and, at the end, of Kingsley and finally Degarmo himself. The point of this formal deduction is to problematize the commonsensical or 'natural' conception of dwelling as such in Chandler; one of its advantages is the way it allows us retroactively to transform our first sub-form – the 'dwellings' of the rich (the hothouse of General Sternwood, the jade collection of old Grayle, Mrs Murdock's port-drinking room) – into spaces of retreat and withdrawal that are somehow more analogous to offices than to houses or even quarters or apartments. There follows, thereby, a prodigious metaphysical or philosophical expansion of the category of the office *per se* in Chandler. We may, thus, return to his other city spaces in order to test them against this one, which is derived (it will be remembered) from the positing of some initial distance between the 'person' and his or her space, in other words, from the structural calling into question of the identity, within the act of 'dwelling', between character and spatial housing or envelope.

But at that point it becomes clear that a second and narratively very significant group of Chandlerian former dwellings all at once explicitly demand subsumption under the enlarged figurative category of the office: these are the sumptuous private houses of the various gigolos, from that of Lindsay Marriott in *Farewell, My Lovely*, hidden away above the coast highway (*FML*, VIII, 168ff.: 'It was a nice little house with a salt-tarnished spiral of staircase going up to the front door . . . ') to that – classically and repetitively 'revisited' in the above sense – in which Vannier lives and dies in *The High Window* (see *HW*, XXIX, 437ff) and its immediate, structurally varied replay in the 'dwelling' of Chris Lavery in *The Lady in the Lake* (*LL*, III, 480ff.; XV–XVI, 531ff.; and XX, 552ff.), both of which include what we may call complementary or mirror-image 'revisits' analogous to that involving the murder in the office next door of Harry Jones by Canino in *The Big Sleep*. That these luxuriously appointed private dwellings are to be considered offices can be persuasively argued from the source of the livelihood of the various males who use them as places in which to meet the wealthy women on whom they prey: at which point the Geiger house in the inaugural *The Big Sleep* retroactively comes to range itself under this category (underscoring the peculiar slippage, in Chandler's unconscious, between male homosexuality and high-class male 'prostitution', whose gigolo practitioners he seems to have felt to be somehow 'effeminate' as well).

Yet if we consider that the Geiger house – itself also like Monet's cathedrals seen under a variety of weathers, from driving rain via afternoon sunlight to moonlit night – is something like a professional office in the way in which it houses Geiger's other line of 'work', namely nude photography with a view towards blackmail, we begin to entertain a new kind of extension, which leads to a further sub-category with a rich new harvest of appropriate examples. Such are indeed virtually any of the institutional spaces that provide for the satisfaction of the (other) 'vices' of the rich: not merely Geiger's 'other' office, the pornographic bookstore, but also and above all the casinos and gambling joints in which Chandler's various heiresses run up illicit IOUs and are subsequently blackmailed – from the Cypress Club (in *The Big Sleep*) through its various avatars in *Farewell, My Lovely* (the Belvedere Club) and *The High Window* (Eddie Prue's Idle Valley Club, which has a virtually posthumous formal reappearance in *The Long Goodbye*): the subsequent wartime *Lady in the Lake* can only offer the London-style male club of Kingsley as a structural substitute. Even here, however, in this general subcategory of the gradual enlargement of the private club or casino into the whole closed enclave of the private development with its gates and private police, we witness something like a replay (or to use the new Chandlerian category, a 'playback') of the transformation in reverse of dwelling into office. Now all at once even more illicit needs associate themselves with these offices, in particular the drug sources: from the relatively high-class doctors' offices (Amthor's in *FML*, Almore's in *LL*) to the Bay City dope houses or 'private hospitals', such as Dr Sonderborg's in *Farewell, My Lovely*. This return movement might well lead us on into the even seedier lobbies of the various Chandlerian hotels (a combination tryst-space and rundown dwelling, the Prescott Hotel in San Bernadino, is extensively explored and deployed in *LL*, XIII, 523ff.), that now eject us back, at the other end of this rather skewed class spectrum, into the lower spheres of the impoverished petty bourgeoisie, into the various offices or dwelling spaces of the down-and-out. (The shift has literally been acted out for us in the illicit transfer of Geiger's pornographic loan library from the bookstore on Las Palmas to the unlucky Brody's rundown apartment on Randall Place [*BS*, X, 32–3].)

As has been suggested above, *The High Window* is uniquely interesting for the way in which it yields a double-barrelled identification of both these variants, in Elisha Morningstar's office and George Anson Phillip's virtually archetypal Bunker Hill murder room, a dwelling that is once again, for a classical loser of his stamp, both private and public all at once and does double duty as an office in the literal sense (he makes an appointment here with Marlowe).

Leaving aside the peculiar extension of this not-so-genteel misery, filled with broken furniture and dust, to the various offices of Chandlerian police officers, crooked and honest alike, we soon see that at the end of this particular structural sequence of forms we have suddenly re-emerged into familiar territory, which is however hereby dramatically and unexpectedly transformed. For the final office we necessarily confront at the conclusion of this lengthy inventory can only be Marlowe's own, the romantic overtones of which are as indistinguishable from his unique persona as the other social character types are from their particular spaces. Which is also to say, as I have repeatedly attempted to demonstrate, that they and he are both at a certain structural distance from these urban places as well. (We have, in other words, neither a Balzacian organic identification, nor a Flaubertian–Sartrean radical contingency, but a kind of substitution of an architectural language for that of individual characters: it is not so much that these 'people' in Chandler are their spaces, as that these spaces in Chandler are 'characters' or *actants*.)

As for Marlowe himself, as is well known,[8] we begin with the classical private eye's office at 615 Cahuenga Boulevard, an ostentatiously empty and dust-filled space without a secretary in the inevitable outer office (where only bills arrive in the mail), which is archetypally a place of waiting (for clients, for phone calls, for envelopes or packages one mails back to oneself) in which, in equally typically Chandlerian displacement, this particular plot function is used as a cover or a structural pretext for urban or ecological perception, a monadic window from which something of the deeper truth of Los Angeles is able to be disclosed:

> It was getting dark outside now. The rushing sound of the traffic had died a little and the air from the open window, not yet cool from the night, had that tired end-of-the-day smell of dust, automobile exhaust, sunlight rising from hot walls and sidewalks, the remote smell of food in a thousand restaurants, and perhaps, drifting down from the residential hills above Hollywood – if you had a nose like a hunting dog – a touch of that peculiar tomcat smell that eucalyptus trees give off in warm weather. (*HW*, XII, 372)

According to the economy I have described above, Marlowe's living quarters (the Bristol Apartments on Bristol Avenue, then the Hobart Arms at Franklin and Kenmore) will become something like extensions of his office in this respect. What it is crucial to observe is that we may deduce a momentous change, not merely in Chandler's narrative form itself, but in the history and the social relations from which the particular narrative shape of his content springs, when, in *The Long Goodbye*, we find that Marlowe has moved from the classic urban apartment building into a private home: 'I was living that year in a house on Yucca Avenue in the Laurel Canyon district. It was a small hillside house on a dead-end street with a long flight of redwood steps to the front door and a grove of eucalyptus trees along the way . . .'[9] It is the end of an era! and the moment at which Marlowe's marriage (to money) and relocation to La Jolla become unexpectedly imaginable.

II

The system we have initially traced here – our first, essentially synchronic one – now suggests two further comments. The first has to do with closure as such. For there can be no question that this particular 'map' of the social totality is a complete and closed semiotic system: unified by the category of the 'office', its various positions and inversions are able in a satisfactory and satisfying manner to span the breadth of the social system from wealth to poverty and (in the area of crime and vice) from public to private. This is, to be sure, an ideologically motivated vision or scale model of the social, which strategically omits or represses production as such, along with the law-abiding, average, peaceful middle classes themselves (although it would be a mistake to imply thereby that any nonideological, 'scientific', representationally adequate map of the social could be imagined to take its place – following Althusser's definition of ideology,[10] all visions of the social in this sense will be equally ideological, although not equivalent in political or even aesthetic value).

But the very closure of this system now presents a problem in its own right. We have so far largely followed the implications of a classic structuralist aesthetic, which tended to conflate structural systematicity and aesthetic value, or at least the aesthetic effect of formal closure and formal satisfaction. Although it is nowhere very explicitly argued (Barthes comes closest in various passing remarks), the suggestion is that a work or a narrative is felt to be completed when it has been able to touch all the bases in some underlying semiotic system; that unconscious cognitive acknowledgement of systematicity is then transferred to the surface of the work of art, which can be pronounced in one way or another a full form, a completed thing.[11] Indeed, all four of Chandler's first novels (with the few specific historical modifications we have noted in *The Lady in the Lake*) do succeed in touching all the relevant bases and are in that sense very complete itineraries through the social system of the Chandlerian cognitive map.

But that is precisely the problem, since we started from the (not merely personal) impression that *The High Window* was somehow, despite the rare quality and intensity of several of its individual episodes, distinctly less satisfying as an overall narrative than the other three. How are we to account for this impression, given that the same social and semiotic system is in operation in this novel as in the others and that it is to this system that we have been tempted to attribute their value and aesthetic effect?

The obvious first step lies in a critique of the limits of what we have done so far: but this must be a twofold critique, both empirical and methodological. We may begin by seeing what was omitted from the previous system, but we should not neglect the possibility that it is the very way in which the semiotic concept of a system is framed that may be at issue here. In the first case, it is conceivable that another system might be constructed and projected that would not be altogether coterminous with the first, and which might allow the difference between *The High Window* and the other novels to become visible. In the second case, the dissatisfaction with our analytic results would tend to move us toward a more general critique of semiotics as such, as a system capable of including or processing certain kinds of materials of a uniform type – whether these be semes or realities. Such a critique would then lead us not automatically to posit an alternative type of system, but rather, more dialectically, to designate conceptualities or reflexivities, negativities, absences, which do not register on the essentially positivistic apparatus of the semiotic recording device.

I think, for example, of some of the truly wondrous effects in *The Lady in the Lake* which can scarcely be conveyed by the socio-spatial notations we have devised so far, since they derive from the swooping sense of a radical shift in worlds. Such an effect is produced, for instance, after Marlowe makes his way down from Fawn Lake, where he has discovered a dead body, explored the tourist village and the cabins, had lengthy encounters with the local sheriff, and finally interrogated the rather seedy bellhops in the hotel in San Bernadino where the fleeing suspect is likely to have spent the night. The very next day, in Bay City (Santa Monica), he visits the expensive home of one of those playboys we have already mentioned, which stands across the street from the equally expensive home (or 'office') of a shady society doctor. The shift from Fawn Lake to Bay City is so extraordinary as to make us imagine we have opened the pages of a different novel. We experience something like a generic–ontological discontinuity, a well-nigh phenomenological substitution of worlds, which cannot, for that very reason, be described in purely social terms. Lavery, for instance, has visited the lake; and the Kingsleys, whose cabin Marlowe went to see, clearly inhabit both worlds, which can scarcely be seen as city and country in the older agricultural sense, but at best in terms of an opposition between tourist industry and workplace. Still, what used to be called nature must somehow be in play here, if only because of the deployment of mountain roads and the extraordinary images of the drowned body, which first 'waves' hesitatingly beneath the water and then boils up to the surface along with accompanying objects ('an ancient rotted plank popped suddenly through the surface, struck out a full foot of its jagged end, and fell back with a flat slap and floated off' [*LL*, VI, 499]). And the ending – the soldiers on guard on the bridge across the Puma Lake dam – bears witness to an unusual semic combination of history, nature and human production rare even in Chandler.

In this respect, it is also worth recalling other combinations of motifs in these novels that one might have been tempted to think of as purely aesthetic or formal, but that in this context now begin to appear as the insistence, through a purely social–typological fabric, of other orders of being or reality. These are the colour motifs, by which people and their settings (Vivian Regan's 'white' apartment, the 'grey' insistently associated with Eddie Mars) are as it were reunified into metaphorical *actants* in which the relationships between characters and space or furniture are relatively more organic and quite different from the tensions and syncopated inconsistencies described above. And they also include the meteorological rhythms, particularly in *The Big Sleep*, where a host of precise and vivid indications signals the change of weather from scene to scene, thereby reuniting the interior chapters, the indoor experiences as it were, to the atmospheric unity of the Los Angeles basin as a whole.[12] Here too, then, a different kind of 'totalization' can be found at work, which has nothing to do with the overall plot itself or with the social-character system, but which somehow sketches in the presence of some vaster, absent natural unity beyond this ephemeral set of episodes in punctual human time.

In any case, Los Angeles has so often been thought of as a different kind of city – sunbelt megalopolis of the future, portending fundamental changes in the classic urban structure and incorporating modern transport media in new structural ways[13] – that it is worth allowing for the possibility that (quite unlike Hammett's San Francisco, for example) this particular deployment of the 'urban' includes nature in a dialectically different way, which may escape the older kinds of semic oppositions.

Everything I have said so far, however, suggests the necessity of thinking these formal peculiarities in Chandler according to some scheme that is capable of flexing dualisms while remaining deeply suspicious of them, and that programmatically avoids the attribution of any *a priori* content to terms hitherto implicitly predefined by such traditional oppositions as subject and object or nature and culture. This is, as is well known, the very programme of Heidegger's philosophical revolution, and I hope it will not be taken as an ideological endorsement of this particular philosophy when I suggest that its speculative machinery – particularly as evidenced in *The Origins of the Work of Art*[14] – may well turn out to offer a theoretical solution to some of the problems posed by Chandler's narrative structures. The juxtaposition of the detective story novelist and the Central European philosopher–sage – rendered even more incongruous by the palpable high-cultural conservatism of Heidegger himself, and his more general suspicion of modernity and technology as such, let alone of formal and aesthetic reproducibility – may be justified, from a different angle, by the way in which the philosopher's aesthetic proposition assimilates in advance the act of poetic inauguration he wishes to think to other forms of the inaugural or the originative: to the philosophical itself, for example, which reopens the question of Being; or to the religious; or to the political, in which a new type of society and new social relations find themselves – from Romulus to Lenin – instituted in what can only be described as a revolutionary act and break.[15] Although Los Angeles lacks any radical legendary foundational act of this kind, the historical novelty of its structure – which has so often been transferred to Chandler, as the writer equally often considered to be that city's epic poet – may encourage us to consider the relevance of Heidegger's argument which, to be sure, mobilizes the far more classical texts of the Greek temple and the more explosive modernity of Van Gogh's oil painting. Any attempt to adapt narrative as such to Heidegger's scheme would seem, however, to do it violence at the same time as (no matter how classical the narrative in question) it would require a good deal of analytical and interpretive ingenuity.

For the terms of Heidegger's aesthetic – which seeks, as we shall see, to include and transcend space as such – are still expressed in a spatial metaphor that tends to immobilize them, to impose on them a kind of static condition that may initially make them seem more suited to the visual arts and architecture (something his own examples, as we have seen, do nothing to overcome). Indeed, he predicates the work of art (and, by implication only, the other inaugural acts I have enumerated) as emerging from a gap or rift between World and Earth. I will of course attempt to name this gap or rift in other ways and with codes quite unrelated to these, but it is initially clear, none the less, that such language continues to figure incommensurability on the model of the mountain crevice, the glacial crack or fissure, the unbridgeable chasm or canyon between plateaux that can no longer be reunited or even recombined in the unity of a single thought: the world of Fawn Lake as it were, versus the world of Altair Street in Bay City. But this is not yet a satisfactory way of reformulating the Heideggerian 'gap', since in its initial version both sides of the tension seemed to be given to us in the terms of one, the Earth, while in our translation it is the opposite term, World, which serves this same function.

Heidegger's deployment of this opposition at the moment he touches on the art object as such points a way out of this dilemma. It is the materiality of the object, he tells us, the sonority of the language, the smoothness of the marble, or the slick density of the oil paint, that marks the part of Earth in it; while it is the semiotic features of the work, the meanings and meaningfulness – what is paraphrasable in the verse, the functions of the building, the object imitated by the painting – that indicate the part of World. What seems crucial here – and specifically Heideggerian – is that the opposition between Earth and World be understood as irreducible in the last instance, no matter how much each becomes implicated in the other, no matter how crushing the preponderance of one term in their struggle. Thus, the work of art itself, exhibited in that worldly place that is the museum, and drawn into a web of social and worldly relationships – those of sale and investment, interpretation and evaluation, pedagogy, tradition, sacred reference – must always somehow scandalously exceed all those worldly relationships by the ultimate and irreducible materiality of its earthly element, which cannot become social: there is a colour that cannot be made altogether human. In the same way, clearly, the work's emergence as a kind of aerolith in sheer space – a meteor from the void, taking a place, being measurable, weighing, being accessible to the physical senses – can never quite entitle it to full inert status as a thing among other things. Allegorically, indeed, this primal opposition in Heidegger's aesthetic can be read as a refusal of fundamental philosophical dualisms while acknowledging the inevitability of their existence and persistence. The meanings of World suggest any number of idealisms in which reality is thought to have been successfully assimilated to Mind once and for all, while the resistance of Earth marks the resurgence of the various materialisms that try to stage their sense of the fragility of meanings in physical reality by way of meaningful words. The ontology that wishes to escape ideological imprisonment in either idealism or materialism can then only do so by foretelling the inevitable temptations of both and using them against each other in a permanent tension that cannot be resolved.

I will suggest, then, that World, from the Heideggerian perspective, be understood in different terms as History itself, that is to say, as the ensemble of acts and efforts whereby human beings have attempted, since the dawn of a human age, to bring meanings out of the limits and constraints of their surroundings. Earth, meanwhile, is everything meaningless in those surroundings and what betrays the resistance and inertia of sheer Matter as such and extends as far as what human beings have named as death, contingency, accident, bad luck, or finitude. What is distinctive about Heidegger's proposal is the insistence not merely that these two 'dimensions' of reality are radically incommensurable with each other, and somehow unrelatable in terms of either, but also that philosophy, and following it, aesthetics, and perhaps even politics as well, must now find its specific vocation, not in the attempt to paper over the difference or to mystify it and theorize it away, so much as to exacerbate and hold it open as an ultimate situation of unresolvable tension. (I avoid the word 'contradiction', since it is so often wrongly felt to promise its own resolution in idealist fashion.)

This is the perspective from which the work of art emerges, not to heal this rift or even to assuage what is seen as an incurable wound in our very being, this gap between History and Matter, or World and Earth. Rather, the great or authentic works (for Heidegger's aesthetic, like aesthetic systems as such, necessarily includes a normative moment) are those whose vocation consists in holding the two incommensurable dimensions apart and in allowing us thereby to glimpse them simultaneously in all their scandalous irreconcilability: to grasp Earth or Matter in all its irreducible materiality, even and particularly there where we have been thinking about it in terms of meaning and human and social events: and to grasp World or History in its most fundamental historicities even where we have been assuming it to be inert nature or nonsocial landscape. Although its aesthetic relevance would have been utterly alien and repugnant to him, Adorno aptly captured the spirit of this alternation-in-tension when in another context he recommended that we constantly defamiliarize our philosophies of human history by rethinking them in terms of natural history, and demystify our positivistic impressions of natural history by thinking them through again in historicist and social ways.[16] But in Heidegger, at least in these privileged instances among which the work of art is numbered, the alternation becomes a blinding simultaneity, both dimensions now momentarily coexisting.

The rift in Chandler, however, if we are able to posit one, can surely not take on so benign an appearance as that of the opening of a human and social drama out onto an essentially natural landscape, particularly since that landscape has already been itself fully humanized by the process of urban construction, and also since the social system we have discoverd at work in Chandler has already tended to endow itself with spatial expression, so that the character types are already at least styles of architecture and gardening, and associated with specific neighbourhoods or even ecologies (as Banham called them). Nothing is indeed quite so depressingly human or social as the tourist industry itself, so that the distinctive phenomenological 'world' we have posited for Fawn Lake cannot have much to do with its survival as the sheerly natural and inhuman, in contrast to the world of human streets and occupations and passions down below. Yet Fawn Lake is in another sense something like the end of a trajectory, a point beyond which neither writer nor character can seem to go, and which marks the end of the road by being somehow beyond it. We may here want to recall the equally memorable ending of *Farewell, My Lovely* which, also couched in the language of distance or space, seems to attempt to transcend it by cancelling it out: 'It was a cool day and very clear. You could see a long way – but not as far as Velma had gone' (*FML*, XL, 315). It is not because Fawn Lake is associated with death after the fashion of this sentence that we reach the end of the road as such but, rather, the other way around: it is because of Fawn Lake's spatial peculiarity and involution that the theme of death can win back such power of evocation.

Farewell, My Lovely is in many ways Chandler's most ambitious novel, as well as his most romantic; and thereby offers as promising an occasion as any other for an examination of what, in the enumeration of the separate and specific episodes, seems to exceed that socio-typological system we synoptically abstracted from the superposition of the four novels upon each other. The novel includes the spaces of the rich (the Grayles, though less fully developed than in *The Big Sleep* or *The High Window*), the spaces of poverty of marginalized people and things (Jess Florian's house); it also includes one of the memorable playboy villas – that of Marriott, whose function can be situated somewhere between Geiger's house and the various gigolo establishments – along with the usual gambling casinos, several distinctive dens of vice (Amthor's oddly modernistic dwelling and Dr Sonderborg's 'hospital'), as well as different police offices, including Marlowe's own. But Chandler tried to move, not always successfully, into new territory here; the unresolved episode of Anne Riordan introduces the possibility of a partnership–romance to which Chandler will not return until after Marlowe's marriage. Meanwhile, Marlowe is in this novel knocked out several times, by a blow to the head and by drugs, something Dick Powell exploited memorably in his film version (*Murder, My Sweet*, 1944), but which is not completely consistent with the premium placed on disabused lucidity by the voice-over format. This may, indeed give us our first clue: in the attempt to draw the nonconscious, the other of conscious observation or of a signed 'point-of-view' into the narrative, Chandler was always careful to keep at a certain generic distance from the adventure format (in which, as with Dick Francis, the hero is regularly beaten up, tortured, pursued, etcetera).

Such moments – which imitate death itself by allowing the conscious or named personality to come into contact with its own end or extinction – also seem to transform the spaces at which they occur. Sonderborg's 'hospital' is, to be sure, not so metaphorically outside the world, but Marlowe's first bout of literal unconsciousness is even more interesting. It takes place literally at the end of a road, at the dead end of an unbuilt street beyond which Marlowe and Marriott are supposed to rendezvous with the thieves who have offered to sell back Mrs Grayle's Fei Tsui jade. The place, called Purissima Canyon, is marked 'by a white fence of four-by-fours' (*FML*, IX, 176) at the end of a paved street; and this white wooden barrier (like the memorable wooden fence in Antonioni's *Blow-Up*, which is neither symbol nor contingent reality-effect, neither expressive, semiotic, nor social sign, is surely one of the most fascinating things in all of Chandler, as though it somehow spelled the very end of space itself.

But, if this is what we are looking for, any reader of *Farewell, My Lovely* knows that its ultimate strong form is to be found elsewhere in that novel: in the dramatic closing sequence on the gambling boats moored beyond the three-mile jurisdictional limit, riding on the open sea in front of Bay City. These boats – immense floating casinos – are indeed virtually as far from Los Angeles as one ever gets in Chandler (save in the last two novels, where we touch down in Kansas and Mexico respectively):

A faint music came over the water and music over the water can never be anything but lovely. The *Royal Crown* seemed to ride as steady as a pier on its four hawsers. Its landing stage was lit up like a theater marquee. Then all this faded into remoteness and another, older smaller boat began to sneak out of the night towards us. It was not much to look at. A converted seagoing freighter with scummed and rusted plates, the superstructure cut down to the boat deck level, and above that two stumpy masts just high enough for a radio antenna. There was light on the *Montecito* also and music floated across the wet dark sea. The spooning couples took their teeth out of each other's necks and stared at the ship and giggled. (*FML*, XXXV, 286)

Although the social relations on board are not much different from those we have left behind (Brunette here standing in for the stock Chandler type of the likeable gangster with a heart of gold), Marlowe's adventuresome approach and final arrival there have all the mythic qualities of the perilous journey, the passage to another realm or world; while the sea itself glitters with all that mineral fascination, that radically nonhuman, cold, even unnatural mystery that the ocean often has for writers like the essentially urban Chandler, who do not specialize in sea stories, or for cultures that are nonmaritime. This is to say that – especially since we do not fantasize Los Angeles as a port city (unlike Hammett's San Francisco which memorably greets the arrival of the *La Paloma*) – the liquid element does not exist here within the narrative world, is not a part of its semiotic system, but rather lies beyond it and cancels it as such. We need a stronger negative for this unimaginable exterior face of that monad (that we can ourselves only witness from within, as a complete world, as precisely *without* limits), particularly since the inner system is itself made up of a host of differentiated negations (contraries and contradictories alike) about which what one wants to say is that they too – negatives and positives alike, all swept up together in a jumble of semic existents – are precisely what this chill outer realm refuses and repudiates. Nor is it really worthwhile pronouncing the term 'Other' (or 'Otherness'), which so strongly reaffirms its secret internal relations with the thing-itself. The sea is here cleansed even of otherness; and it would be tempting to associate it with death itself, that nonplace and nonspace where Velma goes, and where the big sleep of the earlier novel is slept. But even this strikes me as sentimentalism, and the attribution of an inner-worldly content to a nonspace whose function it is, rather – anti-semiotic yet poetic all at the same time – precisely to appropriate even the word *death* itself and to lend it a specific, private, and hauntingly Chandlerian tone.

In other words, death itself is in Chandler something like a spatial concept, a spatial construction; as is nature, when at its farthest verge – staring down into the uncommon depths of Fawn Lake – it touches on the outer edge of Being itself. We find here therefore the operation of a second system or dimension in coordination yet in tension with the first socio-semiotic one. This last organizes people and their dwellings into a cognitive map of Los Angeles that Marlowe can be seen to canvass, pushing the doorbells of so many social types, from the great mansions to the junk-filled rooms on Bunker Hill or West 54th Place. But this dimension – in Heideggerian language, that of World – has no grounding or resonance unless it circulates slowly against the rotation of that other, deeper anti-system which is that of Earth itself, and which can include space and 'nature' only at the price of transcending them and enveloping them in its own global negation, coupling them with the nonspace of the outer limit, the white wooden barrier at the end of the world.

In retrospect, this ultimate dimension can be detected in various places in *The Big Sleep* as well, and not only in the oil derricks that mark the seam between a prehistoric nature and the fitful traces of heroic political history in this social world which, after the deeds of Rusty Regan's IRA or the General's Mexican War ancestor, appears to be in a state or condition of the most feeble survival, warming itself in its own decadence with so many forms of vice. (This will, however, be the last time in Chandler's work that this particular elegiac note is sounded.) But we fail to come to terms with the peculiar form of this narrative, which can at first seem broken-backed and clumsily divided in half, when the search for Eddie Mars's wife is suddenly substituted for the completion of the Geiger matter, unless we see that the garage in which the fugitive is held is itself yet another such place at the very edge of Being:

I drove north across the river, on into Pasadena, through Pasadena and almost at once I was in orange groves. The tumbling rain was solid white spray in the headlights. The windshield wiper could hardly keep the glass clear enough to see through. But not even the drenched darkness could hide the flawless lines of the orange trees wheeling away like endless spokes into the night.

Cars passed with a tearing hiss and a wave of dirty spray. The highway jerked through a little town that was all packing houses and sheds, and railway sidings nuzzling them. The groves thinned out and dropped away to the south and the road climbed and it was cold and to the north the black foothills crouched closer and sent a bitter wind whipping down their flanks. Then faintly out of the dark two yellow vapor lights glowed high up in the air and a neon sign between them said 'Welcome to Realito.'

Frame houses were spaced far back from a wide main street, then a sudden knot of stores, the lights of a drugstore behind fogged glass, the fly-cluster of cars in front of the movie theater, a dark bank on a corner with a clock sticking out over the sidewalk and a group of people standing in the rain looking at its windows, as if they were some kind of a show. I went on. Empty fields closed in again.

Fate stage-managed the whole thing. Beyond Realito, just about a mile beyond, the highway took a curve and the rain fooled me and I went too close to the shoulder. My right front tire let go with an angry hiss. Before I could stop the right rear went with it. I jammed the car to a stop, half on the pavement, half on the shoulder, got out and flashed a spotlight around. I had two flats and one spare. The flat butt of a heavy galvanized tack stared at me from the front tire.

The edge of the pavement was littered with them. They had been swept off, but not far enough off.

I snapped the flash off and stood there breathing rain and looking up a side road at a yellow light. It seemed to come from a skylight. The skylight could belong to a garage, the garage could be run by a man named Art Huck, and there could be a frame house next door to it. I tucked my chin down in my collar and started towards it, then went back to unstrap the license holder from the steering post and put it in my pocket. I leaned lower under the wheel. Behind a weighted flap, directly under my right leg as I sat in the car, there was a hidden compartment. There were two guns in it. One belonged to Eddie Mars's boy Lanny and one belonged to me. I took Lanny's. It would have had more practice than mine. I stuck it nose down in an inside pocket and started up the side road.

The garage was a hundred yards from the highway. It showed the highway a blank side wall. I played the flash on it quickly. 'Art Huck – Auto Repairs and Painting.'(*BS*, XXVII, 110–111)

Indeed, another kind of inquiry might want to make some connections between this spatial involution and the intermittent visions of evil in Chandler (for not the least original feature of his modification of the detective story is that his crimes do without villains; or, if you prefer, the villains are social – police corruption – rather than antisocial in the conventional meaning of this word). But here, in this remote garage, we find the more sinister Canino, who poisoned Harry Jones and prepares to torture Marlowe to death. Canino's function, however, is not finally to supply us with a villain and with evil, but rather, like the space itself, to stand as the Other and the negation of that true but human and inner-worldly murder that is the shooting of Regan (and indeed the source of the other violent crimes throughout the novel). Meanwhile, as for nature itself – as though the remote location of the hideaway were not enough, and in the spirit of the meteorology of the other chapters – Chandler drowns this one pouring rain, deep inland restoring the watery element that is the sign of the nonhuman axis of matter in these novels.

We may now swiftly conclude, for our inquiry has virtually answered itself: *The High Window* (for we began with its problematic features some pages back) fails to have the signal resonance of the other Chandlers – despite its remarkable episodic work – because it utterly lacks this dimension of the spatial outside or underside deployed in them. Did Chandler feel, perhaps, that great height – the fall into the void, not waving but 'screaming with fear' – might somehow complete the centre of his narrative with the necessary absence? The case itself, however, is closed and long since filed away.

NOTES

1. References to the novels are from *The Raymond Chandler Omnibus* (New York: Modern Library, 1975) and will be made within the text by means of the following abbreviations: *The Big Sleep* (1939) = *BS*; *Farewell, My Lovely* (1940) = *FML*; *The High Window* (1942) = *HW*; *The Lady in the Lake* (1943) = *LL*. Since Chandler's novels have been reprinted in many different editions, there follows, for the convenience of the reader, the number of the chapter in question, in Roman numerals; and finally the page reference in the Modern Library edition.

2. See Tania Modleski's brilliant chapter on soaps as an emergent form of decentred narrative in *Loving with a Vengeance* (Hamden, CT.: Archon, 1982), p. 90ff.

3. Quoted in my essay 'On Raymond Chandler', *Southern Review*, vol. VI, no. 3 (Summer 1970), pp. 624–50. The reader of this older text may wish silently to correct an understandable, yet exasperating misprint on page 626; for 'take for example some perfectly significant event', read 'take for example some perfectly insignificant event'.

4. Radio is thus impeccably Sartrean; see the well-known reflections on narrative in J.-P. Sartre, *Nausea* (New York: New Directions, 1964), trans. L. Alexander, p. 38ff.

5. I like this one, which might still 'render' southern California today: 'On the highway the lights of the streaming cars made an almost solid beam in both directions. The big cornpoppers were rolling north growling as they went and festooned all over with green and yellow overhand lights' (*FML*, IX, 176).

6. 'Dwelling' (*Wohnen*) is here a gerundive formation taken in the Heideggerian sense of 'Bauen Wohnen Denken', in *Vortage und Aufsatze* (Neske, 1985), pp. 139–56.

7. Roland Barthes, 'L'effet de réel', *Communications*, vol. 11 (March 1968), pp. 84–9.

8. An indispensable aid to these sites is available in the form of *The Raymond Chandler Mystery Map*, published by Aaron Blake Publishers (1800 S. Robertson Blvd, Suite 130, Los Angeles, CA 90035), 1985.

9. *The Long Goodbye* (Boston: Houghton Mifflin, 1954), p. 4.

10. The reference is to the addendum to L. Althusser, 'Ideological State Apparatuses', in *Lenin and Philosophy* (New York: Monthly Review Press, 1971).

11. But see, for a more orthodox application of the structuralist aesthetic, my 'Spatial Systems

in *North by Northwest'*, in Slavoj Žižek, ed., *Everything You Always Wanted to Know about Lacan but Were Afraid to Ask Hitchcock* (London: Verso, 1992).

12. These motifs are somewhat more fully explored in the first version of this chapter, published as 'L'Éclatement du récit et la clôture californienne', trans. M. Mekies, in *Littérature*, no. 49 (February 1983), pp. 89–101.

13. But see Rayner Banham's wonderful *Los Angeles: The Architecture of Four Ecologies* (London: Penguin, 1971).

14. In R. Hofstadter and R. Kuhns, eds., *Philosophies of Art and Beauty* (New York: Modern Library, 1964), pp. 649–701.

15. Derrida's analysis of this Heideggerian text (in Jacques Derrida, 'Restitutions', *The Truth in Painting* [Chicago: University of Chicago Press, 1987]) identifies the essay's deeper unconscious commitment to 'representability' as an ideological structure in which Heidegger's North American critic, Meyer Schapiro, is also gripped. It may therefore be worth restoring the historical and allegorical level at which Schapiro's essay can be read as a crucial political move and permutation. The essay turned on the suggestion that the footgear depicted in Van Gogh's painting might not be the shoes of a peasant woman at all, but rather the painter's own. It thereby substituted an auto-referential act for a populist or political–foundational one (as in Heidegger himself). Schapiro's reversal thus becomes supremely emblematic of that new post-war, high-modernist ideology with which the members of a formerly left intelligentsia replaced their political commitments during the Cold War period. The reversal, which now rediverts our attention to the painter himself and the act of painting, also conceals its apostate anti-communism beneath a perfectly acceptable repudiation of the defeated Fascist positions.

16. See, on this point, my *Late Marxism* (London and New York: Verso, 1990), p. 94ff.

3

STRANGE PURSUIT: CORNELL WOOLRICH AND THE ABANDONED CITY OF THE FORTIES

David Reid and Jayne L. Walker

I

In 1935 the popular English novelist and playwright J. B. Priestley, travelling in the United States, was alarmed by rumours of a new terrain in the American way of crime. 'It is not a tropical underworld of hot blood and passion, of people too barbaric for the bourgeois virtues,' he wrote in *Midnight on the Desert*. Rather,

> It is a chilly, grey, cellar-like, fungus world, of greed, of calculated violence and a cold sensuality. The more austere writers of American detective stories, such as Dashiell Hammett, seem to show us that world . . . How big is this particular America? Does it exist only in a few big cities. And if there is not much of it, why do we hear so much about it?[1]

Priestley had a sharp, prophetic eye for *noir* effects – he called them telegrams from hell – in newsprint, between hard covers, and on screen, where he claimed to find 'great slabs' of this new regime on display. Perhaps it helped that he was a middlebrow from abroad with little American cultural capital to prejudice his views. Later, in the post-war forties, when *film noir* was in its classic phase and the *Partisan Review* critics were busy discovering America, Mary McCarthy would dismiss *noir* as a childish mythology in which only a gullible existentialist like Simone de Beauvoir could believe. 'We admired and liked our country; we preferred it to that imaginary country, land of the *peaux rouges* of Caldwell and Steinbeck, dumb paradise of violence and the detective story, which had excited the sensibilities of our visitor and of the up-to-date French literary world.'[2] In contrast to McCarthy, who literally could not see what was in front of her eyes ('there were no good Hollywood movies' in 1947, she declared firmly, and no decent players either), Priestley in 1935 had somehow managed to write a passable trailer for a cycle of doomy harsh-shadowed somnabulistic films that was actually ten years in the future.

Midnight on the Desert brings out the essential continuity between *roman noir* and *film noir*: the imagination of disaster in both was Depression-bred. Mike Davis makes this point in *City of Quartz*, when he observes of the Los Angeles novels of the thirties that the 'Depression-crazed middle classes of Southern California became, in one mode or another, the original protagonists of that great anti-myth known as *noir*'.[3] Indeed, the Depression so burdens the sense of the past that even the novels and stories Hammett published before *Crash* now read as if they were prophetic meditations on what came after. But the most dramatic evidence of continuity lies in the thrillers of Cornell Woolrich, the canonical *noir* novelist most often adapted for the movies in the 1940s. In Woolrich's fiction, New York – any big city – is not simply *noir*; literally, it is mad, bad, and dangerous to know. The Depression never lifted and threatens to become eternal; the city is fallen and inescapable. Not an uplifting vision, to say the least, but one that proved answerable to the particular anxieties of the forties. Woolrich recommended himself to audiences and film producers with plots that were like little infernal machines for generating suspense and have now survived the texts in which they appeared. (Compared to Hammett, Raymond Chandler and James M. Cain, he has few readers today.) There is an attractive historical symmetry in the fact that his narratives of the fallen, Depression-bound city rhyme closely with obsessions, in the long-forgotten sensational American fiction of exactly a century before, when the big American city first emerged. But the real literary-historical irony of his case, one that even the Columbia University-educated Woolrich almost certainly did not grasp, was how conventional and in its way respectable his urban apocalypse really was.

The most familiar interpretation of *film noir* presents it as a sort of dark allegory of the post-war 1940s, starring such abstractions as 'the loss of wartime unity' and post-war economic conditions. Or, as Sylvia Harvey writes in her much-quoted article from 1980: 'The hard facts of economic life are transmuted, in these movies, into corresponding moods and feelings. Thus the feelings of loss and alienation expressed by the characters in film noir can be seen as the product both of post-war depression and of the reorganisation of the American economy.'[4] Though there are far more nuanced versions, for example by Dana Polan, this remains in its essentials the standard historical interpretation.[5] (By *film noir* and *roman noir*, we mean the works that are customarily taxonomized as such, for example in standard works such as the encyclopaedic *Film Noir*, of Silver and Ward. The controversy over whether *film noir* represents a genre or a movement [as opposed to the more interesting matter of whether it exists at all], not to mention the terminological niceness that would deny the title of *noir* to any film with an equivocal, let alone happy ending, threatens to become as tiresome as the ancient and now extinct argument over the possibility of bourgeois tragedy.)[6]

In a 1991 essay in the *New York Review of Books*, Geoffrey O'Brien denies that *film noir* ever appealed to the supposedly endemic disillusionments, displacements, anxieties, or nihilism of the Truman years:

> The movies' actual effects might more accurately be considered not so much a 'universe' or a 'sensibility' – and certainly not the 'movement' that one writer calls it – as a particular sheen, a slick new variety of packaging, faddish at the time and subsequently much prized by connoisseurs: a nexus of fashions in hair, fashions in lighting, fashions in interior decoration, fashions in motivation, fashions in repartee.[7]

Thus O'Brien sets straight not only the sort of overambitious critic who straightfacedly pursues the origins of *film noir* all the way back to the theatre of Dionysos, but also the standard view. Even Paul Schrader, who very nicely described *film noir* as 'a nightmarish world of American mannerism', also earnestly supposed that films in this cycle answered to 'the public's desire for a more honest and harsh view of America'.[8]

Up to a point, no doubt, the frankness and disillusionment may have had its appeal, but there has always been something wildly unpersuasive about the notion that *films noirs* continued to attract customers in the late forties, when movie receipts were plunging, principally because times were anxious and people wanted to massage their gloom. Contrary to settled mythology, audiences actually began to drift away from the movie palaces in advance of television; weekly attendances fell from 80 million per week in 1946 to 67 million in 1948, when there were still only 1 million television sets in the country (up to 6,500 in 1945).[9] The combination of grandiosity, self-destructiveness, and panic with which Hollywood reacted to the audience's desertion is the subtext of Nicholas Ray's *In a Lonely Place* (1950), which is set in the jittery Hollywood of 1949. (Bogart, playing a near-psychotic screenwriter, says to restaurateur-conman Mike Romanoff, playing himself: 'How's business?' Romanoff: 'Like show business. There's no business.') For the major studios, particularly Warner and RKO, *film noir* represented simply one of many devices, including in time everything from 'adult' westerns to 3-D, used to captivate the restive mass audience or retain the hardcore one. Sex, death and pop nihilism could be depended upon to accomplish the latter, then as now. A vehicle for social criticism in the hands of a director like Ray, *film noir* was also a set of conventions available to a sturdy hack like Sam Wood (*A Day at the Races*, *Kings Row*), a fanatical right-winger, indeed the man who invited the House Un-American Activities Committee to investigate the movies. (Wood directed *Ivy*, a rare example of period *film noir*, based on a story by Marie Belloc-Lowndes, which came out in 1947.) No doubt, Geoffrey O'Brien's turn to slick packaging and a 'nexus of fashions' to explain why *film noir* crystallized at the moment it did discloses as much about the trend-besotted atmosphere in which he is writing as it does about the forties. But then, something like the same could be said of the interpretations he lampoons – which find in the peculiarly dense, complicated, tragic and sometimes ludicrous politics of 1944–50 a mere rough draft of the cultural wars of the sixties and seventies.[10]

If anything, the mythology that now surrounds World War Two and is regularly invoked in criticism of *film noir* – notably, the chain-mail solidarity that supposedly characterized the home front – confirms that nothing is more changeable than the past. How quickly the conflict that the young Norman Mailer called a 'mirror that blinded everyone who looked into it', was sentimentalized into 'the good war'. How swiftly forgotten were the thousands of work stoppages, including hate strikes, racial strife (hardly limited to Detroit and Los Angeles), John L. Lewis's duel with Roosevelt, the congressional attack on the New Deal, and the bitter and morose 1944 presidential election (now remembered only for FDR's 'Fala' speech).[11]

Paradoxically, it was precisely the success of 'wartime nationalism' and its subsequent deflection into the forty-four-year crusade against communism and the national security state that dissolved these memories. Such giant effects had larger causes and more important authors than the agencies actually charged with wartime propaganda. The principal agencies of this propaganda – the ill-fated Office of Facts and Figures and its successor, the Office of War Information (OWI) – were faction-ridden, unpopular with Congress, and scarcely capable of formulating a coherent line on the war, let alone imposing it. Much of what conservatives found objectionable in the films, radio scripts and pamphlets produced by the New Deal faction in the OWI amounted to premature 'political correctness', as it is now stigmatized, such as monitoring the comic strips for racial attitudes or signs of undue 'individualism' (as demonstrated for example by Terry of 'Terry and the Pirates').[12]

In Hollywood, the Bureau of Motion Pictures vetted scripts, imposed export restrictions on objectionable films, and encouraged an all-consuming concentration on the war effort. The studios were craven on principle, but even in wartime Paramount, whose upper management was violently against the New Deal, usually declined to submit scripts for review. In general, restrictions on camera film and budgets for studio sets had a much larger effect on film-making than exhortations or overt censorship, especially after it became clear that emphasis on the war was leaving the public bored and restless: in July 1943 *Variety* headlined: 'STUDIOS SHELVE WAR STORIES AS THEY SHOW 40% BOX OFFICE DECLINE'. Thus, an early *noir* entry like *Street of Chance* (1942), based on Woolrich's *The Black Curtain*, would have had a novelty appeal, an appeal which may also perhaps explain the surprise success of a more elaborate adaptation, *Phantom Lady* (Robert Siodmak, 1944).[13]

From the potted histories that appear in many studies of *film noir*, one might think that all the worst forebodings of 1945 were actually realized. Indeed, the strike wave of 1945–46 was the largest in American history – it was estimated to have cost 107,475,000 lost days of work – and large portions of the public were horrified or outraged. Immediately after the war there were meat shortages, housing shortages, a thriving black market, startling increases in the price of living, bitter debate over price controls, and a generally sullen public temper. But there was no post-war depression. The GNP dipped to $231 billion in 1947, the lowest since 1942, rebounded to $258 billion the next year, dropped slightly in 1948, then grew for the next twenty-two years until the American Century shuddered to a close in the presidency of Richard M. Nixon (who launched his political career in 1946). Per capita annual income in 1947 was about $1,750, measured in constant 1939 dollars, down from the wartime peak of $1,900; but it was depressed to this extent only because of a vastly increased fertility rate (the beginning of the entirely unanticipated, by demographers at least, baby boom). In 1947 the distribution of income in the United States was more nearly equal (which of course was not very) than before or since. At no time did the economy seriously threaten to contract to the dimensions of the 1930s, nor did the spectre of mass unemployment at Depression levels ever come close to materializing, despite widespread fears that both of these things were virtually inevitable. If the conditions of 1938 (one in five out of work), let alone of 1933, had ever returned, there would have been more dramatic results to reckon with than a vogue for moody genre pictures.[14]

What of the Freudian argument made by Frank Krutnik in *In a Lonely Street*, but not only by him, that *film noir* assisted in restoring a 'phallic order' threatened by the wartime mobilization of women and other such awful spectacles?[15] Perhaps the

Phantom Lady (Robert Siodmak, 1944)

femmes fatales in *film noir*, the sirens portrayed by Jane Greer, Gloria Grahame, Lana Turner and the rest, really did somehow represent the Medusa face of Rosie the Riveter, and Joan Crawford playing Mildred Pierce is punished for Rosie's impudence. But again, it was not during or after World War Two but during the Depression that the prejudice against working women (who were supposedly depriving male bread-winners of jobs) was most acute. Thus, Norman Cousins, that reliable liberal-middlebrow bellwether, observed in 1939: 'There are approximately 10,000,000 people out of work in the United States today; there are 10,000,000 or more women, married and single, who are jobholders. Simply fire the women, who shouldn't be working anyway, and hire the men. Presto! No unemployment. No relief rolls. No depression.' The hobgoblinization of working women was not a product of wartime; nor, contrary to the standard interpretation of *film noir*, is there much evidence that such prejudices were greatly intensified by wartime (since the employment of women in aircraft and other manufacturing sectors was almost universally conceded to be temporary).[16]

Equally to the point, though usually forgotten in these discussions, the Depression dealt extraordinarily harsh blows to the 'phallic' cult of aggressiveness, individualism and self-reliance, as Robert S. McElvaine maintains in his history *The Great Depression: America 1929–1941*; far harsher, it might be added, than anything the war or the postwar years ever brought. It is true that while mobs of jobless ex-GIs never materialized on the streets or at factory gates, as feared, a fair number of fictional veterans did run satisfyingly amok on the film screens of the late forties. On the other hand, the alienated veteran was such a cliché that even Ronald Reagan, who spent the war commuting between west Hollywood and Culver City, felt obliged to represent himself as one. As he relates in the earliest (1955) of his ghostwritten autobiographies, 'Like most of the soldiers who came back, I expected a world suddenly reformed.' How he conceived this illusion at distant 'Fort Hal Roach' is unexplained. 'I discovered that the world was almost the same and perhaps a little worse.' To solace himself, he arranged for the twenty-four-hour rental of a speedboat on Lake Arrowhead, an extravagance that supposedly convinced its owner he was 'crazy'.[17]

Krutnik contends as follows: 'That there was such a market for these dissonant and schismatic representations, as is suggested by the sheer number of noir "tough" thrillers in the mid-to-late 1940s, is perhaps evidence of some kind of crisis of confidence within the contemporary regimentation of male-dominated culture.'[18] And indeed there is no mistaking the appeal in the post-war forties of male leads (and male movie stars) who were deeply confusing figures by traditional standards. But surely the great exemplar of this troubled new construction of masculinity was not the burly, lumpish Tom Neal of *Detour* or the ravaged Bogart of *Dead Reckoning* – let alone Robert Mitchum, insolently phallic even amid the delirium of *Out of the Past* – but rather the beautiful and ephebic Montgomery Clift, who appeared in no *films noirs* at all.

No, the 'phallic regime' emerged from World War Two in surprisingly good shape. Certainly, there was nothing in the cultural politics of the late forties remotely comparable to the great revolt against the fathers – extending to androgynous fashions in clothing and body types, widespread pacifism, defiantly uncloseted homosexuality and bisexuality, and a vast and distinguished literature of disillusionment – that followed on the end of World War One in England and the United States, not to mention Weimar Germany.[19] In literature, there was nothing at all to match Strachey's *Eminent Victorians* (which actually appeared in wartime), Sherriff's *Journey's End*, Owen, Sassoon, Graves; or T. S. Eliot's 'Gerontion', e. e. cummings's *The Enormous Room*, Hemingway's *The Sun Also Rises*, and all the rest. In the post-war forties the novel was still close to the centre of American popular culture. Although the rising young novelists were self-consciously belated in their relation to the rebel-avatars of the twenties, their big war novels either accepted militarism and massification as an irresistible fact of life (Irwin Shaw's *The Young Lions*, Norman Mailer's *The Naked and the Dead*) or actively championed obedience and hierarchy, as in the trick ending of Herman Wouk's *The Caine Mutiny*. But then, in the era of *film noir*, the most popular and universally admired person in the country (as the Gallup Poll duly attested) and the bestselling nonfiction author was Dwight D. Eisenhower, the former Supreme Allied Commander in Europe.

The reconstruction of a long-ago public 'mood', like for that matter the interpretation of an existing one, is a species of mythmaking that deals with a notably inchoate subject; but as with any other kind of fiction, some reconstructions carry more conviction than others. Consider this famous passage from C. Wright Mills's *White Collar*:

> The Second World War was understood by most sensitive observers as a curiously unreal business. Men went away and fought, all over the world; women did whatever was expected of women during war; people worked hard and long and bought war bonds; everybody believed in America and in her cause: there was no rebellion. Yet it all seemed a purposeless kind of efficiency. Some kind of numbness seemed to prohibit awareness of the magnitude and depth of what was happening; it was without dream and so without nightmare, and if there was anger and fear, and there was, still no chords of feeling and conviction were deeply touched. People sat in the movies between production shifts, watching with aloofness and even visible indifference, as children were 'saturation

bombed' in the narrow cellars of Europe . . . There were no plain targets of revolt; and the cold metropolitan manner had so entered the soul of overpowered men that they were made completely private and blasé, deep down and for good.[20]

It is not too much to say that Krutnik's phallic regime, so afflicted by the Depression, actually recuperated itself during the war and its aftermath. The post-war 1940s were something of a golden age for real-estate speculators, developers of tract housing, Wall Street lawyers (one of whom, John J. McCloy, the architect of the Japanese internment, became American proconsul in Germany), professional anti-communists, offshore oil-drillers, uranium prospectors, tobacco growers, 'whiz kids', courthouse politicians from Missouri, and other props of the patriarchy too numerous to mention, almost all of them apparently comfortable with their socially constructed masculinity, and many of them rejoicing in the jeering Republican slogan of 'Had enough?' These were the true inheritors of the American Century, for whom its brave dawn would always be golden. In Allan Gurganus's story 'Minor Heroism', the homophobic war hero father is repelled when his grown-up son's lover raves about the music of the forties. 'Jacques kept saying over and over again, "What a period, what a period!" For a person like myself, who loved the forties, the silliness of this kind of conversation made me sick. As if anybody like that could ever understand what it meant to be alive then.'[21] But then, it should never be forgotten that the great American success story of the late forties was, exactly, Richard M. Nixon, the 'Fighting Quaker' from Whittier, California.

Yet even the corporate *gran signori* that *Fortune* canvassed in 1947 found something to be anxious about, and that was a return to the conditions of 1933. Rather than struggling with a depression, the post-war era lived in fear of one, wrestling with a shadow all the more minatory because it obstinately remained a shadow, a phantasm, not a state of affairs. The Depression visibly lingered in the look of the country, large-scale private construction having been virtually at a standstill in most places since the early thirties. The nightclub symbolically concentrated everything that seemed phant-asmal about the prosperity of the post-war forties and naturally figures as one of *film noir*'s standard settings.[22] This complex mood of apprehension goes farther towards explaining the characteristic air of grim and baffled fatality in *film noir* than any passing downturn, as in 1947 or 1949, that actually occurred. Henry Adams's description of New York in 1905 applied even more exactly – uncannily so – forty years later. 'The outline of the city became frantic in its effort to explain something that defied meaning . . . Prosperity never before imagined, power not yet wielded by man, speed never reached by anything but a meteor, had made the world irritable, nervous, querulous, unreasonable and afraid.'[23] It was obvious that the new world of 1945 would be one of huge scale and bureaucratic rationality, and post-war *film noir* registers both resignation and resentment at the prospect. (Some alarmists on the right terrified themselves with the fear of a social-democratic planet, and that fear, too, found its way into *film noir* with the figure of the labour racketeer.) Yet a more than vestigial fear lingered that somehow the worst conditions of the Depression would return. In August 1932 a journalist had asked John Maynard Keynes if there had ever before been a calamity like the Depression. He replied, 'Yes. It was called the Dark Ages, and it lasted four hundred years.'

II

In a long perspective, the *roman noir* of the late 1920s and 1930s seems to mark less a new departure than something very like a return of the repressed. Almost exactly a century before, in the 1830s and 1840s, American writers were producing a cycle of crime and adventure novels and penny pamphlets of extraordinary violence, perversity and bleakness of outlook. In a crowded literary marketplace, 'American sensationalists quickly earned a worldwide reputation for special nastiness and grossness,' David S. Reynolds writes in his authoritative mapping of this lost continent of dark ephemera.[24] There were, for example, 'Romantic', 'Moral', and of course 'Dark' adventures, and even darker temperance tracts beside which even the absurdly scabrous James Ellroy looks to be a model of decorum. But the most interesting for our purposes were the lurid and conspiracy-minded 'city-mysteries', of which George Lippard's *Quaker City* (1845), 'an illustration of the life, mystery and crime of Philadelphia' as the title page declared, was the most famous. Lippard's exposés vastly outsold anything by Hawthorne, or Melville, or by his friend Poe – in fact, they outsold every other American novelist, genteel or subversive, until Harriet Beecher Stowe. The amazing popularity of his books inspired similarly lurid exposés of New York City and New Orleans, Salem and Worcester, Massachusetts, and Nashua, New Hampshire. As David G. Reynolds notes, Lippard's works were directly modelled on Eugene Sue's *The Mysteries of Paris* and G.M.W. Reynolds's *The Mysteries of London*; but behind them we find the example of Balzac.[25] By 1831, according to Italo Calvino, we find Balzac pursuing 'his first intuition of the city as language, as ideology, as the conditioning factor of every thought and word and gesture, the streets that "impriment par leur physiognomie certaines idées contre lesquelles nous sommes san défense", the city as monstrous as a giant crustacean, whose inhabitants are no more than motor articulations.'[26]

In the 1840s, as again a century later, Europe and the United States were coming into closer orbits. There was a brisk traffic in intellectuals and intellectual fashions, mostly westward, such as Louis Agassiz, the lessons of Balzac, and Fourierism in the 1830s and 1840s, and the Frankfurt School, surrealism, and existentialism in the 1930s and 1940s. Essential figures of *film noir*, including Lang, Wilder, Siodmak, and Preminger, were emigrés from Hitler's Europe. In urban history, the two decades are at either end of a great arc, representing the period when cities were growing in Europe and North America at the fastest rate in history (that is, until the present Third World urban explosion). In the US, the population quadrupled between 1820 and 1860, and the proportion of city-dwellers was increased by about 80 per cent. By 1850, New York was a city of 500,000 people. Abruptly, the nation awoke from Jeffersonian reveries to discover that the city had become a demiurge, as monstrous, in the eyes of a people whose national mythology said they belonged on the farm, as it was irresistible. According to Reynolds, 'It is understandable that the dark city-mysteries genre, portraying the city as a modern "Sodom" populated by depraved aristocrats engaging in nefarious doings in labyrinthine dens of iniquity, would arise in the 1840s, for such novels reflected the profound fears and fantasies of an American population faced with rapid urbanization and industrialism . . . The city was suddenly an overwhelming place, filled with hidden horrors and savage struggles as fascinating as they were appalling.'[27]

In *Quaker City* the 'Monks' (the Philadelphia elite) pursue their vices in a secluded mansion, full of cunning corridors and complete with dungeons, whose entrance is guarded by the evil factotum and assassin, Devil-Bug. Lippard was a rather excitable radical democrat, and his prolix novel combines the thriller and the tract. Larzer Ziff comments thus:

> In Lippard's handling, the conventional castle of gothic horrors becomes a metaphor of the city, in which the wealthiest and most respectable have direct communion with the most vicious, who serve them in exploitation of the majority in the middle. The crew of criminal servants are, in effect, embodiments of the dominating vices of their masters, so that at certain crises the monstrous underling calls the tune for judge, minister, or merchant.[28]

(Raymond Chandler's use of the same situation would be more skilful but no less obsessive.) Like the Dark Adventure novels, the city-mysteries exploited themes of violation, sexual humiliation, madness, mutilation and satanism with an avidity positively contemporary. Such sensational literature (and Poe, Hawthorne and Melville) also drew directly on the New Age enthusiasms and popular pseudoscience of the day – mesmerism, spiritualism , phrenology – in a way that nicely prefigures the influence of vulgar Freudianism on the movies of the forties. 'The sensational, the erotic, and the pseudoscientific were often linked in the antebellum imagination': and in the postbellum imagination of 1945–50.[29]

Since most of the American novels in this vein have been forgotten, the 'Mysteries of . . .' genre in the United States represents merely an interesting precedent for *film noir*, unlike Poe's invention of 1841, the detective story. On a broader view, however, as Calvino writes, 'The myths destined to mold both popular and cultured fiction for over a century all pass through Balzac';[30] and within the traditions of urban melodrama certain continuities and convergences can be traced that lead up to *film noir* on one side and parallel it on the other. In 'cultured' fiction one finds the 'melodramatic imagination' that Peter Brooks traces from Balzac to James to Mailer:

> The world is subsumed by an underlying manicheism, and the narrative creates the excitement of its drama by putting us in touch with the conflict of good and evil played out through the surface of things – just as description of the surfaces of the modern metropolis pierces through to a mythological realm where the imagination can find a habitat for its play with large moral entities.[31]

This is not a bad description of what occurs in the most ambitious examples of the *roman noir*, such as Woolrich, with the proviso that one speaks of large and small amoral entities as well. In popular fiction, Balzac's obsessions with subterranean connectedness, sinister supermen, and so on, carry over directly into the European city-mysteries, achieving their first and greatest realization on film in Fritz Lang's silent Mabuse films in the twenties (based on the novels by Norbert Jacques), which are among the wellsprings of big-city *film noir*. Lang's *films noirs* of the forties are in a very different vein, smaller and more severe than the grandiose Mabuse melodramas.) The relation of *film noir* to the big city that is its standard setting has been interrogated less closely than might be expected, perhaps because it seems so obvious; which in a way it is. Just as the city-mystery registered the dreaded rise of the metropolis, *film noir* registered its decline, accomplishing a demonization and an estrangement from its landscape in advance of its actual 'abandonment' – the violent reshaping of urban life sponsored by the Federal Housing Administration, the Housing Act of 1949, and in New York City the force of nature known as Robert Moses. Around the winter of 1947–48, when classic *film noir* was midway in its career, the United States reached its pitch of urbanization. In terms of both absolute numbers and percentage of the whole population, more Americans lived in central cities than ever before or since. Some 7 per cent lived in New York City alone. But the great dispersal was at hand.[32]

III

Raymond Chandler, writing in 1950, attributed the 'authentic power' of *romans noirs* (a phrase he did not use) to

> the smell of fear which these stories managed to generate. Their characters lived in a world gone wrong, a world in which, long before the atom bomb, civilization had created the machinery for its own destruction, and was learning to use it with all the moronic delight of a gangster trying out his first machine gun. The law was something to be manipulated for power and profit. The streets were dark with something more than night.[33]

Apocalypse is the most compelling parallel, at least for our apocalyptically minded times, between the old urban melodramas and the *roman noir*. For as George Steiner writes with customary plangency, 'It is precisely from the 1830s onward', that is, from the very moment when Balzac began elaborating his vision of the city as logic, grammar, ideology and body of fate, 'that one can observe the emergence of a characteristic "counterdream" – the vision of the city laid waste, the fantasies of Scythian and Vandal invasion, the Mongol steeds slaking their thirst in the fountains of the Tuileries Gardens. An odd school of painting develops: pictures of London, Paris, or Berlin seen as colossal ruins, famous landmarks burnt, eviscerated, or located in romantic emptiness among charred stumps and dead water. Romantic fantasy antici-pates Brecht's vengeful promise that nothing shall remain of the great cities except the wind that blows through them.' As Steiner conscientiously notes, it required exactly a hundred years of progress before Europe realized its fantasy.[34]

The crisis of modern capitalism in the thirties, which Keynes compared to the Dark Ages, followed by the literal urban apocalypse in Europe and Asia during World War Two, vindicated a tradition of cultural pessimism whose great names include Henry Adams, Burckhardt and Spengler, and the antimodern modernists Yeats, Eliot and Pound. The proudly cultivated Chandler at least must have realized how closely the low-rent *Kulturpessimismus* of the pulps during the Depression rhymed with, if it did not exactly echo, the doomsday chic of *The Waste Land* and *Hugh Selwyn Mauberley* after the Great War. Spengler, for whom the 'world-city' like New York was invariably a late, wintry phenomenon, the winding-sheet of civilizations, sold steadily. 'These are ominous times,' Lewis Mumford wrote in 1944, 'and Spengler is like a black crow, hoarsely cawing, whose prophetic wings cast a shadow over our whole landscape.'[35] In the spring of 1943, *The Decline of the West* was being read by Jack Kerouac and Allen Ginsberg (at the insistence of William Burroughs, for whom it was a holy book), and by a herald of a different future, Private First Class Henry Kissinger, on whose 'thought' its imprint was permanent. Arnold Toynbee was a bestseller in 1947–48, and the subject of a pompous *Time* cover story written by Whittaker Chambers.

Variously envisaged, the fated city was the counterpart of the radiant 'White City' of official optimism, as it developed from the Columbian Exposition of 1893, through the technophile science fiction of the thirties, to the atom-powered Tomorrowland projected after World War Two.[36] What we are describing was not only a matter of high culture and low. In fact, the most reliable evidence that the fated city was part of conventional wisdom, and had a niche in dominant discourse, was its malign fascination for middlebrow or, as Dwight Macdonald used to say, Midcult writers like Stephen Vincent Benet, the laureat of the Popular Front, and Archibald MacLeish, Librarian of Congress, head of the OFF, Assistant Secretary of State, and multiple Pulitzer Prize winner. Benet's 1937 story 'By the Waters of Babylon', which pictures a ruined, apparently radioactive Manhattan a hundred years hence, was the lead selection in Donald A. Wolheim's wartime *Pocket Book of Science Fiction*. MacLeish's declamatory radio play 'The Fall of the City' was the first and, it is safe to say, one of the very few full-length verse dramas ever broadcast on American radio. (It was performed on CBS in October 1935, with Orson Welles narrating.)

When Albert Camus made his first visit to New York City in 1946, it struck him immediately that 'Everybody looks like they've stepped out of a B-film.'[37] In the years immediately after the war, when the United States was dispatching proconsuls to Europe and viceroys to Japan, visiting existentialists, oblivious to Mary McCarthy's scorn, always expected and found its capital city, New York, to be an immense *noir* spectacle, whose fall was visibly prefigured. 'A prodigious funeral pyre at midnight, as its millions of lighted windows amid stretches of blackened walls carry these swarming lights halfway up the sky,' Camus wrote, 'as if every evening a gigantic fire were burning over Manhattan, the island with three rivers, raising immense smoldering carcasses still pierced with dots of flame.'[38] And Sartre:

All the hostility, all the cruelty of the world are present in this almost prodigious monument that man has ever raised to himself. It is a *light* city; its apparent lack of weight amazes most Europeans. In this immense, malevolent space, in this desert of rock that supports no vegetation, they have constructed thousands of houses in brick, wood, or reinforced concrete which give the appearance of being on the point of flying away . . . Already [the skyscrapers] are slightly neglected; tomorrow, perhaps, they will be demolished. In any event, to build them in the first place required a faith we no longer feel . . . I see in the distance the Empire State Building or the Chrysler Building pointing vainly toward the sky, and it occurs to me that New York is about to acquire a history, that it already has its ruins.[39]

Neither essay mentioned the atom or hydrogen bomb (Sartre was recording a visit that took place in wartime), and both were translated for affluent American audiences (Sartre's was published in *Town and Country*). The advent of the bomb confirmed and deepened, rather than originating, the forebodings of the post-war forties, especially in so far as they were concentrated on the fate of the big city. In Dawn Powell's 1948 novel *The Locusts Have No King*, a hitherto sheltered medievalist emerges from his researches 'to find New York a strange and terrifying city, the peace now being celebrated as sinister and barbaric as the Dark Ages he has just left'. In *The Lady from Shanghai* (Orson Welles, 1948), the mad pop-eyed lawyer played by Glenn Anders raves to Orson Welles on a bright hilltop in Acapulco: 'Do you think the world is coming to an end?' (Welles replies: 'It's a bright guilty world.') 'It's coming, you know. Oh, yeah. First the big cities and maybe even this. It's just *got* to come . . . ' The novels and stories of Paul Bowles were perhaps the most minatory in post-war fiction. 'Our civilization is doomed to a short life; its component parts are too heterogeneous,' writes the narrator of 'Pages from Cold Point' (1949). 'I personally am content to see everything in the process of decay. The bigger the bomb, the quicker it will be done. Life is visually too hideous for one to make the attempt to preserve it. Let it go.'[40]

In *The Art of the City*, Peter Conrad considers the odd case of the architectural visionary Hugh Ferris, who dreamed in the 1920s and 1930s of the modern metropolis of tomorrow, with aerodromes and golf courses on the tops of skyscrapers, but decided after 1942 that New York should be abandoned for its own good and rebuilt in vaults under the Jersey Palisades.[41] In Elizabeth Bishop's poem of 1946 'The Man-Moth', New York is a sort of metaphysical underground pitched atop the literal underground of the subway.

> Here, above, cracks in the buildings are filled with battered moonlight.
> The whole shadow of Man is only as big as his hat.

The claustral New York of Otto Preminger's 1944 *film noir* of Vera Caspary's novel *Laura* feels somehow subaqueous, 'more submarine than subterranean', as Benjamin said of Baudelaire's Paris, and on the point of abandonment. 'It seemed as if I were the only person left alive in New York', says Waldo Lydecker (Clifton Webb) in voice-over, before Dana Andrews arrives to investigate Gene Tierney's supposed murder. But nowhere is New York more desolate, guilty, abandoned or menacing than in the *noir* fictions that Cornell George Hopley-Woolrich, a failed, closeted imitator of F. Scott Fitzgerald, began publishing in 1934, almost at the bottom of the Depression.

IV

Hammett is a legend, Chandler is a private mythology – both enjoyed seasons of celebrity – and Cain was a career; but Cornell Woolrich (b. New York City, 1903; d. New York City, 1968) was a sort of writing machine, whose horribly uneventful adult life was spent typing in a hotel room as his mother watched. (He dedicated *The Bride Wore Black* to his Remington Portable.) In the twenties, Woolrich attended Columbia University, where he began his career as an imitator of Fitzgerald; his first novel, a jazz-baby chronicle called *Children of the Ritz*, won a prize from *College Humor* of $10,000, an immense sum in those days. Along with it came a ticket to Hollywood, where he married the daughter of a minor film producer. Neither his career as a film writer nor the marriage was a success. Woolrich spent his late nights cruising the waterfront in a sailor suit he kept hidden beneath the bed. The marriage dissolved with surprisingly little rancour, and Woolrich returned to New York and the company of his socialite mother, Claire Attalie, with whom he toured Europe in 1931 – an odd couple, like Sebastian and Violet in *Suddenly, Last Summer*. For most of the next twenty-six years, until her death in 1957, he lived with her in a residential hotel, the Marseilles, at Broadway and 103rd, in Manhattan.[42]

When the Depression came and the bottom dropped out of the market for jazz-baby novels, Woolrich turned to suspense writing for the pulps. His success was immediate, but there were anxious years. (He once wrote a story about a hack writer desperately trying to write a novella in a single night, from which the legend grew that Woolrich had been reduced to that extremity himself.) Thereafter, as his biographer Francis Nevins Jr says, the Depression was the dominant reality in his fiction:

> The New York that Woolrich lived in like a hermit in a cave and wrote about like one who
> knew its every square block as well as he knew his own name is a city of subways, automats,

movie palaces, cheap furnished rooms, cold stone streets, doorways thick with shadows, people sick with terror, loving, clawing, killing, smoking too much, drinking too much, each one trying and failing to keep at bay the certainty of death which marked Woolrich's work and scarred his life.[43]

(Obviously, the example of Woolrich's overheated prose is infectious.) The thanataphobe had come a long way from the Ritz. Toward the end of the thirties he followed Hammett and Chandler into the respectability of hard covers. The 'black' novels of the forties (*The Bride Wore Black, Rendezvous in Black, Black Curtain* and the rest) were respectfully reviewed. More important, his work was being purchased for the movies. He was becoming indecently prolific, at least for the taste of Lippincott's, which in 1942 published *Phantom Lady* under the pseudonym William Irish. *Deadline at Dawn* and 'It Had To Be Murder' (the basis for Hitchcock's *Rear Window*) were also published under the Irish pseudonym. Sales to the movies, radio and eventually television made him a comfortable income, which apparently he hoarded.

In his history of crime films, Carlos Clarens points to the undistinguished early film versions of Hammett's *The Maltese Falcon* and *The Glass Key* and Chandler's *Farewell, My Lovely* and *The High Window*, all of which lacked the distinctive atmosphere and iconography of the famous *film noir* remakes, as evidence that 'noir is more likely to be in the eye of the director than on the printed page'.[44] To the eye unclouded by antique auteurist prejudices, it is not so simple. In the case of Woolrich, the more faithful the translation from the novel or story, the darker the film. In large part this is a matter of Woolrich's powerfully determinist vision, a dime-store philosophy dramatized with greater or less conviction in *film noir* but in which he, at least, completely believed: 'The path you follow is the path you have to follow; there are no digressions permitted you, even though you think there are.'[45] There is, too, the unforgettably sinister and dingy *mise en scène*. And then there are extraordinary visual, auditory, and even synaesthetic effects – one of Woolrich's chief gifts was a surveyor's eye, as the play with parallax in 'It Had To Be Murder', so brilliantly exploited by Hitchcock, confirms.

Nevins, Woolrich's indefatigable booster as well as biographer, divides his suspense fiction (he also wrote romances, adventures, period pieces and supernatural thrillers) into such categories as the Bizarre Murder Method, the *Noir* Cop, the Clock Race, the Oscillation Story, the Headlong Through the Night Story, and the Annihilation Story, whose names are evocative enough.[46] Unlike Hammett and Chandler, Woolrich did not write detective stories as such, although he produced a few grim parodies, most famously 'The Dancing Detective', in which the 'investigator' is a taxi dancer being stalked by a serial murderer. His view of law enforcement was without illusions. Woolrich's ghoulish variation on the police procedural is 'Dead On Her Feet', in which a suspect known to be innocent is driven mad when he is forced by a sadistic detective to dance with the corpse of his lover. Woolrich's protagonists are victims, bystanders, naïfs, the occasional psychopath, never the 'enforcers' of social order – the Sam Spades and the Philip Marlowes – that function as the central intelligences of classic detective fiction, even in their *noir* incarnations.

Always in Woolrich, life is ruled by chance, but its workings hide – barely – the machinations of a more sinister order beyond the visible. 'The hidden identities, mysteries, evils of melodrama are never the result of chance or fate,' says Peter Brooks, 'but of conscious plotting: evil is concerted, volitional – which is not to say it is motivated. Indeed, the more it is unmotivated the more it becomes a pure product of will, demonstrating that the world is inhabited by a Satanism as real as it is gratuitous.'[47] Woolrich's city is fallen, guilty, complicitous, animated by a Jansenist sense of evil (Woolrich was a lapsed Catholic), and ruled by a sinister demiurgic force that thwarts and deforms individual life. The midnight streets, furnished rooms, low bars, dance halls, precinct offices, rain, heat, shadows, whiskey fumes and cigarette smoke – all the familiar elements of New York *noir*'s *mise en scène* – are the sometimes overstrained vehicles for an imagination fundamentally melodramatic and manichean. Which is not to say that Woolrich was (only) a kind of allegorist: these details have their own mad verisimilitude and hypnagogic intensity, brought out by the pell-mell, often lurid, and occasionally ludicrous rush of his prose. They are very much rooted in the experience of the Depression, when the fear (or, in other quarters, hope) arose that capitalism and its incarnation in the modern metropolis had entered some permanent crisis. In Woolrich's fiction the Depression has become a sort of eternal unrelieved dark night of body and soul.

For precisely this reason, Woolrich's fiction was peculiarly answerable to wartime and especially the post-war forties, an anxious time chased by its own shadows. Not only was his work frequently adapted during the classic phase of *film noir*, it also generated seventy-one radio plays on series like 'Molle Mystery Theater' and 'Suspense' (and later nearly as many television adaptations on 'Alfred Hitchcock Presents', an ironic venue, and other suspense series). Woolrich's fiction belongs to a lost literary economy, in which (according to Nevins's count) as many as twelve to thirteen hundred writers competed to supply the mostly male, downmarket audience of *Black Mask, Dime Detective* and other pulps with rawer sensations than those offered by films or the *Saturday Evening Post*. James Joyce spoke of his ideal reader, afflicted with the ideal insomnia: Woolrich's had no immediate job prospects and a hangover.

The Black Curtain, the Woolrich novel so vital in establishing the atmospherics of *film noir*, begins with its protagonist Frank Townsend dazed, unable to remember the last three years of his life, and seized by an unnamable dread. The opening paragraph typifies the rendering of perceptions fragmented and deranged by terror, physical distress or, as here, amnesia, that pervade Woolrich's fiction.

> First everything was blurred. Then he could feel hands fumbling around him, lots of hands. They weren't actually touching him; they were touching things that touched him. He got their feel one step removed. Flinging away small, loose objects like chunks of mortar or fragments of brick, which seemed to be strewn all over him.[48]

It is quickly established that a falling beam has destroyed Townsend's memory. Since Woolrich could be as derivative as the next penny-a-liner, Nevins is probably right to suggest that this beam began falling in *The Maltese Falcon*, in the parable that Sam Spade tells to Brigid O'Shaugnessy. But, in an irony that the austere Hammett would never have permitted himself, it turns out that Townsend had already lost his memory when the beam hit him; the accident that erases the last three years restores him to the life (and marriage) he had unaccountably mislaid. His up-to-date wife is amazingly understanding about his long disappearance ('Amnesia', she explains to him, with the certainty of someone who has read all about it in *McCall's*); and so is his old boss, for whom a 'nervous breakdown' is sufficient explanation. 'Amnesia' = anamnesis is a neat trick, even for Woolrich.

The 1942 B movie *Street of Chance*, based on Woolrich's novel and directed by Jack Hively for Paramount, was apparently the first of many films about amnesia to be produced in the forties. The loss and recovery of memory was a matter of obvious, even overdetermined relevance for a society abruptly sundered from previous routines (the effect first of 1929 and then of Pearl Harbor), then remoulded into a wartime regime whose reticulations went everywhere but were supposed to be temporary; a society, as C. Wright Mills observed, that nightly witnessed, at the movies, enormities from which it remained strangely aloof.

Though understandably anxious to know where and who he was during his lost time, Townsend resumes his suspended life, only to realize that he is being stalked by a stranger – Agate Eyes, as he thinks of him. When Agate Eyes follows him to his bus stop, he changes his route; when Agate Eyes finds out where he works, he quits his job. He is now literally afraid of the dark:

Blue shadows, like tentatively clutching fingers, began a slow creep toward Townsend out from under the trees. Deepening, advancing only furtively when they weren't watched closely, pretending to be arrested when they were. At first azure, scarcely visible in the still-strong light of day. Then dark blue, like ink rolling sluggishly amidst the grass blades and dyeing them from the roots up. At last, freed of the vigilance of the closing red eye of the sun, turning black, showing their true color. (p. 44)

When his house is ransacked, he flees. In the novel, the baroque escape scene is rich in *noir* symbolism: he and his wife Virginia flee down a dumbwaiter, 'in a sort of hideous parody of entombment alive' (pp. 75–6), to a basement that connects to the next apartment building. There they shuffle through the darkness, terrorized by the 'scurry of searching footsteps scattering from room to room' in their own flat, above them (p. 77). In the film version, anticlimactically, Frank simply slips down the fire escape. The novel is filled with bravura passages of melodramatic chiaroscuro (the 'shallow nimbus of a gas flame', a shadow looming 'grim and ominous, like a prophet of doom') and darkness visible:

There seemed to be a man standing there, directly opposite, facing these windows in a surveyor's line of directness. He was in the black silt of a shadow that filled a wall indentation like sand blown into a niche. It might have been just an optical illusion, giving the shadow's border the rounded likeness of a shoulder, then lower down a hipbone.

As he peered, trying to decide, a faint flow of motion had altered the silhouette. The rounded shadows of the shoulder, the hip, drew subtly inward, disappeared into the heart of the shadow mass, leaving a clean-cut knife line of dark that should have been there in the first place but hadn't been. (pp. 69–70)

The auditory effects are similarly, paranoically, heightened: the 'slight, soft grate of straining leather' that a man's heavy brogues 'made each time – nothing so acute as a squeak – the cushioned thud of their incessant fall upon the pavement. The rhythm of the walk – *pat-pat, pat-pat-pat, pat-pat-pat, pat*. You hear the sound at night when the streets are still, when someone's coming toward you in the distance' (p. 65). 'As lifelike, as natural as the moving pavement belt beneath them', yet fraught with signification, the description of Agate Eyes's feet, Townsend's nightmare image of pursuit, fills no fewer than three pages of meticulously detailed prose. This kind of hyper-intensive description, reminiscent of Robbe-Grillet's in its obsessional precision and hallucinatory defamiliarization, is what led Anthony Boucher to praise Woolrich as the 'great living master of what the psalmist calls "the noonday devil" – the infinite terror of prosaic everyday details'.[49]

Woolrich's plots routinely slip the traces of mere narrative coherence, but never more so than in *The Black Curtain*, where he spends two full chapters explaining his explanation and still leaves loose ends dangling. What matters for our purpose is how seamlessly his *mise en scène* melded with the shadowy, low-ceilinged, expressionist sensibility of Theodor Sparkuhl, the film's cinematographer, to create one of the earliest *films noirs*. The *noir* style may have been in the obscure director Jack Hively's eye and is certainly in Sparkuhl's cinematography, but it was also already indelibly present in Woolrich's prose.

By contrast, Woolrich's *Deadline at Dawn* was transmuted into one of the odder entries in the *film noir* canon, through the mismating of one of Woolrich's 'Headlong through the Night' stories with the particular talents and Popular Front sentimentalism of screenwriter Clifford Odets and director Harold Clurman. Woolrich's novel contrasts the empty desolation of New York with the main characters' nostalgia for smalltown America, where '[f]olks say good morning to you from all the way over on the other side of the street, even if you'd never set eyes on them before in your life, and they never had on you'.[50] Even this heavy-handed thematic opposition can barely be glimpsed in Odets' screenplay, in which everything, even the nocturnal city itself, has been conventionalized and sentimentalized.

In Woolrich's novel, Bricky Coleman comes to New York with dreams of becoming an actress and ends up in a dismal job as a taxi dancer. Obsessed with dance, Woolrich wrote often and, contrary to the myth of his misogyny, with great sympathy about taxi dancers, his favourite example of working women, always dramatizing their resilience in the face of economic and sexual exploitation.

> She got up and she went over to a sort of cupboard arrangement, a niche without any closure, gaping against the back wall. It held, on a shelf, a gas-ring, with a rubber tube leading up and cupping onto a jet that protruded from the wall overhead. She struck a match, uncocked the jet, and a little circle of sluggish blue fire jumped into being. She placed a battered tin coffee-pot over this, readied for brewing from earlier in the day, when it had not been so much agony to move about. (p. 331)

Life in the city has been no easier for Quinn, an out-of-work electrician's helper who grew up in the same small town as Bricky. Bricky sees New York as a personal enemy, with a 'half-nelson' on her. When Quinn, whom she meets at the dance hall, literal-mindedly objects that 'houses, stone and cement buildings, they haven't got arms, they can't reach out and hold you back, if you want to go', she replies thus:

They don't have to have arms. When there are so many of them bunched together, they give off something into the air . . . [T]here's an intelligence of its own hanging over this place, coming up from it. It's mean and bad and evil, and when you breathe too much of it for too long, it gets under your skin, it gets into you – and you're sunk, the city's got you. Then all you've got to do is sit and wait, and in a little while it's finished the job, it's turned you into something you never wanted to be or thought you'd be. Then it's too late. Then you can go anywhere – home or anywhere else – and you just keep on being what it made you from then on. (p. 341)

This denunciation of the city goes on for three more long paragraphs, culminating in Bricky's memory of the morning she tried to leave New York by bus: 'When the sun started to creep down from the tops of the buildings, and the people started to thicken along the sidewalks on 34th Street, it kidded me by trying to look familiar, something I was used to, something that wouldn't hurt me, I didn't need to be afraid of.' Lured again, she walked out of the terminal and heard 'the trombones and the saxes razzing me, way up high around the building-tops somewhere. "We've gotcha"' (p. 342).

In Woolrich the metropolis is not only monstrous and monstrously alive, as in Balzac, but actively malevolent, a demiurge brooding over his creation like the gnostic Demogorgon. (Not that all of his protagonists are unequal to it. In *The Bride Wore Black* Julie, widowed on her wedding day by a drunken driver, plots her revenge in a furnished room on Twenty-first Street: 'She seemed to *lean toward* the city, visible outside, like something imminent, about to happen to it.'[51] Woolrich's city is a hallucinatory night town, the definitive *noir* landscape; it can 'look familiar', even humanized in the sunlight, but is incapable of disguising its malice after dark. In *Deadline at Dawn*, chapter headings, featuring a clock ticking off the passage of time, insist on the passing of the hours and the urgency of the deadline: before dawn Bricky and Quinn must prove that Quinn was innocent of the murder with which he will otherwise be charged. (In Woolrich, innocence is relative: out of work and desperate, Quinn has just stolen a stack of bills from a safe in a rich man's house where he had done some electrical work a few months before. With Bricky's help, he decides to re-enter the house and return the money. When he does, he finds the owner murdered.) After they find the murderer, they hope to escape to New York together, that same morning, and return to the small town where they both grew up.

Seeking clues to explain what actually happened in the interval between Quinn's two visits, he and Bricky make separate forays into the darkened streets. In defiance of the conventional logic of mystery plots, these characters follow one clue after another, each leading to a dead end. These loose threads afford brief glimpses of other narratives –

sometimes ordinary (the man whose wife had just delivered a child), sometimes desperate (the woman who had just committed a murder) – a random sampling of life on the streets of the guilty city. Dana Polan has noted how explicit Woolrich is 'in showing the ambivalent possibility of this new space of modernity for the fragmentation of narrativity . . . where each narrative denouement exists alongside the possibility of an equally significant but opposed alternate denouement. Modernity here is the possibility of a generation of endless narratives, all equally possible expansions of initial premises.' In this account, Woolrich's text becomes available for reading as 'a kind of meditation on novel writing'.[52] The idea that *Deadline at Dawn* belongs in the company of, say, Calvino's *If on a Winter's Night* is charming and, on reflection, even plausible.

Bricky's and Quinn's search through a defamiliarized, maze-like nocturnal landscape takes on the air of a walk through a massive, monolithic sepulchre. 'There was no one abroad, nothing that moved. Not even a cat scenting at a garbage-can. The city was a dead thing' (p. 355). As always in Woolrich, hypnagogically exact details, visual and auditory, contribute to an all-pervading thematics of abandonment.

> They came out into a slumbering early-morning desolation, flitted quickly past the brief bleach of the close-at-hand street-light, and were swallowed up again in the darkness on the other side of it. The street-lights, stretching away into perspective in their impersonal, formalized, zig-zag pattern, only added to the look of void and loneliness. (p. 355)

But then, Woolrich's portrait of urban abandonment and desolation is not merely *film noir* atmospherics *avant la lettre*. It is a veridical picture of New York still deeply scarred by the Depression, and a prophetic portrait of its falling, building by building, into ruin.

> Up a tunnel-dim side-street, that had once carried a lateral branch of the Elevated over to Ninth Avenue. It was now shorn of it but permanently stunted in its development by the sixty-year strait jacket it had endured. The slab-like sides of windowless warehouses, the urved back of a well-known skating rink that looked like a cement tank, gaps torn in the building-ranks here and there by the Depression, particularly on corner-sites, and never rebuilt upon, used now for parking lots. (p. 325)

It was not to be expected that Odets, the genius-playwright of *Awake and Sing!*, or Clurman, the cofounder of the Group Theatre, would deal sympathetically or comprehendingly with a work from the author of *I Married a Dead Man*. Odets believed in leftist politics and well-made plays, and to him Woolrich's radically unconventional, logically disjunctive plot could only have appeared as simple incompetence. The 1946 film transforms the out-of-work electrician's helper into a sailor on twenty-four-hour liberty (Bill Williams), thus imparting a plausible urgency to the 6.15 a.m. deadline that Woolrich never bothered to give it, and considerably glamorizes the taxi dancer, played by Susan Hayward. Until big lug Bill Williams appears with his troubles, her biggest problem has been unwelcome marriage proposals from Steven Geray, a prosperous immigrant with a funny accent. Instead of fending for themselves on the mean streets, Williams and Hayward are driven everywhere – for free – by a sententious cabbie, who in the final plot twist is revealed as the murderer, though one whose crime is entirely justified since he has only killed to prevent a vicious woman from hurting others.

Woolrich's 1942 novel *Phantom Lady*, found more sympathetic translators in emigré director Robert Siodmak and cinematographer Woody Bredell. Indeed, *Phantom Lady* the film (1944) launched Siodmak's short, brilliant Hollywood career. The multiple perspectives and radical subjectivity of Woolrich's text furnished a perfect vehicle for Siodmak's expressionist visual sensibility and taut, knotted narrative line. And the *mise en scène* of the film's most gripping visual and auditory sequences was already scripted, in minute detail, in the novel, as it had been in *The Black Curtain*.[53]

In Woolrich's novel, the characters' – and the reader's – hold on what passes for objective reality is more tenuous than in the film. Henderson is a youngish stockbroker whose monstrous wife Marcella is murdered one night while he is out on the town with a mysterious pick-up in an unforgettable hat. One after another, the witnesses who could establish his alibi remember him but deny seeing the woman, whose testimony is somehow necessary to prove his innocence. (As is so often the case in Woolrich, the narrative logic is elusive.) Oddly, Henderson himself cannot remember what the 'phantom lady' looked like, but he is haunted by metonymic associations: 'The rustle of her dress. The words she spoke . . . Where did the liquor go to, that my eyes saw in her glass when she raised it? When it came down, it was empty.'[54] Paradoxically, this memory trace of the empty glass helps to convince him of the woman's materiality. But these phantom memories are useless in the relentless glare of the police investigation. Terrified that no one else can – or will – bear witness to the woman's presence, Henderson fears he is losing his grip on reality: he feels the city turning into a 'never-never land' of 'unreal buildings and unreal streets moving backward past them, like shadows on glass' (pp. 39, 38). Finally he begs the detective to take him back to the detention pen, with its 'walls . . . that you can feel with your hands' (p. 39).

The harsh lighting and stark shadows that characterize the film's visual style direct the viewer toward a stronger and more definite interpretation of these initial events than anything the novel provides. For example, the scenes in which two major witnesses, the bartender and the cab driver, are interviewed by detective Burgess, accompanied by Henderson, both end with close-ups of the witnesses' guilty faces, lit as if by a glaring interrogation lamp, only after Burgess and Henderson have turned away. Later, in prison, the ethereal white light that streams down from a high window to form a cone of radiance around Henderson, trapped inside a corral-line barred structure, and his visitor 'Kansas' (Carol Richmond, his executive assistant) strongly suggests, by conventional symbolic associations, that he is innocent and, further, that the two of them will fall in love or rather realize that they have always been.

In the film Kansas, unlike Carol Richmond in the novel, is shown, from the beginning, to be a competent professional woman, with her own secretary and her own (undefined) responsibilities in Henderson's engineering business. (In Woolrich's novel, Carol is having an affair with Henderson; the Production Code precluded this simple motivation.) Kansas's professionalism, brio, courage and resourcefulness, combined with the tenderness displayed in the prison scene, bear more resemblance to plucky working-women stalwarts of the thirties – like Jean Arthur in Capra films – than to the devouring femmes fatales that supposedly populate the landscape of *film noir*. But Kansas also displays an uncanny capacity for negative capability and metamorphosis, and the form she assumes in the first half of the film is literally that of a femme fatale.

The novel's stalking sequence could not be more different from the conventional images of male pursuit in *film noir*. What Siodmak, closely following Woolrich, creates is an intense psychodrama of stillness, silence and cunning. The camera moves through a crowded bar (the bar in which Henderson met the 'phantom lady'), catches the bartender in a harsh white light, and comes to rest on Kansas, dressed in a white dress with horizontal stripes, sitting at the end of the bar, gazing fixedly into the camera – and at the bartender, who has been suborned into swearing he never saw the woman with Henderson. In the next scene, Kansas sits in the same spot, this time wearing a black dress, her gaze still fixed. First the bar is crowded, then it is empty. Still she sits there, a gorgon with a 'harrowing stare', a 'Medusa-like countenance,' gazing implacably (pp. 66, 68). Then we see her leave the empty bar, wearing a white coat. The bartender, now thoroughly unnerved, calls closing time with his back cautiously turned, only to discover she has disappeared. He closes up and goes out into the rain, where he sees her waiting on the nearest street corner, under a lamppost. He walks toward her, past her. She follows him through deserted streets all the way to the El, her high heels clicking in the silence, pursuing him as if she were one of the Furies, or, as

Woolrich explicitly says, 'Nemesis' (p. 78). The pursuit, prolonged for three days in the novel, is abridged into minutes on screen. The two of them are alone in the deserted station, and she is in front of him on the platform. Tension builds as he finally turns on her and both eye the third rail, then breaks as a black woman in a flowered dress comes clattering in.

Foster Hirsch, in *Film Noir: The Dark Side of the Screen*, praises Siodmak for this 'quintessential moment of *noir* contrivance'.[55] In fact, everything in this sequence, including the intrusion of the black woman that Hirsch so admires, was already scripted in Woolrich's novel, which builds the suspense to an even greater height, and over a longer period of time. At the end of the film sequence, the bartender finally confronts Kansas angrily: 'You have nothing on me.' When his shouts draw a hostile crowd of men, he panics, bolts into the street, and is run over by a car. In the novel, the final confrontation occurs in 'full sunshine', and the bartender, terrified of her rather than guilt-ridden, says he has no idea 'what she's *after*' (p. 77). After she tells the crowd of men to let him go, '[h]e went running away from the scene full tilt . . . running away from the slender girl who stood there looking after him, her coat belted around her waist to the thickness of little more than a man's hand-span. The ultimate in degradation' (p. 78). When she takes off after him again, the narrator underscores the unconventionality of this chase sequence: 'Strange pursuit. Incredible pursuit. Slim young girl hurrying after a stocky barman, in and out, out and in, through the swarming midday streets of New York' (p. 78). The barman's end is the same.

Kansas's search takes her into social worlds, and roles, she has obviously never ventured into before. With tawdry, seductive clothes, garish makeup and chewing gum, she transforms herself into the sort of cheerfully vulgar and available demimondaine who would appeal to the drummer Cliff (Elisha J. Cook Jr), another suborned witness. 'I'm a hip kitten,' she assures him. In the famous jazz cellar sequence, distorted camera angles and rhythmic quick cuts from Kansas to Cliff's masturbatory drum solo and his leering companions build to an orgastic expressionist frenzy that is one of the special glories of forties film-making. The scene is like a trapdoor opening onto a weirdly stylized version of the actual Times Square during that odd seed-time when the Beats were haunting the Angle Bar and buying Benzedrine-laced inhalers at the all-night drugstores: these were the days when Alan Greenspan (currently presiding over the Federal Reserve Board) was a jazz sideman working his way through college, and William Burroughs (now an adornment of the National Institute and Academy of Arts and Letters) was rolling drunks in the subway. As the drummer twitches and grimaces, a tight close-up frames Kansas laughing maniacally, her teeth bared. Caught up in the drugs and the music, she seems to have lost track, for a moment, of her identity and purpose. The scene in the novel is similar – all bebop, gin and marijuana – but Carol remains more of a square. Still, the encounter with Cliff, which needless to say proves fatal to him, testifies to Woolrich's odd, persistent and rather terrifying conviction that by sheer will one can transform oneself into the complete image of another's desire and thereby destroy him – or her. This is the central conceit of *The Bride Wore Black* and *Rendezvous in Black*, which is simply the earlier novel retold with a male avenger. Character is arbitrary and infinitely malleable; dread, desire and will remain. 'Funny how we know these things, all of us,' Kansas thinks as she makes eye contact with poor Cliff across the orchestra pit, 'even when we've never tried them before' (p. 91). The conviction, to put it another way, that there are no limits to self-fashioning, because the self is literally inessential, is somehow evocative of Woolrich's own closeted way of life, and almost suspiciously consonant with certain present-day critical concerns. But it also has an obvious relevance to the flux of identity and status, the desperate obsession with keeping up appearances, and the proud impostures of the Depression.

In a characteristic touch, the actual murderer is revealed to be Henderson's best friend, a moody sculptor named Marlowe, who has been carrying on an affair with Henderson's wife. In the film, Tone plays Marlowe as one of the mad – literally mad in this case – anarchic *Übermenschen* that so fascinated the collectivist forties. (The archetype, of course, is Howard Roark in *The Fountainhead*, which King Vidor, the populist of the silent *The Big Parade*, turned into the astonishing film of 1949.) When he is not busy murdering possible witnesses or tagging unhelpfully along with Ella Raines to milliners' shops, Tone is staring at his hands, or keeling over from migraine, or looking peevish as Thomas Gomez, playing Inspector Burgess, delivers a lecture on the psychology of serial murderers. Marlowe lives in a ludicrously moderne penthouse apartment-studio, white on white with his works (heroic busts in the manner of Hitler's favourite sculptor, Arno Breker) displayed on waist-high pedestals. After Kansas realizes his treachery, she is chased by Marlowe around the arctic vastness for a while until Burgess arrives to rescue her, and he pitches himself out the window. Following on the expressionist *tours de force* of the first half of the film, the second, increasingly dominated by Tone's overwrought performance, has naturally been deemed a disappointment by critics. But it is not unrevealing of the popular prejudices to which Hollywood was playing in wartime, or unfaithful to Woolrich, in whose fictions the treacherous friend (lover, wife, comrade, whoever was capable of the most comprehensive betrayal), was a stock player.

In contrast to the extreme mannerism of *Phantom Lady*, the 1949 film *The Window*, based on Woolrich's story of 1947 'The Boy Who Cried Wolf', appears firmly rooted in the sociology of urban working-class life. (It was directed by Ted Tetzlaff, who had formerly been a cinematographer for Alfred Hitchcock; the screenwriter was Mel Dinelli, who worked with Siodmak on *The Spiral Staircase*.) In the opening sequence, the camera pans through busy daylit streets to rest at last on the partly boarded-up windows of an abandoned tenement building, ironically graced by what seem to be handsome Greek Revival details. It lingers on one window, a gaping black hole in the sunlight, then cuts to the boy, Tommy Woodry, asleep inside on a bed of straw. This abandoned building, at once a principal location and a dominant signifier in the film, is the boy's private playground, where he entertains himself with solitary cops-and-robbers fantasies. Because the stairs are destroyed up to the third floor, he enters from above, by scampering over the adjacent roofs. The camera follows him, opening onto an expansive view of the city from his Lower East Side rooftop.

As his title announces, Woolrich's plot was banality itself. Tommy ('Buddy' in print) is a young fabulist, whose parents naturally do not believe him when he insists that the Kellertons upstairs (Paul Stewart and Ruth Roman in the film) have robbed and murdered a drunken sailor. (He has seen everything from the fire escape onto which he crawled one night in order to sleep during a heatwave.) After the sympathetic but stern Mrs Woodry (Barbara Hale) insists that he confess his tale-bearing to the Kellertons, they set out to murder him too. Gore Vidal relates that the Wise Hack, his guide to moviedom in the old days at MGM, 'truly believed that children in jeopardy *always* hooked an audience', a prejudice that the excellent box office takings of *The Window*, starring the appealing Bobby Driscoll as Tommy, could only have confirmed.[56] (The picture was made under the thrifty regime of Dore Schary at RKO, before he moved on to the by then troubled MGM.)

Unlike most other Woolrich adaptations, *The Window*, for all its routine melodrama, is a more compelling study in the *noir* style than its source, which is slight and formulaic. In *Film Noir*, Blake Lucas praises Tetzlaff for using location shots 'to create an American urban landscape that seems almost infernal',[57] complete with falling-apart tenements, the clatter of the El, heat and squalor – everything but a singing cistern. The city is at once unpeopled and overcrowded. The streets are empty, but the same day that Tommy boasts to some other boys that he and his parents are moving to a ranch 'out west', the building manager materializes at their door, with desperate would-be tenants in tow. Since a flight to the suburbs is obviously not in their calculations, Tommy's parents (Arthur Kennedy plays the well-meaning, hardworking father) are terrified of being evicted. Whether or not the symbolism was intended, *The Window* occurs in the cusp separating wartime and post-war housing shortages from the depredations of 'urban renewal'; we are at the portals of what Marshall Berman calls the 'Expressway World'.[58]

Tommy Woodry's home life is delimited by the bars of the fire escape outside his window. The slatted views favoured by *film noir* cinematographers (the director of photography was William Steiner) are very much in evidence. The murder itself is seen through the narrow band defined by a shade and a window sill. Contrasting with these ominous, constricted views is the bright sunlit street the morning after. With gleaming clouds of honest working-class laundry strung from building to building, the neighbourhood briefly looks to be clean and safe. But Tommy's journey from his street to the local precinct station, after his parents refuse to credit his story, is filmed to look like a desperate and perilous voyage through the underworld shadowed by the El. After his mission fails (the cops are incredulous too), Tommy is locked in his room alone, and darkness and claustrophobia (and Paul Stewart and Ruth Roman) close in. Terror builds until, in a visually spectacular chase sequence, he seeks refuge in the abandoned building, which begins to collapse around him. Paul Stewart, in hot pursuit, is crushed by a falling beam – the falling beam again! – and Tommy is left clinging perilously from another until he leaps to the safety of a fireman's net.

In *The Window*, director Tetzlaff and screenwriter Dinelli, whose pacing is expert, powerfully recreate the claustral atmosphere and apprehensive mood of wartime *film noir*, and of Woolrich's text, using actual New York locations as expressionistically as if they were pieces of scenery on a sound stage. The iconography of the city in early *film noir* was a brilliant minimalist response to the restrictions of wartime production. Hirsch describes these studio-bound cityscapes as 'simplified and semi-abstract . . . deliberately lacking the fullness and density of real life', but 'pregnant with meaning – an evocative background for dramas of entrapment'.[59] After the war, when camera crews were able to move outside the sound stages and venture onto the streets of New York and other cities, in the approved post-war manner, the controlled studio images of urban desolation and abandonment were soon supplanted by the more open documentary style that incorporated the random bustle of pedestrians and vehicular traffic. Jules Dassin's *The Naked City* (1948), the most famous example of pseudo-documentary post-war *film noir*, epitomizes this historical moment. Tetzlaff was one of the relatively few directors in the late 1940s (Fritz Lang was famously impervious to the new mood) who used these new conditions of production to intensify, rather than dilute, the thematics of the abandoned city that pervaded wartime *film noir*.

Blake Lucas writes, 'Such a world represents the inverse of the American dream of freedom; and it is not surprising that when his mother tells him not to go out of the apartment, Tommy replies ingenuously that "There's no place for me to go."'[60] But in so far as *film noir* is, as we have been urging, a meditation on the fate of the city, such criticism is equally ingenuous. The hidden (but not very) subject of the whole exercise is the suburban escape, via the 'Expressway World', which the boy's parents seem too obtuse to grasp. Once again, the *mise en scène* of New York amounts to a demonization of the metropolis in advance of its abandonment by such sturdy strivers as the fictional Woodrys (Mr Woodry seems to be some sort of technician); it is a movement that will be voluntary for some (the lure of suburbia, race-exclusive Federal Housing Administration loans, not to mention the appeal of a new life 'out west'), involuntary for others ('urban removal'). According to Lucas's account in *Film Noir*, the filming of *The Window* was completed in January 1948, but its release was for some reason delayed until August 1949, whereupon it became a surprise hit.[61] On 7 March 1949, on a 1,500-acre former potato field on Long Island, the first Levittown was opened, and despite the cold and lack of advertising, there were a thousand couples like the Woodrys waiting in line to buy. 'Too often we forget that the suburb has been built at a terrifying cost,' say the authors of *American Skyline*, an unpretentious 1955 history that suddenly deflects into outrage:

> This lies not primarily in the *loss of the countryside* before the lengthening superhighway and spreading development; that is perhaps inevitable in the face of a growing population and the very natural desire of the American to own his own home. Rather, it lies in the *abandonment of the city,* the center of our civilization. Like the Mad Hatter at the tea party, who moved around the table using only the clean teacups and leaving the dirty ones behind him, we Americans move on to new land once we have exploited the old. The central city has seemingly been worked for all that it is worth and then abandoned for the suburban fringe.[62]

In this paragraph, the authors, Christopher Tunnard and Henry Hope Reed, may have communicated a good deal more of the facts of the matter than they realized.

By 1955, when *Rear Window* appeared, a new social construction and the routine use of colour film combined with the particular talents of Alfred Hitchcock to create a visual thematics so far removed from the iconography of classic urban *film noir* that this film, although closely based on Woolrich's 1942 short story 'It Had to Be Murder' (originally and more appositely entitled 'Murder From a Fixed Point of View'), is never included in the canon of *film noir*. The interrupted sightlines, the complex interplay of gazes that so fascinate film theorists, are already there in Woolrich, in virtually the same sequence as in the film. Woolrich's 'Rear Window' (as the story is now published in deference to Hitchcock's version) could easily have been adapted as a powerful *film noir*. But while retaining every detail of the suspense plot and visual subtlety of Woolrich's thriller, Hitchcock made several major changes that together created a style and a mood far removed from *film noir*.

Woolrich begins thus:

> I didn't know their names, I'd never heard their voices. I didn't even know them by sight, strictly speaking, for their faces were too small to fill in with identifiable features at that distance. Yet I could have constructed a timetable of their comings and goings, their daily habits and activities. They were the rear-window dwellers around me.[63]

Prose and donnée are (almost) as austere as Beckett. The unnamed, undescribed narrator-protagonist is a man, immobilized, alone in his room except for occasional visits by his houseman. ('The idea was, my movements were strictly limited around this time' (p. 2). In the film, the man is more or less alone in his room – except for the glamorously dressed Grace Kelly, his sweetheart, and Thelma Ritter, his coarse, talkative, good-hearted nurse, playing herself. (However *film noir* is defined, it may safely be asserted that no film prominently featuring Thelma Ritter qualifies as *noir*.) In *Rear Window*, the protagonist's voyeurism, edgily acknowledged in the story ('Sure, I suppose it *was* a little bit like prying, could even have been mistaken for the fevered concentration of a Peeping Tom. That wasn't my fault, that wasn't the idea' – p. 2) is carefully motivated. James Stewart is a bored, restless *Life* photographer laid up with a broken leg. The combination of a virile leading man like Stewart with romantic (Grace Kelly) and comic (Thelma Ritter) elements is sufficient to defeat anything that might have survived of Woolrich in the atmospherics of the film. Structurally, *Rear Window* is almost identical to *The Window*. In the latter, a child witnesses a murder, is disbelieved by his parents and the police, and is menaced by the murderers. In the former, a man temporarily infantilized infers that a murder has been committed, is disbelieved by his lover, surrogate mother, and the police, and is menaced by the murderer. In the comic resolution of *Rear Window*, Jeffries (played by Stewart) persuades lover and cranky mother figure to humour him (though Kelly demurs: 'We're two of the most frightening ghouls I've ever known'), baits the murderer (Raymond Burr) into a confrontation and, once that is over, finds himself with two broken legs and an even firmer engagement to marry Kelly. The optics in Woolrich are retained, the psychological austerity is lightened, and the homosexual subtext, so apparent in the story, is considerably muted, not without leaving a trace in the overtones of homosexual rape when the impossibly goaded Raymond Burr finally barges into Stewart's apartment with murder on this mind.

Like the suspense plot, the setting too is at the same time faithful to Woolrich in every schematic detail (the locations of all the windows in the adjacent building precisely duplicate the description in the story), yet totally different from the claustral atmosphere of the short story – and of *film noir*. In Woolrich's 'Rear Window', set in an anonymous city, the rather dreary apartment buildings face each other, as New York apartments tend to do, over a concrete wasteland, delineated only by a back fence. The film, set at an imaginary New York address (125 West 9th Street), as Peter Conrad has pointed out creates an equally imaginary setting.[64] The apartment houses overlook a beautifully landscaped lawn, with well-tended grass and flowers. The suburbanized vision of city life tends to undercut the thematics of isolation that the iconography of windows renders so powerfully in Woolrich's story and in *The Window* (both story and film). These effects are greatly intensified by Hitchcock's particular use of colour, which intensifies the lushness of the lawn and flowers, and Grace Kelly's beauty. Clearly the distinctive quality of Hitchcock's film, which followed Woolrich's story so faithfully in so many details, had little to do with *film noir* – however it is taxonomized.

Hitchcock neglected to invite Woolrich to the New York première of *Rear Window* in 1955; or so, according to Nevins, Woolrich told the writer Barry Malzberg. 'He knew where I lived. He wouldn't even send me a ticket.'[65]

V

Apart from *film noir* and bebop, the post-war forties enjoy remarkably little purchase on what passes for popular memory; little indeed compared to the hold of the fifties, that cartoonish construction (Ike, Marilyn and the Bomb; beatniks and hula-hoops) superimposed on a cold torpor that passes in national mythology as the United States's golden age. The classic phase of *film noir* – from 1944 to 1950 – coincided with a period in which the United States had gained, and its rulers were determined to secure, a 'preponderance of power' in the world. Despite bravado in the Truman White House, the public mood by any measure (Gallup or even novelistic) was fearful and apprehensive: fearful of a renewed Great Depression (at least up to 1947); fearful afterwards of international communism (the Attorney General's list of 'subversive organizations' was drawn up in 1947). What C. Wright Mills called 'the cold metropolitan manner' and

Rear Window (Alfred Hitchcock, 1959)

W.H. Auden 'the age of anxiety' were cognate. The temper of the times was jittery and skittish. Respectable opinion was pursued by a host of phantasms.

Just as Woolrich and other pulp writers of the thirties were secret sharers in the lofty tradition of cultural pessimism that included Adams and Spengler, just as they continued Balzac's obsessed interrogation of the surfaces of the city, so *film noir* – more than a mere 'nexus of fashions' after all – did register something distinctive about the post-war mood. For example, in his 1992 essay 'The Ends of History', Perry Anderson writes of the German historian Lutz Niethammer's identification of 'an uncanny skein' of European thinkers who at mid-century had arrived at

> something like a collective vision – glimpsed from many angles – of a stalled, exhausted world, dominated by recursive mechanisms of bureaucracy and ubiquitous circuits of commodities, relieved only by the extravagances of a phantasmic imaginary without limit, because without power. In a post-historical society, 'the rulers have ceased to rule, but the slaves remain slaves'.[66]

Surely some such vision of the 'end of history' troubled the sight of others in the forties and early fifties as well (for example, the young Mailer), and indeed is recurrent in the whole career of *film noir*. Rather than dramatizing the ordeal of change, as we are usually told, it would be truer to the mood of these films to say that they melodramatize the ordeal, or at least the fear, of changelessness. In this way the frustrations of the left and the fears of the right both found their way into the mythologies of *film noir*. In Chandler's novel *The Long Goodbye*, for example, the wealthy Mrs Loring (Philip Marlowe's future bride) is convinced the world is well along the road to serfdom. 'We'll have another war and at the end of that nobody will have any money – except the crooks and the chiselers. We'll all be taxed to nothing, the rest of us.'[67]

Psychologically marooned in 1934, possessed (in the full sense of the word) by a melodramatic imagination, Cornell Woolrich in his awful isolation became a master anatomist of Depression-era urban malaise, and a dispiritingly good prophet. 'Among the many images and symbols that New York has contributed to modern culture,' Marshall Berman writes, 'one of the most striking in recent years has been an image of urban ruin and devastation.'[68] In the same way that American city-mysteries of the 1840s surpassed their European counterparts, Woolrich was 'more nightmarish and stylistically wild' than his fellow *romanciers noirs*. In large tracts of the city, his visionary dreariness has been realized in sober fact. Urbanization reached its peak in the US midway through the late 1940s, and almost at once the decline began. As Stanley Aronowitz reports, 'The white working class was fated for dispersal: the center cities were to be reserved for the very poor and relatively affluent.'[69] Paradoxically, to the extent that Woolrich's *noir* vision was realized, its power diminished. But then, its fulfilment was paradoxical as well. The fear of a renewed Depression lifted, and the city was made desolate in its passing.

What became of *film noir* was the fifties. In so far as it represented merely a congerie of fashions, its formal possibilities, or at least those that were formalizable and profitable, were soon exhausted; the studios, for whom it had always represented simply a device to hold a skittish audience, turned to other devices (and eventually returned to old ones, as late *film noir* became neo-). Snubbed by Hitchcock in 1955, Woolrich was a whiskey-sodden wreck and beyond caring when François Truffaut, eager to lionize, invited him to the première of *The Bride Wore Black* in 1968. Woolrich died a millionaire, and one of the five mourners at his funeral was a representative from Chase Manhattan Bank, who brought flowers. As for the infernal machines, his plots, which profitably live on – movie adaptations in Italy, Argentina, Japan, Germany, and endless television reruns – *Habeant sua fata libelli*.

Finally, a large part of the appeal of *film noir* in the forties, when Woolrich's peculiar vision was so often screened is also an explanation of why *film noir* faded in the dull sunshine of the fifties; it is a matter of 'Art and Evil', as Robert Lowell phrased it in an unfinished essay of 1955 about the literary–moral atmosphere after World War Two:

> Old classics no longer pleased; but presently we discovered with relief that supposedly sound authors were much worse than they seemed. We discovered the black, nihilistic, homosexual, almost disintegrating Shakespeare of *Measure for Measure, Troilus, Hamlet* and *Timon*. We discovered a black, gin-drinking Tennyson. We discovered a black, wolfish, wife-deserting Dickens, whose grotesque Hieronymus Bosch world struck us as God's plenty, a richer creation than any English writer's since Shakespeare. Then, a funny thing happened; just as we had labeled our times the Age of Anxiety, and had managed to point out an ample and redeeming shadow of darkness in just about every writer who had ever lived – just at this point we suddenly found we were midway in a second solid, sensible, wealthy, optimistic, child-bearing era, one not unlike the times of Queen Victoria and Prince Albert. Out of the black earth of our evil authors and evil visions, we had somehow rebuilt our own booming 1870s, '80s, and '90s, complete with their dynasties of Republican Presidents.[70]

Since then, yet another dynasty of Republican Presidents has come and gone. The 'ample and redeeming shadow' of New York *film noir* still compels.

NOTES

The authors gratefully acknowledge the urgency of Mike Davis, the resourcefulness of Roland De La Rosa at Movie Image in Berkeley, California, and the forbearance of Stephen Reid.

1. J.B. Priestley, *Midnight on the Desert* (London: Heinemann, 1937), pp.75–6.

2. Mary McCarthy, 'America the Beautiful: The Humanist in the Bathtub', in *On the Contrary* (New York: Farrar, Straus and Cudahy, 1951), pp.6–7. 'She [Beauvoir] did not believe us when we said there were no good Hollywood movies, no good Broadway plays – only curios; she was merely confirmed in her impression that American intellectuals were "negative".' No doubt Beauvoir, for her part, was astonished by McCarthy's suggestion that she spend her time in New York taking in *Rome, Open City* and *Les Enfants du paradis*. See also in the same collection, 'Mlle Gulliver en Amerique'.

3. Mike Davis, *City of Quartz: Excavating the Future in Los Angeles* (London: Verso, 1990), p. 37.

4. Sylvia Harvey, 'Women's Place: The Absent Family of Film Noir', in E. Ann Kaplan, ed., *Women in Film Noir* (London: British Film Institute, 1980), p. 26.

5. Polan's interpretation of *film noir* appears in Dana Polan, *Power and Paranoia: History, Narrative and American Cinema, 1940–1950* (New York: Columbia University Press, 1986). See especially pp. 16–17 and the chapter 'Blind Insights and Dark Passages: The Problem of Placement'.

6. Alain Silver and Elizabeth Ward (Carol Mack and Robert Porfirio, co-editors), *Film Noir* (London: Secker and Warburg, 1980) remains invaluable. For terminological niceness (and much useful learning), see Jon Tuska, *Dark Cinema: American Film Noir in Cultural Perspective* (Westport, CT and London: Greenwood Press, 1984).

7. Geoffrey O'Brien, 'The Return of Film Noir', *New York Review of Books*, vol. 38, no. 14 (15 August 1991), p. 45.

8. It is Tuska who brings in Greek tragedy (p. 7ff.). For Paul Schrader, see his 'Notes on Film Noir', in David Denby, ed., *Awake in the Dark* (New York: Random House, 1977), p. 290.

9. For an atmospheric account of Hollywood in this period, see Otto Freidrich, *City of Nets: A Portrait of Hollywood in the 1940s* (New York: Harper and Row, 1986); the figures quoted appear on pp. 343–4.

10. Friedrich includes material on the red-baiting Sam Wood (see especially pp. 167–8, 318–19), who is also the subject of a monograph by Tony Thomas in *The Hollywood Professionals*, vol. 2 (New York: A.S. Barnes/Tantivy Press, 1974). On the periodization of *film noir*, we are inclined to follow the severe view of Foster Hirsch in *Film Noir: The Dark Side of the Screen* (San Diego and New York: A.S. Barnes/Tantivy Press, 1981) that its 'true heyday', or classic phase as we call it, 'was brief: from Billy Wilder's *Double Indemnity* in 1944 [and Robert Siodmak's *Phantom Lady* in the same year] to Wilder's *Sunset Boulevard* in 1950' (p. 199). *Film Noir* in the fifties became tinctured with camp and was usually destined for drive-ins and grindhouses.

11. For this paragraph, see Richard Polenberg, *War and Society: The United States, 1941–45* (Philadelphia, Lippincott, 1972); John Morton Blum, *V Was For Victory: Politics and American*

Culture During World War Two (New York: Harcourt Brace Jovanovich, 1976); Mike Davis, *Prisoners of the American Dream: Politics and Economy in the History of the US Working Class* (London: Verso, 1986), chapter 2; George Lipsitz, *Class and Culture in Cold War America: 'A Rainbow at Midnight'* (New York: Praeger, 1981); and Norman D. Markowitz, *The Rise and Fall of the People's Century: Henry A. Wallace and American Liberalism, 1941–1948* (New York: Free Press, 1973).

12. Congress effectively gutted the domestic operations of the OWI at the end of 1943. On its beleaguered career, see Blum, pp. 15–52.

13. See Blum and James MacGregor Burns, *The Crosswinds of Freedom*, vol. iii of *The American Experiment* (New York: Knopf, 1989) pp. 193–4, which contains the quotation from *Variety*. Clayton Koppes and Gregory Black, *Hollywood Goes to War* (London: I.B. Taurus, 1988) is a reasonably balanced full-length account. Though Roosevelt knew how to use Hollywood for his purposes, his inner circle was mostly concerned with the image of the President himself, particularly in newsreels (Polan has interesting things to say about FDR's carefully controlled representations and his centrality to the war narrative, pp. 66–8 and 133–6). Of course, the medium Roosevelt made most completely his own was radio. Though fond enough of movies, movie stars, and even the occasional movie mogul, his interest in the medium was sporadic, never approaching his obsession with newspapers and their mostly hostile proprietors. On the whole, the journalists, literary men and former social workers in his entourage were probably less interested in Hollywood than he was. It is suggestive that Lowell Mellett, his emissary to Hollywood, was apparently regarded within the White House as something of a buffoon. See Jonathan Daniels, *White House Witness, 1942–1945* (New York: Doubleday, 1975), p. 142: 'Obviously Mellett is impressed like a child by the glamor of Hollywood.'

14. For a brief discussion of the significance of the strike wave, see Davis, *Prisoners*, pp. 86–7. See also the impressionistic account in Eric F. Goldman, *The Crucial Decade – and After: America, 1945–1960* (New York: Knopf, 1960), an enlarged version of *The Crucial Decade, America, 1945–1955* (1956), pp. 23–7. Goldman's original volume was the first general history of the period written by a respectably tenured academic and is redolent of the conventional wisdom of the time in which he is writing. For a useful overview of the relevant economic figures, see Michael Barone, *Our Country: The Shaping of America from Roosevelt to Reagan* (New York: Free Press, 1990), pp. 147–8.

15. Frank Krutnik, *In a Lonely Street: Film Noir, Genre, Masculinity* (London: Routledge, 1991). See especially chapter 6.

16. Cousins is quoted in Robert S. McElvaine, *The Great Depression: America 1929–1941* (New York: Times Books, 1984), p. 182. McElvaine describes the widespread practices that translated this prejudice into public policy, such as refusing to hire married women to teach in public schools (77 per cent of all school districts) and firing women teachers who did marry (50 per cent); these restrictions provided the supposedly misogynistic Woolrich with a plot twist in *The Bride Wore Black*. See McElvaine, p. 182.

17. On the crisis of traditional male values during the Depression, see McElvaine, pp. 340–41. About Ronald Reagan, confused veteran, see Ronald Reagan (with Richard G. Hubler), *Where's the Rest of Me?* (New York: Duell, Sloan and Pearce, 1955), pp. 160–61.

18. Krutnik, p. 91.

19. Far from witnessing a social revolution, the post-war forties reversed long-standing demographic trends of increased divorce and lowered fertility, which were only restored in the sixties, as Elaine Tyler May reports in 'Cold War – Warm Hearth: Politics and the Family in Postwar America', in Steve Fraser

and Gary Gerstle, eds., *The Rise and Fall of the New Deal Order, 1930–1980* (Princeton, N J: Princeton University Press, 1989), pp. 53–6. 'It might have been otherwise': but it was not. Though *film noir* is often interpreted as registering alarm at various upheavals and assisting in dragooning people back into traditional roles (*Mildred Pierce*, for example, is generally interpreted along these lines), it might equally convincingly be described as a kind of proleptic nightmare vision of a much vaster political, social, sexual and cultural revolution that mysteriously failed to materialize; perhaps the telegrams that Priestley speaks of were coming not from hell but from the political unconscious.

20. C. Wright Mills, *White Collar: The American Middle Classes* (1951; reprinted New York: Oxford/Galaxy, 1956), pp. 328–9.

21. Allan Gurganus, 'Minor Heroism: Something About My Father', in *White People: Stories and Novellas* (1990; reprinted New York: Ballantine/Ivy, 1992), pp. 15–16.

22. The nightclub scenes in *Gilda* (set in Buenos Aires) are a classic locus. A tour of nightspots is a regular feature of the 'soldier's home' genre of post-war fiction, as nostalgically described by Gore Vidal in 'The Art and Arts of E. Howard Hunt' collected in Gore Vidal, *Matters of Fact and of Fiction (Essays 1973–1976)* (New York: Random House, 1977), pp. 211–14. Of course, most of these novels are set in New York ('a glittering Babylon in those days before the writing appeared on Mayor Lindsay's wall', Vidal writes, pp. 211–12), but the nightclub is also an important setting in a grim affair like Ross Macdonald's *Blue City* (1947; reprinted New York: Warner, 1992), set in a city rather like Akron and haunted by the recent strike wave.

23. Henry Adams, *The Education of Henry Adams* (Boston: Houghton Mifflin, 1918), p. 499.

24. David S. Reynolds, *Beneath the American Renaissance: The Subversive Imagination in the Age of Emerson and Melville* (New York: Knopf, 1988), p. 172. See especially chapter 6.

25. On the city-mysteries, see Reynolds, pp. 82–4. Reynolds notes: 'The typical American city-mysteries novel was more nightmarish and stylistically wild than its foreign counterpart, principally because, in America, socialist fervor had by the 1840s become fused with a fierce evangelical emotionalism and a republican rowdiness unknown in Europe' (p. 82).

26. Italo Calvino, 'The City as Protagonist in Balzac', in *The Uses of Literature: Essays* (San Diego: Harcourt Brace Jovanovich, 1982), trans. Patrick Creagh, pp. 184–85.

27. Reynolds, p. 82.

28. Larzer Ziff, *Literary Democracy: The Declaration of Cultural Independence in America* (1981: reprinted New York: Penguin, 1982), p. 96.

29. Reynolds, p. 170.

30. Calvino, p. 183.

31. Peter Brooks, 'The Melodramatic Imagination', *Partisan Review*, vol. XXXIX, no. 2 (Spring 1972), p. 199. The argument in this essay is extended in his *The Melodramatic Imagination* (New Haven: Yale University Press, 1976).

32. See Barone, p. 199. On dispersal, see Stanley Aronowitz, *False Promises* (New York: McGraw-Hill, 1973), p. 383.

33. Originally published in Raymond Chandler, *The Simple Art of Murder* (1950); reprinted in the introduction to *Trouble Is My Business* (New York: Ballantine, 1972), p. viii.

34. George Steiner, *In Bluebeard's Castle: Some Notes Towards the Redefinition of Culture* (New Haven: Yale University Press, 1971), p. 19.

35. Lewis Mumford, 'Spengler: Dithyramb to Doom' (1939–44), collected in *Interpretations and Forecasts: 1922–1972, Studies in Literature, History, Biography, Technics, and Contemporary Society* (New York: Harcourt Brace Jovanovich, 1973), pp. 224–5.

36. On the 'White City', see Spencer R. Weart, *Nuclear Fear: A History of Images* (Cambridge, MA: Harvard University Press, 1988), pp. 5–9.

37. Albert Camus, *American Journals* (1978; trans. London: Abacus, 1990), trans. Hugh Levick, p. 32.

38. Albert Camus, 'The Rains of New York' (1947), trans. Ellen Conroy Kennedy, in Philip Thody, ed., *Lyrical and Critical Essays* (1968; reprinted New York: Vintage, 1970), p. 183.

39. Jean-Paul Sartre, 'Manhattan: The Great American Desert' (1946), collected in Alexander Klein, ed., *The Empire City* (New York: Rinehart, 1955), pp. 455, 456–7.

40. The quotation regarding Dawn Powell's novel *The Locusts Have No King* is from the original jacket copy. See the introduction by John Guare to the reprint (New York: Yarrow Press, 1990), p. ix. Guare asks: 'But doesn't that sound more like *Double Indemnity*, more like a Fritz Lang *Woman in the Window* hurling an innocent to the film noir wolves of fate?' Indeed it does – but Powell was a satirist, whose target in this novel was the publishing industry. On her work, see Gore Vidal, 'Dawn Powell: The American Writer', in *At Home (Essays 1982–1988)* (New York: Random House, 1988). Paul Bowles's 'Pages from Cold Point' appeared in his *The Delicate Prey and Other Stories* (New York: Random House, 1950).

41. Peter Conrad, *The Art of the City: Views and Versions of New York* (New York: Oxford University Press, 1984), p. 265.

42. The standard source on Woolrich's life and literary production is Francis M. Nevins Jr's *Cornell Woolrich: First You Dream, Then You Die* (New York: Mysterious Press, 1988), to which we are much indebted. For a wide-ranging collection of Woolrich's shorter fiction, see *Rear Window and Other Stories*, selected by Maxim Jakubowski (New York: Simon and Shuster, 1988) in the Blue Murder series,

which includes a terse and instructive introduction by Richard Rayner.

43. Nevins, p. 127.

44. Carlos Clarens, *Crime Movies: From Griffith to The Godfather and Beyond, An Illustrated History* (New York: Norton, 1980), pp. 193–4.

45. Nevins, pp. 112–13,

46. Ibid., p. 117.

47. Brooks, p. 206.

48. Cornell Woolrich, *The Black Curtain* (New York: Simon and Shuster, 1941), p. 3.

49. Quoted in Nevins, p. 318.

50. Cornell Woolrich ['William Irish', pseud.], *Deadline at Dawn* (Philadelphia: Lippincott, 1944), p. 339.

51. Cornell Woolrich, *The Bride Wore Black* (1940; reprinted New York: Ballantine, 1984), p. 76.

52. Polan, p. 233.

53. The brief but informative entry for *Phantom Lady* by Robert Porfirio in Silver and Ward, pp. 225–6, notes the nice melding of sensibilities and the 'boost' the film gave to Siodmak's brief passage through Hollywood.

54. Cornell Woolrich [William Irish, pseud.] *Phantom Lady* (1942), reprinted in *The Best of William Irish* (Philadelphia: Lippincott, n.d.), p. 39.

55. Hirsch, p. 115.

56. See 'The Top Ten Bestsellers', in Vidal, *Matters of Fact*, p. 3.

57. Entry for *The Window* in Silver and Ward, p. 314.

58. Marshall Berman, *All That Is Solid Melts Into Air: The Experience of Modernity* (1982; reprinted New York: Penguin, 1988), pp. 290–91.

59. Hirsch, p. 15.

60. Blake Lucas, '*Rear Window*', in Ward and Silver, p. 313.

61. Ibid., p. 312.

62. Christopher Tunnard and Henry Hope Reed, *American Skyline: The Growth and Form of Our Cities and Towns* (New York: Mentor, 1956), p. 184.

63. 'Rear Window', in Cornell Woolrich, *Rear Window and Other Stories*, p. 2.

64. Conrad, pp. 293–4.

65. Nevins, p. 477.

66. Perry Anderson, 'The Ends of History', collected in *A Zone of Engagement* (London: Verso, 1992), pp. 279–80.

67. Raymond Chandler, *The Long Goodbye* (1953; reprinted New York: Vintage, 1988), p. 362.

68. Berman, p. 290.

69. Stanley Aronowitz, *False Promises* (New York: McGraw-Hill, 1973), p. 383.

70. Robert Lowell, 'Art and Evil', collected in *Collected Prose*, ed., Robert Giroux (New York: Farrar, Straus and Giroux, 1987), pp. 129–30.

4

THE MYSTERY OF *THE*

BLUE GARDENIA

Janet Bergstrom

Peter Bogdanovich, commenting on *The Blue Gardenia*: 'This is a particularly venomous picture of American life.'

Fritz Lang: 'The only thing I can tell you about it is that it was the first picture after the McCarthy business, and I had to shoot it in twenty days. Maybe that's what made me so venomous. [Laughs]'

In the fall of 1965, Peter Bogdanovich interviewed Fritz Lang at his home in Beverly Hills, California. Over the course of six days, Bogdanovich questioned Lang about each of the twenty-five films he had directed since he came to America under contract to MGM in 1935, the last one completed just four years before. These interviews were published in 1967 as *Fritz Lang in America*.[1] Bogdanovich could not have imagined that this brief account, Lang's own, of his history in the American film industry would be used as the most reliable source of information on this subject for over twenty-five years. Despite Lang's favoured status with critics and scholars, no one has undertaken the archaeology of his involvement with the American studio system, much less the more daunting task of establishing his biography and professional history across five national contexts (Austria, Germany, France, America and post-war West Germany). Not that charting Lang's course through the studio system would be an easy task.

Whether a sign of strength or weakness (critics have different opinions about this), Lang changed studios almost continuously between 1935 and 1956, from *Fury* to *Beyond a Reasonable Doubt*. His filmography shows affiliations with MGM, United Artists, Paramount, Twentieth-Century Fox, RKO, Universal, Warner Brothers, Republic, and Columbia. Moreover, about half of Lang's American films were independent productions, in which the studio became involved at a relatively late date for release and distribution. Although today we have access to production files maintained by the studios in a way that was once unimaginable, for these hyphenate productions the studio records document, at best, only half of the production history.[2] The records of independent productions are much more difficult to locate. Generally they have not survived or their whereabouts are unknown.[3] Such is the case of *The Blue Gardenia* (1952–53).

The first part of this chapter represents a preliminary effort to trace the production history of this film, based on an interpretation of studio records and clippings files available in the research libraries of Los Angeles as well as the wealth of documents that Lang donated to the Cinémathèque Française in the 1950s.[4] The second part uses the same sources to suggest ideas about the film itself, as distinct from the project to make it and promote it. From the production history of *The Blue Gardenia* we can gain some insight into Lang's work as a 'Hollywood professional' in the early 1950s, and we can also see how Lang attempted to live up to his self-image as a particular kind of creative artist, one charged with the responsibility of translating socially significant ideas into intelligent cinematic expressions. Deception, betrayal and psychological terrorism thoroughly permeate this McCarthy-era film, not only those scenes presented in the nightmarish visual style of *film noir*. *The Blue Gardenia* is a nightmare from one end to the other, no matter how wholesome the 'women's world' featured in many scenes appears to be, with its flat lighting style, as if simulating the look of television.[5] One could almost say that the film is structured around a struggle to re-establish clear lines of demarcation between social expectations for men and those for women. But, on the other hand, the film has been seen as progressive, by E. Ann Kaplan first and others more recently, precisely because of its crystalline representation of sex role limitations for women. I will return to these issues later.

Lang's career in the early 1950s, as described to Bogdanovich, presents a puzzling sequence of events. No one offered him a job after he finished *Clash by Night* (1951–52), and he was unable to find out the reason. Months passed without an offer or an explanation until finally, after a year of anxiety, he learned that he had been blacklisted. Lang described the moral and political confusion at this time, when anti-fascist activities during World War Two, such as Lang's involvement with the Anti-Nazi League, could be reinterpreted as pro-communist, regardless of the political allegiances of the individuals involved. All it took was a rumour for work to disappear. Lang said that although he had never been a member of the Communist Party, unlike many people he knew, he discovered that there was no way to clear his name – no court where he could be heard – because there was no specific charge against him. Lang also reported that his lawyer went to New York to see an official of the American Legion on his behalf, with no clear results. 'Well, finally,' Lang concluded, 'after a year and a half, Harry Cohn gave me the first job.'[6] The exchange between Bogdanovich and Lang on *The Blue Gardenia* cited above ('it was the first picture after the McCarthy business') follows this statement and constitutes the entire entry on that film.

Here is the puzzle: if Harry Cohn was the solution to Lang's blacklisting problem, why was his next film, *The Blue Gardenia*, an independent production released by Warner Brothers? For it was only after Lang finished *The Blue Gardenia* that he went to work for Harry Cohn at Columbia Studios, where he directed *The Big Heat* (1953) and *Human Desire* (1954).

Lotte Eisner, in the French edition of *Fritz Lang*, modifies the account Lang gave Bogdanovich as follows:

> After 13 months of forced idleness, a producer by the name of Alex Gottlieb finally gave Lang a chance, offering him *The Blue Gardenia*. Lang accepted so that he could get back to work. In 1953, Harry Cohn, the head of Columbia, would give him a one-year contract and act as Lang's political guarantor.[7]

According to this, it was a producer named Alex Gottlieb – the man who did, indeed, hire Lang to direct *The Blue Gardenia* in 1952 – who gave Lang his first job after the 'McCarthy business'. But if Lang was already back at work, why would it have been necessary for Harry Cohn to act as his political guarantor the following year? Or was it possible that Cohn gave Lang a contract before Gottlieb, but one that was to begin after *The Blue Gardenia* was completed?

Eisner tells us that *Clash by Night* was finished on 3 November 1951; here began Lang's thirteen months without work. But this date, for which she gives no source, cannot be accurate. Although there are no files on this film in the RKO Collection to establish the dates of the production (*Clash by Night* was an independent production released by RKO), another important collection of documents does provide useful information.[8] The Production Code Administration documented the progress of the film in monitoring the script and all of its revisions throughout the course of shooting.[9]

The PCA file on *Clash by Night* shows a continuous exchange of correspondence about recommendations and changes in the script between the producer and Joseph Breen from 11 July 1951, when the first script was submitted for approval, until 18 March 1952. This is four and a half months after the date given by Eisner for the film's completion. The PCA reviewed the film and granted a seal of approval number on 8 February 1952. Subsequently two more sets of letters were exchanged about 'added scenes', the last one dated 18 March.[10] *Clash by Night* was 'tradeshown' at RKO Studios on 12 May and released in June.

As early as the following September, notices about *The Blue Gardenia*, featuring producer Alex Gottlieb's name, began to appear in the trade papers.[11] On 16 October *Variety* announced: 'Fritz Lang, who has been signed to direct, checked in with Gottlieb at Motion Picture Center yesterday to start work on final screenplay with [Charles] Hoffman.' If Lang finished shooting *Clash by Night* in February or March 1952 and began working on the script for *The Blue Gardenia* in October, his period of inactivity was much shorter than he remembered: at most, seven or eight months. This would not have been considered a long time between films in Hollywood, although it might have seemed like an eternity in the midst of the career-destroying rumours and allegations of the McCarthy era. (The House Committee on Un-American Activities – HUAC – hearings on Hollywood had recommenced in 1951.[12]) According to Columbia Studios' legal department, Harry Cohn did give Lang a one-year contract, but not until after he had finished shooting *The Blue Gardenia* (24 December): on 8 January 1953 Lang signed a contract with Columbia to make three pictures for $15,000.[13] *The Blue Gardenia* was released on 28 March. If Lang's career was ever endangered because he was suspected of being a 'fellow traveller', it was Alex Gottlieb, Blue Gardenia Productions incarnate, who put him back to work.[14]

The man who produced the first ten Abbott and Costello comedies for Universal would seem to be an unlikely match for Fritz Lang.[15] Gottlieb, who started out in publicity, had built a reputation since the 1930s as a writer and producer of low-budget comedies and musicals.[16] In 1952 and 1953, besides *The Blue Gardenia*, Gottlieb produced two more Abbott and Costello films for Warner Brothers and a Frank Tashlin comedy for RKO (*Marry Me Again*). His screen credit as producer of Sternberg's *Macao* for RKO (1950; released 1952), a darker, more ambitious film, was only nominal (the production was run by Howard Hughes).[17] It does not help us to understand why Gottlieb decided to produce a film like *The Blue Gardenia* or why he chose Lang as the director. Perhaps Gottlieb recognized Lang as another seasoned professional, someone who could be relied on to get the job done on time and within budget: here was an opportunity for a low-budget investment to pay off in a quality product. As Gottlieb stated to the press, 'We started with a good story, got Fritz Lang to direct, looked for the best possible actors, and got them.'[18]

Gottlieb moved the entire production along very quickly, keeping his name and the film's progress in the trade journals continuously. (Gottlieb seemed to be personally involved at every step.) He bought the rights to Vera Caspary's story 'The Gardenia' on 3 September 1952. Three weeks later he had a script to send to Breen for PCA approval; by 15 October Lang was working on revisions with Hoffman, which gave him about six weeks for pre-production.[19] On 24 November Gottlieb confidently sent the 'revised final version' of the script to Breen ('Dear Joe . . .') with a note indicating that shooting was scheduled to begin 'on Saturday of this week, so haste will be in order regarding any changes your office recommends that we make'.[20] On 27 November Gottlieb concluded the distribution deal with Warner Brothers.[21] Lang began shooting the next day, finishing on Christmas Eve.[22] Near the end, Gottlieb helped out by delivering 'wild lines' of dialogue and appearing briefly in front of the camera as a newspaperman; his wife, Polly Rose Gottlieb, came in to play a steno typist.[23] Although Lang complained to Bogdanovich and Eisner that he had to shoot the film in twenty days, he actually finished the film one day ahead of his 21-day schedule. The trade papers presented this as a directorial coup, no doubt thanks to Gottlieb's publicity releases: 'Lang established a kind of record in bringing in *The Blue Gardenia* in 20 days . . . by diagramming scenes in advance and using a new kind of quick working dolly for the camera.'[24]

In *The Blue Gardenia*, circumstantial evidence points to Los Angeles telephone operator Norah (Anne Baxter) as the murderer of commercial artist Harry Prebble (Raymond Burr), a notorious womanizer. In an unguarded moment following the news that her fiancé, in Korea in the army, has fallen in love with a nurse, Norah accepts a date with Prebble and later, intoxicated, goes home with him only to realize that she has made a mistake. To fend off his advances, she strikes him with a poker from the fireplace and then blacks out. The next day she remembers nothing about the seduction or the struggle or even about coming home. When she hears that Prebble has been murdered, she panics, assuming she did it (the clues point to her). Disoriented and afraid, she begins to quarrel with her roommates Crystal and Sally (Ann Sothern and Jeff Donnell), accusing them of spying on her. Star newspaper reporter Casey Mayo (Richard Conte), also renowned for his success with women, competes with the police for the prize story; he entices Norah to confess to him by extending to her a calculated promise of sympathy and protection in 'Casey Mayo's Letter to an Unknown Murderess', advertised by a headline that fills the front page of the *Chronicle*. Casey's investigation draws the police to her. As Norah is led off, she accuses him of betrayal. Now in love with her, Casey joins Captain Haynes (George Reeves)[25] to find another woman, Rose Miller (Ruth Storey), who had also gone to Prebble's apartment on the night of the murder. About to be questioned by the police, Rose slashes her wrist, but she is still able to confess from her hospital bed in Norah's presence. At the end, Norah emerges smiling from the courthouse with her protective roommates, who now give Casey their approval.

Never one to improvise on the set, Lang took special care to organize this shoot for maximal efficiency. The documents he donated to the Cinémathèque Française give us a good idea of how he accomplished this. Mapping camera positions, angles and corresponding shot numbers onto architectural drawings of the sets, scene by scene, allowed Lang to visualize shooting out of continuity more easily, keep track of the daily production, and form a condensed picture of shot changes within a scene. Some of these diagrams show elaborate camera movements planned for the crab dolly, a new device for holding the camera that allowed it to be manoeuvered easily on rubber wheels, thus eliminating the expensive, time-consuming process of laying tracks and allowing a new flexibility in shooting.[26] Lang also drew up master charts for each location that showed at a glance the order of the shots he wanted to take, organized to minimize the time spent in setting up the camera and lighting. The chart opposite for the most frequently used set, of the girls' apartment, shows the kind of efficient, logical organization behind the detailed preparations for the film's quick shooting schedule. These visual aids referred to the master document, Lang's heavily annotated copy of the shooting script (key to the shot numbers), on which added shots and changes in dialogue and action, even very small ones, were scrupulously noted, occasionally in the hand of an assistant. Vertical lines were drawn through the shots as they were filmed, with dates and shot numbers noted. Not surprisingly for a director so inclined toward montage, Lang's most frequent notes and sketches added screen direction, especially the direction of an actor's look. Lang's script provided him with a detailed continuity record, the closest thing possible to a replica of the day's shoot that he could take home to use in planning for the next day and that would doubtless facilitate editing later.[27]

Lang's script shows evidence of typical last-minute changes in dialogue: words or lines crossed out or changed to avoid redundancy, improve the pace, or suit the actors' delivery. More substantial revisions can also be seen, one of the most important

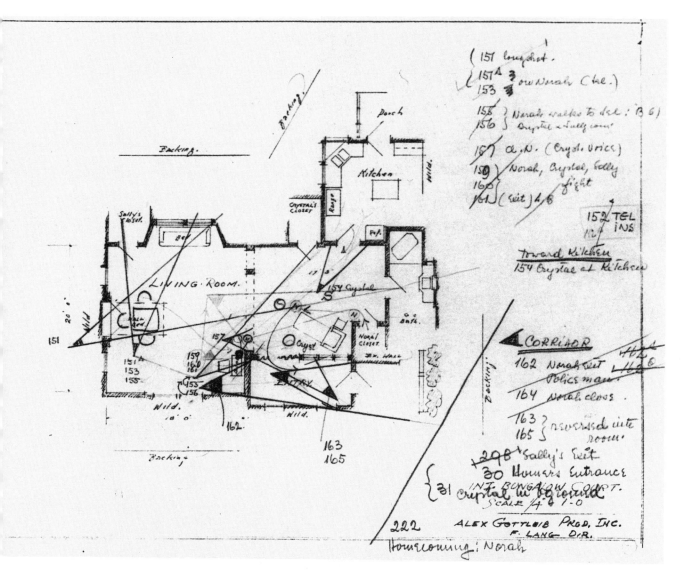

The Blue Gardenia (Fritz Lang, 1952–3)

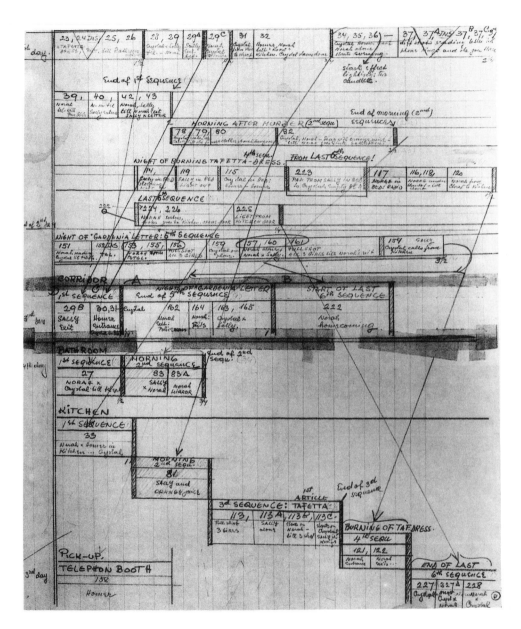

The Blue Gardenia (Fritz Lang, 1952–3)

concerning the murder scene in Prebble's apartment. Several subjective shots from Norah's point of view that are described in detail in the script are not present in the finished film: as Norah tries to regain consciousness, bits of dialogue and shadows reveal that another woman is in the apartment arguing with Prebble. Eisner, after examining Lang's copy of the script, understood these omissions as a wise decision on his part to maintain suspense, so that the audience would not know the murderer's identity until the end of the film.[28] One might state this another way: with no information to the contrary, we are encouraged to believe, along with Norah and on the basis of the same circumstantial evidence, that she is guilty. Perhaps this is meant to increase a paranoid sort of identification with her – until we are proven wrong much later.

Other important departures from the 'Final Shooting Script' are noted in pencil on Lang's copy. On examination, all the late changes involving Rose Miller, the woman who quarrelled with Prebble after Norah blacked out, are significant. In a brief telephone conversation between Rose and Prebble at the beginning of the film, the dialogue was edited in a way that did more than improve the pace: it served the interests of censorship. In so doing, Rose's motive for killing Prebble dropped out of the film. In these few moments on screen (this is the only time we see Rose or hear about her until almost the end of the film), she is reduced to the cliché of the hysterical woman. She murdered Prebble, one assumes, because she has been seduced by him and then callously discarded. According to the script as written, however, Rose has a stronger reason for being desperate.

Rose calls Harry at the telephone company. He makes up an excuse about why he has not called her.

ROSE I don't believe you, Harry. You haven't worked three nights in a row in your life! (*rushes on*) I have to see you and talk to you. I've just been to the doctor and he . . .
HARRY (*interrupts*) All quacks. Don't believe any of 'em. (*listens – bored, then*) Rose, I'm tied up now. Call me later. At home.
(*Rose is on the verge of hysteria.*)
ROSE How can I? You changed the number and I can't get it from the operator. (*pleading*) You have to help me, Harry. You promised. You told me that if anything happened . . .
HARRY (*remains calm and unmoved*) Suresuresure. But you're too smart to believe what a guy tells you – aren't you? I just can't talk now. Take it easy. I'll be seeing you.
ROSE (*close-up in phone booth, frantically*) Harry! (*She flicks the phone desperately, then collapses against the phone as she realizes he's hung up on her.*)

This is not inspired dialogue, but it delivers the information: Rose is pregnant. The synopsis prepared by Warner Brothers is unequivocal on this point: 'Rose Miller, whom [Prebble's] trying to jilt, is hysterical as she tells him she is going to have a baby. Prebble coldly brushes her off.'[29] In the film, their conversation has been reduced to the following exchange (the other lines have been crossed out in Lang's copy of the script):

ROSE   I don't believe you, Harry. You haven't worked three nights in a row in your life! I've got to see you and talk to you.
HARRY   Rose, I'm tied up now. Call me later. At home.
(*Rose is on the verge of hysteria.*)
ROSE   How can I? You changed the number and I can't get it from the operator. (*pleading*) You've got to help me, Harry.
HARRY   I just can't talk now. Take it easy. I'll be seeing you.

The camera remains on Harry, who hangs up, preoccupied with his sketch of another woman.[30]

The basis for Rose's desperation is also kept out of the flashback at the end of the film when she is allowed to tell, so to speak, 'her story'. A letter from Joseph Breen was responsible for excising a few words here that added another dimension to her situation: 'We would like to suggest you eliminate Harry's line " . . . Money to help you –", to avoid the possible interpretation that he is suggesting an abortion.'[31] We can assume that a similar concern, expressed in the name of morality, about negative reactions that could hurt profits was behind the elimination of Rose's pregnancy. As if dispossessed of a body, Rose is reduced to a negative female stereotype ('a woman scorned'). This sanitizing procedure weakened the script: Rose looked like a *deus ex machina* to contemporary reviewers.

Although Rose is older than Norah and appears less attractive because of her strained demeanour, the two women look very much alike: they are the same height, they have the same figure, and the same short, blonde hairstyle.[32] They are dressed almost identically on three occasions, most notably the night they go to Prebble's apartment, where they use the same weapon against him (a poker from the fireplace) after Prebble plays a special record for each of them: for Norah he chooses Nat 'King' Cole singing the romantic title song (they had heard it sung by Cole in person earlier at dinner), while for Rose, he puts on Wagner's 'Liebestod'.[33] It is the music that eventually differentiates them and leads to Rose's discovery. The two women mirror each other again during Rose's confession scene in the prison ward of the hospital: both of them wear anonymous institutional uniforms (Norah a prison dress, Rose a hospital gown) as guilt is exchanged from one to the other. According to a logic of narrative and symbolic condensation especially evident in Lang's American films, Rose functions as a double for Norah. Norah is not found innocent independently, not even in the eyes of the audience. It is only because of Rose that Norah is saved from the law, which is (as usual in Lang's American films) threatening, arbitrary, inhuman and misdirected: in the most striking dissolve in the film, closing the scene of Rose's confession, the insignia of the Hall of Justice appears to descend over Norah's head like a noose.[34] Norah never regains her memory of that night with Prebble; she accepts Rose's story as the truth of her own past. It is Rose, not one of the male representatives of truth or justice, who allows Norah to be innocent – at least innocent of murder.

Lang also establishes an equivalence between three of the men in the film, men who betray trusting women: Prebble, Casey and Norah's fiancé. In two of the most carefully staged scenes in the film, Norah is joined at her modest dinner table by a fantasized male presence as his off-screen voice reads a letter to her. The first scene is that of Norah's birthday. Refusing to go out with her roommates, she sits down to an intimate candlelight dinner at home wearing a new evening dress she has bought for the occasion. Her fiancé's place setting at the table is accompanied by his photograph and a letter. Norah opens a bottle of champagne so that she can share a toast with him, at least in spirit. These romantic touches seem extravagant in this practical apartment where three working women use the same room as a living room, dining room and bedroom, thanks to a folding table and convertible couches. As we read the letter with Norah (an insert shot), we hear her fiancé's voice. What she expects to be a love letter turns out to be an impersonal note written to end their engagement: he has fallen in love with a nurse and they are going to be married.[35] Surprised by this cruel turn of events, Norah is suddenly vulnerable; her idealistic self-sacrifice has been for nothing (she has not gone out with a man since he left). At this moment repression speaks with the voice of coincidence: the telephone rings and Prebble invites her to dinner, thinking she is Crystal. Like Professor Wanley in *The Woman in the Window* (1944), Norah lets herself go and spends the rest of the film terrified of the law (policemen keep turning up in her path) because of an indiscretion that, like a moralistic nightmare, becomes magnified into a capital offence.

Later, Norah is on the verge of hysteria (not unlike Rose earlier). Unable to tell her friends what happened, she tries to hide her emotions and her guilt from them. The tiny apartment, where everything used to be shared with affectionate give and take,

becomes a nightmarish spider's web for Norah (despite its flat lighting) as she tries to assert a sudden, inexplicable need for privacy, even accusing her room-mates of spying on her. In this state, Norah sits alone at her dinner table a second time and reads another letter. This one has been published in the news-paper by Casey Mayo and is addressed to 'an Unknown Murderess'. Casey's voice enters from off-screen, reading the letter as if it were meant for Norah alone, reassuring her that he understands her loneliness and fear, and that she can trust him. The letter is signed 'yours very earnestly, Casey Mayo'. The script continues:

> *Voice Fades. Norah looks up and across the table, as when she concluded reading letter from Korea, and repeating half-aloud to herself:* Yours very earnestly.

This closing, which earlier seemed like the ultimate proof of her fiancé's insensitivity, is here taken by Norah as a sign of just the opposite: Casey Mayo's sincerity.

As the script indicates: 'The situation is almost the same as where Norah read the letter from Korea.' So is the *mise en scène*: the camera frames Norah looking up to-ward the camera as she had after she finished the first letter. As before, she

The Blue Gardenia (Fritz Lang, 1952–3)

appears feminine, sensual, inviting, and defenceless. She is set up, in other words, by a preliminary, imaginary, incomplete scene of seduction to be helped by a man, not by her able and trustworthy roommates. In this, the director's presence – and perhaps his collusion – is strongly felt because of the stylish enunciation leading to the pivotal moment of vulnerability when she looks into the camera. Norah reacts to this letter as if it can cancel the effect of the first one and give her a man to whom she can entrust her future. Little does she know that Casey is counting on his ability to take advantage of a woman's feelings to advance his career. If he does not denounce her to the police, it is only because he stands to gain by publishing his story (or rather, her story) before they do.[36]

Where earlier Prebble took advantage of Norah's emotional state, now Casey does the same, beginning in an improbable scene that makes their first encounter a metaphor of control and entrapment. Casey's 'letter' succeeds in getting Norah, now desperate, to call his number from a phone booth and ask for his help, on the pretext that she is a friend of the murderess. She agrees to meet him at his office. (It is the middle of the night in downtown Los Angeles!) Waiting for her, Casey inexplicably turns out the lights in the large outer newsroom and hides. As Norah enters, a rectangle of light behind her marks the doorway at the far side of the room, making her seem small, defenceless and blind as she tries to find her way.[37] A neon light outside flashes a huge shadow of the word 'CHRONICLE' above her head, an ominous reminder that her story is being transferred from a private to an institutional context, the antithesis of Norah's safe apartment with her warm and generous woman friends. 'I'm sorry. I didn't mean to frighten you,' Casey says disingenuously when he finally steps forward, still in the dark, to take her into his office.

There are noticeable differences, then, between the supportive, uncomplicated, domestic world of women, who are powerless, and the representation of men as calculating, insidious quislings who jockey for privilege and public recognition (appearing to be friends, they turn out to be enemies). Here we should recall Ann Kaplan's analysis of *The Blue Gardenia*, in which she points out that the film is divided into two different kinds of scenes: those that belong to the male world of *film noir* and others that are centred on the female characters and resemble the Hollywood 'woman's film' of the 1930s.[38] Within the context of Lang's work, the *noir* aspects of the film are hardly unexpected; it is the quality screen time devoted to the women, especially when they are together at home, that seems remarkable. Eric Rohmer went so far as to praise *The Blue Gardenia* for its neo-realism because of these scenes.[39]

This mixture of *film noir* and the 'woman's film' are already present in the story on which *The Blue Gardenia* was based. The writer Vera Caspary was the celebrated author of *Laura* and many other best-selling mystery novels.[40] Her subject was the working woman, her difficulty in maintaining independence, and her internal conflicts about her values and self-image as a woman carrying a traditional American past into a modern urban environment. Caspary, a feminist, ended her autobiography in 1979 with these strong lines:

> This has been the century of The Woman and I know myself to have been part of the revolution. In another generation, perhaps the next, equality will be taken for granted. Those who come after us may find it easier to assert independence, but will miss the grand adventure of having been born a woman in this century of change.[41]

The script follows large parts of Caspary's story (she was not involved with the film), but there are a number of important differences.

Agnes (Norah in the film) did murder Prebble, by accident, almost exactly as we are led to believe that Norah did, in a scene that includes *noir* lighting and a misleading, elliptical presentation similar to that of the film. Like Norah, Agnes does not realize this until the next day. Rose was invented for the film, as were the scenes with the deceptive 'love letters' and the late-night meeting in Casey's office. What the film version ignores entirely are the many references to family, religion, sexuality, the social environment of the workplace, and the women neighbours who share the courtyard and their daily experiences with Agnes and Crystal. Absent, too, are all the details addressed to initiates of women's magazines that emphasize the story's very specific woman's point of view. Thus, if the film seems remarkable for its emphasis on a 'woman's world', it is a world devoid of the sense of personal and socio-economic history that defines and largely determines Caspary's female characters. Perhaps the most telling difference between the story and the film is that Caspary keeps the woman's point of view throughout, while the film appears to switch from a female to a male protagonist when Casey Mayo begins his investigation, not unlike Lang's *Secret beyond the Door* (1947).[42]

In 'The Gardenia', Agnes is the product of a repressive, small-town environment dominated by her mother, her mother's fundamentalist religion and the Women's Temperance League: a moralistic community of women enforcing conformity. Anything that can lead to a loosening of morals or to sex has been forbidden Agnes: swearing, dancing, drinking. Her only knowledge of men, in this sense, comes from advice columns in women's magazines and newspapers. Agnes has never had a date. It is in this context that the issue of innocence is first articulated. Agnes has come to believe that innocence is a liability.

Many of the girls who worked with [Agnes and Crystal] were married; some, like Crystal, had been divorced; others were knowing. Most of them treated innocence, or ignorance or chastity . . . it was the same thing whatever you called it . . . as a disability. It was ignorance that made Agnes unimportant.[43]

Because of her ignorance of men, Agnes is excluded from the social world of women. This is one of the frank insights of Caspary's story about these post-war working women. None the less, despite their focus on men (Caspary sees this as a product of socialization), the women are loyal to each other in a way that has nothing to do with professional advancement.

The story is structured around a conflict between Agnes's past and her uncertain new identity in the city where, again, it is the voices of women that dominate the imaginary comments that echo in her mind: those of the other telephone operators at work, her roommate and neighbours at home. Agnes is troubled and heavily self-absorbed from the outset (this self-absorption does not begin, as in the film, after the news of Prebble's murder); she vacillates between conflicting images of the kind of woman she should be. This conflict constitutes Agnes. It is inseparable from her. She seems trapped within an internalized discourse directed against herself, no matter whether it is her mother's stern voice that she hears, condemning social interaction with men as sin, or the voice of the 'other girls' and ready-made images from advertising that she thinks ridicule her old-fashioned prudishness. She seems to have no independent sense of self. Prebble's murder is an accident (a plot device) that brings the two sides of Agnes's self-image into more brutal contact with each other and that forces a strange, disturbing and *noir* cinematic resolution that is completely different from the film.

In *The Blue Gardenia* the principal conflict turns on whether or not Norah will escape the consequences of the accidental murder we assume she has committed. The narrative is thus dominated by incidents that demonstrate misplaced trust and betrayal, and by a mood of paranoia. Norah embodies conflict in the same general way that Lang's characters almost always do; anyone, male or female, has the potential to be subjected to a drastic reversal – a sudden transformation into one's opposite or mirror image or double – when they least expect it and have done almost nothing to deserve it. This was a motif dear to Lang long before the McCarthy period. (Think of *Fury*, made in 1936.) When Norah finds out that Prebble is dead, she becomes consumed by doubts, secrets and dread. She feels helpless, and makes mistakes at every turn (unconscious slips), which seem, in her new, self-conscious state, to become symptoms, signs and clues that she fears make her guilt visible to everyone around her. Overnight, the circumstances of her daily life spiral disastrously out of control. The film can resolve this nightmare, in one sense at least, by displacing the conflict onto Rose, who can externalize Norah's dark side, allowing Norah, in an epilogue, to revert to the 'normal', open, friendly side of her personality. Once again she is in harmony with her women friends, as she was in the film's opening scenes, and she can start over with a new fiancé, too. The more pervasive nightmare, although it was never perceived as such by contemporary reviewers, persists, however, in the prison-like confines of the social conventions governing the 'positive' scenes, scenes in the film that look like they could be part of a women's television series.

Caspary's story pushes the *noir* dimension much further than the film, especially in its unsettling conclusion. Agnes unites in a perverse but not cynical way her desire to be important with her revived, fundamentalist religious convictions: to be known as a murderer would make her even more important than to be known as a woman who is experienced with men. She prepares her appearance scrupulously to match the way she looked the night she went out with Prebble, with detailed attention to her hair and makeup, dressing again in the taffeta suit she had bought for that occasion. Then she proceeds to exhibit the proof of her guilt publicly by standing on a stage, flanked by the two witnesses to her evening at the Blue Gardenia supper club: a Chinese waiter and the blind woman who sold her the gardenia. Calm and self-assured for the first time, she declares herself a sinner, and repents publicly before the police and the press, who have been summoned by her to witness this revelation. Her warring identities seem to have taken over in a way that is beyond her control in this moment that she feels is her greatest triumph.

Caspary's analysis of the ways her protagonist's aspirations and fantasies were channelled into limiting, conventional behaviour was not far from Lang's: story and film share an implicit critique of American society.[44] Caspary's story turns on the negative consequences of sexual repression. Agnes fights the influence of her past even as her mother's injunctions echo in her mind. Interestingly, her mother's fears are exactly the same as those addressed by the Production Code Administration: the relationship of alcohol, sex and crime. It is more strongly suggested in the story than in the film that Prebble's murder is really a screen, or displacement, for the more probable transgression following an evening of exotic drinks, namely sex. When Agnes wakes up the morning after her first date:

> Memory brought confusion. Nothing came into her mind whole or clean. The sense of

difference persisted within her, irrevocable, as if she had been married or given herself in the fog.[45]

Censors in the cities of Cincinnati and Cleveland saw the possibility of sex in the scene in Prebble's apartment, as well as a suggestion of rape, and required cuts in the release print before allowing the film to be shown:

> Eliminate all scenes of drinking of wine by the girl 'Norah,' and eliminate all the kissing as she lies on couch and reduce the violent struggle between the girl and the man.[46]

According to this code, one might observe, illicit sex is a crime worse than murder.

In *The Blue Gardenia*, the double standard is flaunted: men brag about their record of sexual success while women take pride in their fidelity. Rose represents a cautionary example of what Norah could become after just one false move. She also actualizes male fears about sexual violence directed against them, although that story is largely elided: Rose is the image of defeat, not a femme fatale.[47] *The Blue Gardenia*, with its condensed, indirect presentational style and its elaborate work of doubling (involving dialogue, costumes, scenes, characters, actions, *mise en scène*), demonstrates an environment in which betrayal is well-motivated and easy, whilst clearing oneself is a matter of last-minute chance and coincidence, and very difficult.[48] The climate of paranoia encouraged by the political denunciations of the McCarthy period coincided with fear, especially for men, of the destabilization of traditional sex roles. From Lang's vantage point, as if he positioned himself at a distance from this world of entrenched emotional stakes and valueless prizes, both sexes – not just women – are prisoners within a confining, inherently repressive and capricious system. His American films are remarkably consistent in their cinematic demonstration of a series of procedures that the media and the judicial system depend on and exploit 'blindly' – without regard for truth in a higher sense: knowledge is inferential, evidence circumstantial, belief provisional, justice a matter of coincidence. If this is a cynical view, or a 'venomous picture of American life', contemporary reviewers did not see that. To most of them, *The Blue Gardenia* was a routine melodrama.

Lang celebrated his sixty-second birthday on 5 December 1952 during the shooting of *The Blue Gardenia*. Among the documents he sent to Lotte Eisner for the Cinémathèque Française, he included photographs of himself with cast, crew and birthday cake, and a rather touching explanatory note: 'It is customary in Hollywood that the crew, if they like you, invite you to coffee and birthday cake and celebrate with you, when your birthday happens to be during shooting time.' The sentiment expressed here, while it may seem uncharacteristically personal, is consistent with the way in which Lang expressed a sense of respect for – and reciprocity with – his audience throughout his entire career:

> I was always opposed to the American line, 'An audience has the mentality of a sixteen-year-old chambermaid.' If this would be true, I would be ashamed to work for such an audience. I like audiences, but I don't think you should give an audience something fifty steps ahead of them. I asked myself – why is the first work of a writer, of a screenwriter, or of a playwright almost always a success? Because he still belongs to an audience. The more he goes away from the audience, the more he loses contact. What I tried to do my whole life long was not to lose contact with the audience.[49]

There are essentially two views of Fritz Lang's American films since *Cahiers du cinéma* sparked controversy in the 1950s over Lang's 'second career': whilst everyone who understands the history of the cinema can agree that his films demonstrate a masterful conceptual and aesthetic integration of subject and *mise en scène*, as well as constituting virtual essays on meta-cinema and abstraction, critics are divided into those who see Lang as a promulgator of radical social criticism and those who see him as a pessimist or a cynic, even if a modernist one. Ann Kaplan and those who concur with her analysis of the place of women in *The Blue Gardenia* would be among the first group, arguing that the starkness of the imbalance of power and potential for social action between women and men in the film constitutes an implicit argument against the status quo, in favour of women. The most powerful formulation of the opposite view was made by Jean-Louis Comolli and François Géré, who ended their brilliant study of *Hangmen Also Die* (1943) with the shocking conclusion that the film is a 'fiction about hate, but first and foremost hatred of the spectator'.[50] The spectator is bound to identify with the Czech partisans on ideological grounds (they are oppressed, their cause is just), but is bound to identify with the Nazis in an emotional sense, despite himself/herself because of Lang's cinematic rhetoric, which one has no choice but to internalize in the process of following the narrative.

In neither case is it likely that the audiences for whom these films were made would arrive at the same conclusions as these critics. Douglas Pye, writing a decade later about the role of the spectator in *The Blue Gardenia*, considered as a modernist film, brings the argument back to the issue raised by Lang: contact with the audience. He quotes George Wilson on *You Only Live Once* (1937) to make his point about *The Blue Gardenia*:

> The film's power cannot be fully felt until the viewer recognizes that the dramas of misperception enacted on the screen have been replicated still one more time in his or her

theater seat. Realizing this, we come to recognize that *You Only Live Once* has a kind of complexity and a kind of insight that we, unsurprisingly, are not likely to see.[51]

Can Lang's statement that it was important to him to maintain contact with his audience be reconciled with his agreement with Bogdanovich, with which this essay began, that *The Blue Gardenia* represented a 'venomous picture of American life'? Did Lang misjudge his audience – was he, after all, 'fifty steps ahead of them' – or was his design more cynical, that is, did he know that the film would appear to be just the opposite of what it was: that it would appear to show a healthy society with an unscrupulous newspaperman who reforms at the end of the film, when, in fact, it was the entire system of institutionalized relationships that was out of time? In my view, Lang's sense of politics toward the end of his career was deeply ambivalent. Are these films oriented toward exposing problems of American institutions and social conventions with a view toward social change through education? Or do they depict, cynically, a fundamentally static society that is ultimately, as Jean Douchet put it, distilled into pure concept or abstraction?[52] The films can be read both ways. Yet the structural faults that Lang points to again and again in the social institutions on which American society is based are not subject to liberal reform. One must imagine that Lang made films that were, in some sense, at cross purposes with his own intellectual views, as if in the hope that he might be wrong, just as he probably operated with two diametrically opposed estimations of his audience (respect/disdain). This is not an unfamiliar position within cultural politics. In my opinion, it is this absolutely fundamental ambivalence, running throughout the cinematic experience of this relatively 'light' film, that makes *The Blue Gardenia* so disturbing.

NOTES

I would like to thank Bernard Eisenschitz for his generous assistance, as well as Dominique Brun, Catherine Ficat at the Cinémathèque Française; Howard Prouty, Sam Gill, Michael Friend at the Margaret Herrick Library of the Academy of Motion Picture Arts and Sciences; Ned Comstock, Stuart Ng, Leith Adams at the University of Southern California (Warner Brothers Collection). An abridged version of this chapter was published in Paulo Bertetto and Bernard Eisenschitz, eds., *Fritz Lang: la messa in scena* (Turin: Lindau, 1993).

1. Peter Bogdanovich, ed., *Fritz Lang in America* (New York: Praeger, 1967), quotation from p. 84.

2. Of course, studio files, like other kinds of evidence, can raise as many questions as they answer. In 'Fritz Lang Outfoxed: The German Genius as Contract Employee' (*Film History* [vol. 4; no. 4, 1990]) Nick Smedley offers a disappointing, reductive polemic for their use in his effort to prove that the three films Lang made for Twentieth-Century Fox were 'mere contract jobs' in which '[Lang] simply put onto celluloid ideas and themes worked up by others without any of his own input'. Arguing that 'it is not adequate to assess films on the basis of visual style alone', he ignores representation entirely. For a counter-argument that addresses one of Smedley's own examples and is based on the same kind of documentation, see Bernard Eisenschitz's essay in Eisenschitz, ed., *Man Hunt de Fritz Lang* (Crisnée, Belgium: Editions Yellow Now, 1992).

3. The Walter Wanger Collection at the University of Wisconsin represents an important exception for Lang's career. A biography of Wanger by Matthew Bernstein, based on these papers, is forthcoming from the University of California Press. See Bernstein's interesting article 'Fritz Lang, Incorporated' on Wanger's association with Lang and Joan Bennett in Diana Productions (*The Velvet Light Trap*, no. 22, 1986).

4. Several books have been published that reproduce documents and photographs from this collection. Two of them consist mainly of production stills taken by Horst von Harbou, Thea von Harbou's brother, sometimes documenting missing scenes or shots: *Metropolis: Un film de Fritz Lang (Images d'un tournage)* (Paris: Centre National de la Photographie and Cinémathèque Française, 1985); *M. le Maudit: Un film de Fritz Lang* (Paris: Editions Plume and Cinémathèque Française, 1990). Two others are critical analyses of films, which use and reproduce a variety of documents, such as letters, sketches and pages from Lang's shooting scripts: Gérard Leblanc and Brigitte Devismes *Le Double scénario chez Fritz Lang* (Paris: Armand Colin, 1991) a luxury format book devoted to *The Big Heat*; and Eisenschitz (see note 2).

5. The lighting is characterized by Robert Porfirio and Alain Silver as follows: 'An indication of the changing aspect of the noir cycle is that *The Blue Gardenia* as directed by Lang and as photographed by Nicholas Musuraca was largely composed of flat, neutral gray images most representative of 1950s television with its overhead lighting. The diminished influence of a particular studio or visual style is evidenced by Musuraca, whose presence helped define the noir style at RKO but who contributes only a few expressionistic moments in *The Blue Gardenia*.' In Alain Silver and Elizabeth Ward, eds., *Film Noir* (Woodstock, NY: Overlook Press, 1979), p. 38.

6. Bogdanovich, p. 84.

7. Lotte Eisner, *Fritz Lang* (Paris: Cahiers du Cinéma/Cinémathèque Française, 1984), p. 368 (my translation). This contradicts the information found in the English edition of Eisner's book, which retains the sequence found in Bogdanovich's interview. The English edition includes many errors that were subsequently corrected in the French edition: for instance, that Harry Cohn testified before the House Committee on Un-American Activities on behalf of Lang, which he did not; Alex Gottlieb is called Adolf; HUAC was said to have been founded in 1947, whereas that was the year that the hearings on Hollywood began; the Black Dahlia murder case is said to be recent, whereas it dated back to 1947. In the English edition, Lang was idle for eighteen months, compared to thirteen in the French edition. Eisner's manuscript, written in German, was

published first in English translation (ed. David Robinson, London: Secker and Warburg, 1976). Eisner did not see the final version of the manuscript for review. For French publication, the text was revised substantially by translator and editor Bernard Eisenschitz working in collaboration with Eisner, as described in the book's preface.

8. The RKO Collection at UCLA generally does not contain clipping files or anything pertaining to release and distribution. A great deal of material is held by Turner Productions and is not currently accessible.

9. The PCA's role as the industry's agency for self-regulation was designed to forestall potentially expensive problems that a finished film might encounter from state censorship boards, religious or educational agencies, or foreign markets by recommending changes before shooting. See Lea Jacobs, *The Wages of Sin: Censorship and the Fallen Woman Film, 1928–1942* (Madison: University of Wisconsin Press, 1991). The PCA files are located in the Margaret Herrick Library at the Academy of Motion Picture Arts and Sciences, hereafter referred to as Academy.

10. These additions were probably adjustments based on reactions to preview screenings. The PCA allowed them without a second review. A separate source shows that the producer filed 20 February 1952 as the date of completion with the Academy of Motion Picture Arts and Sciences. See the 'Data for Bulletin of Screen Achievements Awards', dated 20 June 1952. The data sheet submitted by Alex Gottlieb for *The Blue Gardenia* shows 24 December 1952 as the date of completion; this was the last day of shooting. (Academy clipping files.)

11. *Hollywood Reporter*, 3 September 1952.

12. The House Committee on Un-American Activities hearings on Hollywood began in 1947; they recommenced in 1951 after the appeals of the so-called Hollywood Ten had been exhausted, and continued through 1953.

See Victor S. Navasky, *Naming Names* (New York: Penguin, 1980).

13. They were to be *China Venture* (also known as *Operation 16-Z*), *The Big Heat*, and *The Human Beast* (later changed to *Human Desire*). On 17 March the contract was amended to relieve Lang of *Operation 16-Z*, making *The Big Heat* the first picture. The third picture named in the amended contract, *Ten Against Caesar*, was apparently abandoned. The contract commenced on 12 January 1953 and expired on 11 January 1954 with no option to renew.

14. I found no confirmation that Lang had been blacklisted. Alex Gottlieb Productions is the name that appears on correspondence and documents relating to the film until the agreement with Warner Brothers, when it becomes Blue Gardenia Productions.

15. The Abbott and Costello unit at Universal 'was composed of B-picture personnel who were used to working at top speed . . . turning out a picture every three or four months'. See Thomas Schatz, *The Genius of the System* (New York: Pantheon, 1988), pp. 342–7.

16. Gottlieb's career charts the movement of comedy and entertainment shows through radio, film, Broadway theatre and television. The Russian-born Gottlieb (1906–88), a 1928 graduate of the University of Wisconsin, became publicity director for Walter Wanger Productions. Early on a writer for radio comedians Al Jolson, Eddie Cantor, Edgar Bergen, and George Jessel, he made an easy transition from low-budget film to television, producing more than fifty television shows, mostly in the variety and comedy format, including 'The Gale Storm Show', 'The Tab Hunter Show', 'The Bob Hope Chrysler Theater', 'The Donna Reed Show', and 'The Smothers Brothers Show' (*Variety*, 11 October 1988). Though Gottlieb was a successful businessman, his name never became famous and the location of his papers, if he kept them, is unknown. Judging from the press

clippings on *The Blue Gardenia*, Gottlieb's production history was well documented by news items in the Hollywood trade journals. See the Warner Brothers Collection and Academy clipping files.

17. In a production marked by revolving personnel held in a state of confusion by Howard Hughes (including the uncredited Nicholas Ray), Sternberg had more to do with the executive producer, Samuel Bischoff, than Gottlieb. See Bernard Eisenschitz, *Roman américain: Les vies de Nicolas Ray* (Paris: Christian Bourgeois, 1990), pp. 212–13. See also Sternberg's autobiography, *Fun in a Chinese Laundry* (New York: Macmillan, 1965), p. 283.

18. *Los Angeles Daily News*, 30 March 1953.

19. PCA files, 6 October 1952, Academy. Charles Hoffman was a lacklustre screenwriter who had worked with Gottlieb several times before on Warner Brothers films. We do not have a copy of the script before Lang started to work on it.

20. PCA files, Academy.

21. *Variety* and *Hollywood Reporter*, 28 November 1952.

22. Lang's detailed log of the shoot, in which he listed by number the shots that were completed each day, is in the Cinémathèque Française collection.

23. *Variety*, 23 December 1952; *Variety* and *Hollwood Reporter*, 24 December 1952; and *Los Angeles Times*, 26 December 1952. Gottlieb's many releases to the press about hiring actors for minor parts appeared during the first week of shooting. (Warner Brothers, clipping files.)

24. *Los Angeles Times*, 25 December 1952; see also *Variety*, 26 December 1952; *Los Angeles Examiner*, 28 December 1952; *Los Angeles Examiner*, 11 January 1953.

25. George Reeves was already known as Clark Kent in television's 'Superman' series. A news item in *Variety* on 12 December drew attention to the fact that five of the film's main actors were currently appearing on television, most notably, aside from Reeves, Ann Sothern in 'Private Secretary'. See the Warner Brothers clipping files for other connections to television.

26. Even when operating on an extremely tight shooting schedule, Lang, as was typical of him, found time to reflect on the aesthetic and psychological uses to which a new technological device could be put. 'My new camera carriage assures the attainment of a fluid film picture. The photographic apparatus becomes the constant companion of the actor; it becomes a sharp observer of the events, capturing the drama more intensively as it draws quickly nearer when something decisive is done or said. As soon as it becomes important, it can then go immediately to focus on some characteristic event or significant object. The camera in motion, therefore, becomes an important and "living" participant in the film.' From an interview with Friedrich Porges, 'Eine Kamera, die alles sieht: Fritz Lang erfand das "Opernglas" System', *Berliner Morgenpost* (27 February 1953), cited in Frederick Ott, *The Films of Fritz Lang* (Secaucus, NJ: Citadel Press, 1979).

For a thoughtful consideration of Lang's use of this invention, see Raymond Bellour, 'Sur l'espace cinématographique', in *L'Analyse du film* (Paris: Editions Albatros, 1979).

27. Lang was in the habit of working each evening when he was shooting a film, making notes and sketches to prepare for the next day.

28. Eisner, *Fritz Lang*, French edition, p. 370; English edition, pp. 323–4. According to the notations on Lang's script, however, the visuals for this missing scene were shot.

29. 'Synopsis of "The Blue Gardenia"', Warner Brothers Collection.

30. The sketch anticipates Rose's double: a position match sets up the dissolve to what the script describes as 'Norah, in almost the same pose as the girl in Harry's sketch'.

31. PCA files, 2 December 1952, Academy.

32. Ruth Storey, the wife of Richard Conte, dyed her hair to play the part of Rose, according to the *Los Angeles Daily News* (1 January 1953). Another news item drew attention to the fact that all four female leads had blonde hair. This is one of the many ways in which the women seem almost interchangeable. Despite their individualized personalities, they represent a standardized image of wholesome, domestic femininity. Rose, too, seems to desire this image.

33. The record of the title song had been released commercially and was advertised with the film. There is virtually nothing about Nat 'King' Cole's participation in either the Warner Brothers Collection or the materials Lang gave the Cinémathèque Française. According to the *Los Angeles Examiner* (11 December 1952) this popular singer received $10,000 for one day's work.

34. See Frieda Grafe and Enno Patalas, *Fritz Lang* (Munich: Hanser, 1976) in which these frame enlargements were published as part of an eloquent illustration of Lang's methods of visual and symbolic condensation.

35. The male voice appears to be given life by Norah as we share her psychological and visual point of view, reading the beginning of the letter in an insert shot, listening to her fiancé. But when the content of the letter makes it clear that he does not share her fantasy, the camera is positioned opposite her, as if in his place. The anguished expression on Norah's face then makes his voice seem like a foreign presence pressing in on her from outside. (There is no change in the audio level.)

36. First Casey competes with the police, then he joins them (Haynes and Mayo are on a first-name basis). The news after Norah's arrest underlines Casey's complicity: 'Read all about it. Blue Gardenia police trap. Beautiful murderess caught by columnist.' The front page reads: 'Casey Mayo Captures Blue Gardenia', where earlier it announced the duplicitous 'Casey Mayo's Letter to an Unknown Murderess'.

37. This visual configuration, one of Lang's favourites, translates an unequal power relationship into the internalized language of *mise en scène*. Compared to Norah's unwise date with Prebble, the danger here looks more obvious and more serious, although the audience can see that it is just a teaser for Casey. Cutaway shots show him watching Norah from his hiding place with the undisguised curiosity of a voyeur.

38. E. Ann Kaplan, 'The Place of Women in *The Blue Gardenia*'. In this respect, as Kaplan notes, her essay resembles Pam Cook's analysis of *Mildred Pierce*. Both were published in *Women in Film Noir*, edited by Kaplan (London: British Film Institute, 1972).

39. Maurice Scherer [E. Rohmer], 'Un réalisme méchant', *Cahiers du cinéma* 36, June 1954. On the other hand, see Frieda Grafe's essay 'Für Fritz Lang: einen Platz, kein Denkmal', (For Fritz Lang: A Place not a Monument), in which she compares Lang and Brecht on realism: 'What united them, these two specialists in distanciation, momentary differences aside, was a horror of nature, of pseudo-nature, and it was this that they attempted to analyse, each with the means proper to his respective medium. Brecht had the easier task: in the cinema, it is more difficult to destroy appearance than reality' (Grafe and Patalas, p. 17, my translation).

40. Vera Caspary (1904–87), a playwright as well as a novelist, earned many screen credits for adaptations, among them *Easy Living* (1937) with Preston Sturges; *A Letter to Three Wives* (1948) with Joseph L. Mankiewicz; and *I Can Get It for You Wholesale* (1951) with Abraham Polonsky. 'The Gardenia' was published in a

women's magazine, *Today's Woman* (February–March 1952). The manuscript is included in Caspary's papers at the Wisconsin State Historical Society. Attached to it is this note: 'I do not have screenplay of final movie ("The Blue Gardenia") which I had nothing to do with.' In 1949 she married producer I.G. Goldsmith. They formed an independent production company called Gloria Pictures. Although Caspary was not involved with the script or the production of *The Blue Gardenia*, apparently Gloria Pictures had a financial stake in it. This would explain the production credit seen in Lang's filmographies: 'Blue Gardenia Productions/Gloria Films for Warner Bros'. Blue Gardenia Productions is listed as the sole copyright claimant. Gloria Films does not have a screen credit on the film itself.

41. Vera Caspary, *The Secrets of Grown-ups* (New York: McGraw-Hill, 1979). Also quoted (with minor errors) in Caspary's obituary in the *New York Times*, 17 June 1987.

42. Reviewers saw this as the script's biggest problem; the script was routinely pointed to as the film's greatest weakness.

43. Caspary, 'The Gardenia', ms. p. 5.

44. Caspary, unlike Lang, had been a member of the American Communist Party during the 1930s. To avoid answering questions during the McCarthy era, she moved to Europe for several years. See *The Secrets of Grown-ups*.

45. Caspary, 'The Gardenia', ms. p. 45.

46. Warner Brothers Collection.

47. Alison McKee writes about female characters whose stories are elided in 'To Speak of Love: Female Desire and Lost Narrative in the Woman's Film, 1939–1949' (PhD dissertation, UCLA, forthcoming 1993).

48. The musical clue that leads to Rose's discovery and eventually frees Norah is represented as a truly ridiculous coincidence: Casey and his news photographer are at the airport about to leave to witness a hydrogen bomb explosion (!) when Casey happens to hear the 'Liebestod' again over the loudspeaker. 'What's that song?' he asks his friend, remembering it from Prebble's record player the morning after the murder. 'Canned music.' As it builds to a climax, Casey realizes that Norah can't be the murderer because the record Prebble played for her, and that Casey played for her, too, in the diner when he started flirting with her in earnest, was 'The Blue Gardenia'.

49. *The American Film Institute Dialogue on Film* (April 1974), p. 11 (edited slightly for punctuation).

50. Jean-Louis Comolli and François Géré, 'Deux fictions de la haine', (part one) *Cahiers du cinéma* 286 (March 1978), p. 47 (my translation). This essay appears in English in Steve Jenkins, ed., *Fritz Lang: The Image and the Look* (London: British Film Institute, 1980).

51. George Wilson, *Narration in Light* (Baltimore: Johns Hopkins University Press, 1986), p. 38; cited in Douglas Pye, 'Seeing by Glimpses: Fritz Lang's *The Blue Gardenia*', *CineAction!* (Summer 1988), p. 74.

52. Jean Douchet, 'Le Piège considéré comme l'un des Beaux-Arts', *Arts* (Paris), 1–7 July 1959, p. 6.

5

FILM NOIR AND WOMEN

Elizabeth Cowie

Whether it is a genre, a cycle of films, a tendency or a movement, *film noir* has been extraordinarily successful as a term. As 'the genre that never was' – since the term was not used by the studios themselves, or by audiences at the time, except perhaps in France where the term originated – the claims for the category lie in a *post hoc* analysis of similarities and in a set of elements that provide a 'core' of characteristics that are identified in certain films. The term has succeeded despite the lack of any straightforward unity in the set of films it attempts to designate. Unlike terms such as the 'western', or the 'gangster' film, which are relatively uncontroversial (and were industry categories), *film noir* has a more tenuous critical status. This tenuousness is matched by a tenacity of critical use, a devotion among *aficionados* that suggest a desire for the very category as such, a wish that it exist in order to 'have' a certain set of films all together. *Film noir* as a genre is in a certain sense a fantasy: it is something that is never given a pure or complete form; the 'first' *film noir*, *The Maltese Falcon* (John Huston, 1941), is usually described as 'atypical', while it is the much later *Out of the Past* (Jacques Tourneur, 1947) which is often cited as the quintessential *noir* film. Though only ever realized in some incomplete form, the 'true' form is nevertheless discerned across a series of films. The desire for *film noir* can be seen, too, in the tendency by film reviewers to discover contemporary examples – colour cinematography notwithstanding – a recent example is Denis Hopper's film *The Hot Spot* (1990).[1] What is centred by this fantasy is almost always a masculine scenario, that is, the *film noir* hero is a man struggling with other men, who suffers alienation and despair, and is lured by fatal and deceptive women.[2]

THE DESIRE OF THE CRITIC

In a widely quoted passage James Damico proposes a model of *film noir*'s plot structure and character type:

> Either because he is fated to do so by chance, or because he has been hired for a job specifically associated with her, a man whose experience of life has left him sanguine and often bitter meets a not-innocent woman of similar outlook to whom he is sexually and fatally attracted. Through this attraction, either because the woman induces him to it or because it is the natural result of their relationship, the man comes to cheat, attempt to murder, or actually murder a second man to whom the woman is unhappily or unwillingly attached (generally he is her husband or lover), an act which often leads to the woman's betrayal of the protagonist, but which in any event brings about the sometimes metaphoric, but usually literal destruction of the woman, the man to whom she is attached, and frequently the protagonist himself.[3]

This same core theme is presented by Marc Vernet in his discussion of the openings of *films noirs*, though it is now identified as having an 'incest form':

> The 'triangle' has often been pointed out as a principal form of relation among the characters: the young hero desires and conquers a rich woman who is quite often tied to an older man or some other representative of patriarchal authority (*Double Indemnity, The Lady From Shanghai, Out of the Past, The Big Sleep, The Maltese Falcon*). However, in most of these films the woman is made guilty and despite her protestations she is either abandoned or killed by the hero. In this manner, the resolution of the intrigue is guaranteed by the annulment of the incestuous relations.[4]

Although, as the translator David Rodowick notes, in this essay Vernet 'is concerned less with a generic definition of *film noir* than with the elaboration of the general conditions of hermeneutic development and narrative suspense in the classic American film, of which the *noir* is an extreme example', he nevertheless assumes that *film noir* is a genre with a relatively homogenized form: '*films noirs* are characterized by their singular brutality and surfeit of violence . . . the *film noir* insists on the transparency of the disguise . . . when the *film noir* takes off . . . ' and so on.

Foster Hirsch in his book *Film Noir: The Dark Side of the Screen* claims that 'The three major *noir* character types – the sleuth, the criminal, the middle-class victim and scapegoat – all inhabit a treacherous urban terrain filled with deceiving women and the promise of money easily and ill-gotten.'[5] These figures are clearly male, and he goes on to say that while there are other kinds of women – meek wives or a few like Lauren Bacall 'who achieve something like parity with the men they fall for' – nevertheless 'the dominant image is the one incarnated by Barbara Stanwyck in *Double Indemnity*: woman as man-hating fatal temptress'. Moreover he says, 'The force and persistence of this image of women as amoral destroyers of male strength can be traced, in part, to the wartime reassignment of roles, both at home and at work.'[6] Hirsch attempts here to attach this image to a little bit of reality, but this very attempt only confirms its actual status – as fantasy. While he appeals to a social reality which gives rise to the fantasies, I would like to emphasize their *psychical* reality. The *mise en scène* of these fantasies is provided by elements from the contingent social reality, just as in the dream-work. This very clothing of contingent social reality can then become the basis or alibi for a disavowal thus: the image of woman as devouring is not, or not merely, my fantasy, but really true – women have substituted for men at home and at work, and it is social reality that produces a crisis in my masculine identity. Freud, in a discussion of fantasy in neurosis and psychosis, says that both the neurotic and the psychotic draw upon a 'world of phantasy' which functions as the

> storehouse from which the materials or the pattern for building the new reality are derived. But whereas the new, imaginary external world of a psychosis attempts to put itself in the place of external reality that of neurosis, on the contrary, is apt, like the play of children, to attach itself to a piece of reality – a different piece from the one against which it has to defend itself – and to lend that piece a special importance and a secret meaning which we (not always quite appropriately) call a *symbolic* one.[7]

What must be explained is the continuing fascination with this fantasy long after the historical period that is supposed to justify it. Accompanied now by a disavowal of the 'anti-woman bias' of the films, this fascination nevertheless valorizes their themes and visual style, which, Hirsch says 'is both varied and complex, and in level of achievement it is consistently high. *Film noir* is one of the most challenging cycles in the history of American films.'[8]

The pleasure and fascination of the fantasy of the duplicitous woman in *film noir* are, no doubt, as varied – or limited – as the different forms the fantasy takes. In certain films the fascination seems close to the compulsively repeated pattern Freud describes in 'A Special Type of Object-choice Made By Men' (1910),[9] that of falling in love with a woman who is another man's 'property', that is, his wife or mistress, but who is sexually promiscuous, giving rise to the lover's suspicions and jealousy. This jealousy is not, however, directed at the 'lawful' possessor of the woman, but at all the other men she associates with (seen, for example, in Johnny's behaviour in *Gilda* [Charles Vidor, 1946]). Moreover the man seeks to 'rescue' the woman he loves from moral decline, or from poverty, or from a vicious lover or husband. Freud connects this type of object-choice to the man's oedipal desires, so that the duplicitous woman is a mother surrogate. This explains the condition that the woman not be unattached, as well as the over-valuation of her as love-object, and the condition of her unfaithfulness for, after all, she has betrayed the son by granting her sexual favours to his father, rather than to him. This is not a straightforward fantasy, however, for the mother is both punished for her betrayal by being cast as promiscuous and at the same time becomes available to her son, for Freud says, 'the lover with whom she commits her act of infidelity almost always exhibits the features of the boy's own ego, or more accurately, of his own idealized personality, grown up and so raised to a level with his father'.[10] The injured third party 'is none other than the father himself'.[11] And, Freud says, 'in the rescue-phantasy [the boy] is completely identifying himself with his father. All his instincts, those of tenderness, gratitude, lustfulness, defiance and independence, find satisfaction in the single wish *to be his own father*.'[12] Here, too, can be found a basis for the homoerotic relations often noted in *film noir*, namely in the identification between the male characters, whether as rivals as in *Out of the Past*; or as substitutes, notably in *Dead Reckoning* (John Cromwell, 1947) in which the hero, played by Humphrey Bogart, falls in love with the girlfriend of his newly murdered best friend and war buddy; in *Gilda* it is the repression of this wish that is figured, and which then forms the basis for Johnny's sadistic punishment of Gilda.

Freud's essay 'On the Universal Tendency to Debasement in the Sphere of Love' (1912)[13] suggests another motive for the fantasy of the duplicitous woman, namely that it is her very 'promiscuity' (however veiled to accommodate the Production Code) that secures her as a sexual object. It is only as a whore that she becomes desirable, but as such she is not worthy of love – a split most visible in *Out of the Past*, but also evident in *Murder, My Sweet* (Edward Dmytryk, 1944) and *Double Indemnity* (Billy Wilder, 1944), where the bad girl is counterposed to another, purer woman, but who usually remains unattainable.

The scenario of the duplicitous woman as femme fatale affords as well as the pleasures of passivity which arise from being in thrall to her promise of love, pleasures which are no doubt also masochistic. The violent retribution so often enacted upon the femme fatale by the plot and/or the male hero bears witness not so much to patriarchal ideology as to the man's inverse desire to control and punish the object of desire who has unmanned him by arousing his passive desire. Of course, desire itself always involves the risk of loss, of losing the object of desire to whom one has surrendered a part of oneself. Hence Hirsch's image of 'women as amoral destroyers of male strength' in the *film noir*. But 'femme fatale' is simply a catchphrase for the danger of sexual difference and the demands and risks desire poses for the man. The male hero often knowingly submits himself to the 'spider-woman' – as Neff does in *Double Indemnity* – for it is precisely her dangerous sexuality that he desires, so that it is ultimately his own perverse desire that is his downfall.

Frank Krutnik is another writer for whom the 'core' *film noir* involves a male protagonist, exemplified by the male 'tough' thriller. He sees this as having three forms:

> Each of the three modes of the 'tough' thriller tends to be structured around a testing of the hero's prowess – not merely a testing of his ability as a detective or criminal, but of how he measures up to more extensive standards of masculine competence. For it is through his accomplishment of a crime-related quest that the hero consolidates his masculine identity.

Krutnik goes on to emphasize, however, that 'while seeking ostensibly to dramatise a positive trajectory . . . the "tough" thrillers tend to subject [it] to a series of inversions, delays, and schisms'. As a result, these films offer a range of alternative or 'transgressive' representations of male desire and identity.[14] This argument opens up important insights, but nevertheless it too makes of *film noir* a male preserve.

Even where there is a broader definition of the *film noir* it is still assumed to be a masculine form. Richard Maltby, for example, writes thus:

> The hero of these films, who was not always the central protagonist, was the investigator, the man assigned the task of making sense of the web of coincidence, flashback and unexplained circumstance that comprised the plot. Uncertainly adrift in a world of treachery and shifting loyalties, the investigator of the noir movie was himself less than perfect, frequently neurotic, sometimes paranoid, and often managed to re-establish a stable world in the film only by imposing an arbitrary resolution on the other characters.[15]

A QUESTION OF GENRE

These films then appear to be the antithesis of the 'woman's film', for although *film noir* often features strong, independent women with determined and determinate desires, it has been argued that this figure is invariably destroyed, either literally, or metaphorically, and replaced by her inverse, the nurturing woman.[16]

Things are not, however, so simple. The number of films that fit this model is comparatively small (although this immediately begs the question of what is meant by 'fitting' the model, an issue to which I will return). For example *Laura* (Otto Preminger, 1944), one of the original films designated by Nino Frank as a *film noir* when he coined the term,[17] has no such deceptive woman; on the contrary, it is the villain who is the source of the deception. But this film does have a number of other characteristics in common with the group of films Frank cites: it contains an investigation (here a policeman investigating a murder); its narrative is convoluted (the film opens with the assumption that Laura is dead and then reverses this assumption); it uses voice-over (Lydecker narrates at the beginning); it shifts point of view (from Lydecker to the detective, McPherson); its visual style is recognizably *noir*; and, finally, the motivations of its two main male characters are psychologically perverse (Lydecker's obsession with Laura is matched and paralleled by that of McPherson, who falls in love with a dead woman's portrait).

Film noir is now identified by a range of elements, not only thematic, such as the role of fate or of a duplicitous woman, but also formal: the use of flashback, for example, and hence of voice-over, the frequent undermining or shifting of character point of view, and the investigative narrative structure, which requires the posing of an enigma, or several, which the film attempts to resolve. The narrative complexity of these films stems from the doubling of the investigative structure, with stories within stories, so that the investigation of one enigma frames another, as for example in *The Big Sleep* and *Murder, My Sweet*. Characters are given psychological motivation, and this is often in some way perverse or acknowledged as psychotic. Fate, the arbitrary and accidental event that brings diverse dangers and the risk of death, together with a hero falsely accused are used as narrative motivation.

Finally, *film noir* is said to be identified by its visual style:[18] low-key lighting; the use of chiaroscuro effects; strongly marked camera angles, either low or high; jarring and off-balance shot composition; tight framing and close-ups that produce a claustrophobic sense of containment. The films are predominantly urban, the action taking place at night and filmed night-for-night on location, to produce a strong contrast between the enveloping dark and intermittent pools of light.

This style was clearly recognized within the industry and was deliberately used and developed, especially by the small independent production companies – for whom the style offered spectacular and distinct effects for little cost while producing a style associated with 'quality' – but also by the major studios, for projects not necessarily determined by low budgets.[19] The self-conscious use of the style is confirmed by *Reign of Terror* 1949 directed by Anthony Mann and photographed by John Alton, which reproduces the *noir* style very closely, but here for a story set in Paris during the French Revolution. Similarly, the use of this visual style motivates the inclusion of Ophuls's *Caught* and *The Reckless Moment* (both 1949) in the category of *film noir*, although they were clearly also seen as 'women's pictures'.[20]

The sense of alienation and fatalism in many of the films was recognized at the time within the film industry. Richard Maltby cites two articles in which John Houseman,[21] writing in the 1940s, expressed reservations about a new kind of post-war crime film he described as the 'tough' movie, taking as his examples *The Big Sleep* (Howard Hawks, 1946) and *The Postman Always Rings Twice* (Tay Garnett, 1946).

> What is significant and repugnant about our contemporary 'tough' films is their absolute lack of moral energy, their listless, fatalistic despair.[22]

> One wonders what impression people will get of contemporary life if *The Postman Always Rings Twice* is run in a projection room twenty years hence. They will deduce, I believe, that the United States of America in the year following the end of the Second World War was a land of enervated, frightened people with spasms of high vitality but a low moral sense – a hungover people with confused objectives groping their way through a twilight of insecurity and corruption.[23]

All this does not add up to a genre, however, at least not a genre in the sense that the term is applied to other cinematic forms such as the western, or the gangster film, which have a specific iconography of objects and milieux as well as a limited set of narrative themes or problematics.[24] Although genre studies in film has many pitfalls, it is possible to posit sets of elements that are obligatory or forbidden in the western or the gangster film, but this is much less easy in the case of *film noir*.[25] The latter has no unique elements, and whilst it has some obligatory elements, notably narrative elements of the suspense mystery or thriller form, it does not have any forbidden elements, except perhaps the requirement that the period of the story be contemporary. Whilst *films noirs* are not typically about family relations and children, these relations are central to *The Pitfall* as well as to *Mildred Pierce* and *The Reckless Moment*, whilst in *The Prowler* (Joseph Losey, 1951) the threat to the couple is the wife's pregnancy and its testimony to the couple's sexual relations prior to her first husband's death.

The concept of genre invoked in film studies is derived from a literary and dramatic tradition of categories which, by the time film arrived on the scene of representations at the end of the nineteenth century, had already been fundamentally undermined as discrete forms, challenged by new forms such as the novel, and by romanticism. The adoption of the term, from scientific studies such as botany at the turn of the nineteenth century, to refer to groups of literary works with definable similarities, does not simply signal the imperialism of the discourse of science in the study of literature. Rather, it marks the point at which the classes can no longer be assumed, but must be explained, described and differentiated.[26] This crisis of identity is not merely a matter of labels; also at issue is the determining of the value of literary and dramatic works, a value that had earlier depended on a work's embodiment of a genre–epic, lyric, drama, or tragedy. Adherence to genre, that is, to the forms and conventions by which genre was recognized and hence constituted, ceases to be a simple criterion of value, but it is not abandoned. As Paul Hernadi's overview in *Beyond Genre: New Directions in Literary Classification* shows, the discussion of genres proliferates.[27]

The definition of genre as an adherence to a fairly fixed set of conventions has given rise to a tendency to see genre works as stereotyped or formulaic; hence some critics see the term as appropriate only to the study of 'popular' or mass literature, which is seen as similarly stereotyped. 'Literature' is then marked as those works that challenge our existing conceptions. The elitism implicit here is not the only problem with such an approach. The rules of a genre may be viewed not as restrictions on creativity but as a frame and a stimulus.[28] Moreover, as Todorov has persuasively argued, a concept of genre remains necessary in so far as it names the relation of a particular work to the field of literature as a whole. Any work of representation will 'manifest properties that it shares with all literary texts, or with texts belonging to one of the sub-groups of literature (which we call, precisely, genres)'. In other words, in order to be recognizable as different from the old, the work must also be recognizable as in some way like it, as similar to previous works. Todorov concludes, 'Genres are precisely those relay-points by which the work assumes a relation with the universe of literature.'[29]

A major aspect of genre and hence of genre study is therefore the extent to which any particular work exceeds its genre, how it reworks and transforms it, rather than how it fits certain generic expectations. The theorist constructs an ideal type in order to show not only how any particular work fulfils its criteria of the ideal, but also how it deviates from it.

If *film noir* is not a genre, it is nevertheless recognizable. It names a certain inflection or tendency which emerges in certain genres in the early 1940s, notably in the gangster film, the crime thriller and the detective film. The common element of this inflection is not so much, or not only, visual style, as melodrama. It must be admitted, however, that melodrama, too, is a highly imprecise genre and though, unlike *film noir*, the term was used by the film industry, this was not the way in which modern criticism has applied the term to films.[30] In the trade papers, from the 1910s onwards, the term 'melodrama' referred to 'thrills and spills' films, to adventure, suspense and action and even – in the 1940s – to prison films, rather than to Joan Crawford vehicles. It appears that it was in this sense too, that films later considered *films noirs* were described as 'crime melodramas'.[31] The term 'melodrama' has a long critical history, and the rather specialized use of the term by the film trade press is both justified by and distinct from that history. The 'thrills and spills' definition of melodrama derives from what Ben Singer has referred to as the 'lowbrow' sensational or 'blood and thunder' melodrama that dominated popular theatre and cheap literature around the turn of the century. Singer describes the serial-queen melodramas such as *The Perils of Pauline* as an attempt to stave off the emergence of the feature film, and he sees them as direct cinematic descendants of the 'sensational' popular melodrama.[32] By contrast, the up-and-coming, and up-market, feature film sought to associate itself with 'serious' literature and theatre and hence eschewed the term 'melodrama'. (Suspense – as well as thrills and spills – was nevertheless also integral to the films of a prestigious director such as D. W. Griffith, who adapted a number of earlier classic stage melodramas, including *Orphans of the Storm*.[33]) The melodramatic plot had been used by many nineteenth-century writers concerned to depict contemporary social reality and its moral consequences for society, such as Dickens or Balzac.[34] As a result the devices of melodrama – extremes of emotional experience, chance and coincidence, a compression of dramatic time – are allied with a socially realist representation, giving rise to a quite different cinematic tradition, exemplified in films such as Borzage's *Seventh Heaven* as well as *The Mortal Storm*, King Vidor's *The Crowd* as well as *Duel in the Sun*, and the so-called 'family melodramas' of the 1950s and 1960s, such as Nicholas Ray's *Rebel without a Cause*.

The connection between *film noir* and melodrama has been made by a number of writers, but usually in order to distinguish *film noir* as a form of male melodrama, in contrast to the woman's film and female melodrama. Maureen Turim, for example, points out that '*noir* and the woman's film are two sides of the same coin in Hollywood's forties symbolic circulation'.[35] Murray Smith suggests that the investigation of the woman in *film noir* is mirrored in the female gothic melodrama's investigation of the man.[36] Frank Krutnik also argues in terms of parallel genres:

> The 'tough' thrillers tend to treat the drama of their 'dislocated' heroes seriously . . . . Just as the dramatic representation of the realm of women – issues of the family, home, romance, motherhood, female identity and desire – has been approached . . . in terms of the generic category of the 'women's picture melodrama', one could consider the 'tough' thriller as representing a form of 'masculine melodrama'.[37]

This is no doubt the case in some films, so that in the 'male *film noir* melodrama' the man triumphs over a threatening and dangerous feminine element and thereby resolves his conflict with the law. Nevertheless, I want to examine the melodramatic in *film noir* in order to overturn this rigid sexual division, not to affirm it.

In *film noir*, a narrative of an external enigma, a murder or theft, replaces the melodrama's plot of an external event of war, poverty or social circumstance; in both cases, however, this narrative is interwoven with or supplanted by another which focuses on the personal and subjective relations between the characters. In *film noir* melodrama, these relations are characterized not only, if at all, by heterosexual desire, but also by perverse, sadistic, obsessive or possessive desire.[38] Additionally, the element of fate, of chance and coincidence, which produces the characteristic under-motivation of events in melodrama, is also central to the *film noir*. Characters feel compelled by forces and passions beyond their reason to act as they do – in a form of *amour fou*. *Film noir* can therefore be viewed as a kind of development of melodrama so that whereas earlier the obstacles to the heterosexual couple had been external forces of family and circumstance, wars or illness, in the *film noir* the obstacles derive from the characters' psychology or even pathology as they encounter external events. It is just such an emphasis that links the forties films of Nicholas Ray – usually termed *films noirs* – such as *In a Lonely Place* (1950) and *They Live by Night* (1948) with his later films, such as *Bigger Than Life* and *Rebel without a Cause*, which Thomas Elsaesser describes as melodramas. The emphasis on psychological motivation, including psychoanalytic theories of psychology (the 1940s saw the adoption of so-called vulgar Freudianism by Hollywood), was often associated with or presented as an increased realism. It provided spectacular and extraordinary characters and situations, which nevertheless could be set in very ordinary and familiar contexts (for example, in *Christmas Holiday*, which is about a soldier's leave, or *Lost Weekend*, about an alcoholic).

This type of hybridization or inflection of existing forms or genres is characteristic of Hollywood film-making. For whilst genre emerged early in cinema as an important factor in product differentiation and standardization, it was marked – particularly in 'quality' films – by the transformation of generic expectations as much as by the fulfilment of generic norms. This happened because although Hollywood cinema is a form of popular entertainment, it is also a mass form, and the studios were concerned to maximize audiences for their films; specialized genres such as the horror film were apt to draw too narrow an audience, while generic conventions tended to become stale for all but the committed *aficionados*.[39]

Strongly marked genre films were primarily low-budget or B pictures.[40] Whilst many *films noirs* were made as B films, they were also often developed as potential A films – especially by independent companies – since the strong visual style offset low production values, and the 'realism' similarly justified or narratively motivated low production values.

Whilst these films were not recognized by the studios as a genre in the way in which the gangster film was, the hybridity they offered the studios in the forties does seem to have been recognized, even if no single term was used to designate it. Thus what has come to be called *film noir*, whilst it does not constitute a genre itself, does name a particular set of elements that were used to produce 'the different' and the new in a film; hence the term *film noir* names a set of possibilities for making existing genres 'different'. With this view of genre and of *film noir* it is no longer possible to speak of 'the' *film noir*, as so many writers seek to do. This view also accords more closely with the way in which Hollywood itself treated these films. Studios had for some years sought to adapt the 'hard-boiled' thriller writers; MGM, for example, bought the rights to James M. Cain's *The Postman Always Rings Twice* in 1935, but the constraints of the Production Code forced the studio to abandon plans to film it. The detective film had been intermittently successful, but was primarily a B picture format. It was hoped that by drawing on the hard-boiled style of fiction writing of the thirties, Hollywood might transform the detective film. In Raoul Walsh's *They Drive by Night* (1940), often cited as a precursor to *film noir*, elements of the Warner gangster film format are reworked with themes from its thirties 'woman's pictures'. The film's stars, Humphrey Bogart and George Raft, play family men caught up in the rackets around trucking, resolved when Raft takes a job managing a bigger firm. He is menaced, however, by the unwelcome but desperate attentions of the boss's wife, played by Ida Lupino, who kills her husband and attempts to implicate Raft. Lupino's role as the neurotic and obsessed wife could be seen as an element of 'melodrama', or as prefiguring the obsessive, psychotic characters of *film noir*.

In the 1940s the elements later identified as *film noir* allowed Hollywood to reintroduce themes of sexuality within the terms of the Production Code. In the film version of *Mildred Pierce* (Michael Curtiz, 1945), for example, the use of flashback narration and the introduction of a murder as the opening enigma motivate from the beginning the tragedy and grief brought upon the characters, and particularly upon Mildred herself, as punishment for the adultery and technical incest of the story. Columbia's *Gilda* and *Dead Reckoning* both present many of the elements of *film noir*, particularly sexual perversion, suggesting that these elements were now fairly well known and conventionalized.[41] A British reviewer, writing in the *Tribune* commented

> Every pattern in art, if used too often, tends, I suppose, to caricature itself. The slope is easy and logical from Mansfield Park to Mrs Miniver, the tough felicities of *The Glass Key* must inevitably have degenerated into the sentimental–sadistic inanities of the new Bogart thriller, *Dead Reckoning*.[42]

WOMEN AND *FILM NOIR*

The *film noir*'s world of alienation and angst is associated in critical writing with the male protagonists, and hence it is seen as portraying a masculine problem of the forties. For Silver and Ward, *film noir* is characterized by 'two key character motifs', obsession and alienation, of which the second was the most important

> The darkness that fills the mirror of the past, which lurks in a dark corner or obscures a dark passage out of the oppressively dark city, is not merely the key adjective of so many *film noir* titles but the obvious metaphor for the condition of the protagonist's mind.[43]

Of the films they cite, all involve male protagonists. A woman protagonist is cited only in relation to the 'explicitly psychotic figures' in *The Dark Mirror* (Robert Siodmak, 1946). The inflection that *film noir* represented was not so exclusively masculine, however, as writers often imply.

Whilst there are no female equivalents to Philip Marlowe, this may be due more to the demands of verisimilitude than to those of patriarchy in Hollywood, in so far as studios assumed that audiences would find a female detective improbable in the 1940s.

But women do feature in the position of the investigator who 'seeks to restore order', Frank Krutnik's first form of the thriller,[44] notably in *Phantom Lady* (Robert Siodmak, 1944), from the novel by Cornell Woolrich. Here the male protagonist is the victim, falsely convicted for the murder of his wife. He is incarcerated in prison, and it is his secretary who takes on the role of the investigator who will restore order; this situation corresponds to Krutnik's second form, the 'suspense thriller', which is the inverse of the 'investigative thriller' in that the protagonist is in a marked position of inferiority in relation to the conspiracy and/or the police and 'seeks to restore himself to a position of security by eradicating the enigma'.[45] The film considerably increases the centrality of the woman investigator, and whilst she is helped by a sympathetic policeman, and has to be rescued after she has uncovered the real killer, this same device was also used for male protagonists. In *The Dark Corner* (Henry Hathaway, 1946), for example, the detective is saved only by the killer's wife, when she shoots her husband dead.

I Wouldn't Be in Your Shoes (Marvin Mirsch, 1948), also from a novel by Woolrich, similarly has a woman – the hero's wife – carry on the investigation in order to clear her husband, again aided by a detective, but one who this time proves himself to be the killer. In *Woman on the Run* (Norman Foster, 1950) it is again the wife who is the investigator, together with a reporter who, she discovers, is the real killer. In *The High Wall* (Curtis Bernhardt, 1947) the woman psychiatrist becomes the investigator for the male hero. These films contain the figure, cited by Hirsch, of the male middle-class victim who does not effect his own rescue – and this raises the question of how to determine 'whose story' the film centres on – an issue which will be considered in more detail in relation to *Raw Deal*.

Such examples of female investigators are usually dismissed on the grounds that the women are never shown to be 'as good as' equivalent male figures in some way (all of which reminds me of cases brought by women for equal pay in which the exact equivalence of work is always disputed, again to the woman's disadvantage). Not only does this beg questions of the comparability of criteria – each film gives rise to new criteria for assessment – but it also privileges an implied ideal of narrative dominance that the female protagonists always lack, yet which is frequently absent where the protagonist is male. For example, in *Murder Is My Beat* (Edgar G. Ulmer, 1955) the victim falsely convicted is a woman, her police guard believes her story and helps her escape, but he in turn must be helped by his partner. Here the figure of the victim–protagonist is played by a woman. Similarly, in *The Accused* (William Dieterle, 1949), the female protagonist is the victim of events unwittingly entered into: Wilma Tuttle, a psychology professor, accidentally kills one of her students when he attempts to seduce her and the film follows her efforts to evade discovery, in a way reminiscent of Professor Wanley in *The Woman in the Window* (Fritz Lang, 1945). Lang's later film *The Blue Gardenia* (1953) figures a woman, Norah Larkin, as the victim – accused of a crime she did not commit but believes that she did. The real killer is uncovered through the efforts of a journalist, not directly but as a result of the murderess's attempted suicide.

The obsessed or psychotic character, as already noted, is considered by many writers to be a central figure in *films noirs*. This figure may be someone other than the central protagonist: for example, in *Crossfire* (Edward Dmytryk, 1947) the story centres on the innocent suspect, but reveals the murderer to be Robert Ryan's Jew-hating psychopath. And the obsessed character may as frequently be a woman as a man. The obsession is usually motivated by sexual desire, most obviously in *Possessed* (Curtis Bernhardt, 1947) with Joan Crawford, or *So Dark the Night* (Joseph H. Lewis, 1946), where it is a male protagonist who murders. In *The Dark Past* (Rudolph Maté, 1948), the obsession stems from the criminal's unconscious guilt over his father's death, whilst in *The Locket* (John Brahm, 1947) the heroine's kleptomania is traced to a false accusation of theft in her childhood. In *Gun Crazy* (Joseph H. Lewis, 1950), Bart Tare's fascination with weapons is more than matched by Annie Laurie Starr's 'gun-craziness'. *Born to Kill* (Robert Wise, 1947) reverses this plot, with a heroine who is uncontrollably drawn to the psycho-pathic man, even after she realizes that he has committed a murder.

Women may also fall victim to their involvement with the underworld, in an equivalent to the male criminal 'tough guy' thriller, using their beauty of course, but also and necessarily their intellectual talents for deceit, as Joan Crawford does in *The Damned Don't Cry*; or, as Lizabeth Scott does in *Too Late for Tears* (Byron Haskin, 1949), who murders two husbands in order to 'move out of the ranks of the middle-class poor', as she says in the film.

The duplicitous woman is, of course, never cited as a central protagonist, except where the film is designated a 'woman's picture' (which seems to be the fate of *The Strange Love of Martha Ivers* (Lewis Milestone, 1946), and the criteria by which this figure is isolated are much less consistent than critics pretend. First of all, a confusion exists between the requirement that characters be duplicitous in order for the suspense to be created and sustained – which frequently involves male characters as well as female characters – and the narrative function of the woman's *sexual* duplicity, for example in the use of her sexuality to dupe the male hero. This latter is also distinct from the narrative function of the woman as object of the male hero's desire; this desire may result in the hero being drawn into criminal or self-destructive activities without the woman herself being in any way duplicitous. This is the case in *The Prowler*, in which the wife does not realize that her lover deliberately killed her husband; similarly, in *The Postman Always Rings Twice*, it is not the woman's duplicity that is the couple's undoing. In *Nora Prentiss* (Vincent Sherman, 1947) the heroine of the title is not duplicitous in the usual sense of this term, for though she fails to save the hero at the end, this is on his own insistence (his downfall arises from his own duplicity and weakness rather than Nora's ensnarement). *This Gun for Hire* (Frank Tuttle, 1942) presents a particularly tricky variation on the theme of duplicity. Veronica Lake plays Ellen, a government spy who nevertheless falls in love with the hired gun, Raven (Alan Ladd), who is eventually killed. Robert Porfirio claims that 'stripped of her patriotic guise, Ellen is revealed as a noir *femme fatale* who leads Raven to his destruction',[46] even though Ellen's motives are blameless. Moreover, her function in the narrative affords Raven the chance to redeem herself through his self-sacrifice for her – as does Donnelly, the male hero in *The Reckless Moment*. Barbara Stanwyck as Thelma in *The File on Thelma Jordan* (Robert Siodmak, 1950), is also redeemed in death, for she refuses to name her partner in the murder, thereby protecting the district attorney she had seduced into helping her (she, like Raven, a psychologically disturbed hired assassin, and Donnelly, a blackmailer, is already on the wrong side of the law). Duplicity is not always and only on the side of the woman; in *Southside 1–1000* (Boris Ingster, 1950) it is the woman protagonist, Nora Craig, who runs a gang of counterfeiters, who is duplicitously romanced by Nick Starns, whom she betrays in turn.

Finally, the duplicitous woman is essential neither to the group of films designated *noirs*, nor to the thirties crime fiction from which many were derived. For example, *Fast One* by Paul Cain, published in 1933 after serialization in *Black Mask*[47], involves a gunman gambler and his alcoholic lover, whose intelligence and ingenuity are loyally put in his service; both perish in the final conflagration that concludes their rearrangement of the Los Angeles underworld.

What I am attempting to challenge here is the tendency to characterize *film noir* as always a masculine film form. Even though this masculine bias is considered critically, the tendency is still to see women characters as occupying a subordinate position in the films. This obscures the extent to which these films afforded women roles which are active, adventurous and driven by sexual desire. Nor is this observation necessarily discounted by the fact that these roles were frequently undertaken by villainesses. As Janey Place has pointed out, in these films 'women are deadly but sexy, exciting, and strong'.[48] If the women die as a result, they suffer a fate no different from that of the men: the Production Code was egalitarian on this point. Moreover, for the woman as well as the man the crucial relation is between desire and death; of *Double Indemnity*,

Claire Johnston notes, 'the eroticisation of death in the final scene of the flashback confirms a universe where access to desire is only through repression'.[49] The fantasy of the woman's dangerous sexuality is a feminine as well as masculine fantasy, and its pleasures lie precisely in its forbiddenness. To argue that it is only patriarchy, or the Production Code, that requires its punishment is to misunderstand that it is the fantasy itself that demands the punishment, for in the punishment the reality of the forbidden wish is acknowledged.

Neither *films noirs* nor the thriller novels they drew upon are a preserve of male writers. A number of films were scripted, co-written or adapted by women or derived from stories by women – including *Desperate, Railroaded* and *Raw Deal*, all directed by Anthony Mann (his collaboration with women writers was extensive: 'Follow Me Quietly', an unpublished short story by Mann and Francis Rosewald was scripted for the film by Lillie Hayward). *In a Lonely Place* is based on the novel by Dorothy B. Hughes; *Private Hell 36* was co-scripted by Ida Lupino and Collier Young; additional dialogue in *The Pretender* was by Doris Miller, and Chandler's novel *The High Window*, filmed as *The Brasher Doubloon*, was scripted by Dorothy Hannah and adapted by Dorothy Bennett and Leonard Praskins. *The Reckless Moment* was based closely on the story 'The Blank Wall' by Elisabeth Sanxay Holding, who was described by Raymond Chandler as 'the top suspense writer of them all'.[50]

There are also a number of films in which it is a man who is revealed as duplicitous, and who may also be a murderer – for example, *Laura* – or who will attempt to murder the heroine; these films are as a result centred on the female figure, for example *Sleep My Love*, or *My Name Is Julia Ross*, and *The House on Telegraph Hill, Undercurrent, Sudden Fear, When Strangers Marry, Shadow of a Doubt* or *Sorry, Wrong Number*, and *Danger Signal*.[51] In *The Reckless Moment* and *Mildred Pierce* the duplicitous man is the murder victim. The man here is similar to the 'spider-woman' figure in that he uses his sexuality to prey on women; he is therefore generally more like Kitty in *Scarlet Street*, ensnaring a gullible Professor Wanley, than Phyllis Dietrichson (who teams up with the willing Walter Neff in *Double Indemnity*) – although in *Born to Kill* it is just such dangerous sexuality, represented by his willingness to kill, which attracts the heroine to the man. In all these films the woman protagonist is victim to events that are beyond her control and from which she must be rescued, though this rescue is not always effected by a man: in *The House on Telegraph Hill* and *Undercurrent* accidental circumstances, aided in the former by another woman, bring about the heroine's release. In this the films directly parallel other *films noir* with male victims, notably *Fear in the Night*.

These films have often been considered as primarily 'woman's pictures' or 'gothic romance', and therefore characterized by the questioning of the heroine's perceptions. Yet, as Diane Waldman notes, these films 'represent a substantial departure from the 19th century Gothics, the earlier films in the cycle, and the modern Gothics and contemporary romances where the moody Byronic lover emerges as someone who truly loves the heroine'.[52] For in them the man is really seeking to kill the heroine – and her perceptions are thus proved correct. A central component of the *noir* inflection, however, namely the suspense thriller, involves just such a questioning of the protagonist, since the suspense film, unlike the classic detective film, always involves the production of a narrative hesitation about the truth concerning the enigma and about the protagonist's perception of reality.

A WOMAN'S STORY

Implicit in the arguments I have been advancing are questions of narrative focus. Whose story does the film tell? On which character does the narrative centre? Does it centre on more than one character? Does it tell a man's or woman's story? Finally, what does it mean to ask this last question? Certainly, these questions are raised by the authors of the anthology *Women and Film Noir*, and by most contemporary commentators on *film noir*. Behind these questions there lies the whole issue of reading and interpretation, of discerning whether and how the woman is subordinated in *film noir*. Yet it is clear that while many narratives ostensibly tell the tale of a protagonist and his or her adventures, for the spectator the film's 'story' is more than that of any one character; it is also a fantasy scenario. This fantasy is not produced by the spectator but by the filmic text itself, which must 'move' the spectator to occupy his or her place within it.

The following discussion seeks to explore the question of the woman's voice and her story in relation to *film noir* by taking two films, *Raw Deal* and *Secret beyond the Door*, which exhibit a feature singularly associated with *film noir*, namely, first-person narration. Voice-over narration, together with the narrative device of flashback, was comparatively rare prior to the 1940s in American film, but it became common in that decade, then fell in popularity in the fifties and again in the sixties. This popularity was not confined to the *film noir*, or even to the detective film, and it precedes the *film noir* slightly – being strongly established from 1940, and gaining pre-eminence with Welles's *Citizen Kane* and Ford's *How Green Was My Valley* in 1941;[53] the first *films noirs* to use it are *Laura, Double Indemnity, The Mask of Dimitrios* and *Murder, My Sweet*, all released in 1944. Subsequently voice-over is more commonly used for films in other genres. It is nevertheless featured in many of the films that have become the key examples of *film noir*, including not only those just listed above, but also *Gilda, The Killers, The Postman Always Rings Twice* and *Out of the Past*.

In *film noir* the use of voice-over narration is associated with the male hero, often a detective or 'tough guy' investigator whose dialogue is 'hard-boiled' – clipped and cynical. It functions to place the spectator subjectively with the character, allowing us to enter his world through his words. The authority of the voice-over tends to be assumed by convention; but it also conventionally includes the voicing of hesitations and doubts about the hero's perception and interpretation of events, including self-doubt (notably in *Gilda*, and in *Dead Reckoning*). The flashback voice-over narration of *Mildred Pierce*, as of *Possessed* also starring Joan Crawford, markedly lacks a hard-boiled style and as a result is associated with melodramas or 'woman's pictures', many of which also use this device in this period. In *Raw Deal*, however, the first-person, present-tense narration by a woman does follow the hard-boiled style of the male *film noir* hero – though in this film the narrator is not the ostensible protagonist of the film.

Raw Deal was directed in 1948 by Anthony Mann, who had earlier made *Railroaded* and *Desperate*, which are also usually recognized as *films noirs*. *Raw Deal* tells the story of Joe Sullivan who, convicted for a crime he did not commit, escapes from prison aided by his loyal girlfriend Pat, by his ex-partner (who hopes he will be killed in the escape) and – though unwillingly – by his lawyer's legal assistant, Ann. The film features his ex-partner, a sadistic gangster boss played by Raymond Burr; obsessed with fire, he wantonly throws hot coffee at the girlfriend who has annoyed him (this scene was later imitated by Fritz Lang in *The Big Heat*). The film also features, in the hard-boiled style, two sidekicks named Fantail and Spider; it is filmed by John Alton in the singularly *noir* style with which he was particularly associated: marked high or low camera angles, strong chiaroscuro lighting, and emphatic use of shadows (marked camera angles are a feature of Anthony Mann's films in general and not only those photographed by Alton).

Considered as Joe's story, *Raw Deal* fits Krutnik's category of the 'criminal adventure thriller', in which the hero 'usually with the aid of a woman, becomes engaged in either a wilful or an accidental transgression of the law, and has to face the consequences of "stepping out of line"'.[54] In this case there are two women, Pat and Ann, but they do not simply fall into the good versus bad girl pattern. While it is clearly Pat who is from the 'wrong side of the tracks', it is Ann, the good girl, who appears ready to betray Joe, to believe him capable of cold-blooded murder. The two women are more like Marie and Velma in Raoul Walsh's *High Sierra* (1941), though Ann, after shooting but not killing Fantail to defend Joe, is revealed truly to be in love with Joe. And Pat, whilst concealing the information until the eleventh hour, finally reveals to Joe that Rick is holding Ann hostage. Both women are also involved in crucial narrative actions.

Joe's story is not, however, the story of his struggle for justice against Rick Coyle, although this, together with making good his escape from jail, is his initial goal. A secondary goal, which finally supersedes the first, emerges in the central conflict between Joe and Ann, or in a sense between a former Joe, who as a kid had rescued some people from a burning building, and the present Joe, apparently ruthless, hardened and cynical, whom Ann believes to be capable of cold-blooded murder. At the film's end Joe will act to redeem his past and also to affirm the truth of his childhood bravery, to become the 'real' Joe, whom Ann always believed in (Joe thereby following the nineteenth-century melodrama tradition of the villain turned hero who sacrifices himself for the heroine).

The film opens with a shot of prison gates and a woman's voice-over in the present tense 'This is the day, this is the day!' There are no flashbacks in the film, and the narrative structure is comparatively straightforward, presenting events in chronological order, covering just a couple of days. (Complexity is introduced on another level through the use of parallel montage, with cutaways on the one hand to Rick and his increasingly hysterical response to Joe's continuing success at evading the dragnet, and on the other hand to the police themselves. As a result of this complexity, a cutaway to a posse of police in the woods when Joe, Pat, and Ann are at Oscar's is initially read as the hunt for Joe; only later is it revealed to be a quite unrelated pursuit, involving a wife-killer. The pursuit is relevant to the story of Joe, however, since in a humanitarian gesture Joe gives the man shelter inside Oscar's Tavern.)

The first-person narration by Pat, intensely personal and subjective, is used to present her thoughts, rather than to narrate events. Pat's voice-over constitutes a subjective point of view on the events. In this sense *Raw Deal* becomes her story, the story of how Joe will be free to be with her. But this story, which she narrates obliquely through her fears about what is happening, turns out to be about Joe's falling in love with another woman. So it is Pat's tragedy that we participate in at the end; as Ann cradles the dying Joe and receives his love, Pat looks on, losing Joe twice over, in death and to Ann.

Pat's voice-over occurs on eleven occasions, but always very briefly, usually for the duration of only one shot, and never more than three. Her voice-over is, then, both strongly marked – through its recurrence – and relatively intermittent. It is also frequently interrupted. Sometimes Pat's voice moves from voice-over to spoken dialogue, as in shots 116, 117, 118:

Voice-over
'We've made it all right, we've gotten out of town. For some strange reason I feel worse than before. Like a two-time loser. Maybe it's . . .' (CUT)

' . . . the let down, though there is still the roadblocks up ahead.' (CUT)

'Or maybe it's because of her, sitting next to Joe where I should be. Where I would be if she weren't there. If she weren't . . .' (CUT)

Dialogue
'Why don't we ditch her now, Joe?'

The voice-over often carries information but, as here, it is usually information also given by the image track, which shows that they have left town. More important, it functions to voice Pat's hopes, at the opening, and subsequently her fears, especially in relation to Ann. Yet Pat's perceptions of the events are never questioned. The poignancy of Pat's position is shared by the spectator not only through her voice-over but also in one scene through a privileged sharing of information.

The three have escaped the roadblocks and have reached Oscar's Tavern where they will change cars. Pat sprains her ankle as they walk to the house and Joe picks her up in his arms and carries her in. The next scene contains three shots (shots 215, 216, 217). The first shows Pat lying on a couch in medium long shot while Joe is standing looking out of a window rear centre; Pat begins to speak in voice-over, 'Deep down I guess I have no real beef at what I know is happening. Watching him.' The music that accompanies Pat's voice-over begins at the end of this shot. The next shot frames her in close-up as she looks up off-screen right. Her voice-over continues. 'Only one thing keeps ringing inside of me. He's never really told me he loved me. Funny how that keeps coming back now. I haven't minded it before. I'd always been more than ready to take him at any terms.' Her voice-over continues into the next shot with the words, 'But now . . .', then she begins to speak to Joe. This third shot is as the first shot of the sequence, and shows Joe pacing up and down right to left in mid-ground; reflected in a mirror as he paces, he walks into the window arch then back to Pat as she talks to him; he is not listening. Pat lights a cigarette while Joe searches for his pack; finding it empty, he says he will go down and see if Oscar has any. Pat answers, 'Hey, I've got some right here. No, mine's all gone too.' We can see, however, that she does have cigarettes, that

Leaving town, Pat, Joe and Ann in shots 116, 117, 118 (*Raw Deal,* Anthony Mann, 1948)

she is lying. Her lie gives Joe an excuse to leave the room and shows us that Pat realizes that this is what he wanted, and that she will not try to stop him. That it is Ann who is the cause of his restlessness is confirmed for the spectator (though not for Pat) in the next shot: Joe enters Ann's room and when he sees that she is not there, he leaves to search for her outside. Though Pat's lie is spoken in dialogue, it functions like her voice-over to give the spectator knowledge of her internal thoughts; this focalization through Pat is supported by the fact that her voice-over music continues until the end of the scene.

Neither Ann nor Joe is given any equivalent subjective point of view in the film; instead their subjective views and feelings are presented through their dialogue or that of others; for example, Joe and Pat discuss Ann's motives, whilst Pat voices what she understands to be Joe's feelings. We also come to understand the characters through their actions and reactions as these are presented by the film, for example in the use of shot/reverse-shot alternations, by which a character's reactions to the adjacent shot is implied. These are seen especially at the opening of the film where Ann's talk to Joe at the prison is presented in a series of alternating close-ups of each of them. This alternation is repeated and varied later when Pat sees Ann leave and then goes to talk to Joe herself.

Ann, of course, is a powerful alternative focus in the film. From the point of view of the other characters, she is Pat's rival for Joe's love, and she represents for Joe the respectable world he is basically part of but cannot reach from the slum where he grew up, Corkscrew Alley; in responding to Ann's arguments and in falling in love with her, Joe narratively affirms his decency. The spectator is therefore aligned variously with these three characters, even though only Pat is given a direct subjective point of view. There is, then, no simple hierarchy between the characters in which the story is mainly Joe's, partly Pat's and to a lesser extent Ann's. Rather Ann's story, her concern and love for Joe are crucial to the poignancy of Joe's predicament: though he is doomed, he can see through her the decent life that remains beyond his grasp. And Ann's rivalry with Pat is not resolved by a simple eviction of Pat; rather, the film focuses on the tragedy of Pat's position in relation to Ann and Joe. Nevertheless, at the film's end Ann functions primarily to resolve Joe's and Pat's stories; at the end, as Ann cradles Joe, he says, 'Hey, hey, none of that. I got my breath of fresh air. You . . .' his speech breaking off in mid-sentence as he dies. It is Pat's voice-over that then closes the film. 'The police picked me up and brought me here. There's my Joe in her arms. A kind of . . . (CUT) happiness on his face. In my heart I know that . . . (CUT) this is right for Joe. This is what he wanted.' In an extraordinary move, the narrative emphasis shifts to Joe's finally having what he

Pat is carried into Oscar's by Joe after hurting her ankle, and shots 215, 216, 217 follow.

wanted, Ann, rather than focusing on his death, and at the same time emphasizes Pat's self-sacrifice, and her loss. In telling Joe's story, Pat also tells her own.

Along with this shift from an exclusive concern with the male protagonist, in *Raw Deal*, there is an emphasis on the interaction between characters, and this is presented in a way more usually associated with melodrama. Joe's hard-boiled style is cracked by moments of concern and sympathy; learning that the police have the details of the car they are using, Pat panics and Joe responds to her acerbically, only to apologize after a short pause. His apology shifts the way in which we understand Joe and his relationship to Pat, suggesting that he does not take her help for granted. Joe makes his own sacrifice later when he sends Ann away after their night together, a sacrifice made either to protect Ann or out of loyalty to Pat. But Pat is unable to talk Joe out of meeting Rick to get the money he is owed, and so she retorts bitterly that he would not go if it were Ann who asked him to stay. A terrible row ensues. Joe ends it by slapping Pat on the face; she walks out. On her return she sits weeping on the bed and admits that she almost called the police. Joe responds to this confession with a fumbling attempt to explain: 'About Ann . . . I don't know how to . . . that's the trouble, I don't know how to . . . OK . . . ' In the next shot Pat and Joe embrace and he says, 'Okay, you've forgiven me a thousand things before without my asking . . . (*long pause*) C'mon. Let's go! Get your things.' Pat: 'My things?' Joe: 'Sure, sure, the clothes that you bought for us this afternoon. A fellow and his girl going to take a boat trip, they usually dress for it, don't they?'

This scene is intercut with shots of Rick, who is now holding Ann hostage. The reconciliation between Joe and Pat is therefore qualified by the expectation that Joe will have to rescue Ann. A narrative irony now structures the events: it is Pat who takes the call threatening that if Joe does not meet Rick, Ann will be killed. Pat does not report the call to Joe. As the boat is about to set sail, Joe suddenly suggests that he and Pat get married. 'Have a house. Kids, maybe. Bring 'em up right.' Pat's voice-over is anguished. 'Why didn't he stop talking? Or the clock stop moving? He was saying everything I had ever wanted to hear. All my life. The lyrics were his all right. But the music, Ann's. Ann's! Suddenly I saw that every time he kissed me he'd be kissing Ann. Every time he held me, spoke to me, danced with me, ate, drank, played, sang, it would be Ann, Ann!'[55] Finally she tells Joe about the threat to Ann.

The penultimate sequence of the film is again conventionally *noir* action. It is night, there's a fog, and Rick's men are waiting to jump Joe in a dark city alley. But he outshoots Fantail and Spider, then enters Rick's apartment through a window and begins a final struggle to the death with him; though fatally wounded in the struggle, Joe is nevertheless able to rescue Ann from the now-burning apartment.

In the final sequence, Joe has collapsed on the steps outside and Ann is leaning over him, as a police car arrives with Pat; in the final shot (485, credits in 486), she says, 'This is right for Joe. This is what he wanted,' and as she does so the camera pans right to reveal the road sign: 'JANE STREET/CORKSCREW ALLEY' introducing a final irony and ambiguity.

No doubt this analysis of *Raw Deal* begs more questions about the category of melodrama than it can answer here. Nevertheless, I think it is clear that it is not only as some uniquely masculine form that melodrama appears in *film noir*, and thus, too, that *film noir* is not exclusively a form in which a particular masculine fantasy of sexual difference is played out.

DEATHLY DESIRES

> I, insofar as I can sense the pattern of my mind, write of the wish that comes true, for some reason a terrifying concept, at least to my imagination. Of course, the wish must have terror in it; just wanting a drink wouldn't be quite enough. I think my stories have some quality of the opening of a forbidden box, and that it is this, rather than violence, sex, or any of the other things usually cited by way of explanation, that gives them the drive so often noted.
>
> James M. Cain, preface to *The Butterfly*

Secret beyond the Door (1948) is the third in Fritz Lang's trilogy of films with Joan Bennett, but though the first two, *The Woman in the Window* (1945) and *Scarlet Street* (1945), centre on a male protagonist – played by Edward G. Robinson in both films – in *Secret beyond the Door* the central protagonist is a woman, Joan Bennett herself, and her centrality is emphasized by her voice-over narration. (This is the only Lang film that uses voice-over narration in this way.) Moreover, as Stephen Jenkins points out, in this film it is the woman who investigates the man, inverting the structure of the earlier two films, and implying that Celia is in the narrative position previously taken by the Edward G. Robinson characters). That position is not, however, one of dominance, for the male character becomes a victim of his own desire, which brings him into conflict with the law. This situation produces a relationship between the male figure and the law that is mediated by the woman as object of desire. Similarly, Celia throws caution to the wind

The knife fight. (*Secret beyond the Door*, Fritz Lang, 1948)

and pursues her desire, marrying Mark Lamphere after a seventy-two-hour acquaint-ance. Celia, however – unlike Chris Cross in *Scarlet Street* who wilfully refuses to realize what Kitty is, but like Vern in *Rancho Notorious* and other Lang protagonists – is required to discover the meaning of the mysterious signs with which she is presented, namely Mark's strange behaviour and, later, the locked seventh room which she equates with Mark's locked mind, or unconscious.

There is no simple inversion of gender in *Secret beyond the Door*, but this is not because Celia's discourse is subverted by the filmic enunciation or by Mark's ascendancy in the film.[56] On the contrary, Celia's discourse remains dominant at the end of the film: she arrives at the truth of Mark's neurotic disturbance, she correctly reads the signs and contributes to his cure (she also literally has the last word in the film). But since for Lang such psychological veracity is never the point, it is important to note that it is Celia's return to the house and to the locked room to face her possible death at Mark's hands that resolves the problem of her desire and thereby makes possible the 'happy ending'. The film does have a masculine project: to bring Celia to the position from which she can 'understand' Mark and hence rescue him from his neurosis. This is brought about, however, not because Celia 'submits to Mark's fantasy' as Jenkins argues, but because the link between her desire and danger or death has been broken. The film makes Celia the subject of her own desire and narrates the story of its vicissitudes; this brings her to a position where, instead of fearing death, which is equivalent to her desire, Celia now fears the loss of desire, of Mark, in preference to which she would rather die.

The connection of desire with death is central to *film noir*, for it is with *film noir* that American cinema finds for the first time a form in which to represent desire as something that not only renders the desiring subject helpless, but also propels him or her to destruction. It was this aspect of the work of the hard-boiled school of writers that may have provoked censorship, not the fact of illicit sexual relations alone. In *Double Indemnity*, Neff's attraction to Phyllis Dietrichson is inextricably linked to his knowledge of her desire to kill her husband for his life insurance money; to gratify this desire she wants Neff to help her take out a policy without her husband's knowledge. The sexual tension between them is bound up with bringing this off, but is lost later as Neff becomes more involved in duping his mentor and father figure, Keyes.

The connection of desire with danger or death is visible in *Secret beyond the Door*, though few writers consider it a *film noir*, unlike the earlier two films in the Bennett trilogy. Instead the film is associated with the 'woman's film' and the gothic.[57] Paul M. Jensen observes in his book-long study of Lang's films: 'The story is akin to those modern Gothic novels about a young girl who marries after a whirlwind courtship, and then notices that her new husband starts acting mysterious after they move into his large, gloomy mansion.'[58] And indeed Lang himself claimed that Hitchcock's *Rebecca* – adapted from Daphne Du Maurier's gothic novel – was a direct inspiration. Certainly an array of gothic elements can be found in the film:[59] a former wife who died of an unnamed illness; a son who hates his father and who, he believes, has killed his mother; a gloomy ancestral home; and a scheming woman employee lurking at a window. There is also Celia's foreboding, the dark voice in her heart that she hears just as she is about to be married, but does not heed, and the story centres on her sense of doubt and uncertainty about Mark, at first about whether he loves her or not, then about the possibility that he may have killed his first wife, and finally about his desire to kill her. At Mark's home in Levender Falls, new suspicions arise and further suspense is created, expressively reinforced by Celia's point-of-view shots and the *mise en scène*, for example the chiaroscuro lighting that half obscures the long corridor that Celia investigates just before her discovery of Miss Robey.[60]

Other elements in the film, however, contradict or disturb the genre expectations of the gothic. Celia is not very young, and not at all inexperienced – she is the darling of her set, she breaks an engagement at the drop of a hat, and is revealed never to have intended to marry the man in the first place; she is sophisticated, self-possessed and self-assured, as well as assertive, defending her psychoanalyst friend to her brother; later, in Mexico, she speaks of sending away her friend Edith in order to meet Mark on her own ground. Their honeymoon at an idyllic hacienda is shown to be not only romantic but also highly sexual, as is their eventual reunion at Levender Falls when Celia tells Mark that she is collecting on his raincheck from their honeymoon. She too has independent means, so when she becomes furious at Mark for his treatment of her at the train station in Levender Falls, she plans straightaway to return to New York. She ultimately rejects this course of action because it would be a return to loneliness, and because she loves Mark; but her more rational evaluation is prefaced by a wish, a wish for her brother Rick: 'If only Rick were alive – I could go home to Rick.' She says to Mark later, however, that when she conjured Rick up, it was to 'read her the riot act', that is, to make her see reason, to see that she had committed herself to Mark and should stick by that commitment. Here is conjoined an image of her brother as incestuous love-object with an image of him as representative of the law to which she must submit. She does not question her own worth, but she is puzzled, and put out, so that when Mark arrives home that evening, she questions him directly. Celia is not yet or not sufficiently a victim of her circumstances.

As a result, the gothic elements in *Secret beyond the Door* appear marked; they function as a device which refers not only to the conventional expectations of the gothic as a genre, but also to the category of the gothic as such. Thus the device becomes a symbolic referent. When Lang cited *Rebecca* as an influence what he pointed to was not the similarity of plot, the death of a first wife in mysterious circumstances, the scheming woman servant at the window, the film's ending with a burning house, but something else:

> I'll tell you what the whole idea was. You remember that wonderful scene in *Rebecca* where Judith Anderson talks about Rebecca and shows Joan Fontaine the clothes and fur coats and everything? . . . Talk about stealing – I had the feeling that maybe I could do something similar in this picture when Redgrave talks about the different rooms. Now let's be very frank – it just didn't come through for me.[61]

What Lang is describing is Mrs Danvers's morbid obsession with Rebecca, visualized through her careful preservation of Rebecca's possessions, tangible signs of a lost object. It is this obsession that is the basis for Lang's presentation of Mark's perverse passion for collecting rooms that have been the scene of a murder. By emphasizing the details of reconstruction, the glass from which the wife drank before being knifed, the chair to which the mother was tied, the scarf with which Don Antonio killed – Mark/Lang make objects stand for a murder which is itself absent. Lang, then, inverts Mrs Danvers's obsession, for while she wished to recover the living Rebecca through the objects, Mark seeks to recover the deaths in his.

Further, Lang has replicated Mrs Danvers's gesture, with not one but seven rooms of revered objects. In doing so he introduces another reference, and one which is also part of the gothic tradition, namely the reference to Bluebeard, his murdered wives, and the one forbidden, locked room of his castle. So, too, the seventh of Mark's rooms is forbidden to his visitors, and to his new wife.[62] It immediately becomes necessary, then, for Celia to gain entry to the room, to discover its contents and thereby the contents locked away in Mark's mind, or unconscious. What she finds there is a replica of her own room, which had formerly belonged to Mark's late wife Eleanor. At first Celia assumes that the room's secret is Mark's morbid fear that he was responsible for his wife's death, but she reassures herself that he had no hand in her death and is about to leave when the mantle clock chimes, causing her to glance at it, and thus to notice the candlesticks on either side of the clock. One of them is shorter than the other, just like the candlesticks in her room now, since she herself shortened one in order to make a wax impression of the key to the seventh room. This is a replica of *her* room, and it awaits, it is the harbinger of, her own death. Terrified, Celia dashes out, only to discover that Mark is in the adjacent room. She runs on, followed by Mark, who is carrying the scarf that had been Don Antonio's murder weapon. Unlike the gothic heroine, however, Celia is not an innocent player in this *mise en scène* of murderous desire. She too is touched by the passion of death and by a desire to transgress the law. She is, in fact, a veritable *noir* protagonist.

Secret beyond the Door opens with a dream-like image (filmed through gauze and patently unrealistic) of a pool with a paper boat floating in it, while Celia's voice-over says, 'I remember. Long ago I read a book that told the meaning of dreams. It said that if a girl dreams of a boat or ship she will reach a safe harbour but if she dreams of daffodils she is in great danger. [The camera pans across from the boat to daffodils under the water.] But this is no time for me to think of danger. This is my wedding day.' The scene cuts to high and low angle shots of a church, and Celia's voice-over continues; she repeats Mark's words about the felicitous structure of the church, then adds 'and love is new for me'. The scene then cuts to the first shot of Celia, in a bridal gown, entering the church. She says, still in voice-over, 'It's said that when you drown, your whole life passes before you like a fast movie,' which is a cue for the flashback to the events leading up to her marriage; the scene cuts to her brother's office where he is berating 'my gaudy young sister' for breaking another engagement. Celia refers to her brother as her 'mother, father, and cheque-signer', pointing to an overdetermined relationship to which the film adds overtones of incestuous desire when Bob, her brother's young assistant lawyer, breaks in upon their embrace, only to be told by the brother that 'it's strictly legal', before he introduces Celia as his sister.

After her brother's death, Bob proposes to Celia, who gladly accepts; but Bob urges her first to take the trip to Mexico suggested by friends. The scene cuts to a busy market square in Mexico, and the camera pans to reveal Celia and Edith at a leather stall, discussing the purchase of a wallet for Bob; as Edith chats about a former fiancé of her own who looked like Bob but who broke off their engagement, a scream is heard from a girl off-screen. Edith urges, 'Let's get out of here. I don't want to be an innocent bystander. Celia, come on! Come on! What's wrong with you?' But Celia remains transfixed by the scene before her. Her voice-over narration begins again: 'There was nothing wrong, but I was strangely held,' and while she admits that she had seen men fight before, she protests, 'This was different. A woman, and two men . . . fighting over her with naked knives. Death was in that street. And I felt how proud she must be. [One of the men's knives strikes the table, beside her hand.] Suddenly I felt that someone was watching me. [Celia looks around her to frame left and right, then left again.] There

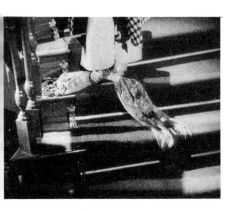

Celia, using a duplicate key, has entered the locked room number 7, only to find that it is the double of her own room, that is, the room of Mark's first wife; she assumes that Mark's secret is that he believes he is responsible for his first wife's death. The clock's chime causes her to turn towards the mantelpiece, and, seeing the candles, one shorter than the other, she realizes with horror that it is indeed her own room. She runs out, only to find Mark has been in the adjacent room. Mark emerges carrying the scarf which the Count used to kill his mistresses. In the house, Miss Robey gives Celia the key to the car to drive to town, but as Celia leaves she finds the scarf – implying that Mark has followed her – and runs wildly out into the mist-filled garden, until she confronts a male figure. The film cuts to Mark's voice-over and his imagined trial for Celia's murder. Discovering Celia has returned to the house, Mark is afraid to remain alone with her and attempts to leave, but is drawn back. Meanwhile Celia has made her preparations, and complete with a bouquet of lilacs, returns to the room to await Mark.

was a tingling at the nape of my neck as though the air had turned cool. I felt eyes touching me like fingers. [Celia looks off-frame left as the camera cuts to a man we later discover is Mark Lamphere, who is looking up off-frame right. The camera cuts back to Celia looking frame-left. Cut-back to Mark, and the voice-over resumes.] There was a current flowing between us. Warm and sweet. And frightening too. [Cut back to Celia looking frame left.] Because he saw behind my makeup what no one had ever seen. Something I didn't know was there.'

Eventually, Edith and Celia leave; later at a café Edith recalls, 'When you finally snapped out of your trance you looked as though you'd seen death himself'. 'That's not how he looked,' Celia replies and sends Edith off on a pretext in order to allow Mark, whom we see as the camera follows her look off-frame right, to join her at her table.

'You're not a bit like you,' he tells her, then compares her to cyclone weather in wheat country, remarking that behind her smile he sees turbulence. Celia's voice-over resumes, saying that she no longer heard his voice (which ceases on the soundtrack though we see him talking): 'Because the beating of my blood was louder. As if this were what I searched for all those foolish years in New York. I knew before I knew his name or touched his hand. Strange, I thought then of daffodils.' Her voice-over ceases and we again hear Mark's voice, now saying that Celia had been living the fight between the two men herself. 'You've been starved of feelings, any real feelings. A twentieth-century sleeping beauty.' His reference here to her absorption in the fight confirms that Celia was indeed no innocent bystander.

Once again her voice-over resumes to summarize their next few days, and the next shot shows Mark and Celia at a wishing well, where she announces that she is leaving the next day. Mark declares his need for her, they kiss, and then her voice-over resumes. 'One door closed and another opened wide and I walked through and never looked behind. Because wind and space and sun and storm – everything was beyond that door. [cut to Celia in the church] That night I wrote to Bob.' Then, over images of the marriage, Celia's voice-over registers her sudden fear: 'I'm marrying a stranger.' (The doors suggest a reference to Hitchcock's *Spellbound*, but also more specifically to the rooms in the Bluebeard's castle of Bartok's opera.) The film is marked by a sense of fatality, by dark passions and psychological disturbances in which the heroine as well as the hero participates: all the traits, in fact, of certain *films noirs*.

Celia's voice-over bears an extremely complex relation to the diegetic time of the film. Conventionally, such a voice-over is taken to be the character's internal thoughts, and Celia recounts her dream in the present tense at the film's opening. She repeats Mark's earlier words about the church, then – having entered bodily into the scene –

she relates, over a visual flashback, all the circumstances leading up to her forthcoming marriage in the church; hence these scenes are shown as belonging to the past. The return to what appears to be the present time in the film is accompanied by Celia's presentiment of danger as she takes Mark's hand in marriage. Yet this voice-over continues across into the diegetically discontinuous scene that follows: the first shot of which shows a fountain in the wall of the hacienda where Mark and Celia are spending their honeymoon. The voice-over continues: 'Maybe I should have followed the dark voice in my heart. Maybe I should have run away. It started on our honeymoon. [The camera starts to track in to a close-up of the fountain.] Legend says . . .' Celia goes on to say that if lovers drink from the fountain they will keep no secrets, and their two hearts will be one, anticipating the film's story and conclusion.

The use of the voice-over here implies that the scene – and indeed the whole film – unfolds in the past tense, as a flashback. But subsequently Celia's voice-over presents her thoughts and fears in the present time of the film and no longer recounts events as past. Following this opening scene at the hacienda, there is no subsequent marking of the whole film as flashback, so that the rest of the film appears as '*histoire*', unnarrated by Celia, whose thoughts and fears we are nevertheless allowed to hear and understand. The film thus resumes the cinematic convention by which the textual system 'speaks' the story, in its ordering and disposition of its codes of narration, in particular in its visual codes, so that we see the film as an 'objective' story and no longer as solely the subjective view of Celia. There are then two Celias, one who is the author of the flashback but who ceases to be marked as such and thus comes to be aligned with the omniscient narrator, and Celia the character in the film. In neither case does 'Celia' directly acknowledge her 'desire for death'; instead the film effectively proposes her speech as a 'manifest' text in contrast to which it offers a 'latent' text to be read or deciphered through a series of repetitions, symbols and coincidences. This distinction between latent and manifest text follows the same division Freud describes for two aspects of the dream-work whereby the latent meaning of the dream is discovered indirectly through the associated thoughts and memories of the analysand as he or she recounts the manifest text of the dream. The film's opening images of Celia's dream implicitly motivate our reading the film in this way.

At the same time as the filmic system narrates the conscious and unconscious thoughts of Celia – she too is neurotic, as Humphries points out – it also displays an 'unconscious' of its own. Its conscious project is the organization of the film as a series of signs, so that while Celia interprets the signs of Mark's neurosis, the spectator interprets the signs of Mark's *and* Celia's neurosis. This organization breaks down after

Celia's flight from the locked room; her story 'disappears' and it is Mark's story that now becomes dominant, it is his childhood trauma that will be understood and resolved in the seventh room. We are given not Celia's voice-over but his, through which we come to understand his feelings. This – together with his sharp exchange with Carrie about his having been dominated by women – serves to bring his point of view into direct focus. Again, logically or technically there should be an ambiguity as to how we are given this understanding, through Celia as author of the flashback as a whole, or by the objective, omniscient narrator, the textual system. By this time in the film, and since Celia's disappearance has not been explained, the narration is implicitly 'objective'. Yet it reveals itself immediately as highly manipulative: we are led to believe she has been murdered by Mark, but this is not the case. At the same time, since the film occludes the scene of Celia's change of mind, we can read this elision as a sign of the textual system's own 'unconscious', a gap that remains undermotivated in the narrative. Its very convenience for the plot only draws attention to its undermotivation by it.

As a result of these developments Celia has, it seems, become only a narrative function in the service of the male hero's story. But let us reconsider this in the light of the Bluebeard tale; in that, too, the question is: whose story does the tale tell, Bluebeard's or his bride's? The early versions of this tale centred on the bride's transgression of a prohibition – which is implicitly a sexual transgression, since it is a taboo related to marriage – which brought about her punishment by death. The development of the happy ending, in which she cunningly achieves her escape from Bluebeard, or is rescued by someone else, presents the overcoming of the taboo. It is in this later version of the tale, centred on the bride and her escape, that the characteristics of the gothic can be discerned. In Bartok's version of the tale, his opera *Bluebeard's Castle*, the wife's punishment is reinstated and Bluebeard himself comes to figure centrally, which makes the tale the story of *his* tragedy, his loss of Judith to her insistent curiosity. Her demand for knowledge destroys her, or rather destroys her ability to be the new love Bluebeard desires, and she becomes, royally garbed and bejewelled, a glowing memory.[63] Serge Moreux, in an explanation of the opera that he claims Bartok himself sanctioned, comments thus:

> In man's interior world, perhaps, there are secrets locked away; each one of us contains the best and the worst, by our material condition . . . Only the shining intoxication of fresh love can sometimes dissipate this dark threat: but let the new woman in a man's life be discreet; the hidden places of the masculine self are forbidden to her and, above all, those where . . . past love lives.[64]

Opening the doors, 'the woman who with her faith, confidence and adoration had gradually lightened the darkness and sorrow of the soul, now begins to doubt. She begins to feel the man's secrets as an intolerable burden just at the very moment when Bluebeard has given her everything that could be shared.'[65] Her punishment is not so much death, as the consignment to memory.

Bartok's opera centres on the man and tells his side of the story. Similarly, Lang's film represents the man as something more than brutish and nefarious; but the secret beyond the door, the problem of Mark's desire which is uncovered by Celia, does not bring her death – rather it frees them both. For Celia rescues herself not by escaping from Mark but by releasing him from the 'spell' – the neurosis – of which the locked room is a sign and a symptom. Celia goes through the fantasy of the gothic romance, both as a narrative device and as a psychological symptom, by resolving the conflict central to the gothic scenario of an ambivalent desire for the primal father (or parent composite), a conflict expressed in the split figure of the masculine, the sadistic and dangerous husband or suitor and another, who is gentler and who protects and rescues. Mark is both of these and, finally, neither. Celia, too, has had to undertake a journey, and it is equally oedipal, namely from a desire forbidden to a desire permitted; this journey dissipates the threat of punishment or retribution which the desire originally provoked. But it is not only a problem of a forbidden incestuous desire; her brother Rick, the implicit object of this desire, embodies both the law and enjoyment. As Celia says, 'If only Rick were alive – I could go home to Rick.' The fantasy that Celia must go through is that of the enjoyment or *jouissance* that Rick signifies and which she is excluded from and therefore desires. The repeated association of death and its correlative, danger, with her desire is the symptom of Celia's fantasy. For *jouissance* cannot be symbolized; instead it intrudes as the 'real', as the death drive. In pursuing this *jouissance* Celia finds her own death, to which she draws close a couple of times. Thus Mark represents both her heart's desire and a danger. The repetition characteristic of the death drive is seen, too, in the repeated pattern of her running away or wishing to do so (namely her broken engagements and her attempts to leave Mark).

The transformation in Celia is signified first of all by the calm with which she greets Mark the morning after her flight from the locked room, in contrast to her hysteria of the night before, then later, when she returns to the locked room, by her determination to confront Mark's neurosis by seeking to interpret the signs of his symptoms. She thus encounters his desire from within the order of the signifier and no longer finds in his murderous longings the real of her own desire. The film, however, occludes the scene of her transformation, which can only be inferred secondarily. Instead it is implied that she may be dead, for the film cuts from Celia running headlong into a male figure on the lawn as she attempts to escape from the house, to Mark's voice-over the next morning, in which he imagines his trial for her murder. Her appearance as Mark wanders through her room surprises the spectator as much as it does Mark, but for different reasons, and her explanation – that she ran into Bob – is meant for the audience rather than for Mark, who presumably knows that he did not kill her. That she is able to return is therefore implicitly connected to Bob, who is both her lawyer and the rejected/repressed stand-in for her brother Rick, suggesting a transference through which she finally accedes to the law. Her avowed reason for returning, that she loves Mark, transparently veils rather than motivates her change of mind. The occlusion marks a repression in the film's text, of something that cannot be spoken or represented but which enables the heroine to bring about the happy conclusion. It is therefore, as suggested earlier, a mark of the text's own 'unconscious'.

Celia is able to read the signs of Mark's neurosis, including the key's turning in the lock, and thus brings about in Mark the 'conviction' necessary to therapeutic success.[66] Celia releases Mark from the tyranny of the hidden places of his masculine self, and rescues him from his past. For both, the fantasy of the dangerous sexual other who will either kill or be killed is successfully overturned. The bad omen of the daffodils is nevertheless realized, in an ironic Langian gesture; for whilst the key is turning in the lock – which precipitates Mark's murderous impulse and which Celia correctly connects to the story of his sister Carrie locking him in his room – serves to unlock Mark's unconscious memory and thereby dissipate his desire to kill, it also serves as the sign of another murderous intent, that of Miss Robey, who has just set fire to the rooms. The characters are propelled from their immersion in the real, in the death drive, to the reality of an impending incendiary death that parodies the image of the 'burning desire' of the two lovers. From this emerges the fantasy through which the terror of the wish that might come true is overturned, and thus through which '*jouissance* is domesticated'.[67] This is of course the fantasy of the heterosexual couple as a complementary union of reciprocal desire. Celia resolves Mark's unconscious conflict, whilst Mark rescues Celia from the burning house. A postscript shows the couple once more at the romantic hacienda of their honeymoon; Mark, with his head on Celia's lap, is saying that he still has a long way to go. Her reply, that they both do, is the only element that refers back to the film's beginning and the disturbance in her own desire. The reinscription of the fantasy of the romantic couple with which the film closes is therefore undermined by the reference to Celia's story which opened the film, but which was left behind in the shift of emphasis to Mark's story. As Bellour noted, 'Because Lang plays a highly perverse game, it is through the lacunae, the lack he establishes, that he seems intelligible. And it is this which requires decipherment at all levels.'[68]

A WOMAN'S INTEREST IN *FILM NOIR*

Interviewed in 1990 about her latest film, *Blue Steel*, Katherine Bigelow had this to say:

I find B-movies inspiring because they delve into a darkness and talk about the demons that exist in all of us. They take a lot of chances. When I was moving away from the art world and into the world of film, I stumbled on to *noir* films and couldn't get enough of them. I was fascinated by them, riveted to them. I found Joseph H. Lewis' *Gun Crazy* extraordinary, lurid, very brave, with characters who were willing to transgress, who were so far beyond the edge that they were almost in a sort of Z world of vicarious thrills. *Detour's* another picture that I think is a flawless masterpiece. I'm a huge fan of *film noir*, but I'm less interested in updating it than in reinventing it, or perhaps just using it as a point of departure.

She cited her earlier film *The Loveless* as a 'sort of biker-*noir*', and said of *Blue Steel*:

I wanted to do a 'woman's action film', putting a woman at the centre of a movie predominantly occupied by men.
    When women go to see *Lethal Weapon*, many of them will identify with Mel Gibson. I was interested in creating a person at the centre of an action film who represents an Everyman that both women and men could identify with. At our initial screenings at the Berlin Film Festival, some men at the press conference commented that they found themselves for the first time in their lives identifying with a woman. I found this very interesting because finally the notion of self-preservation is universal. I wanted to create a very strong, capable person who just happens to be a woman, using the context of the police genre.[69]

Blue Steel seems fundamentally *noir* in style, achieving through the use of colour a lighting style that is the equivalent of *film noir*'s chiaroscuro world of black and white. Instead of a world of shadows, we see the passageways of the police station, veiled in bars of light, as dust reflects sunlight in streams across faces. Megan is a rookie cop who kills an armed robber on her first patrol. The robber's gun is never found, but subsequently a series of murders are committed using bullets engraved with Megan's name. Her wish to be on the side of the law, to partake of its powers, turns into a nightmare when the man she has been dating proves to be the murderer. He is obsessed with her precisely as the woman with the gun/phallus, which he desires as an absolute and pure violence, as the power of death rather than life. He has identified with her – they are two halves of one person, he says – in a grotesque inversion of the romantic language of ideal union between lovers. The film presents a story not merely of self-preservation on Megan's part, but of her confrontation with her own identification with the law – revealed most graphically in the image of her donning a Smith and Wesson at the beginning of the film – and thus of her confrontation with the distorted reflection of herself embodied by Eugene. He comes to represent her own desire for violence, which is psychologically motivated – though schematically – with reference to her wife-beating father.

If both men and women identify with Megan, it is not because she represents some notion of Everyman from which the question of sexual difference is absent, but because the problem of sexuality posed by the film is not fitted up in the conventional codes of gender. The conjoining of desire and destruction familiar in the 1940s *film noir* is present here, too, and is equally a matter for women as for men.

NOTES

I would like to thank colleagues and students at the University of Kent, Canterbury, who worked on the shot breakdown of *Raw Deal* on which this chapter has drawn. I would also like to thank Lea Jacobs for her helpful comments and Steven Neale, who read an earlier draft of the article.

1. Alain Silver and Elizabeth Ward include a 'Filmography of Film Noir in the Eighties', pp. 375–9 in *Film Noir: An Encyclopedic Reference Guide* (London: Bloomsbury, 1980).

2. *Black Widow* (Bob Rafelson, 1987) has a woman investigate the duplicitous woman, while *Jagged Edge* (Richard Marquand, 1985) fully inverts the classic structure: the desirable man is duplicitous.

3. James Damico, '*Film Noir*: A Modest Proposal', *Film Reader*, no. 3 (1978) p. 54.

4. Marc Vernet, 'The Filmic Transaction: On the Openings of *Films Noirs*', *Velvet Light Trap*, no. 20 (Summer 1983), p. 8.

5. Foster Hirsch, *Film Noir*: *The Dark Side of the Screen* (New York: A. S. Barnes, 1981), p. 13. The fourth and less important figure for Hirsch is the psychotic or obsessed character; this is, however, frequently a woman.

6. Hirsch, pp. 20–21.

7. Sigmund Freud, 'The Loss of Reality in Neurosis and Psychosis' in *The Standard*

Edition of the Complete Psychological Works of Sigmund Freud (henceforth referred to as *SE*), vol. XIX (London: Hogarth Press, 1961), p. 187.

8. Hirsch, pp. 20 and 21.

9. Freud, *SE*, vol. XI. Freud also cites this as the basis for the obsession of his female patient in 'The Psychogenesis of a Case of Homosexuality in a Woman', *SE* vol. XVIII. As Mandy Merck has pointed out, 'this allusion fleetingly reopens the question of early mother love only briefly mentioned thus far in the homosexual case study', but it is nevertheless not pursued by Freud (Mandy Merck, 'The Train of Thought in Freud's "Case of Homosexuality in a Woman",' in Parveen Adams and Elizabeth Cowie, eds., *The Woman in Question* (London: Verso, 1991), p. 332.

10. Ibid., p. 171.

11. Ibid., p. 169.

12. Ibid., p. 173.

13. Freud, *SE*, vol. XI. These two essays, together with 'The Taboo of Virginity', were published together in 1918 under the collective title 'Contributions to the Psychology of Love'.

14. Frank Krutnik, *In a Lonely Street: Film Noir, Genre, Masculinity* (London and New York: Routledge, 1991), pp. 86 and 89. The three forms he describes are: (1) *the investigative thriller*, where the hero, often a professional detective, seeks to restore order – and to validate his own identity – by exposing and countermanding a criminal conspiracy; (2) *the male suspense-thriller*, which is the inverse of the above, in that the hero is in a marked position of inferiority, in regard both to the criminal conspirators and to the police, and seeks to restore himself to a position of security by eradicating the enigma; and (3) *the criminal adventure thriller*, where the hero, usually with the aid of a woman, becomes engaged in either a wilful or an accidental

transgression of the law, and has to face the consequences of stepping out of line (p. 86).

15. Richard Maltby, 'Film Noir: The Politics of the Maladjusted Text', *Journal of American Studies*, vol. 18, no. 1 (1984), p. 53.

16. Janey Place, 'Women in Film Noir', in E. Ann Kaplan, ed., *Women and Film Noir* (London: British Film Institute, 1978), p. 50, and Mary Ann Doane, '*Gilda*: Epistemology as Striptease', *Camera Obscura*, no. 11, p. 15. This article is reprinted in her collection entitled *Femme Fatales* (London and New York: Routledge, 1991) in which she argues: 'Since feminisms are forced to search out symbols from a lexicon that does not yet exist, their acceptance of the femme fatale as a sign of strength in an unwritten history must also and simultaneously involve an understanding and assessment of all the epistemological baggage she carries along with her' (p. 3).

17. The other films were *Murder, My Sweet* (UK title *Farewell, My Lovely*), *Double Indemnity* and *The Woman in the Window* (Fritz Lang, 1945), Nino Frank, in *Ecran français*, no. 61 (28 August 1946).

18. These features are all listed in almost all books on *film noir*; see for example the introduction to Silver and Ward, p. 3. Discussions of the origins and antecedents of this style usually invoke German expressionism, the influx of emigrés from the German film industry, and Welles's *Citizen Kane*. David Bordwell has challenged many of these assumptions in *The Classical Hollywood Cinema Film Style and Mode of Production to 1960* (London and New York: Routledge and Kegan Paul, 1985), pp. 74–7. He points to realistic motivation as the alibi for these stylistic devices, and notes that low-key lighting was already a staple of genres such as the horror film.

19. This view is argued by Frank Krutnik, who suggests that the style of German expressionism was associated with quality and with art. He cites Phil Karson, a director

working for Monogram in the 1940s, who commented, 'No matter what I did in the smaller studios, they thought it was fantastic, because nobody could make pictures as fast as I could at that time, and get some quality into it by giving it a little screwier camera angle or something' (Phil Karson, interviewed in Todd McCarthy and Charles Flynn, eds., *Kings of the B's: Working within the Hollywood System* [New York: E. P. Dutton, 1975], p. 335, and quoted by Krutnik, pp. 21–2).

20. Richard Winnington, writing in *The Chronicle*, a British daily newspaper, of 10 December 1949, claimed that, 'but for the grace of Max Opul's [*sic*] [there] would have gone the dread "woman's film"'.

21. John Houseman was a writer and director for the stage and screen, as well as an actor. He set up the Mercury Theater with Orson Welles in 1937 and developed the original story for *Citizen Kane*. He later worked as a producer. He was, as Richard Maltby points out, a liberal.

22. John Houseman, 'Today's Hero: A Review', in *Hollywood Quarterly*, vol. 2, no. 2 (1947), p. 163.

23. John Houseman, in *Vogue*, 15 January 1947, quoted in Lester Asheim, 'The Film and the Zeitgeist', *Hollywood Quarterly*, vol. 2, no. 4 (1947), p. 416.

24. Steven Neale provides a review of recent discussions of film genre in 'Questions of Genre', *Screen*, vol. 31, no. 1 (Spring 1990), pp. 45–66.

25. Marc Vernet discusses the obligatory and the forbidden in his essay, 'Genre' in *Film Reader*, no. 3 (1978).

26. The use of the term in English to refer to the classification of literary works seems more recent, however. The *Oxford English Dictionary* gives 1818 as its first use, but with reference to kinds of character. Thackeray uses it in 1840 to refer to a 'story in this genre'. The phrase 'genre painting' is used from 1873 to refer to works in which 'scenes and subjects of ordinary life are depicted' and the term 'genre' seems to have subsequently acquired a pejorative sense in this connection. The term 'species' is used by the *OED* in its entry for 'epic', which it defines as a 'species of poetical composition', and it cites under the uses of the term Milton's reference (1644), to the teaching of 'what the Laws are of a true Epic Poem'.

27. Paul Hernadi, *Beyond Genre: New Directions in Literary Classification* (Ithaca and London: Cornell University Press, 1972).

28. Hernadi cites Pierre Kohler's views that artistic creation may be regarded as a process of 'ordering' 'that starts with selection and leads to construction. The idea of genre stimulates and guides the artist in both creative phases' (Hernadi, p. 21). See Pierre Kohler, 'Contribution à une philosophie des genres', *Helicon*, 1 (1938), pp. 233–44; 2 (1940), pp. 135–47.

29. Tsvetan Todorov, *The Fantastic: A Structural Approach to a Literary Genre* (Cleveland: Case Western Reserve, 1973), pp. 6–7 and 8.

30. Modern critical attention to the category of melodrama can be traced in part at least to Thomas Elsaesser's landmark essay 'Tales of Sound and Fury: Observations on the Family Melodrama', which first appeared in the British film journal *Monogram*, no. 4 (1972) and has been widely reprinted, including in Christine Gledhill, ed., *Home is Where the Heart Is* (London: British Film Institute, 1987). Elsaesser's essay also recognizes *films noirs* as melodramas (Gledhill, p. 56) in so far as they involve 'psychologised, thematised representations of the hero's inner dilemmas' (p. 55).

31. Steven Neale has pointed out that the most common term for the films later called *films noirs* was 'melodrama' or 'meller' – *Variety*'s slang term. He notes that these terms cross over into the so-called gothic melodramas such as *Gaslight*, and that the gothic films and

thrillers with a contemporary setting are all described in the same way. This material was presented in a paper 'Melo Talk: On the Meaning and Use of the Term "Melodrama" in the American Trade Press', at the *Screen Film Studies Conference*, Glasgow, 1991. Raymond Durgnat, in 'Ways of Melodrama', *Sight and Sound*, vol. 21, no. 1 (1951), maintains that the notion of melodrama centres on thrilling action, while taking account of 'emotional melodrama'.

32. Ben Singer, 'Female Power in the Serial-Queen Melodrama: The Etiology of an Anomaly', *Camera Obscura* no. 22 (1990), p. 91.

33. Made in 1922, it was adapted from the play *The Two Orphans*, written by Adolphe d'Ennery and Eugene Cormon, first performed in 1874.

34. Peter Brooks's study *The Melodramatic Imagination: Balzac, Henry James, Melodrama and the Mode of Excess* (New Haven: Yale University Press, 1976) also suggests a wider application of the term, although his emphasis on the 'melodramatic imagination' gives priority to textual analysis rather than to generic conventions.

Patrice Petro's study *Joyless Streets: Women and Melodramatic Representation in Weimar Germany* (Princeton, Princeton University Press, 1989) argues that 'melodrama was an important representational mode in Weimar Germany' (p. 26). Heide Schlüpmann, however, argues for a distinction between social drama and melodrama in her article 'Melodrama and Social Drama in the Early German Cinema', *Camera Obscura*, no. 22 (1990).

35. Maureen Turim, 'Flashbacks and the Psyche in Melodrama and Film Noir', in *Flashbacks in Film* (New York: Routledge, 1989), p. 182.

36. Murray Smith, '*Film Noir* and the Female Gothic and *Deception*', *Wide Angle*, vol. 10, no. 1 (1988), p. 64.

37. Krutnik, p. 164.

38. Obsession was a central element in many melodramas as well, for example in *The Seventh Veil* (Compton Bennett, 1945), James Mason is a crippled music teacher and sadistic guardian of the heroine, a brilliant pianist. He refuses to recognize his love for his ward, which she reciprocates, while his pathological jealousy begins to destroy her.

39. The example of the western is interesting here. Audience research prior to 1950 indicates that, whilst westerns were regularly produced in large numbers by the studios, the genre was popular only with adolescent boys and sectors of America's rural population, and that it was actively disliked more than it was liked by the viewing population as a whole (Garth S. Jowett, 'Giving Them What They Want: Movie Audience Research Before 1950', in Bruce A. Austen, *Current Research in Film: Audience, Economics and Law*, vol. 1 [Norwood, NI: Ablex Publishing, 1985]). At the same time, from John Ford's *Stagecoach* on, the A western as directed by Ford, Hawks, Walsh and later Antony Mann was extremely successful at the box office. These films not only drew upon the western formula, they also extended the genre, using it in a way that would come to be seen as recognizably Fordian, Hawksian, etcetera.

40. The term B picture can be understood in two different ways. As an exhibition category – in the US and the UK between the early to mid 1930s and the 1950s – it made up the second half of a double bill and was sold on the basis of a flat rental fee, in contrast to the first-half, or A, picture, which was sold on the basis of a percentage of the gross return on receipts. A B picture thus had a very reliable return, but could never become a blockbuster for the producers, however popular it was. A slightly more complex picture emerges, however, when we consider the term B picture as a production category. Production categories were specials, or one-off pictures. A projects were assigned big budgets, whilst B projects had smaller budgets. A studio's B projects

were not necessarily released on a flat rental basis, that is, they might become A pictures on exhibition. Moreover, a film might start out as an A picture and be released as a B, depending on pre-release audience reports, changes in studio control, etcetera. For example, Twentieth Century Fox initially assigned *Laura* a budget in its lowest bracket, but then raised its budget in the preview stages and reshot some scenes.

In addition, releases in New York, Los Angeles and other big cities were often handled differently from the rest of the United States. Large cities had cinemas that specialized in certain types of films in a way not possible in smaller locations; as a result B horror films, westerns, etcetera, could appear as feature films. If successful, the film might be reassigned by the distributor for exhibition in the rest of the country. In the 1940s, B production was not a ghetto of poor talent and limited expectations; rather it was a training ground whereby new young directors might prove themselves on cheaper productions. Lea Jacobs has examined the structures of distribution/advertising and exhibition of low budget A pictures and B pictures in the 1930s in 'The B Film and the Problem of Cultural Distinction', *Screen*, vol. 33, no. 1 (1992). My thanks to Ben Brewster for information on the nature of B picture production, distribution and exhibition.

41. Glenn Ford, who co-starred in *Gilda*, has confirmed in interviews that the psycho-sexual overtones of *Gilda* were intentional.

42. *Tribune*, 21 March 1947.

43. Silver and Ward, p. 4.

44. Krutnik, p. 86; see my note 14.

45. Ibid.

46. Silver and Ward, p. 291.

47. Paul Cain, *Fast One* (reprinted Harpenden: No Exit Press, 1989).

48. Place, p. 54.

49. *Women in Film Noir*, Claire Johnston, 'Double Indemnity', in E. Ann Kaplan, ed., (London: British Film Institute, 1978), p. 110.

50. Quoted on the cover of the Ace Giant Double Novel edition, 1947 of Elisabeth Sanxay Holding's 'The Blank Wall', which first appeared in the *Ladies' Home Journal* (motto: 'Never Underestimate a Woman'). Also published in this edition was another story 'The Girl Who Had to Die', about a beautiful woman who believes her boyfriend wants to kill her – he does not, but others, whom she is blackmailing, do. The story is told in the first person by the boyfriend, who thus investigates the woman.

51. These films have also been associated with films not included as *films noirs*, such as *Rebecca, Suspicion, The Two Mrs Carrolls, Gaslight, Dragonwyck, Jane Eyre*, and with *Secret beyond the Door, Experiment Perilous*, and *A Woman's Vengeance*, described variously as female gothic or gothic romance. Mary Ann Doane also describes these as 'paranoid woman films' (*The Desire to Desire: The Woman's Film of the 1940s* [Bloomington: Indiana University Press, 1987], p. 123). Thomas Elsaesser cites them as Freudian feminine melodramas. *The Spiral Staircase* is not mentioned, perhaps because the murderer is discovered and despatched by his elderly and ailing stepmother, who had previously suspected her own son.

52. Diane Waldman, 'At Last I Can Tell It to Someone! Feminine Point-of-view and Subjectivity in the Gothic Romance Film of the 1940s', *Cinema Journal*, vol. 23, no. 2 (1983), p. 34.

53. Information here was drawn from Sara Kozloff's valuable investigation of voice-over in the American fiction film, *Invisible Storytellers* (University of California Press, Berkeley and Los Angeles: 1988).

54. Krutnik, p. 86; see my note 14.

55. Nevertheless, the music we hear continues to be Pat's voice-over music.

56. For the opposing view see Steve Jenkins, *Fritz Lang: The Image and the Look* (London: British Film Institute, 1981), p. 104. Reynold Humphries, *Fritz Lang: Genre and Representation in His American Films* (Baltimore: Johns Hopkins University Press, 1988) also sees the film as reasserting a phallocentric order: 'The split subject position manifested by Celia through the voice-off was there all along to show that a woman cannot occupy such an active role' (p. 152). I shall present a different view of Celia's role and function in the following discussion.

57. It is placed in this category by Diane Waldman; see note 52.

58. Paul M. Jensen, *The Cinema of Fritz Lang* (London: Zwemmer, 1969), p. 165.

59. Diane Waldman describes the female gothic thus: 'a young and inexperienced woman meets a handsome older man to whom she is alternately attracted and repelled. After a whirlwind courtship (seventy-two hours in Lang's *Secret beyond the Door*, two weeks is more typical), she marries him. After returning to the ancestral mansion of one of the pair, the heroine experiences a series of bizarre and uncanny incidents, open to ambiguous interpretation, revolving around the question of whether or not the Gothic male really loves her. She begins to suspect that he may be a murderer' (pp. 31–2).

60. Reynold Humphries sees these stylistic effects as in keeping with *film noir* conventions which, he suggests, 'Lang exploits here against a simplistic reading' (p. 147).

61. Cited in Jenkins, p. 163.

62. Bluebeard is the villain of a widespread European folk tale in which he marries, one after the other, three (or seven) beautiful sisters. He hands his latest young wife the keys to the castle and departs, saying that she may unlock any door except one. She disobeys, opens the forbidden door, and beholds some sign of Bluebeard's bloody misdeeds. Her transgression is betrayed by another sign and she is put to death. Only the youngest and last wife saves herself or is rescued by a man she then marries (though this happy ending is thought to be a comparatively recent addition).

63. In Bartok's opera, Judith has abandoned her betrothed and her family to go with Bluebeard to his castle. She sings, 'Darling Bluebeard! If you reject me
And drive me out, I'll never leave you.
I'll perish on your icy threshold.' At this, Bluebeard embraces her. Bluebeard shows her his castle, but forbids her to open the doors of seven of the rooms, but Judith insists, and Bluebeard acquiesces. The story is wholly metaphoric, Gyorgy Kroo argues: 'Bluebeard's castle is the symbol of the male soul. Each of the seven doors represents one particular aspect of the life of man as well as individual character traits.' Gyorgy Kroo, *A Guide to Bartok* (Budapest: Corvina Press, 1971), p. 63.

64. Serge Moreux, *Bela Bartok* (London: Harvill Press, 1953).

65. Kroo, p. 65.

66. Sigmund Freud, 'Beyond the Pleasure Principle', *SE*, vol. XVIII, p. 19.

67. 'Fantasy conceals the fact that the Other, the symbolic order, is structured around some traumatic impossibility, around something which cannot be symbolised – i.e. the real of *jouissance*: through fantasy *jouissance* is domesticated' (Slavoj Žižek, *The Sublime Object of Ideology* [London: Verso, 1989]), p. 123.

68. Raymond Bellour, 'On Fritz Lang' in Jenkins, p. 36.

69. Pam Cook, 'Blue Steel', *Monthly Film Bulletin*, vol. 57 (November 1990), p. 312.

6

THE PHENOMENAL NONPHENOMENAL: PRIVATE SPACE IN *FILM NOIR*

Joan Copjec

THE ACTUARIAL ORIGINS OF DETECTIVE FICTION

Barton Keyes is a first-rate detective, so we learn from Walter Neff, whose voice-over narration addressed to Keyes is dense with praise for him and with recollections of his remarkable talent for detection. Of these recollections, one stands out particularly, and not only because the case on which it bears is the very one in which Neff is himself guiltily entangled. This scene of Keyes's magisterial display of reason is clearly invested with all the emotions of fear and relief that stem from Neff's involvement in the insurance scam under investigation, but it is also invested with the emotions of admiration and pride that characterize Neff's involvement with Keyes. Dramatizing, then, the full ambivalence of Neff's relation to the mentor whom he will not choose to follow, the scene is nevertheless unambivalent with respect to its evaluation of this mentor's logic.

Keyes's superior, the man with the biggest 'office' at the Pacific All-Risk Insurance company, is Mr Norton. An extremely foolish man, he has just pompously and precipitously announced to Keyes, Neff and the newly-widowed Mrs Dietrichson his ill-founded conclusion: Mrs Dietrichson is not entitled to collect any insurance money from her husband's death since it was obviously a suicide and a clear attempt to defraud his company. It is precisely by exposing the foolishness and ill-foundedness of this conclusion that Keyes's performance derives its power. Delivered with great rhetorical flair and punctuated by the frenetic gestures of a man impatient with, even contemptuous of, his opponent, Keyes's counterargument begins with what is meant to be an outright dismissal of his opponent's reasoning. The devastating charge? You are ignorant of statistics:

> You've never read an actuarial table in your life, have you? Why there are ten volumes on suicide alone. Suicide: by race, by color, by occupation, by sex, by season of the year, by time of day. Suicide, how committed: by poison, by firearms, by drowning, by leaps. Suicide by poison, subdivided by types of poison, such as corrosives, irritants, systemic gases, narcotics, alkaloids, proteins, and so forth. Suicide by leaps, subdivided by leaps from high places, under the wheels of trains, under the wheels of trucks, under the feet of horses, under steamboats. But, Mr Norton, of all the cases on record, there's not one single case of suicide by someone jumping off the back end of a moving train.

Appearing in what is arguably the climactic scene of *Double Indemnity* (Billy Wilder, 1944), this speech by Keyes is presented as decisive. But all the rhetorical force and narrative consequence of this argument should not prevent us from observing that there is, nevertheless, something unsatisfying about it. How is it that an appeal to statistics can come to be taken as a devastating argument? What power can possibly issue from a recourse to mathematical probability? Every investigation begins when we cease to be able to take something for granted. Mine begins here with this scene and with this question: what, in the final analysis, do numbers have to do with detection?

It would seem at first that we could begin answering these questions by linking detective fiction to the advent of rationalism. Marjorie Nicolson, for example, makes this link in her description of the detective, who, she says

> ignores . . . clues in order to devote himself to thought. Having like his great predecessor [namely, Descartes] thought away all the universe, nothing remains but the culprit. By the strength of logic alone, he has reconstructed the universe, and in his proper place has set the villain of the piece.[1]

While she is referring specifically to the French tradition of detectives as opposed to the English, whose prime exemplar, Sherlock Holmes, 'laboriously and carefully accumulate[s] all possible clues, passing over nothing as too insignificant, filling his little boxes and envelopes with everything that comes his way', it has often been argued that even Holmes, who always looks a little out of place at the scene of the crime, is not primarily a man of experience. If he sees things that others miss, this is because his investigation takes off from rational categories that they do not seem to possess. From C. Auguste Dupin to Ironside, then, the tradition of detectives is that of the armchair rationalist, known less for his perceptiveness than for his scepticism; the detective is one who withdraws from the world of the senses, of which he remains infinitely suspicious, in order to become more attentive to the clear and distinct prescriptions of *a priori* ideas.

Keyes is a detective in this mode: suspicious of everything and everyone, including the one woman he ever got close to, unwilling even to state what day of the week it is until he consults his calendar and then checks to see if the calendar is this year's; he trusts only the feeling he gets in the pit of his stomach that tells him when something is wrong. This feeling – his 'little man', he calls it – that never errs, how are we to understand it if not as a remnant of the Cartesian tradition, a somewhat hypochondriacal version of the *cogito*? If Keyes's recitation of a list of statistics from an actuarial table leaves us somewhat unsatisfied, we might attribute this to nothing more than the fact that the rationalist, as compared to the man of experience, is always less exciting, more colourless. Detectives, in so far as they are rationalists, are never far from insurance men, claims adjustors. This seems to have been the insight of James M. Cain, who equated detection with insurance in *The Postman Always Rings Twice* as well as in *Double Indemnity*.

But this insight overruns the work of Cain, for the connection between detection and insurance can be established historically. The origins of detective fiction coincide, it turns out, with what Ian Hacking has termed 'the avalanche of numbers'. According to Hacking, there was an exponential increase in the printing of numbers between 1830 and 1848[2] (the precise moment at which the detective story emerges) as a passion for counting – both things and people – incited the Western nations. This new numberlust was an immediate response to the various democratic revolutions which demanded that people be counted. The increased interest in numbers had a double-edged effect. The first was corrosive: statistics had a mordant effect on the image of the monarchical body that had held the old, premodern nations together.[3] The second was constitutive: statistics served to individualize the mass of the citizens, to create more and more kinds of people. As Keyes's speech illustrates, after the avalanche of numbers, there were no longer simply people who attempted suicide and others who did not. Instead there were those who attempted suicide by poison, subdivided by types of poison and subdivided again by race, by colour, by occupation, and so on – and all sorts of others who did not.

Entire bureaucracies grew up around these numbers to count, cross-reference, and analyse them. But it was not merely numbers that were being manipulated by these bureaucracies; it was people, their happiness and well-being, that were primarily at issue. The interest in numbers was part of the modern nation state's concern for the welfare of its population, with whose well-being the state's own was now intimately linked. What statistics calculated was the 'felicity'[4] of citizens and what they aimed at was indemnification against every sort of infelicity, every accident and misfortune. Statistics structured the modern nations as large insurance companies that strove, through the law of large numbers, to profit from the proliferation of categories of people, the very diversity of its citizens, by collectivizing and calculating risk.[5]

Murder is one of the risks that increased at an alarming rate as modern cities grew ever more populous. It would seem that one could never protect oneself from the randomness of a violence such as this; Quetelet once observed that 'nothing would seem more to escape foreknowledge than murder', but as a statistician he demonstrated that there was more stability in the area of 'moral deviancy' than in procreation or mortality.[6] 'The terrifying exactness with which crimes reproduce themselves', was a matter of enormous fascination to populations who were made aware for the first time of the statistical regularities of crime. The frequency distribution of kinds of murder, murderers, and instruments used were all charted to reveal amazing uniformities when correlated with variables such as sex, class, nationality, and so on. Statistics, then created a mathematical expectation within which we could come to believe in the calculability of risk. Before statistics this sort of expectation was strictly impossible, and so, I would argue, was detective fiction. For it was statistics that formed the basis of classical detective fiction's narrative contract with its reader; the nineteenth century's fictional belief in the solvability of crime was specifically a mathematical expectation.

The thesis that modern bureaucracies and detective fiction spring from the same source lends itself to a Foucauldian interpretation. It could be argued that statistics and the bureaucracies that are sustained by them are, like detective fiction, techniques of surveillance, mechanisms of a disciplinary form of power. Each of these techniques isolates minute, differentiating and therefore incriminating details which give access to the most intimate secrets of the individuals they investigate. It is, in fact, the very passion for counting, recording and tabulating that deposits many of the clues used by detectives to track their suspects. Laundry lists, insurance records, telephone bills, parking tickets, the criminal and the criminal act always turn up as figures in some bureaucracy's accounting. When Walter Neff attempts to avoid detection, he establishes his alibi by making a long-distance call that he knows will be recorded and thus help to place him at home at the hour of the crime. Keyes begins to unravel the case when he notes that Mr Dietrichson did not put in a claim for his broken leg, though he was insured against such an accident. *In detective fiction, to be is not to be perceived, it is to be recorded.* This is one of the fundamental differences between the realist novel (with its emphasis on the intersubjective network of perceptions) and detective fiction.

In *The Novel and the Police*, D. A. Miller emphasizes not the differences between the detective and the realist novel so much as their 'radical entanglement'.[7] Taking the detective novel as a special case of the novel in general, Miller sees them as the bad cop and the good cop of modern surveillance. Because the detective novel is set in a bounded space and deals with a limited and, by convention, closed set of characters, it passes off its deployment of investigative techniques as extraordinary, that is, as special and temporary. The ordinary novel, or the novel as such, thus appears as a space vacated by detectives, a space that no longer requires or is exempted from the intervention of any special policing power. Detective novels, then, fill an ideological function by lulling us into the belief that everyday life – the one we ordinarily live and the one we read about in realist novels – is free of surveillance. This blinds us to the fact that our ordinary life is structured by the very diffusion or dispersal of the same techniques found in detective novels. In the more subtle, discreet form of the realist novel the detective function is permitted to go undetected.

But what is meant here by the 'detective function'? What actions does it perform? It scrutinizes, it invades, but above all, it constitutes the very people into which it comes into contact. It 'makes up people'.[8] The function of the nineteenth-century novel, detective and otherwise, is the invention of character, not simply as a literary category but character as such. Here we may stop to note a certain similarity between the rationalist project and that of new historicism. Both believe that categories of being subsume being itself. As the Cartesian 'I think' is supposed to subsume the 'I am', so the categories of people invented in the nineteenth century are supposed to subsume the actual people who came to be numbered in them. It is this new historicist conviction that Hacking wants to reinforce through his reference to Frege's work on numeration: 'as Frege taught us, you can't just print numbers. You must print numbers of objects falling under some category or other.'[9] Hacking's point is that statistics did not simply count varieties of people, it accounted for them, that is to say, it created them. Beneath the categories actual people came into being.

Making a similar point (for example, 'It is not just that, strictly private subjects, we read about violated, objectified subjects, but that, in the very act of reading about them, we contribute largely to constituting them as such'[10]), Miller refines this argument by rendering an account of the subtlety of this constitutive panoptic power. For this power to function properly, it must make itself invisible, it must conceal its own operation. The function of detection, then, is not only to construct various categories of the self, of character, but to construct character *as* quirky, *as* resistant to categorization, to construct the self, finally, *as* private. In this way, the knowledge in which he is held is concealed from the subject. Secrecy is here conceived of as a necessary ruse of modern power, simply that; for there can in fact be no secret that keeps itself from power, no self that is not always already known. Keyes's argument is a corollary of this principle: Mr Dietrichson cannot have attempted suicide by jumping off the back end of a train since there exists no such statistical category. If there is no secret self, no hidden or private domain that is not always already public, then there is no deception, no ignominy other than that which attaches itself to the law. How then is crime possible? How is it possible to transgress territories that have no private boundaries, to steal something which belongs to no one?

THE LOCKED-ROOM PARADOX AND THE GROUP

In his famous interview with François Truffaut, Alfred Hitchcock described a scene he planned to include in *North by Northwest*, but never actually shot:

> I wanted to have a long dialogue scene between Cary Grant and one of the factory workers [at a Ford automobile plant] as they walk along the assembly line. They might, for instance, be talking about one of the foremen. Behind them a car is being assembled, piece by piece. Finally, the car they've seen being put together from a simple nut and bolt is complete, with gas and oil, and all ready to drive off the line. The two men look at each other and say, 'Isn't it wonderful!' Then they open the door to the car and out drops a corpse.[11]

What we have here is one of the defining elements of classical detective fiction: the locked-room paradox. The question is: where has the body come from? Once the complete process of the car's production has been witnessed, 'once the measures of the real are made tight, once a perimeter, a volume, is defined once and for all, there is nothing to lead one to suspect that when all is said and done',[12] some object will have completely escaped attention only later to be extracted from this space. So, if no hand on the assembly line has placed the corpse in the car, how is it possible for another hand to pull it out? The Foucauldian solution would be to consider this paradox a deception of panoptic power, to treat the corpse as a fiction necessary to the discreet functioning of the law. One merely subscribes to the illusion of depth created by this fiction when one believes that something can escape power's meticulous inspection.

Lacan devotes his 'Seminar on "The Purloined Letter"' to a completely different treatment of the locked-room paradox. He argues that those who consider conceal-ment to be simply a matter of depth, those who think that that which lies hidden must lie *underneath* something else, subscribe to 'too immutable a notion of the real',[13] since what is concealed may just as easily lie on the surface. Lacan, then, like Foucault, believes there is nothing but surface, but maintains, nevertheless, that the corpse, the private 'self', the purloined letter are not simply fictions; they are real.

To understand this position, let us return to our original observation that detective fiction arises in tandem with a passion for counting. We have so far left unchallenged the lesson Hacking derives from Frege, that counting registers more than numbers, it registers objects – in this case people – falling under categories. If Lacan argues, on the contrary, that there are real objects that are not reducible to any category, this is because he seems to draw a different, a more basic lesson from Frege: in order for counting to be possible in the first place, the set of numbers must register one category under which *no* objects fall. The category is that of the 'not-identical-to-itself'; the number of objects subsumed by it is zero. Our argument will be that it is precisely this principle that establishes the link between detective fiction and statistics. The group of suspects that forms around the murdered corpse and the paradox of the locked room are two different phenomena that emerge simultaneously in detective fiction to confirm this hypothesis.

The implications of Frege's theory of numeration for Lacanian psychoanalysis have already been clearly spelled out by Jacques-Alain Miller in his influential article 'Suture (Elements of the Logic of the Signifier)'. But since this article has been so often misinterpreted, it will be necessary to repeat its main points here. Miller begins by noting that Frege initiated his theory by rigorously excluding from consideration the subject who counts; more precisely, Frege began by excluding the empirical subject, 'defined by attributes whose other side is political, disposing . . . of a faculty of memory necessary to close the set without the loss of any of the interchangeable elements'.[14] From this exclusion two interrelated consequences follow:

1. Numbers can no longer be considered the neutral tool of a subject who wants to designate empirical things.
2. The question of how the no-longer-closed set of numbers, a pure and infinite series of numbers, can come to subsume objects is raised. How does the series close itself, in other words?

From the first point to the second it is clear that a distinction between things and objects is being made: objects are defined as logical entities as opposed to things, which are empirical; but what is it that allows the abolition of the thing, the suppression of all its attributes, to give rise to a logical object – to something which can be substituted for another without loss of truth?

Do not let the reference to the suppression of attributes ('whose other side is political') fool you; this question is not at all apolitical. It is, on the contrary, one of the most fundamental questions of political modernism. How, after destroying the body of the king, which formerly defined the boundary of the nation and thus closed the set of subjects belonging to it, how then does one constitute a modern nation? What is it that allows the nation to collect a vast array of people, discount all their positive differences, and count them as citizens, as members of the same set, in logical terms as identical? This question poses itself within detective fiction which, classically, begins with an amorphous and diverse collection of characters and ends with a fully constituted group. What we want to know is: what happens to produce this entity, the group? What is the operation that renders these diverse entities . . . countable?

As Miller tells us, this reduction to a purely logical object, that is, to a countable entity, requires us to conceive the concept that subsumes objects as a redoubled concept, as a concept of identity-to-a-concept. Thus, members of a modern nation do not fall under the concept 'citizens of X', but under the concept 'identical to the concept: citizens of X'. While the simple concept 'citizens of X' seeks to gather the individuals it subsumes by 'picking out' the common attribute that qualifies them for inclusion in the set, the redoubled concept gathers by reducing individuals to their identity to themselves. The circularity of this definition should alert us to the fact that we have entered the dimension of the performative. The attribute that distinguishes the objects of a numbered set does not pre-exist, but subsists in the very act of numeration. And since this attribute is simply tautological, their retroactive belonging to the nation confers on its citizens no other substantial identity or representational value.

So far this theory of numeration may not seem incompatible with the one Hacking presents. In both cases an object's existence is made to depend on its falling under a concept. The difference stems, as I have said, from the introduction of the concept 'not-identical-to-the-concept'. With this addition, first, the performative operation of subsumption which appears to close the set is made visible as an *effect* of this closure and, second, numbers or signifiers can no longer be thought to subsume the entire universe of objects. For the performative does not, in fact, resolve the problem we cited above, namely with the expulsion of the empirical subject, the set of numbers remains open. To any number appearing at the end of the series it is always possible to add one more. If we can detect a performative dimension in numeration, this must mean that some limit has been applied to the series of numbers. And since no exterior limit is conceivable (this is, after all, the point of the exile of the empirical subject), only one possibility remains: the limit has to be conceived as *interior* to the series. This is what the concept 'not-identical-to-itself' is: *the interior limit of the series of numbers*. That which is unthinkable within the logical functioning of numbers has to be *conceived* as unthinkable for the set of numbers to be closed, or as Miller says, *sutured*. The fact that this suturing concept does not subsume any objects should clarify any ambiguity that may persist. What is thought is not the unthinkable, but the impossibility of thinking it. The suturing concept is empty of content. In marking the limit of the series of numbers this concept at the same time severs the numbers from empirical reality and solders them to each other; in a phrase, it establishes the autonomy of the numerical field. Henceforth, the value of the numbered objects will not be determined empirically but differentially, through their relation to other numbered objects.

As we have stated, Frege's theory reveals the logic not only of the foundation and operation of the series of numbers but also of the modern state, which was, from the moment of its emergence in the nineteenth century, conceived in actuarial terms. The statistical accounting of citizens resulted in their normalization by assigning to each citizen a value that was merely the translation of its relation to the others. The modern social bond is, then, differential rather than affective; it is based not on some oceanic feeling of charity or resemblance, but on a system of formal differences.

The group forming around the corpse in detective fiction is of this modern sort; it is logically 'sustained through nothing but itself'. The best proof of this, the most telling sign that the social world of the detective is in this sense a sutured space, is the fiction's foregrounding display of the performative: in classical detective fiction it is the narrative of the investigation that produces the narrative of the crime. On this basis we will want to claim that the relations of the suspects to each other are not emotional, familial, or economic; they are not 'the molecular affinities which structure bourgeois society, the ones that reveal themselves to be the last sociological cement between individual persons in a situation in which class divisions no longer exist and despotic methods are not yet binding'.[15]

But if the relations among the suspects are, as we are arguing, differential, what then is their relation to the corpse? It is here that detective fiction appears to offer a more sophisticated explanation of these differential relations than that offered by historicists. For by producing a corpse at the very centre of the group, detective fiction acknowledges that the differential relations that sustain the group depend on an internal limit to the series of suspects. Representing this limit, the corpse becomes, in Helmut Heissenbüttel's words, 'the trace of the unnarrated': that without which the narrated world and the groups of suspects would cease to exist.[16]

Suture, in brief, supplies the logic of a paradoxical function whereby a supplementary element is *added* to the series of signifiers in order to mark the *lack* of a signifier that could close the set. The endless slide of signifiers (hence deferral of sense) is brought to a halt and allowed to function 'as if' it were a closed set through the inclusion of an element that acknowledges the impossibility of closure. The very designation of the limit is constitutive of the group, the reality the signifiers come to represent, though the group, or the reality, can no longer be thought to be entirely representable. At the risk of repetition, I would like to underline the point that must not be missed in all this argumentation: *the modern phenomenon of statistics, of counting people, would be impossible (that is, one could never convert a disparate array of persons within the empirical field into categories of persons) without the addition of a nonempirical object* (Lacan calls this the object *a*) *which closes the field. Within detective fiction the strongest evidence of the obligatory addition of this object by statistics is the paradox of the locked room.*

We may now return to the assembly line scene that Hitchcock planned for *North by Northwest* to observe this paradox at work. Although the corpse that tumbles out of the car – whose assembly we witness, piece by piece, whose elements are joined before our very eyes – appears to be the very surplus element that haunts every symbolic structure and thus allows the articulation of its parts, this corpse does not function in the same way as the one that organizes the group of suspects. For the locked-room paradox is only comprehensible if we view the surplus element not as the corpse itself, but as that which allows the corpse to be pulled out of an apparently sealed space. The logic that says that an element is added to the structure in order to mark what is lacking in it should not lead us to imagine this element as an isolatable excess hidden beneath the structure. The excess element is instead located on the same surface as the structure, that is, it is manifest in the latter's very functioning. It is under the species of default that the excess marker of lack appears, in the internal limitation that prevents the signifier from coinciding with itself. It is in the fact that a signifier is unable to signify itself, but must always call on another in an infinite appeal to one signifier more, that language's internal limit is located.

This means what? That if one person, to take a classical example, says 'X went to the well', and another reports that 'X went to the place where ruffians gather', we cannot treat the two statements as substitutable on the grounds that they have the same referent, for this constitutes the purest form of the realist imbecility. What this error imagines is that the referent contains all its possible descriptions. But if the logic of the signifier follows Frege's elucidation of it, then it is the fact that the two statements are treated as substitutable that allows us to say they have the same referent, and not the other way around. What happens then to the referent? Simply this: it is no longer able to contain all its possible descriptions. For if there is no metalanguage, no external limit to the set of signifiers, if every signifier must appeal to another for interpretation, then it is no longer possible to complete the description of any space, to imagine a space that would contain all its possible descriptions.

It is for this reason that the locked room is always breached in detective fiction. Not because every private space has always already been intruded upon by the public forces of the symbolic, but because in the symbolic the real always intrudes. The room cannot be locked because its details can never be completely enumerated; their list is never countable. The detective, therefore, is not, as is commonly believed, on the side of metalanguage, of the reparation of the signifier's default. He is, instead, on the side of the failure of metalanguage, he represents the always open possibility of one signifier more. Out of every locked room he is always able to extract a letter, a corpse, a clue that was literally undetectable before he arrived on the scene. It is the signifying description of the scene and not the 'scene itself', the referent, that is submitted to the work of detection. And not in order to penetrate the language of the description to discern the scene beneath, but to demonstrate that the surface of language never covers a depth: the clue is always found in the most conspicuous place.

We might even argue that the detective distinguishes himself from the police by virtue of his passion for ignorance, not for eliminating it. For while the police search for the telling clue, the index, in the belief that at this point reality 'impresses' itself on the symbolic, 'brushes up against' and thereby disambiguates it, the detective approaches the index as the point where the real makes itself felt in the symbolic, that is as the point at which the symbolic visibly *fails* to disambiguate itself. Dashiell Hammett's 'Bodies Piled Up' contains an excellent illustration of this point; here the *modus operandi* of detection is explicitly described thus:

> From any crime to its author there is a trail. It may be . . . obscure; but since matter cannot move without disturbing other matter along its path, there always is – there must be – a trail of some sort. And finding such trails is what a detective is paid to do.[17]

While this description sounds as though it belongs more readily to the genre of the police procedural, the clue upon which the solution pivots belies this assumption. As long as it is believed that it was these bodies piled up in room 906 that were the murderer's targets, the investigation remains stalled. In order to solve the crime, someone must first realize that the murderer mistook room 906 for the room of his intended victim, who was actually registered in room 609. How does the investigation arrive at this realization? By noting that the murderer would, when he glanced at the hotel register, be looking at it upside-down. But 609 read upside-down still reads 609. Yes, the reasoning goes, but the murderer in his furtive haste would have forgotten this and would have automatically made an adjustment for the error which, in fact, did not exist.

The detective, like the police, believes that the criminal leaves traces in endless incriminating details; what he denies – and what is denied by the example above – is the possibility of deducing the criminal from his traces. The detective does not refute the belief that the criminal author reveals himself completely and exclusively in his criminal works; he simply, but critically, denies that the evidence itself can account for the way it gives evidence. There is a gap, a distance between the evidence and that which the evidence establishes, which means that there is something which is *not* visible in the evidence: the principle by which the trail attaches itself to the criminal. The registration of the room number 906 does provide a clue essential to the solution of the crime, but however exhaustively we examine this piece of evidence, we will never arrive at the principle of how it leads us to the criminal perpetrator.

Here interpretation must intervene – interpretation which, Lacan says, is desire. All of a sudden it becomes possible to understand what he means. To say that the detective manifests his *desire* in interpreting the clues is not to say that in the absence of complete knowledge a historical or personal bias directs the interpretation. Desire is not an impurity that threatens the 'objectivity' of the detective, but the quasi-transcendental principle that guarantees it. In other words, desire does not impose a bias but supposes a gap: the detective reads the evidence by positing an empty beyond, a residue that is irreducible to the evidence while being, at the same time, completely demonstrated in it. Interpretation means that evidence tells us everything but how to read it. Beyond the evidence, in other words, there is no other reality, nothing – except the principle that guides our reading of it. One of the primary imperatives of detective fiction may be stated in the following way: desire must be taken literally. This imperative is a positive and more complete restatement of the well-known stricture against the introduction in detective fiction of some new reality – a trapdoor or a suspect who is not already known to the reader – for the purpose of solving the crime. This stricture does not mean simply that the culprit must be one from the known gallery of suspects, it also means that he is himself not to be reintroduced as another reality, a substantial entity beyond the trail of evidence he leaves. The culprit is consubstantial if not with the evidence *per se*, then with a reading of it; he is no more nor less than this. The desiring detective, then, concludes by taking the culprit's desire literally, seeing the way it manifests itself in the clues. In this way does the detective make buffoons of the police, who busy themselves with the senseless task of ignoring desire and taking the *evidence* literally, conflating signifiers and signifieds.

The gap that necessitates interpretation, that prevents the signifier from signifying itself, is caused, as I have argued, by the absence of one signifier, a final signifier that would establish an end to the chain. It is because this final signifier (or number) is missing that detective fiction and statistics are, as we have been arguing, possible. On the other hand, the absence of this signifier makes the sexual relation impossible. This signifier, if it existed, would be the signifier for woman. As anyone with even a passing acquaintance with the genre knows, the absence of this signifier is evident in detective fiction not only in the nontotalizable space that produces the paradox of the locked room, but also in the unfailing exclusion of the sexual relation. The detective is structurally forbidden any involvement with a woman.

In the middle of writing this, I take a break to watch *Columbo* on television. He is badgering, patronizing one of the characters, which means, according to the formula, that this character is the guilty suspect. Columbo asks this man, who is running for Congress, for an autograph for his wife. As everyone knows, the wife of this most uxorious of detectives is simply the condition of the impossibility of his involvement in any sexual relation; she never appears, must never appear, in the diegetic space. The congressman agrees to the autograph. Taking a piece of paper from his drawer and beginning to write on it, he asks Columbo, 'What is your wife's name?' – 'Mrs Columbo', is the only, and from the matter-of-fact look on the detective's face, the only possible reply.

DETOUR THROUGH THE DRIVE

Whilst this elision of the signifier for woman can be shown to define the fictional space of classical detective fiction, the very presence of Phyllis Dietrichson, *Double Indemnity*'s femme fatale, reminds us that the film constructs a different sort of fictional world. Although it is inconceivable for Keyes, as a classical detective, to have any involvement with a woman, it is equally inconceivable for Neff, as a *noir* hero, to escape such involvement. One of the most theoretically compelling aspects of *Double Indemnity* is its inscription not only of this difference, but of the very topological incompatibility of classical detective fiction and *film noir*. In one scene Neff receives a call from Phyllis while Keyes is in his office. Since Keyes seems disinclined to leave, Neff must conduct the entire conversation in his mentor's presence. The uncomfortableness of this situation, combined with the shot/reverse-shot cutting between Phyllis on one end of the line and Neff (together with Keyes) on the other, serves to underline this incompatibility. In another scene, as Neff awaits a visit from Phyllis, Keyes drops by his apartment unexpectedly. While Neff attempts to usher Keyes out, Phyllis arrives and has to wait behind the door until Keyes walks down the corridor toward the elevator before she can slip, unseen, into Neff's apartment. Throughout the film, Phyllis and Keyes have a 'revolving door' relationship; they do not and cannot occupy the same space. But this relationship is trivialized, its real stakes obscured if one interprets its either/or dimension in strictly narrative terms. The choice that Neff faces is not one between two people, a mentor and a lover, but between the world of classical detection and *film noir*.

One of the most common descriptions of the historical shift between these two worlds makes identification the pivotal term; that is, it is argued that the detective comes to identify more and more closely with his criminal adversary until, at the end of the *film noir* cycle he has become the criminal himself, as here in *Double Indemnity*, where Neff is both investigator and murderer. The moment Neff stops 'watching the customers to make sure that they don't crook the house' and gets to thinking how he could crook the house himself 'and do it smart', he enters the *noir* world. But if the reversal were that simple, the choices that symmetrical, if *film noir* depended merely on the hero's rejection of a lofty goal for a base one, one would be forced to wonder why the hero always ends up not getting the money and not getting the woman.

Double Indemnity (Billy Wilder, 1944)

I would like, then, to offer a different explanation of Neff's choice to try to 'crook the house'. This explanation is derived from the *fort/da* game that Freud describes in *Beyond the Pleasure Principle*. I propose that we consider this little game of hide-and-seek as the elementary cell of detective fiction – in both its incarnations. A few pages after his original analysis of it, Freud adds that his grandson later developed a variant of the game. In this later version the child himself functioned as the cotton reel; hiding beneath the mirror for a time, he would suddenly jump up to observe the emergence of his mirror reflection. Now there is, it would seem, a fundamental distinction to be made between the two versions of the game. For when the child throws the cotton reel, he throws that part of himself that is lost with his entry into language. The child thus situates himself in the field of language; he chooses *sense* rather than the being that sense continually fails to secure. He thus becomes a subject of desire, lacking-in-being. But when the child takes up the position of the cotton reel, he situates himself in the field of being; he chooses being, *jouissance*, rather than sense.

This distinction causes us to note a difference in the two forms of repetition that the games instantiate. In the first game it is failure, or desire, that propels the repetition. Something escapes, or to use one of Lacan's phrases, something 'does not stop *not* writing itself', in the field of representation structured by the game, and so the game is repeated endlessly with the hope, but without the possibility, of capturing that which escapes it. In the second game repetition is driven not by desire but by satisfaction: some satisfaction is repeated, 'does not stop *writing* itself' in the game.

I am proposing that the inversion that defines the shift from classical detection to *film noir* is to be understood not in terms of identification but in terms of the choice between sense and being, or – in the dialect of psychoanalysis – between desire and drive.[18] Lacan has argued that this shift describes a general historical transition whose process we are still witnessing: the old modern order of desire, ruled over by an oedipal father, has begun to be replaced by a new order of the drive, in which we no longer have recourse to the protections against *jouissance* that the oedipal father once offered. These protections have been eroded by our society's fetishization of being, that is of *jouissance*. Which is to say: we have ceased being a society that attempts to preserve the individual right to *jouissance*, to become a society that commands *jouissance* as a 'civic' duty. 'Civic' is, strictly speaking, an inappropriate adjective in this context, since these obscene importunings of contemporary society entail the destruction of the *civitas* itself, of increasingly larger portions of our public space. We no longer attempt to safeguard the empty 'private' space that counting produced as a residue, but to dwell within this space exclusively. The ambition of *film noir* seems to have been monitory: it sought to warn us that this fetishization of private *jouissance* would have mortal consequences for society, would result in a 'rise of racism',[19] in ever smaller factions of people proclaiming their duty-bound devotion to their own special brand of enjoyment, unless we attempted to reintroduce some notion of community, of sutured totality to which we could partially, performatively belong. Thus, of all the admonitory ploys in the arsenal of *film noir* surely the most characteristic was its insistence that from the moment the choice of private enjoyment over community is made, one's privacy ceases to be something one savours when sheltered from prying eyes (so that, as is the case with Keyes, no one can be sure that he even has a private life) and becomes instead something one visibly endures – like an unending, discomfiting rain. In *film noir* privacy establishes itself as the rule, not as a clandestine exception. This changes the very character of privacy and, indeed, of 'society' in general – which begins with the introduction of this new mode of being to shatter into incommensurable fragments.

THE VOICE AND THE VOICE-OVER

If there is one feature of *film noir* that seems to stand in the way of the acceptance of our thesis, it is the voice-over narration, which definitively links the hero to speech and hence, we would suppose, to community, to sense. Speech, as we know – language – is the death of the thing, it contributes to the drying up of *jouissance*. And nothing has seemed more obvious in the criticism of *film noir* than this association of death with speech, for the voice-over is regularly attached to a dead narrator, whether literally as in *Sunset Boulevard* and *Laura*, metaphorically as in *Detour*, or virtually as in *Double Indemnity*.

But before we can contest this reading of the voice-over in *film noir*, we must first confront a certain theorization of the voice in cinema. In an excellent article entitled 'The Silences of the Voices', Pascal Bonitzer makes a distinction, which will form the basis of a great deal of subsequent theorizing, between the disembodied voice of the documentary voice-over – a voice that remains off-screen throughout the film and thus never becomes anchored to a body imaged on screen – and the voice-over that at some point becomes attached to a visible body. Neff's voice, and that of other *noir* narrators, belongs to the latter category and, in fact, Bonitzer uses the example of a late *film noir*, *Kiss Me Deadly* (Robert Aldrich, 1955), to great advantage in furthering his argument. Throughout most of the film Dr Soberin, the arch criminal, is absent from the screen, we hear only his off-screen voice and see only his blue suede shoes. At the end of the film, however, he appears bodily in the space for the first time and, almost immediately, is shot and falls dead to the bottom of the frame. That is to say, at the moment the voice is anchored to a body, it relinquishes its apparent omnipotence and is instead 'submitted to the destiny of the body'; corporealized, it is rendered 'decrepit and mortal'.[20] The voice, we could say, dies in the body. In opposition to this, the noncorporealized voice of the classical documentary issues from a space other than that on the screen, an unrepresented, undetermined space; thus transcending the visible, determined field, the voice maintains its absolute power over the image, its knowledge remains unimpugned.

This distinction between the disembodied voice, which conveys knowledge and power, and the embodied voice, which conveys the limitation of both, is underwritten by a simple opposition between the universal and the particular, the latter being conceived as that which ruins the possibility of the former. The embodied voice, particularity, and lack of knowledge line up on one side against the disembodied voice, universality, and knowledge on the other. Within this framework of nestled oppositions, another notion is introduced toward the end of the article, that of the 'body of the voice'. Bonitzer effortlessly sweeps this notion beneath the 'particular' flank of his oppositions, using it to argue that any voice at all, any commentary, threatens the assumption of universality upon which documentary realism depends. For though the voice may never become visibly anchored in a place, place may be audibly anchored in the voice, thus betraying it through accents that indicate its regional, class, sexual, or some other rootedness. By 'the body of the voice' Bonitzer means any accent that particularizes the voice, spoiling its ideal atony, hence the omniscience and authority that are assumed to define the neutral, unaccented voice-over. Once the body of the voice becomes audible, it betrays 'a subject fallen to the rank of an object and unmasked. . . . [The body of this voice is] its death to meaning. . . . The voice . . . "labors". It is perceived as an accent . . . and this accent neutralizes meaning.'[21]

But the films of Marguerite Duras, which Bonitzer mentions in his article, manage to perturb his argument more than they bear it out. Consider *India Song*. In this film the images are almost completely silent. The voices all issue from off screen (as in a documentary), though they are all heavily 'accented'. We can speak properly here of the 'laboring' of the voices, their grain. Distinctly female, except for one at the end, they seem to suffer throughout the film. One could say that they are the very embodiment of everything the documentary voice is not supposed to be: they are 'burning' voices, seemingly 'ephemeral, fragile, troubled'. But while they appear to comment on the images on the screen, there is in what they say a constant ambiguity of reference, since they may also be commenting on their own situation. 'The heat!' 'Can't bear it. No, can't bear it!' We begin to be unsure whether it is the heat that suffuses the diegetic space or the off-screen space that these voices find insupportable. Sometimes they dispense altogether with any pretence of commenting on what we see on screen and speak to each other of their own situation.

What are we to make of the fact that these voices are situated permanently off screen? that they are so painfully, burningly 'grainy'? The standard argument would probably try to convince us that they were 'desiring' rather than omniscient voices; that they express a yearning and loss rather than power; that they reduce their bearers to a merely mortal, corporeal existence. Yet this description clearly misses its mark, for these off-screen voices cannot be construed as mortal. They are, as Duras defines them, *intemporal voices*; they cannot be situated in – nor submitted to the ravages of – time or place. This is not to deny that the voices are associated with death, but to note that this death brings no expiry; rather, in them, death persists. The voices bear the burden of a living death, a kind of inexhaustible suffering.

Though *film noir* does not, like Duras, acoustically mark the break between image and voice, it does, I would argue, similarly tear the voice from the image in a way that remains unexplained – is effaced even – by the commonplace observation that the *noir* hero's voice-over narration simply diverges from the *truth* of the image. Seeing in *film noir* the evidence of a post-war waning of masculine self-certainty and power, this observation reads the grain or labouring of the voice-over as well as its periodic diegeticization as proof of the faltering of the hero's knowledge, his inability to control or comprehend the image, which then often seems to belie what he says. It is the pertinence for *film noir* of this definition of the voice-image relation that must be challenged, together with the pop-psychological diagnosis of post-war male malaise that has lent it credibility. I will continue to argue instead that the aspect of this period that most concerns the development of *film noir* is the perceptible ascendancy of drive over desire. To this shift a whole range of 'social' policies encouraging suburban expansion and ethnic and racial segregation (mandated most notably, but not exclusively, by the Federal Housing Administration, which was founded in 1934 and gained momentum only after the World War Two) clearly bear witness.

There is no need, however, to limit our observation to these policies, for a number of other phenomena will just as readily attest to this shift, including the vogue for existentialism, which also reached its peak after the war. From the moment the first hard-boiled novels were translated into French in the Série noire, the existentialists recognized in this new type of detective novel something of their own philosophy. What they must have recognized in the novels was their commitment to the priority of being – or, in existentialist parlance, the in-itself – over sense. Existentialism is, in this regard, a philosophy of drive, unthinkable before drive's historical overturning of desire. The problematic of duty or responsibility so crucial to existentialism is equally central to *film noir*, from Sam Spade's moral code (his ultimate refusal, for example of Brigid O'Shaunessy: 'I won't because all of me wants to') to the extravagant, delirious form it takes in Mike Hammer's contempt for death itself, his mad vengeance against injustice. The particular treachery of these ethical vocations (and it is the articulation of this treachery that so fascinates us in both the philosophy and the films) stems from the extreme difficulty of fathoming the Other, society itself, from the perspective of the drive.

How does this diagnosis of the post-war period bear on our understanding of the voice in *film noir*? It supports our perception that however contiguous it is with the diegetic space, the space of the voice-over is nevertheless radically heterogeneous to it. It is to this fact – and not to the limited knowledge of the bearer of the voice – that we ascribe the apparent incompatibilities between image and voice. What is most questionable about standard interpretations of *film noir* is their insistence on subsuming the function of the voice under the category of commentary, since what seems to me distinctive about this voice-over narration is the way it refuses to spend itself as commentary. Certainly this narration performs the same function that every speech does: it vehicles a message addressed to another. In *Double Indemnity*, for example, the voice-over is explicitly addressed to Keynes. But the film also deliberately severs this speech from its addressee in order to return us repeatedly to the image of a solitary Neff, seated in an empty office at night, speaking into a dictaphone. In these scenes the destiny of the voice-over seems not to be exhausted by its function as message. An excess of pleasure, a private enjoyment, seems to adhere in the act of speaking as such as Neff contents himself, beyond the content of the message, with the act itself. This is to say that the voice-over narration serves less to describe or attempt to describe the world that the narrator inhabits than to present that world at the point where he is abstracted from it. Neff clings not to the community with which speech puts him in touch, but to the enjoyment that separates him from that community.

We can begin to grasp what is at stake here by returning to our discussion of the 'body of the voice'. Though Bonitzer offers this notion as the equivalent of Roland Barthes's 'grain of the voice', the two notions are, in fact, quite different. The body of which Barthes speaks 'has no civil identity, no "personality"'.[22] In no way, then, can it be considered the 'accent of an era, a class, a regime',[23] in no way can it be imagined to betray anything like the caricatured types appropriately indicated by Bonitzer in quotation marks: 'the paranoid anticommunist', 'the jovial Stalinist'.[24] The grain is not the index of a particularity with any content, social or otherwise, it is the index of a *particular absolute*. This means that it marks the voice as belonging to *this* speaker, uniquely, even though the grain must not be considered 'personal: it expresses nothing' of the speaker.[25]

The grain of the voice has no content; it appears only as the 'friction' (Barthes's word) one hears when one perceives the materiality of language, its resistance to meaning. The grain works in the voice as index in the same way as the index works in detective fiction: to register a resistance to or failure of meaning. It is this friction that prompts interpretation. *Don't read my words; read my desire!* This is what the grain of the voice urges. That is, don't take me literally (that is, universally), but realize that these words are the unique bearers of my desire. Functioning as limit, the grain of the voice does spell the collapse of the universal, of the universality of sense; some excess of being over sense suggests itself and begins to undermine knowledge. But it is the knowledge of the listener that is in question here, not that of the enunciator. The enunciator becomes all at once not unknowing (as in Bonitzer's account), but unknown, voluptuously an X. The phenomenon just described, and fully exhibited in Barthes's essay, is that of transference. Confronted with the limits of our knowledge, we fictively add to the field of the Other, to the voice, an X, the mark of our nonknowledge. This simple addition is enough to eroticize the voice, to transform our relation to it to one of desire, of interpretation. As Barthes attempts to elucidate the difference between two singers, Panzera and Fischer-Dieskau, we come at first to see his distinction as completely arbitrary, subjective. He isolates in the voices no positive feature that would help us to understand his preference for Panzera, in whose voice he hears 'the tongue, the glottis, the teeth, the mucous membranes, the nose'. One cannot be trained to hear vocal 'features' such as this; we learn nothing that might be called 'music appreciation' from Barthes's essay. And yet there is clearly a difference between the two voices; it amounts basically to this: the addition of an X to Panzera's voice which turns Barthes's relation to it into one of desire. One must be careful, however, not to dismiss this relation as simply subjective: because the X is the cause of desire and not the other way around, we cannot claim that Barthes imposes something of himself onto the voice. He simply 'sets up a new scheme of evaluation which . . . certainly . . . is individual'.[26] Thus do relations of desire preserve particularity, difference, by supposing, via the grain of the voice, a private beyond, a being that does not surrender itself in speech.

When desire gives way to drive, this private beyond no longer remains hidden. What is involved in the drive, Lacan tells us, is a 'making oneself heard' or 'making oneself seen';[27] that is to say, the intimate core of our being, no longer sheltered by sense, ceases to be supposed and suddenly becomes exposed. It thrusts itself forward, pushing through the surface of speech to take up a position alongside it. This does not mean that the merely supposed, hence empty, domain of private being emerges unveiled, its contents finally visible for anyone to see. In shifting its topological position, being does not lose its essential nature as resistance to sense: what is made audible – or visible – is the void as such, contentless and nonsensical. The 'making oneself heard' or 'making oneself seen' of the drive must not be confused with a desire to hear/be heard or a desire to see/be seen, since the very reciprocity that is implied by desire is denied in the drive. The intimate kernel of our being is susceptible neither in its hidden nor in its exposed form to 'objective' knowledge; in exposing itself it does not seek to communicate itself. Or, we might put it this way: surfacing within the phenomenal field, private being, *jouissance*, nevertheless does not take on a phenomenal form. Phenomenal/nonphenomenal – this (more accurately, perhaps, than inside/outside) names the division troubled by drive. It does not communicate itself by exposing itself.

In *film noir* the grain of the voice surfaces alongside the diegetic reality. Issuing from the point of death, it marks not some ideal point where the subject would finally be absorbed into his narrative, used up; it materializes rather that which can never be incorporated into the narrative. Death becomes in *film noir* the positivization of the narrator's absence from the very diegetic reality his speech describes.

LOCKED ROOM/LONELY ROOM

In *Double Indemnity*, Neff's absence from the narrative – that is, from the social space – is imaged as I have said in the repeated scene of a confession that we are refusing to take purely as such. The clue that allows Keyes to begin to unravel the Dietrichson case should not be lost on us; Keyes realizes that the fact that Mr Dietrichson did not put in a claim when he broke his leg is clear proof that the man who boarded the train on crutches must have been someone else. The one detail that trips Neff up, his 'blind spot', is the one that ultimately distinguishes him as a *noir* hero: he cannot think of claiming the protection of the law. For Neff, and his like, the benevolent–impotent Other no longer exists and Neff can, then, no longer seek from it what it is able to provide: protection from *jouissance*. Neff is thus a man who enjoys too much: too much to surrender his words to another, when they hold for him such exquisite pleasure. The difference between the crime film and *film noir* amounts to this question of enjoyment: in the crime film, despite their transgressions of the law, the criminals are still ruled by the impotent Other whom they, understandably, try to cheat; in *film noir* the reign of the Other has been superseded, its law is not so much transgressed as disbanded. The emergence of the enunciation on a level with the narrative statement constitutes our proof of this.

But there exists further evidence. Since it is the cloaking of the enunciative instance, its marked retreat from the phenomenal field, that defines the very space of classical detection, we would expect the surfacing of the enunciation to produce within *film noir* a wholly different sort of space. This is exactly what happens; the infinite, inexhaustible space of the older model – exemplarily realized in the paradox of the locked room – gives way in *film noir* to its inverse; the lonely room, such as the one in which Neff utters his confession. For Neff sits in one of those vacant office buildings, those plain and, for the moment, uninhabited spaces that constitute the characteristic architecture of *film noir*. Office buildings late at night, in the early hours of the morning; abandoned warehouses; hotels mysteriously untrafficked; eerily empty corridors: these are the spaces that supplant the locked room. One is struck first of all by the curious depopulation of these spaces, and then by their spareness. In *The Big Heat* (Fritz Lang, 1953), Debbie Marsh, looking around the woefully underdecorated hotel room in which Dave Bannion temporarily resides, delivers an accurate appraisal of this typically *noir* interior. 'Oh, early nothing!' she quips. But it would be wrong to stop at the observation that these lonely rooms are simply empty of people and decoration. More fundamentally, what *film noir* presents to us are spaces that have been emptied of desire. Or: the emptiness of the room indicates less that there is nothing in them than that nothing more can be got out of them. They are no longer interpretable, in the strict sense: that is, they will never yield anything new and cannot, therefore, hide anything.

Primarily, it is the hero himself who suffers the loss of a hiding place. Think, for example, of Al Roberts in *Detour* (Edgar Ulmer, 1945), who at the end of the film walks resignedly, without wondering how he has been found, toward the police car that stops to pick him up; or Vincent Parry in *Dark Passage* (Delmer Daves, 1947), who is recognized wherever he goes, no matter how late at night or that he has been totally transformed by plastic surgery. Or, think of an earlier moment in *Detour* when Roberts's private voice-over contemplation of the events leading up to his current desperate situation is cut short by this venomously delivered question from the hitchhiker he has recently picked up: 'Where did you put the body?' All of a sudden the voice-over no longer contains his privacy, the seam separating it and him from this cruel passenger melts as the hiss of her viciousness marks the edges of their beings coming into contact. It is almost as if she has read his thoughts and yet she does not really respond directly to his words on the soundtrack. Here we find ourselves in that paranoid universe which *film noir* is so often taken to be. But while this paranoia is usually assumed to indicate an erosion of privacy that permits the Other to penetrate, to read one's innermost thoughts, *film noir* helps us to see that the opposite is true. It is on the public level that the erosion has taken place. No social distance separates individuals, no social 'clothing' protects their innermost being. But since there is no distance to traverse, no layers of disguise to penetrate, the exposure of being is not preceded by any ignorance or curiosity. *Noir* heroes may never successfully hide out in their urban spaces, but neither are they seriously pursued. Nor does their being become readable, in the proper sense, that is, no discursive knowledge is gained by its exposure. It is not Roberts's words, his thoughts, that are revealed to Vera, but rather that which his thinking ordinarily preserves: his being.

In *Double Indemnity* Neff's decision to try to 'crook the house' issues in a situation that is not comprehensible in strictly narrative terms. Henceforth Neff and Phyllis will refrain from meeting in private and will be forced to rendezvous only in public places. Jerry's Market becomes their meeting place. This narrativized description of what takes place does not quite make sense. Wouldn't there be more rather than less risk in their public encounters? Wouldn't the hatching of the plan require private consultation? What this description fails to grasp, however, is that within the terms of the *noir* universe Jerry's Market *is* a private space. It is empty except for a few shoppers who take no interest in their existence, and Neff and Phyllis are in little danger of discovery here, though they are equally incapable of concealing themselves. Phyllis's dark glasses are as humorously ineffectual, and unnecessary, as Vincent Parry's plastic surgery. This seems, in fact, to be the point of both the glasses and the surgical bandages. Every disguise turns out to be futile within a space defined by the drive, where what is at stake is making one's private being seen.

But how does *film noir* exhibit the workings of drive, the exposure of being, when, as I have noted, this being has no phenomenal form, when it is and remains essentially contentless? How is the intrusion of the nonphenomenal private realm into the public, that is, phenomenal world made apparent in *film noir*? As Neff's crepuscular office, Jerry's Market, and the many abandoned sites in these films demonstrate, this is accomplished by adding to public spaces the very emptiness I have already described. The intrusion of the private – the object *a*, the grain of the voice – into phenomenal reality, its *addition*, is registered in the *depletion* of this reality. Lost, thereby, is the sense of solidity that ordinarily attaches to the social field, as well as the illusion of depth that underwrites this solidity. This illusion is simply the perception – unnegatable by any counter-perception – that we have never got to the bottom of our reality. It is *film noir*'s suspension of this illusion that renders it incapable of concealing anything, least of all its heroes. This is the logic that leads me to argue that Jerry's Market is a private space, that *film noir* continually exposes the landscape of privacy. In such a landscape, where private being exhibits itself as complete, as independent of the desire of others, the hero's encounters with other people will be jarring, at least (the series of women whom Marlowe meets in *The Big Sleep*), threatening

Double Indemnity (Billy Wilder, 1944)

Dark Passage (Delmer Daves, 1947)

at most. This is why the palpable claustrophobia of *noir* spaces is not at all inconsistent with their visible emptiness.

Jerry's Market is the result, then, of Neff's choice of private being, *jouissance*, rather than the signifying network that structures social reality. What he gets is being, but deprived of the inaccessibility that gave it its value: in short, he gets nothing. It would be an error, however, to think that the consequences of this choice stir in the hero a kind of 'disappointment', for it is precisely this nothing that satisfies. And therein lies the problem, the potential fatality of this choice. Despite some attempts by Hollywood – for example, the revised ending of *Double Indemnity*, which eliminates Neff's ultimate isolation in the gas chamber and substitutes instead the reciprocity of the cigarette lighting ritual between Neff and Keyes – to disguise the unabatedness of this satisfaction, there is still evidence that the heroes in these films often cling to the satisfactions of this nothing to the bitter end.

LETHAL *JOUISSANCE* AND THE FEMME FATALE

This is not to say that there are no defences against the drive, no means of curbing its satisfactions. Drive is, of course, not instinct, and just as in the symbolic realm some real is manifest (in the failures of the signifier), so in the realm of the real some symbolic makes itself felt (in the very repetitions of the drive's circuits). That is: the drive is not indifferent to symbolic intervention, which is available in *film noir* on two different levels. The first level is that of the filmic system. Here we encounter the deep-focus photography and the chiaroscuro, 'expressionist', lighting that pervade this cycle of films. The function of these devices only becomes clear when we consider them in relation to the empty, private spaces that compose the primary territory of *film noir*.[28] Through the use of wide-angle lenses and low-key lighting these spaces are represented as deep and deceptive, as spaces in which all sorts of unknown entities may hide. One must distinguish between the genuine illusion of depth – which is a matter of desire, of not knowing something and wanting, therefore, to know more – and the ersatz representation of depth – which is simply a matter of a technical skill in rendering, of verisimilitude – if one wants to avoid being misled by the shadows and depth of field that so famously characterize the *noir* image. The visual techniques of *film noir* are placed in the service of creating an artificial replication of depth *in the image* in order to make up for, to compensate for, the absence of depth *in the narrative spaces*; that is, these techniques are placed in the service of a defence against the drive. The makeshift domain of illusion that they create erects a façade of nonknowledge and thus of depth, as a substitute for and protection against their dangerous, and potentially lethal lack in the *noir* universe itself. These techniques of deception install a kind of ersatz symbolic as bulwark against its diegetic collapse. It is only because this distinction between the technical replication or representation of depth and the illusion of depth that depends on the signifier's failure has not been taken into account in the analysis of these films that the *noir* universe has been perceived as essentially deceptive, though it is, in fact, a world in which nothing can lie hidden, everything must come to light. This is really the dark truth of *film noir*.

On the narrative level the defence against the drive takes another, but no less genre-defining form: that of the femme fatale. The femme fatale is in everyone's estimation one of the most fascinating elements of the *noir* world. As such she has provoked a great deal of critical attention, especially from feminists who have wanted to see in this powerful female figure some proof that Hollywood's tendency toward a 'minorization' of women was not absolute. These women had a kind of strength, a kind of privilege and command over the diegetic space that most of their cinematic sisters did not. And yet they seemed always to be presented from the point of view of the male protagonists. Christine Gledhill was able to see in their strength a sort of rebellion against the point of view that could only barely contain them:

> Thus, though the heroines of film noir, by virtue of male control of the voice-over, flash-back structure, are rarely accorded the full subjectivity and fully expressed point of view of psychologically realist fiction . . . their *performance* of the roles accorded them . . . fore-grounds the fact of their image as an artifice and suggests another place behind the image where the woman might be.[29]

The quasi-Brechtian interpretation of the women's tenuous habitation of their roles is questionable, but an important perception underlies this interpretation: the femme fatale does have an initially dependent and visibly artificial existence within this nightmarish world.

Consider the scene of Neff's second visit to the Dietrichson home, arranged by Phyllis so that her husband can hear Neff's sales pitch. Her husband is not in, of course, nor is the maid, though Phyllis plays it – unconvincingly – as if she had forgotten that it is Nettie's day off. She has not forgotten at all; her deceit is transparent to us and to Neff. If the femme fatale is the embodiment of deceit, it is always a deceit of this order: transparent, painted on; a deceit that does not disguise itself. Theoretically, nothing precludes this visible deceit from hiding another, but in the world of *film noir* this second-order deception never takes hold. The femme fatale remains a two-dimensional figure with no hidden sides; the deception is *only* up-front. In other words, although she, too, seems to function, for the hero this time, as a sort of proto-illusionistic element in *film noir*'s nonillusionist field, she usually fails to become a proper barrier, to protect him in the way real illusion does. Rather than screening *jouissance*, she hoards it.

For the femme fatale also functions in another strategy of defence. Having chosen *jouissance*, the *noir* hero risks its shattering, annihilating effects, which threaten his very status as subject. In order to *indemnify* himself against these dangers, he creates in the femme fatale a *double* to which he surrenders the *jouissance* he cannot himself sustain. That is, he tries to take some distance from himself, to initiate some alterity in his relation to himself: to split himself, we could say, not as the desiring subject between sense and being, but between knowledge and *jouissance*. Giving up his right to enjoyment, the hero contracts with the femme fatale that she will henceforth command it from him, as levy.

In *Double Indemnity* we are not left simply to surmise the existence of this contract, we actually witness its drawing up in the scene in which Mr Dietrichson is tricked into signing a document other than the one he thinks he is signing. The document he in fact signs is the contract that binds Neff to the will of Phyllis. Initially entered into through an act of the hero's own volition and in order to forestall his ruin (that is, to impose restrictions on the drive's satisfactions), this document nevertheless fails to secure the hoped-for stability and instead leads Neff to his absolute destruction.

The problem stems from the greediness of the femme fatale. In *Double Indemnity* as well as in *Detour, Gilda, Kiss Me Deadly, The Maltese Falcon* (to name only those films that come immediately to mind), explicit reference is made to the femme fatale's greed, her constant demand for more and more satisfaction. The more the hero devotes himself to procuring it for her, the more she delights in hoarding it. The contract thus binds the hero to a lethal relation, one that goes from bad to worse. Neff's turning-down of his promotion is only the first step toward his eventual abdication of life itself. It is this progressive instability – which is enabled, but not necessitated by the contract – that accounts not only for the regularity of the final, mutually destructive encounter between hero and femme fatale, but for the escalation of violence in the *film noir* cycle as a whole. The social contract between the *noir* hero and the femme fatale – social because it attempts to erect some community within the private space of *jouissance* – turns out, in these cases, to be an ineffectual and ultimately deadly stand-in for the social bond that classical detective fiction had earlier described.

Slavoj Žižek, following up remarks made by Lacan in his 'Seminar on "The Purloined Letter" ', has noted that one of the differences between classical detection and the hard-boiled/*noir* variety is that in the former the detective accepts money for his services, while in the latter he does not.[30] It is Al Roberts (in *Detour*), however, who supplies the most revealing reason for the *noir* protagonist's inability to deal with symbolic currency. Reluctant to accept a ten-dollar tip for his piano-playing, he spits out his definition of money: 'a piece of paper crawling with germs'. What happens, I have tried to argue, is this: the neutral, dead system of symbolic community and exchange that had supported the classical world has given way in *film noir* to a world that crawls with private enjoyment and thus rots the old networks of communication. Something similar happens to numbers. Where formerly the counting of people, statistics, had established a network of relations that protected – and protected us from – private enjoyment, *film noir* allows us to witness the spoiling of this network that takes place when privacy comes to the surface. Seen from Keyes's perspective, statistics enable the discovery of new facts; from Neff's perspective they threaten annihilation since, to him, they represent the existence of other people. And in the *noir* world, this is the greatest horror.

NOTES

1. Marjorie Nicolson, 'The Professor and the Detective' (1929) in *The Art of the Mystery Story* (New York: Simon and Schuster, 1946), p. 126.

2. Ian Hacking, 'Biopower and the Avalanche of Printed Numbers', *Humanities in Society*, vol. 5, nos. 3/4 (Summer/Fall 1982), p. 281.

3. Hacking's work does not acknowledge this effect of statistics; it is Claude Lefort's remarks on numbers in *Democracy and Political Theory* (Minneapolis: University of Minnesota Press, 1988, pp. 18–19) which directed my attention to this important effect.

4. Ian Hacking, 'How Should We Do the History of Statistics?', *I & C*, no. 8 (Spring 1982), p. 25.

5. For a concise statement of this thesis, see François Ewald, 'Norms, Discipline and the Law', *Representations*, 30 (Spring 1990), pp. 138–61.

6. Ian Hacking, 'Nineteenth-Century Cracks in the Concept of Determinism', *Journal of the History of Ideas*, July 1983, p. 469.

7. D. A. Miller, *The Novel and the Police* (Berkeley: University of California Press, 1988).

8. The phrase is Hacking's; see his 'Making Up People', in *Reconstructing Individualism* (Stanford: Stanford University Press, 1986), pp. 222–36. Especially interesting for this discussion of *Double Indemnity* is the following passage: 'Every fact about the suicide becomes fascinating. The statisticians compose forms to be completed by doctors and police, recording everything from the time of death to the objects found in the pockets of the corpse. The various ways of killing oneself are abruptly characterized and become symbols of national character. The French favor carbon monoxide and drowning; the English hang or shoot themselves.'

9. Hacking, 'Biopower', p. 292.

10. Miller, p. 162.

11. François Truffault, *Hitchcock* (New York: Simon and Schuster, 1983), p. 257.

12. Jacques Lacan, *Book II: The Ego in Freud's Theory and in the Technique of Psychoanalysis, 1954–55*, ed. Jacques-Alain Miller (New York and London: W. W. Norton, 1988), pp. 32–3.

13. Jacques Lacan, 'Seminar on "The Purloined Letter" ', *Yale French Studies*, no. 48 (1972), p. 54.

14. Jacques-Alain Miller, 'Suture (Elements of the Logic of the Signifier)', *Screen*, vol. 18, no. 4 (Winter 1877–78), p. 27.

15. Helmut Heissenbüttel, 'The Rules of the Game of the Crime Novel', in Glenn Moste and William W. Stowe, eds., *The Poetics of Murder* (San Diego: Harcourt, Brace, and Jovanovich, 1983), p. 88.

16. It is interesting to compare Roman Jakobson's description of the differential relation. As Jakobson demonstrates, the relation between /pa/ and /ma/ is not to be understood as a simple opposition, but as *two sets of oppositions*:

between /pa/, which is itself an opposition, pure self-opposition or diacriticality, and the opposition between /pa/ and /ma/. In other words, /pa/ appears twice in these sets of oppositions, as the only element of the first opposition and as one of the elements of the second; although the second appearance retroactively effaces the first. Joel Fineman, in 'The Structure of Allegorical Desire' (*October*, no. 12, Spring 1980), p. 59, summarizes Jakobson's argument thus: ' . . . /pa/ loses its original status as mark of pure diacriticality when it is promoted to the level of the significant signifier within the system as a whole. This new significant /pa/ is utterly unrelated to the first simply diacritical /pa/ that it replaces . . . And it is precisely this occultation of the original /pa/, now structurally unspeakable because revalued as something else entirely, that allows the system to function as a structure in the first place.'

In other words, the articulation of /pa/ and /ma/ can only take place by rendering visible a certain empty place, a certain structural impossibility, which is not purely excluded from the system. A diagram of Jakobson's description would look like this:

The shaded area represents the empty place, the structural excess produced by the articulation of the two signifiers; in short, the logic of suture is discernible in Jakobson as well as in Frege.

17. Dashiell Hammett, 'Bodies Piled Up', collected in William Nolan, ed., *Black Mask Boys: Masters in the Hard-boiled School of Detective Fiction* (New York: William Morrow, 1985), p. 84.

18. Jacques-Alain Miller's unpublished 1987–88 seminar 'Ce qui fait insigne' provides the most

complete analysis to date of Lacan's distinction between desire and drive.

19. Jacques Lacan, *Television: A Challenge to the Psychoanalytic Establishment*, ed. Joan Copjec (New York and London: W. W. Norton, 1990), p. 74. The filmed interview is more explicit on this point than is the published text.

20. Pascal Bonitzer, 'The Silences of the Voice', in Philip Rosen, ed., *Narrative, Apparatus, Ideology* (New York: Columbia University Press, 1986), p. 323.

21. Bonitzer, pp. 329, 328.

22. Roland Barthes, 'The Grain of the Voice', in *Image/Music/Text*, trans. Stephen Heath (New York: Hill and Wang, 1977), p. 182.

23. Bonitzer, p. 328.

24. Ibid., p. 329.

25. Barthes, p. 182.

26. Ibid., p. 188.

27. Jacques Lacan, *The Four Fundamental Concepts of PsychoAnalysis, Seminar XI*, ed. Jacques-Alain Miller (London: Hogarth Press and the Institute of Psychoanalysis, 1977), p. 195.

28. The introduction of the notion of two different *levels* in *film noir*'s defining characteristics – one primary and the other secondary, a reaction against the first – also helps to clarify some of the confusion that surrounds the theory of *film noir*. The earlier presence of *noir*-like lighting techniques does not invalidate the belief in the specific, discrete phenomenon of *film noir*, since their earlier use was descriptive and not 'restorative', as they are in *film noir*; that is, chiaroscuro lighting functions differently in *film noir* than it did previously. Additionally, the absence of chiaroscuro lighting and deep focus cannot automatically disqualify a film from inclusion in the *film noir* catalogue, since this list of films must obviously include those that demonstrate little or no defence against the drive as well as those that build an elaborate defence.

29. Christine Gledhill, '*Klute*: A Contemporary Film Noir', in E. Ann Kaplan, ed., *Women in Film Noir* (London, British Film Institute, 1978), p. 17.

30. Slavoj Žižek, *Looking Awry* (Cambridge, MA: October Books/MIT Press, 1991), pp. 60–61.

7

'THE THING THAT THINKS': THE KANTIAN BACKGROUND OF THE *NOIR* SUBJECT

Slavoj Žižek

I

One of the ways to take note of the historical gap that separates the eighties from the fifties is to compare classical *films noirs* to the new wave of *noir* films produced in the eighties. What I have in mind here are not primarily direct or indirect remakes (the two *DOAs*, *Against All Odds* as a remake of *Out of the Past*, *Body Heat* as a remake of *Double Indemnity*, *No Way Out* as a remake of *The Big Clock* etcetera, up to *Basic Instinct* as a distant remake of *Vertigo*[1]) but rather those films which attempt to resuscitate the *noir* universe by combining it with another genre, as if *film noir* were today a vampire-like entity which, in order to be kept alive, needed an influx of fresh blood from other sources. Two cases are exemplary here: Alan Parker's *Angel Heart* (1987), which combines *film noir* with the occult–supernatural, and Ridley Scott's *Blade Runner* (1982), which combines it with science fiction.

Film theory has for a long time been haunted by the question: is *film noir* an independent genre or is it a kind of anamorphotic distortion affecting different genres? From the very beginning, *film noir* was not limited to hard-boiled detective stories: reverberations of *film noir* motifs are easily discernible in comedies (*Arsenic and Old Lace*), in westerns (*Pursued*), in political (*All the King's Men*) and social dramas

Angel Heart (Alan Parker, 1987)

(*Weekend's End*), etcetera. Do we have here a secondary impact of something that originally constitutes a genre of its own (the *noir* crime universe), or is the crime film only one of the possible fields of application of the *noir* logic, that is, is '*noir*' a predicate that entertains towards the crime universe the same relationship as towards comedy or western, a kind of logical operator introducing the same anamorphotic distortion in every genre it is applied to, so that the fact that it found its strongest application in the crime film is ultimately a historical contingency? To raise these questions is in no way to indulge in hair-splitting sophistry: my thesis is that the 'proper', detective *film noir* as it were *arrives at its truth* – in Hegelese: realizes its notion only by way of its fusion with another genre, specifically science fiction or the occult.

What do, then, *Angel Heart* and *Blade Runner* have in common? Both films deal with memory and subverted personal identity: the hero, the hard-boiled investigator, is sent on a quest (in pursuit of a former pop singer suddenly and mysteriously proclaimed dead, in the one case, and of a group of replicants at large in the Los Angeles of 2012, in the other) whose final outcome is that he himself was from the very beginning implicated in the object of his quest. In *Angel Heart*, the hero ascertains that the dead singer is none other than himself (in an occult ritual performed long ago, he exchanged hearts and souls with an ex-soldier who he now thinks he is). In *Blade Runner*, he is told that he is himself a replicant. The outcome of the quest is therefore in both cases the radical undermining of self-identity masterminded by a mysterious, all-powerful agency, in the first case the Devil himself ('Louis Cipher'), in the second case the Tyrell corporation, which succeeds in fabricating replicants who remain unaware of their replicant status, who misperceive themselves as humans. The world depicted in both films is the world in which corporate capital has succeeded in penetrating and dominating the very fantasy kernel of our being: none of our features are really 'ours'; even our memories and fantasies are artificially planted. It is as if Fredric Jameson's thesis – that postmodernism is the epoch in which capital finally colonizes the last-resort holdouts against its all-inclusive logic – were here brought to its hyperbolic conclusion. The fusion of capital and knowledge brings about a new type of proletarian, the absolute proletarian, as it were, bereft of the last pockets of private resistance:

verything, up to the most intimate memories, is planted, so that what remains is literally the void of pure substanceless subjectivity (*substanzlose Subjektivität* – Marx's definition of the proletarian). Ironically, one might say that *Blade Runner* is a film about the emergence of class-consciousness.

This truth is concealed, however, in one case metaphorically, in the other metonymically. In *Angel Heart*, corporate capital is substituted by the metaphorical figure of the Devil, whereas in *Blade Runner*, a metonymical impediment prevents the film from carrying out its inherent logic. That is to say, the director's cut of *Blade Runner* differs in two crucial respects from the initially released version: there is no voice-over and at the end Deckard (Harrison Ford) discovers that he too is a replicant.[2] Yet even in the released version, a whole series of features point towards the latter fact: the

Blade Runner (Ridley Scott, 1982)

accentuated visual parallelism between Deckard and Leon Kowalski, a replicant questioned in the Tyrell building at the beginning of the film; after Deckard proves to Rachael (Sean Young) that she is a replicant by quoting her most intimate childhood recollections, not shared with anyone else, the camera provides a brief survey of *his* personal myth (old childhood pictures on the piano, his dream recollection of a unicorn), with a clear implication that they also are fabricated, not 'true' memories or dreams, so that when Rachael mockingly asks him if he also underwent the replicant test, the question resounds with ominous undertones; the patronizing–cynical attitude of the policeman who serves as the contact with the police chief clearly indicates his awareness that Deckard is a replicant (we can safely surmise that in the original version, he viciously informs Deckard of it). The paradox here is that the subversive message hinges on the metaphorical narrative closure (when, at the beginning of the film, Deckard replays the tape of Kowalski's interrogation, he is unaware that at the end he will himself occupy the same place), whereas in the released version the evasion of the narrative closure functions as a conformist compromise which cuts off the film's subversive edge.

How, then, are we to diagnose the position of the hero at the end of his quest, after recollection deprives him of his very self-identity? It is here that the gap that separates classical *film noir* from the *noir* of the eighties can be perceived in its purest form. Today, even the mass media are aware of the extent to which our perception of reality, including the reality of our personal self-experience, hinges on symbolic fictions. Suffice it to quote from a recent issue of *Time* magazine: 'Stories are precious, indispensable. Everyone must have his history, her narrative. You do not know who you are until you possess the imaginative version of yourself. You almost do not exist without it.' Classical *films noirs* remain within these confines: while they abound with cases of amnesia – the hero 'does not know who he is', what he did during his blackout – this amnesia is here a deficiency measured against a standard of integration into the field of intersubjectivity, of symbolic community. Successful recollection means that, by way of organizing my life experience into a consistent narrative, I exorcize the dark demons of the past. In the universe of *Blade Runner* or *Angel Heart*, on the contrary, recollection designates something incomparably more radical: the total loss of my symbolic identity: I am forced to assume that I am not what I thought myself to be, but somebody or something else entirely.

One of the critical commonplaces about classical *film noir* concerns its philosophical background in French existentialism. In order to grasp the implications of this shift at work in the *film noir* of the eighties, however, one has to reach further back to the Cartesian–Kantian problematic of the subject *qua* pure, substanceless, 'I think'.

II

Descartes was the first to introduce a crack in the ontologically consistent universe: the contraction of absolute certainty to the punctuality of the 'I think' opens up, for a brief moment, the hypothesis of an evil genius (*le malin génie*) who, behind my back, dominates me and pulls the strings of what I experience as reality. He is the prototype of the scientist–maker who creates an artificial man, from Dr Frankenstein to Tyrell in *Blade Runner*. But with his reduction of the *cogito* to *res cogitans*, Descartes as it were patched up the wound opened up in reality; it remained for Kant to articulate fully the inherent paradoxes of self-consciousness. What Kant's 'transcendental turn' renders manifest is the impossibility of locating the subject within the 'great chain of being' in which every element has its own place. The subject is in the most radical sense out of joint – it constitutively lacks a place, which is why Lacan designates it by the mathem $, the barred S.

In Descartes, this out-of-jointness is still concealed, since his philosophy remains within the confines of what Foucault, in his *The Order of Things*, baptized as the 'classical episteme', the epistemological field regulated by the problematic of representations (ideas in the subject), their casual enchainment, their clarity and evidence, the connection between representation and represented content, etcetera. After reaching the point of absolute certainty in his *cogito ergo sum*, Descartes does not yet conceive it as correlative to the whole of reality, as the point external to reality, exempted from it, which as such delineates its horizon (in the sense of Wittgenstein's well-known metaphor, in his *Tractatus*, of the eye which cannot ever be part of the seen reality), that is, as the autonomous agent that spontaneously constitutes the objective world opposed to it. The Cartesian *cogito* is a representation which, following the inherent notional enchainment, leads us to other, superior representations. The subject first ascertains that, doubt being an index of imperfection, the *cogito* is a representation belonging to an inherently deficient being. As such, it entails the representation of a perfect being; and since it is obvious that a deficient, inferior being cannot be the cause of a superior being, this perfect being (God) has to exist. The veracious nature of God furthermore assures the reliability of our representations of external reality, etcetera. In Descartes's final vision of the universe, the *cogito* is therefore one among the representations in an intricate totality, *part* of reality and yet not (or, in Hegelese, only 'in itself') correlative to reality in its entirety.

According to Kant, Descartes falls prey to the 'subreption of the hypostasized consciousness': he wrongly concludes that, in the empty 'I think' that accompanies every representation of an object, we get hold of a positive phenomenal entity, *res cogitans* (a 'small piece of the world', as Husserl would have put it) which thinks and is transparent to itself in its capacity of thinking, that is, that self-consciousness renders self-present and self-transparent the 'thing' in me that thinks. What is lost thereby is the (topological) discord between the form 'I think' and the substance that thinks. Kant here logically *precedes* Descartes: he brings to the light of day a kind of 'vanishing mediator', a moment that has to disappear if the Cartesian *res cogitans* is to emerge. This Kantian distinction between the analytical proposition on the identity of the logical subject of thought, contained in 'I think', and the synthetical proposition on the identity of a person *qua* thinking thing–substance, is revived by Lacan in the guise of the distinction between the subject of the enunciation and the subject of the statement. The Lacanian subject is also an empty, nonsubstantial, logical variable (not a function), whereas 'person' consists of the fantasmatic 'stuff' that fills out its void.

The act of 'I think' is transphenomenal, it is not an object of inner experience or intuition, yet for all that it is not a noumenal Thing-in-itself, but rather the void of its lack. It is not sufficient to say about the I of pure apperception that 'of it, apart from them [the thoughts which are its predicates,] we cannot have any concept whatsoever' (A 346[3]); one has to add that *this lack of intuited content is constitutive of the I – the inaccessibility to the I of its own 'kernel of being' makes it an I*.[4] This gap that separates the empirical I's self-experience from the I of transcendental apperception coincides with the distinction between existence *qua* experiential reality and existence *qua* logical construction (that is, existence in the mathematical sense – 'there exists an X which . . . '). The status of Kant's I of transcendental apperception is that of a *necessary* and simultaneously *impossible* logical construction (impossible in the precise sense that its notion can never be filled out with intuited experiential reality); in short, it has the status of the Lacanian *real* – Descartes's error was precisely to confuse experiential reality and logical construction *qua* real-impossible.[5]

When, consequently, Kant remarks that, 'in the synthetic original unity of apperception, I am conscious of myself, not as I appear to myself, nor as I am in myself but only that I am' (B 157), one must grasp the fundamental paradox inherent in this formulation. I encounter *being* devoid of all determinations-of-thought at the very moment when, by way of the utmost abstraction, I confine myself to the empty form of *thought* that accompanies all my representations. In other words, the empty form of thought coincides with being, which lacks any formal determination-of-thought. Here, however, where Kant seems closest to Descartes, the distance that separates them is infinite. In Kant, this coincidence of thought and being in the act of self-consciousness in no way implies an access to myself *qua* thinking substance:

> Through this I or he or it (the thing) that thinks, nothing further is represented than a transcendental subject of the thoughts = X. It is known only through the thoughts which are its predicates, and of it, apart from them, we cannot have any concept whatsoever. (A 346)

In short: there is no answer possible to the question 'How is the Thing-that-thinks structured?' The paradox of self-consciousness is that it is possible only against the background of its own impossibility. I am conscious of myself only in so far as I am out of reach to myself *qua* the real kernel of my being ('I or he or it (the thing) that thinks'). I cannot acquire consciousness of myself in my capacity as the Thing-that-thinks. We can see, now, how the very notion of self-consciousness implies the subject's self-decentrement, far more radical than the opposition between subject and object. This is what Kant's theory of metaphysics is ultimately about: metaphysics endeavours to heal the wound of the 'primordial repression' (the inaccessibility of the Thing-that-thinks) by allocating to the subject a place in the 'great chain of being'. What metaphysics fails to take notice of is the price to be paid for this 'cure': the loss of the very capacity it wanted to account for, namely, human freedom. Kant himself commits an error when, in his *Critique of Practical Reason*, he conceives freedom (the postulate of practical reason) as a noumenal Thing. What is thereby obfuscated is his fundamental insight according to which I retain my capacity as a spontaneous–autonomous agent precisely and only in so far as I am not accessible to myself as a Thing.

On closer inspection, in what do the inconsistencies which emerge when the I of pure apperception is identified with the noumenal self (the 'Thing-that-thinks') consist? As Henry Allison put it in his perspicacious résumé of Strawson's critique of Kant,[6] in the case of this identification, the phenomenal I (the empirical subject) has to be conceived simultaneously as something that (in the guise of an object of experience) appears *to* the noumenal subject (that is, everything that appears as part of the constituted reality appears to the transcendental subject, which is here conceived as identical to the noumenal subject) and as the appearance *of* the noumenal subject (that is, the empirical subject is, as is the case with every intuited reality, a phenomenal appearance of some noumenal entity, in this case of the noumenal subject). This doubling, however, is a nonsensical, self-cancelling short circuit: if the noumenal subject appears *to itself*, the distance that separates appearance from noumena collapses. In other words, the agency that perceives something as an appearance cannot itself be an appearance – in which case, we would find ourselves in the nonsensical vicious circle described by Alphonse Allais where two appearances mutually recognize themselves as appearances. (Raoul and Marguerite make an appointment at a masked ball. In a secret corner, they both take off their masks and utter a cry of surprise – Raoul because his partner is not Marguerite, after all; Marguerite because her partner does not turn out to be Raoul.) The only way out of this impasse is to maintain the distinction between the I of pure apperception and the Thing-that-thinks: what I experience, what is given to me phenomenally in my intuition, the content of my person (the object of empirical psychology), is, of course, as with every phenomenon, the appearing of a Thing (in this case of the Thing-that-thinks), *but this Thing cannot be the I of pure apperception, the* transcendental subject to which the Thing-that-thinks appears in the guise of the empirical I.

With this crucial point in mind, we can give a precise account of the difference between the inaccessibility of the noumenal self and that of any other object of perception. When Kant says about the transcendental subject that it 'is known only through the thoughts which are its predicates, and of it, apart from them, we cannot have any concept whatsoever' (A 346), does not the same hold also for the table in front of me, for example? This table is also known only through the thoughts which are its predicates, but apart from them, we cannot have any concept of it whatsoever. However, because of the above-described self-referential doubling of the appearing in the case of the I, *'I think' must remain empty also on the phenomenal level* — the I's apperception is by definition devoid of any intuitional content, it is an empty representation which truncates, carves a hole into the field of representations. To put it in a concise way: Kant is compelled to define the I of transcendental apperception as neither phenomenal nor noumenal because of the paradox of *auto-affection*: if I were given to myself phenomenally, as an object of experience, I would simultaneously have to be given to myself noumenally.

Another way to arrive at the same result is via the duality of discursive and intuitive intellect: on account of his finitude, the subject disposes only of discursive intellect. He is affected by Things-in-themselves, and he makes use of the discursive intellect (the network of formal transcendental categories) to structure the multitude of formless affects into objective reality; this structuring is his own 'spontaneous', autonomous act. If the subject were to possess intuitive intellect, the abyss that separates intellect from intuition would be filled out and the subject would gain access to things as they are in themselves. However, 'while I can coherently, if vacuously, claim that if I had an intuitive *instead* of a discursive intellect, I could know *other* things (objects) as they are in themselves I cannot similarly claim that I could know myself as object in my capacity as a spontaneous, thinking subject'.[7] Why not? If I were to possess an intuition of myself *qua* Thing-that-thinks, that is, if I were to have access to my noumenal self, *I would thereby lose the very feature which makes me an I of pure apperception* — I would cease to be the spontaneous transcendental agent that constitutes reality.[8]

III

Lacan's reformulation of Descartes's *cogito*, 'I am not where I think', is to be conceived against the background of this gap between the void of pure apperception and the noumenal self *qua* Thing-that-thinks. How, precisely, are we to understand this 'I am not where I think'? Let us recall a symptomatic act described in Freud's *The Psychopathology of Everyday Life*:

> During a session a young married woman mentioned by way of association that she had been cutting her nails the day before and 'had cut into the flesh while she was trying to remove the soft cuticle at the bottom of the nail'. This is of so little interest that we ask ourselves in surprise why it was recalled and mentioned at all, and we begin to suspect that what we are dealing with is a symptomatic act. And in fact it turned out that the finger which was the victim of her small act of clumsiness was the ring-finger, the one on which a wedding ring is worn. What is more, it was her wedding anniversary; and in the light of this the injury to the soft cuticle takes on a very definite meaning, which can easily be guessed. At the same time, too, she related a dream which alluded to her husband's clumsiness and her anaesthesia as a wife. But why was it the ring-finger on her *left* hand which she injured, whereas a wedding ring is worn [in her country] on the right hand? Her husband is a lawyer, a 'doctor of law' ['*Doktor der Rechte*', literally 'doctor of right(s)'], and as a girl her affections belonged in secret to a physician (jokingly called '*Doktor der Linke*' ['doctor of the left']. A 'left-handed marriage', too, has a definite meaning.[9]

A trifling slip, a tiny cut on the ring-finger, can well condense an entire chain of articulated *reasoning* which concerns the subject's most intimate fate: it bears witness to the knowledge that her marriage is a failure, to the regret at not choosing her true love, the 'doctor of the left'. This tiny bloodstain is the place where her unconscious thought dwells, and what she is unable to do is to recognize herself in it, to say 'I am there', at the place where this thought is articulated. If she is to retain the consistency of her self-identity, the stain has to remain a blot that means nothing to her. Or, as Lacan would have put it, there is no I without the stain: 'I am' only in so far as I am not where I think, that is to say, only in so far as the picture I am looking at contains a stain that condenses the decentred thought – only in so far as this stain remains a stain, that is, in so far as I do not recognize myself in it, in so far as I am not there, in it. It is for that reason that Lacan returns again and again to the notion of anamorphosis: I perceive 'normal' reality only in so far as the point at which 'it thinks' fails to become visible and remains simply a formless stain.

The theoretical temptation to be avoided here, of course, is that of identifying too hastily this stain with the object *a*: *a* is not the stain itself but rather the gaze in the precise sense of the point of view from which the stain can be perceived in its 'true meaning', the point from which, instead of the anamorphotic distortion, it would be possible to discern its true contours. For that reason, the analyst occupies the place of the object *a*: he is supposed to know – to know what? The true meaning of the stain, precisely. Consequently, Lacan is quite justified in claiming that in paranoia object *a* 'becomes visible': in the person of the persecutor, the object *qua* gaze assumes the palpable, empirical existence of an agency which 'sees into me', is able to read my thoughts.

In this sense, *a* stands for the point of self-consciousness: if I were able to occupy this point, it would be possible for me to abolish the stain, to say that 'I am where I think'. It is here that the subversive potential of the Lacanian critique of self-consciousness *qua* self-transparency becomes visible: *self-consciousness as such is literally decentred*; the slip – the stain – bears witness to the *ex*istence of a certain decentred, external place in which I *do* arrive at self-consciousness (Freud's patient articulates the truth about herself, her failed marriage, at a place that remains *ex*ternal to her sense of self-identity). Therein consists the scandal of psychoanalysis, unbearable for philosophy: what is at stake in the Lacanian critique of self-consciousness is not the commonplace according to which the subject is never fully transparent to itself, can never arrive at full awareness of what is going on in its psyche (that is, full self-consciousness is not possible since there is always something that eludes the grasp of my conscious ego), but the far more paradoxical thesis that this decentred hard kernel that eludes my grasp is ultimately self-consciousness itself. As to its status, self-consciousness is an external object out of my reach.[10]

We can see, now, why self-consciousness is the very opposite of the subject's self-transparency: I am aware of myself only in so far as there is, outside of me, a place in which the truth about me is articulated. What is not possible is for these two places to coincide: the stain is not an unreflected remainder, something one could abolish via self-reflection, via a deeper insight into one's psychic life, since it is the very product of my self-awareness, its objective correlative. This is what Lacan has in mind when he writes down symptom as 'sinthome': symptom *qua* ciphered message waits to be dissolved by way of its interpretation, whereas sinthome is a stain correlative to the very (non) being of the subject. In order to exemplify this distinction, suffice it to recall the two versions of *Cape Fear*, J. Lee Thompson's original from the early 1960s and Martin Scorsese's remake of 1991. Even those reviews that were repelled by Scorsese's patronizingly self-conscious attitude towards the original noted that Scorsese accomplished a crucial shift. In the original version, the ex-convict (Robert Mitchum) is simply a figure of evil invading from outside the idyllic all-American family and derailing its daily routine, whereas in Scorsese's remake, the ex-convict (played by

Robert de Niro) materializes, gives body to traumas and antagonistic tensions that already glow in the very heart of the family: the wife's sexual dissatisfaction, the daughter's awakened femininity and sense of independence . . . In short, Scorsese's version has built into it an interpretation homologous to that reading of Hitchcock's *Birds* that conceives of the birds' ferocious attacks as the materialization of the maternal superego, of the disturbance that dwells in family life. Although such a reading may appear 'deeper' than the allegedly 'superficial' reduction of the force of evil to an external threat, what gets lost is precisely the remainder of an outside. This outside cannot be reduced to a secondary effect of inherent intersubjective tensions, since its exclusion is constitutive: an object which always adds itself to the intersubjective network, as a kind of 'fellow-traveller' of every intersubjective community. Are not the birds in Hitchcock's films, notwithstanding their intersubjective status, at their most radical, just such an overblown stain on a finger? When, upon crossing the bay for the first time, Melanie (Tippi Hedren) is attacked by a gull which strikes her head, she feels her head with her gloved hand, looks at her fingers and perceives on the tip of her forefinger a small red bloodstain. All the birds that later attack the town could be said to arise out of this tiny stain, just as in *North by Northwest* the plane that attacks Cary Grant on the empty cornfield is first perceived as a tiny, barely visible spot on the horizon. This original doubling of self-consciousness provides the foundation of 'intersubjectivity': if, as the Hegelian commonplace goes, self-consciousness is self-consciousness only through the mediation of another self-consciousness, then my self-awareness – precisely in so far as this self-awareness is not the same as self-transparency – causes the emergence of a decentred 'it thinks'. What is lost in the translation of the split between 'I am' and 'it thinks' into the standard motif of intersubjectivity is the radical *asymmetry* of the two terms – the 'other' is originally an *object*, an opaque stain that hinders my self-transparency, that is, that which gives body to what has to be excluded if I am to emerge. In other words, the ultimate paradox of the dialectics of self-consciousness is that it inverts the standard doxa according to which 'consciousness' relates to a heterogeneous, external object, whereas self-consciousness abolishes this decentring. *The object is* stricto sensu *the correlate of self-consciousness*, there is no object prior to self-consciousness, since the object originally emerges as that opaque kernel that has to be excluded if I am to gain awareness of myself. Or, to put it in Lacanian terms, the original intersubjective correlate of the subject – of the barred \$ – is not another \$, but S, the opaque, full Other possessing what the subject constitutively lacks (being, knowledge). In this precise sense the Other – the other human being – originally is the impenetrable, substantial Thing.

There is a radical conclusion to be drawn from this: intersubjectivity *senso strictu* becomes possible, thinkable, only with Kant, with the notion of subject qua $, the empty form of apperception that needs S as the correlative of its non-being. What we have prior to the Kantian subject is not intersubjectivity proper, but a community of individuals who share a common universal–substantial ground and participate in it. It is only with Kant, with his notion of the subject as $, as the empty form of self-apperception, as an entity that constitutively 'does not know what it is', that the Other Subject is needed to order for me to define my own identity. What the Other thinks I am is inscribed into the very heart of my own most intimate self-identity. The ambiguity that sticks to the Lacanian notion of the big Other – another subject in its impenetrable opacity, yet at the same time the very symbolic structure, the neutral field in which I encounter other subjects – is therefore far from being the result of a simple confusion: it gives expression to a deep structural necessity. Precisely in so far as I am $, I cannot conceive of myself as participating in some common substance, that is to say, this substance necessarily opposes itself to me in the guise of the Other Subject.

IV

The irreducible gap between the I of apperception and the noumenal Thing-that-thinks opens up the possibility of a 'paranoiac' attitude according to which noumenally – *qua* Thing-that-thinks – I am an artefact, a plaything in the hands of an unknown Maker. This accounts for a crucial component of the *film noir* renewal of the eighties: a new type of father which characterizes 'post-industrial', corporate late capitalism, a father epitomized by Tyrell in *Blade Runner*, a lone figure of uncanny, ethereal, frail materiality, devoid of a sexual partner. This father clearly materializes the Cartesian evil genius: he is a father who exerts domination over me not at the level of my symbolic identity, but at the level of what I am *qua* Thing-that-thinks.[11] In other words, he is a father who is not anymore S_1, a master-signifier whose Name guarantees my symbolic identity, my place in the texture of symbolic tradition, but S_2, Knowledge which created me as its artefact – the moment father changes his status from S_1 to S_2, from empty master-signifier to Knowledge, I, the son, become a monster.[12] The hysterical questions monsters address to their Makers, from Dr Frankenstein's creature to the Rutger Hauer character in *Blade Runner*, ultimately vary one and the same motif: 'Why did you screw me up? Why did you create me the way you did, incomplete, crippled?' Or, to quote the lines from Milton's *Paradise Lost* that served as the motto to the first edition of *Frankenstein*:

> Did I request thee, Maker, from my clay
> To mould me man? Did I solicit thee
> From darkness to promote me?[13]

This paradox of the 'subject who knows he is a replicant' renders clear what the 'non-substantial status of the subject' amounts to: with regard to every substantial, positive content of my being, I 'am' nothing but a replicant, that is, the difference that makes me 'human' and not a replicant is to be discerned nowhere in 'reality'. Therein consists the implicit philosophical lesson of *Blade Runner* attested to by numerous allusions to the Cartesian *cogito* (as when the replicant character played by Darryl Hannah ironically points out 'I think, therefore I am'): where is the *cogito*, the place of my self-consciousness, when everything that I actually am is an artefact: not only my body, my eyes, but even my most intimate memories and fantasies? It is here that we again encounter the Lacanian distinction between the subject of enunciation and the subject of the enunciated: everything that I positively am, every enunciated content I can point at and say 'that's me', is not 'I' – I am only the void that remains, the empty distance towards every content.

Blade Runner thus gives a double twist to the commonsense distinction between human and android. Man is a replicant who does not know it. Yet if this were all, the film would involve a simplistic reductionist notion that our self-experience *qua* free 'human' agents is an illusion founded upon our ignorance of the causal nexus that regulates our lives. For that reason, one should supplement the former statement: it is only when, at the level of the enunciated content, I assume my replicant status, that, at the level of enunciation, I become a truly human subject. 'I am a replicant' is the statement of the subject in its purest – the same as in Althusser's theory of ideology where the statement 'I am in ideology' is the only way for me to truly avoid the vicious circle of ideology (or the Spinozian version of it: the awareness that nothing can ever escape the grasp of necessity is all that allows us to be truly free). In short, the implicit thesis of *Blade Runner* is that replicants are pure subjects precisely in so far as they experience the fact that every positive, substantial content, inclusive of the most intimate fantasies, is not 'their own' but already implanted. In this precise sense, the subject is by definition nostalgic, a subject of loss. Let us recall how, in *Blade Runner*, Rachael silently starts to cry when Deckard proves to her that she is a replicant. The silent grief over the loss of her 'humanity', the infinite longing to be or to become human again although she knows this will never happen; or (the reverse of this) the eternally gnawing doubt about whether *I* am truly human or just an android – these are the very undecided, intermediate states that make me human.[14]

What is of crucial importance here is that we do not confuse this radical 'decentring' that characterizes the replicants and the decentring of the subject of the signifier with regard to the big Other, the symbolic order. It is, of course, possible to read *Blade Runner* as a film about the process of subjectivization of the replicants: notwithstanding the fact that their most intimate memories are implanted, not 'true', replicants subjectivize themselves by way of combining these memories into an individual myth, a narrative that allows them to construct their place in the symbolic universe. Further-more, are not our, 'human', memories also 'implanted' in the sense that we all borrow the elements of our individual myths from the treasury of the big Other? Are we not, prior to our speaking, *spoken* by the discourse of the Other? As to the truth of our memories, does not, according to Lacan, truth have the structure of a fiction: even if its ingredients are invented or implanted, not 'really ours', what is 'ours' is the unique way we subjectivize them, the way we integrate them into our symbolic universe. In this perspective, the lesson of *Blade Runner* is that manipulation is ultimately doomed to fail; even if Tyrell artificially implants every element of our memory, what he is not able to foresee is the way replicants will organize these elements into a mythical narrative which will then give rise to the hysterical question.[15] What Lacan has in mind with *cogito* however, is the exact opposite of this: the 'subject' *qua* \$ emerges not *via* subjectivization–narrativization (that is, the construction of the 'individual myth' from the decentred pieces of tradition), but *at the very moment when the individual loses its support in the network of tradition* – the subject coincides with the void that remains after the framework of symbolic memory is suspended.

The emergence of the *cogito* thus undermines the subject's embeddedness in the symbolic tradition by opening up an irreducible gap between the horizon of meaning, of narrative tradition, and an impossible knowledge the possession of which would enable me to gain access to the Thing I am in the Real, beyond all narrativization, that is, symbolization/historization. A full recollection ('total recall') would therefore amount to filling out the void that constitutes me *qua* \$, subject of self-consciousness, it would amount to identifying–recognizing myself as 'he/it, the thing, that thinks'. In Lacanian terms, 'total recall' would amount to 'knowledge in the Real'.

Replicants know their life span is limited to four years: this certainty which saps the openness of their 'being-towards-death' bears witness to the fact that they have arrived at the impossible point of knowing how they are structured *qua* 'thing-machine that thinks'. For that reason, replicants are ultimately the impossible fantasy-formation of us, human mortals: the fantasy of a being conscious of itself *qua* Thing, of a being that does not have to pay for its access to self-consciousness with $, with the loss of its substantial support. A crack in this fantasy can therefore enable us to approach the question of 'artificial intelligence': do computers think?

What is crucial in the debates on artificial intelligence is that an inversion has taken place which is the fate of every successful metaphor: one first tries to simulate human thought with the computer, bringing the model as close as possible to the human 'original', until at a certain point matters reverse and the question emerges: *what if this 'model' is already a model of the 'original' itself*, what if human intelligence itself operates like a computer, is 'programmed', etcetera? (Therein consists also the intriguing implication of computer-generated virtual reality: what if our 'true' reality itself has to be virtualized, conceived as an artefact?) The computer raises in pure form the question of semblance, of a discourse that would not be that of a semblance: it is clear that the computer in some sense only 'simulates' thought; yet how does the total simulation of thought differ from 'real' thought? No wonder, then, that the spectre of 'artificial intelligence' appears as an entity that is simultaneously prohibited and considered impossible. One asserts that it is not possible for a machine to think, at the same time as one prohibits research in this direction on the grounds that it is dangerous, ethically dubious, etcetera.

And the reason the computer 'does not think' holds precisely to this logic of the reversal of the metaphor where, instead of the computer as the model for the human brain, we conceive the brain itself as a 'computer made of flesh and blood', where, instead of defining a robot as an artificial man, we conceive man himself as a 'natural robot'. This reversal could be further exemplified by an example from the domain of sexuality. One usually conceives of masturbation as an 'imaginary sexual act', that is, an act where the bodily contact with a partner is only imagined. Is it not possible to reverse the terms and to conceive the 'proper' sexual act, the act with an 'actual' partner, as a kind of 'masturbation with a real (instead of only imagined) partner'? The whole point of Lacan's insistence on the 'impossibility of the sexual relation' is that this, precisely, is what the 'actual' sexual act is: man's partner is never woman in the real kernel of her being, but woman *qua a*, reduced to the fantasy object (let us just recall his definition of the phallic enjoyment as essentially masturbatory)!

It is against this background that we can provide a definition – one of the possible definitions – of the Lacanian real: real designates the very remainder that resists this reversal (of the computer as model of the human brain into the brain itself as flesh-and-blood computer; of masturbation as imaginary sexual act into the actual sexual act as masturbation with a real partner). The real is that X on account of which this squaring of the circle is ultimately doomed to fail. This reversal relies on a kind of realization of the metaphor: what at first appears as a mere metaphor, a pale imitation, of true reality (the computer as a metaphor for the brain, etcetera), becomes the original paradigm imitated by flesh-and-blood reality (brains follow in an always imperfect way the functioning of the computer, etcetera). What we experience as 'reality' is constituted by such a reversal: as Lacan puts it, 'reality' is always framed by a fantasy, that is, for something real to be experienced as part of 'reality', it must fit the preordained coordinates of our fantasy space (a sexual act the coordinates of our imagined fantasy scripts, a brain the functioning of a computer, etcetera). In this way, we can propose a second definition of the real: a surplus, a hard kernel, that resists metaphorization.

Let us recall how, apropos of *Alien 3*, some reviewers quoted a series of features (the action takes place in a closed male community where even Ripley has to shave her head in order to become part of it; humans are utterly defenceless against the threat of the 'alien', etcetera) as an argument for conceiving the 'alien' as a metaphor for AIDS. What one has to add, from the Lacanian perspective, is that all the talk about the 'alien', the monster, as a metaphor for AIDS falls short of the crucial fact that AIDS itself owes its tremendous impact not to its raw reality as an illness, to its immediate physical impact, however horrifying it may be, but to the extraordinary libidinal energy invested in it (AIDS is perceived as irresistible, it strikes all of a sudden, as if from nowhere, it seems to fit perfectly the role of a punishment from God for our promiscuous way of life) – in short, AIDS occupies a certain preordained place in our ideological fantasy space, and the monstrous 'alien' ultimately just materializes, gives body to, this fantasy dimension which from the very beginning was at work in the AIDS phenomenon.

V

My point is thus a very elementary one: true, the computer-generated 'virtual reality' is a semblance, it does foreclose the real; but what we experience as the 'true, hard, external reality' is based upon exactly the same exclusion. The ultimate lesson of virtual reality is the virtualization of our 'true' reality: by the mirage of virtual reality, 'true' reality itself is posited as a semblance of itself, as a pure symbolic edifice. The fact that 'a computer doesn't think' means that the price for our access to 'reality' is that *something must remain unthought.*

To make this point clear, let us turn to Fritz Lang's *noir* western *Rancho Notorious* (1950), which begins where a Hollywood story usually ends: with the passionate kiss of a couple awaiting their marriage: immediately thereupon, brutal bandits rape and kill the bride, and the desperate bridegroom (played by Arthur Kennedy) commits himself to an inexorable revenge. His only clue as to the identity of the bandits is the word 'chuck-a-luck', a meaningless signifying fragment. After a long search, he unearths its secret: 'Chuck-a-luck' designates a mysterious place whose very name it is dangerous to pronounce in public, a ranch in a hidden valley beyond a narrow mountain pass, where Marlene Dietrich, an aged saloon singer, former femme fatale, reigns, offering refuge to robbers for a percentage of their booty. Wherein consists the irresistible charm of this film? Undoubtedly in the fact that, beneath the usual western plot, it stages another mythical narrative, the one articulated in its pure form in a series of adventure novels and films whose action is usually set in Africa (*King Solomon's Mines, She, Tarzan*): they narrate the story of an expedition into the very heart of the dark continent where white man has never set foot (the voyagers are lured into this risky trip by some incomprehensible or ambiguous signifying fragment: a message in a bottle, a fragment of burned paper or the confused babbling of some madman hinting that beyond a certain frontier, wonderful and/or horrible things are taking place). On the way, the expedition is confronted by diverse dangers, it is threatened by combative aborigines who at the same time strive desperately to make the foreigners understand that they should not trespass across a certain frontier (river, mountain pass, abyss), since beyond it there is a damned place from which nobody has yet returned. After a series of adventures, the expedition goes beyond this frontier and finds itself in the Other Place, in the space of pure fantasy: a mighty black kingdom (*King Solomon's Mines*), the realm of a beautiful and mysterious queen (*She*), the domain where man lives in full harmony with nature and speaks with animals (*Tarzan*). Another mythical landscape of this kind was of course Tibet: the Tibetan theocracy served as a model for the most famous image of the idyllic world of wisdom and balance, Shangri-la (in *Lost Horizon*), which can be reached only through a narrow mountain passage; nobody is allowed to return from it, and the one person who does escape pays for his success by madness, so that nobody believes him when he prattles on about the peaceful country ruled by wise monks.[16] The mysterious 'Chuck-a-luck' from *Rancho Notorious* is the same forbidden place: it is by no means accidental that all the crucial confrontations in the film take place at the narrow mountain pass that marks the frontier separating everyday reality from the valley where 'she' reigns – in other words, at the very place of *passage* between reality and the fantasy's 'other place'.[17]

What is crucial here is the strict formal homology between all these stories: in all cases, the structure is that of a Möbius strip – if we progress far enough on the side of reality, we suddenly find ourselves on its reverse, in the domain of pure fantasy.[18] Let us pursue this line of associations: do we not encounter the same inversion in the development of a great number of artists, from Shakespeare to Mozart, where the gradual descent into despair all of a sudden, when it reaches its nadir, changes into a kind of heavenly bliss? After a series of tragedies which mark the lowest point of his despair (*Hamlet, King Lear*, etcetera), the tone of Shakespeare's plays unexpectedly changes, we enter the realm of a fairytale harmony where life is governed by a benevolent Fate which brings all conflicts to a happy conclusion (*The Winter's Tale, Cymbeline*, etcetera). After *Don Giovanni*, this ultimate monument to the impossibility of the sexual relationship, to the antagonism of the relation between sexes, Mozart composed *The Magic Flute*, a hymn to the harmonious couple of man and woman (note the paradox of how the criticism *precedes* the panegyric!).

The horrifying, lethal and at the same time fascinating borderline that we approach when the reversal into bliss is imminent is what Lacan, apropos of Sophocles' *Antigone*, attempts to indicate by means of the Greek word *ate*.[19] There is a fundamental ambiguity to this term: *ate* simultaneously denotes a horrifying limit that can never be reached, the touch of which means death, and *the space beyond it*. The crucial point here is the primacy of the limit over the space: we do not have two spheres (that of reality and that of pure fantasy) that are divided by a certain limit; what we have is just reality and its limit, the abyss, the void around which it is structured. The fantasy space is therefore strictly secondary, it 'gives body', it materializes a certain limit or, more precisely, it changes the *impossible* into the *prohibited*. The limit marks a certain fundamental impossibility (it cannot be trespassed across, if we come too close to it, we die), while its beyond is prohibited (whoever enters it cannot return, etcetera). We have thereby already produced the formula of the mysterious reversal of horror into bliss: by means of it, the *impossible limit* changes into the *forbidden place*. In other words, the logic of this reversal is that of the transmutation of the real into the symbolic: the impossible-real changes into an object of symbolic prohibition. The paradox (and perhaps the very function of the prohibition as such) consists of course in the fact that, as soon as it is conceived as prohibited, the impossible-real changes into something *possible*, that is, into something that cannot be reached not because of its inherent impossibility but simply because access to it is hindered by the external barrier of a prohibition. Therein lies, after all, the logic of the most fundamental of all prohibitions, that of incest: incest is inherently impossible (even if a man 'really' sleeps with his mother, 'this is not *that*', the incestuous object is by definition lacking), and the symbolic prohibition is nothing but an attempt to resolve this deadlock by a transmutation of impossibility into prohibition – *there is One* which is the prohibited object of incest (mother), and its prohibition renders all other objects accessible.[20] The trespassing across the frontier in the above-mentioned series of adventure films follows the same logic: the forbidden space beyond *ate* is again constituted by the transmutation of impossibility into prohibition.

By means of the reversal of the (impossible) limit into (prohibited) space, of *Don Giovanni* into *The Magic Flute*, we thus elude the real *qua* impossible: once we enter the domain of fantasy, the trauma of inherent impossibility is replaced by a fairy beatitude. Mozart's *Magic Flute*, its image of the amorous couple forming a harmonious whole, exemplifies perfectly the Lacanian thesis that fantasy is ultimately always the fantasy of a successful sexual relationship: after the couple of Tamino and Pamina successfully undergoes the ordeal of fire and water, that is trespasses the limit, the two of them enter symbolic bliss. The logic of this symbolic bliss enables us to articulate one of the fundamental mechanisms of ideological legitimization: we legitimize the existing order by presenting it as the realization of a dream – *not of our dream, but of the Other's, the Dead Ancestor's dream*, the dream of previous generations. That was, for example, the reference that determined the relationship towards the Soviet Union in the 1920s and 1930s: in spite of the poverty and wrongs, numerous Western visitors were fascinated by this very drab Soviet reality – why? Because it appeared to them as a kind of palpable materialization of the dream of millions of past and present workers from all around the world. Any doubts about the Soviet reality thus entailed instant culpabilization: 'True, we in the Soviet Union make numerous mistakes, but when you criticize our efforts with ironic disdain, you are making fun of and betraying the dreams of millions who suffered and risked their lives for what we are realizing now!'[21] The situation here is not unlike that of Zhuang Zi, who dreamt of being a butterfly, and after his awakening posed a question to himself: how did he know that he was not now a butterfly dreaming of being Zhuang Zi?[22] In the same way, post-revolutionary ideology attempts to make us understand that what we now live is a dream of our ancestors come true; the worker in the Soviet Union of the 1930s, for example, is a pre-revolutionary fighter dreaming of being a worker in the socialist paradise: if we complain too much, we might disturb his dream. This detour through the dead Other is necessary for the ideological legitimization of the present to take effect.

A further formal homology might set us on the right track concerning the logic of this reversal: do we not encounter the same matrix in Freud's most famous dream, that of Irma's injection?[23] Do not the three stages of this dream correspond to the imaginary dual relationship, its 'aggravation' into an unbearable antagonism which announces the encounter with the real, and the final 'appeasement' via the advent of the symbolic order? In the first phase of the dream, Freud is 'playing with his patient',[24] his dialogue with Irma is 'totally stuck within the imaginary conditions which limit it';[25] this dual, specular relationship culminates in a look into her open mouth:

> There's a horrendous discovery here, that of the flesh one never sees, the foundation of things, the other side of the head, of the face, the secretory glands *par excellence*, the flesh from which everything exudes, at the very heart of the mystery, the flesh in as much as it is suffering, is formless, in as much as its form in itself is something which provokes anxiety. Spectre of anxiety, identification of anxiety, the final revelation of *you are this – You are this, which is so far from you, this which is the ultimate formlessness.*[26]

Suddenly, this horror changes miraculously into 'a sort of ataraxia' defined by Lacan precisely as 'the coming into operation of the symbolic function'[27] exemplified by the production of the formula of trimethylamin, the subject floats freely in symbolic bliss – as soon as the dreamer (Freud) renounces its narcissistic perspective. Jacques-Alain Miller was quite right to subtitle this chapter of Lacan's *Seminar II* simply 'The Imaginary, the Real and the Symbolic'.[28] The trap to be avoided here is of course to oppose this symbolic bliss to 'hard reality': the fundamental thesis of Lacanian psychoanalysis is on the contrary that what we call 'reality' constitutes itself against the background of such a 'bliss', that is, of such an exclusion of some traumatic real. This is precisely what Lacan has in mind when he says that fantasy is the ultimate support of reality: 'reality' stabilizes itself when some fantasy frame of a 'symbolic bliss' forecloses the view into the abyss of the real. Far from being a kind of dreamlike cobweb that prevents us from 'seeing reality as it effectively is', fantasy is constitutive of what we call reality: the most common bodily 'reality' is constituted via a detour through the cobweb of fantasy. In other words, the price we pay for our access to 'reality' is that something – the real of the trauma – must be 'repressed'.

What strikes the eye here is the parallel between the dream of Irma's injection and another famous Freudian dream, that of the dead son who appears to his father and addresses him with the reproach, 'Father, can't you see that I'm burning?' In his interpretation of the dream of Irma's injection, Lacan draws our attention to the appropriate remark by Erik Erikson that after the look into Irma's throat, after this encounter with the real, Freud *should have awakened* – like the dreamer of the dream of the burning child who awakens when he encounters this horrifying apparition: when confronted with the real in all its unbearable horror, the dreamer awakens, that is, escapes into 'reality'. One has to draw a radical conclusion from this parallel between the two dreams: what we call 'reality' is constituted exactly upon the model of the 'symbolic bliss' that enables Freud to continue to sleep after the horrifying look into Irma's throat. The anonymous dreamer who awakens into 'reality' in order to avoid the traumatic real of the burning child's reproach proceeds in the same way as Freud who, after the look into Irma's throat, 'changes the register', that is, escapes into the fantasy that veils the real.

VI

How does this situate *film noir*? The art of René Magritte enables us to formulate a precise answer to this question. Upon hearing the name 'Magritte', the first thing one thinks of is his notorious *Ceci n'est pas une pipe*: a drawing of a pipe with an inscription below it, 'This is not a pipe.' Taking as a starting point the paradoxes implied by this painting, Michel Foucault wrote a perspicacious little book with the same title.[29] Yet perhaps another of his paintings can serve even more appropriately to establish the elementary matrix that generates the uncanny effects that pertain to his work: *La Lunette d'approche* (1963), the painting of a half-open window where, through the windowpane, we see external reality (a blue sky with some dispersed white clouds), while in the narrow opening that gives direct access to the reality beyond the pane we see nothing but a dense black mass. The frame of the windowpane is, of course, the fantasy frame that constitutes reality, whereas the narrow opening between the panes opens onto the 'impossible' real, the Thing-in-itself.

This painting renders the elementary matrix of the Magrittean paradoxes by way of staging the Kantian split between (symbolized, categorized, transcendentally consti-tuted) reality and the void of the Thing-in-itself, of the real, which gapes in the midst of reality and confers upon it a fantasmatic character. The first variation that can be generated from this matrix is the strange, inconsistent element that is 'extraneous' to the depicted reality, which is, uncannily, placed in it, but does not 'fit': the gigantic rock that floats in the air close to a cloud, its heavy counterpart, its double, in *La Bataille de l'Argonne* (1959); the unnaturally large bloom that fills out the entire room in *Tombeau des lutteurs* (1960). This strange, 'out of joint' element is precisely the fantasy object filling out the blackness of the real that we perceived in the crack of the open window in *La Lunette d'approche*. The effect of uncanniness is even stronger when the 'same' object is redoubled, as in *Les Deux Mystères* (1966), a later variation of the famous *Ceci n'est pas une pipe*. The pipe and the inscription underneath it 'Ceci n'est pas une pipe' are both depicted as drawings on a blackboard; yet on the left of the blackboard, the apparition of another gigantic and massive pipe floats freely in a nonspecified space. The title of this painting could also have been 'A pipe is a pipe', for what is it if not a perfect illustration of the Hegelian thesis that tautology is the ultimate contradiction: the coincidence between the pipe located in a clearly defined symbolic reality, and its uncanny, shadowy double. The inscription under the pipe on the blackboard bears witness to the fact that the split between the two pipes, the pipe which forms part of reality and the pipe as real, that is, as a fantasy apparition, results from the intervention of the symbolic order. It is the emergence of the symbolic order that splits reality into itself and the enigmatic surplus of the real, making each the derealization of its counterpart. The Lacanian point not to be missed is that such a split can occur only within an economy of desire: it designates the gap between the inaccessible object-cause of desire – the pipe floating freely in the air – and the 'empirical' pipe which, although we can smoke it, is never it. The massive presence of the free-floating pipe, of course, turns the depicted pipe into a 'mere painting', yet, simultaneously, the free-floating pipe is opposed to the domesticated symbolic reality of the pipe on the blackboard and as such acquires a phantomlike, surreal presence. This is precisely equivalent to the emergence of the 'real' Laura in Otto Preminger's *Laura* (1944): the police detective (Dana Andrews) falls asleep staring at the portrait of the allegedly dead Laura. Upon awakening, he finds the 'real' Laura by the side of the portrait, alive and well. This presence of the 'real' Laura accentuates the fact that the portrait is a mere 'imitation'; on the other hand, the 'real' Laura emerges as a non-symbolized fantasmatic surplus, a ghostlike apparition. Beneath the portrait, one can easily imagine the inscription 'This is not Laura'.[30]

This, then, is the *'noir'* that defines the *noir* universe: that crack in the half-open window that shakes our sense of reality and is as such correlative to the subject *qua* void, gap in reality. Eventually, everything that has been said is given a condensed expression in Frank Capra's *It's a Wonderful Life* (1946), a film whose unmistakable *noir* undertones belie the common reduction of Capra's universe to a New Deal populist humanism. When, out of utter despair, the hero (James Stewart) is on the brink of committing suicide, the angel Clarence stops him and submits him to a Kripkean mental experiment with possible universes: he sends him back to his small Massachusetts town, but renders him unrecognizable, depriving him of all aspects of his identity, including his past history, so that he can witness how things would have turned out had he never existed. In this way, the hero regains his optimism, since the catastrophic consequences of his absence are made evident to him: his brother has drowned long ago (the hero was not there to save him), the good-hearted old pharmacist is rotting in jail (the hero was not there to warn him against inadvertently mixing in poison when preparing a prescription), his wife is a lone, despairing old maid, and, above all, his father's small loan society, providing credits to working-class families and thus serving as the last shield of the popular community against the ruthless local capitalist who wants to control the entire town, has gone bankrupt (the hero was not there to take his father's business over, so, instead of a town where solidarity prevails and every poor family has a modest home of their own, the hero finds himself in a bursting, violent American small town, full of rude drunkards and noisy nightclubs, totally controlled by the local magnate). What immediately strikes the eye here is the fact that the America encountered by the hero when he witnesses the way things would turn out in his absence is the actual America, that is, its features are those of the contemporary grim social reality (the dissolution of its communal solidarity, the boastful vulgarity of its nightlife, etcetera). The relationship of dream and reality is thus reversed: what the hero, in the mental experiment he is subjected to, experiences as a nightmarish dream is actual life; in other words, we encounter the real in the filmic dream, and it is precisely in order to escape this traumatic real that the hero takes refuge within the (diegetic) reality structured by the ideological fantasy of the idyllic community still able to resist the ruthless pressure of big capital. This is what Lacan means when he says that the traumatic real is encountered in dreams; this is the way ideology structures our experience of reality.

What we are primarily interested in, however, is the Cartesian dimension of this mental experiment. That is to say, when Stewart is sent back to his town as a stranger, he is bereft of his entire symbolic identity, reduced to a pure *cogito*, as the angel Clarence points out. He has no family, no personal history, even the small wound on his lips has disappeared: the only remaining kernel of certainty, the kernel of the real that remains 'the same' in the two different symbolic universes, is his *cogito*, the pure form of self-consciousness devoid of any content. *Cogito* designates this very point at which the I loses its support in the symbolic network of tradition and thus, in a sense which is far from metaphorical, ceases to exist. This pure *cogito* corresponds to the fantasy gaze: in it, I find myself reduced to a nonexistent gaze, that is, after losing all my effective predicates, I am nothing but a gaze paradoxically entitled to observe the world in which I do not exist (like, say, the fantasy of parental coitus where I am reduced to a gaze that observes my own conception, prior to my actual existence, or the fantasy of witnessing my own funeral). In this precise sense one can say that fantasy, in its most basic dimension, implies the choice of thought at the expense of being: in it I find myself reduced to the evanescent point of a thought contemplating the course of events during my absence, my non-being. In short, I find myself reduced to a *noir* subject.

Usually, the opposition of *film noir* to the classical logic-and-deduction detective fiction is conceived along the axis of being versus thought (or, as it is usually put; action versus contemplation): the logic-and-deduction narrative centres on the mental exercise of the detective who maintains his disengaged distance, who is present just to give body to the 'grey matter', thus whose being is not involved in the affair, whereas in *film noir* the detective is himself caught up in events, to the point of putting his very life at stake. What our analysis ultimately indicates, however, is the exact opposite: classical detective fiction is based on the choice of being at the expense of thought, whereas the shift to *film noir* involves the choice of thought. That is to say, the underlying libidinal matrix of the shift from logic-and-deduction narrative into *noir* narrative is that of the shift of *desire* into *drive*.[31] 'Desire and Its Interpretation', the title of Lacan's seminar of 1958–59, is to be taken as tautological: what this seminar aims to demonstrate is that desire *is* its interpretation, that interpretation of a desire is always already the desire of interpretation – *desire* is that very force that compels us to progress infinitely from one signifier to another in the hope of attaining the ultimate signifier that would fix the meaning of the preceding chain. In opposition to desire, drive is not 'progressive' but rather 'regressive', bound to circulate endlessly around some fixed point of attraction, immobilized by its power of fascination. In short, the opposition of desire and drive corresponds to that of symptom and fantasy: symptoms are ciphered messages to be interpreted, fantasies are to be gazed at, they resist interpretation. In this precise sense symptom is based on the choice of being, it presents the case of 'I am, therefore it thinks', that is, it is the decentred place at which my 'repressed', unconscious thought is articulated, the thought that I have renounced by way of choosing being; fantasy, on the contrary, presents a case of 'I think, therefore it is': in it, I am reduced to a pure thought intuiting the being of *jouissance* in its imbecility.

   Classical logic-and-deduction narrative stages desire in its purest: the effort to interpret symptomatic 'clues' and thus to reconstruct the 'primal scene' of the crime.

In clear contrast to this, the *noir* narrative reduces the hero to a passive observer transfixed by the succession of fantasy scenes, to a gaze powerlessly gaping at them: even when the hero seems 'active', one cannot avoid the impression that he simultaneously occupies the position of a disengaged observer, witnessing with incredulity the strange, almost submarine, succession of events in which he remains trapped.

NOTES

1. *Basic Instinct* also, in a very specific way, bears witness to a fundamental change in the logic and function of the narrative frame. A decade or two ago, the effect of the sudden shift in the last shot (the tracking from the love-making couple on the bed to a close-up of the ice-pick under the bed) would have been shattering, it would have caused a vertiginous turnabout compelling us to reinterpret the entire previous content. Today, however, it loses its dramatic impact and basically leaves us indifferent. In short, the 'Hitchcockian object', a 'little piece of the real' condensing an intense intersubjective relationship, is today no longer possible.

2. The version released in 1992 as the 'director's cut' is a compromise, not yet the true original: whilst it does eliminate the voice-over and the imbecilic happy ending, it still abstains from disclosing Deckard's own replicant status.

3. All quotations from Kant's *Critique of Pure Reason* are from Norman Kemp Smith's translation (London: Macmillan, 1992).

4. Which is why the expression 'self-in-itself' used by some interpreters of Kant (Findlay, for example) is inherently nonsensical: in so far as we conceive self as an intelligible thing, it loses the very feature that defines it, namely its transcendental 'spontaneity' and autonomy, which belong to it only within the horizon of finitude, that is, of the split between intelligible and intuitive. (This is ultimately confirmed by Kant himself who always insisted on leaving open the possibility that free human activity is actually regulated by some inaccessible intelligible nature – God's Providence, for example – which makes use of us for the realization of its unfathomable plan.)

5. The same paradox could also be formulated by way of the ambiguous ontological status of possibility which, in its very capacity as 'mere possibility' as opposed to actuality, possesses an actuality of its own: the Kantian transcendental apperception designates a pure possibility of self-consciousness which, *qua* possibility, produces actual effects, that is, determines the actual status of the subject. Once this possibility is actualized, we are no longer dealing with the self-consciousness of the pure I, but with the empirical consciousness of the self *qua* phenomenon, part of reality. Another way to formulate this difference is via the gap that separates 'I' from 'me': the Kantian transcendental apperception designates the I of 'I think', whereas Descartes surreptitiously substantivizes the 'je pense' (I think) into 'moi qui pense' (me who thinks).

6. Henry E. Allison, *Kant's Transcendental Idealism* (Cambridge: Cambridge University Press, 1983), p. 289.

7. Ibid., pp. 289–90.

8. Towards the end of Part One of *Critique of Practical Reason*, the same logic re-emerges at the ethical level: if I were to have a direct insight into God's nature, this would abrogate the very notion of ethical activity.

9. Sigmund Freud, *The Psychopathology of Everyday Life*, Pelican Freud Library, vol. 5 (Harmondsworth: Penguin, 1976), p. 248.

10. It is against this background that computer-phobia can be properly situated: the fear of a 'machine that thinks' bears witness to the foreboding that thought as such is external to the self-identity of my being.

11. One of the early stories of Philip Dick, the author of *Do Androids Dream of Electric Sheep* on which *Blade Runner* is based, is 'The Father-thing'. Charles Walton, a ten-year-old boy, realizes that his father Ted was killed and replaced by an alien, malignant form of life. This thing, which is 'in father more than father', an evil embodiment of the superego, can be discerned in those rare moments when the expression of Charles's father's face suddenly changes, losing the features of an ordinary, weary middle-class American and irradiating a kind of indifferent, impersonal evil.

12. In this respect, the consequences of the Orlando, Florida, court ruling in September 1992, in favour of compliance with the wishes of the ten-year-old boy who wanted to remain with his foster parents instead of returning to his biological mother, are more radical than may appear, since they concern the very relationship of S_1 and S_2: when a child can win a divorce against his mother, as the newspapers put it, he can ultimately choose who his mother (or his father) is with regard to their respective positive properties (the quality of care, etcetera). In this way, motherhood as well as fatherhood ultimately cease to be symbolic functions independent of positive features: the very logic of 'Whatever you do, you remain my mother/father and I shall love you . . . ', of *qua* master-signifier which designates a symbolic mandate, not a simple cluster of properties, is undermined.

13. The correlate to this reduction of the father to non-phallic Knowledge, of course, is the fantasy notion of mother *qua* self-reproducing monster which generates its offspring without the mediation of the phallus: it was Marx who, in an enigmatic metaphor in *Capital*, vol. III, determined capital as a self-reproducing mother-thing.

14. Was not the same gesture accomplished by Kierkegaard apropos of belief? We finite mortals are condemned to 'believe that we believe'; we can never be certain that we actually believe. This position of eternal doubt, this awareness that our belief is forever condemned to remain a hazardous wager, is the only way for us to be true Christian believers: those who go beyond the threshold of uncertainty and preposterously assume that they really do believe are not believers at all but arrogant sinners. If, according to Lacan, the question that animates the compulsive (obsessional) neurotic is 'Am I dead or alive?', and if the religious version of it is 'Am I really a believer or do I just believe I believe?', here, as we can see, the question is transformed into 'Am I a (dead) replicant or a (living) human being?'

15. For such a reading, see Kaja Silverman, 'Back to the Future', *Camera Obscura*, 27 (1991), pp. 109–32.

16. This utopian world is, of course, structured as a counterpoint to the aggressive, patriarchal, Western civilization: the realm of matriarchy (*She*), of black rule (*King Solomon's Mines*), of harmonious contact with nature (*Tarzan*), of balanced wisdom (*Lost Horizon*). The message of these novels is, however, more ambiguous than it may seem. For the heroes who enter this idyllic world, life in the domain of saturated desire soon becomes unbearable and they strive to return to our corrupted civilization; the universe of pure fantasy is a universe without surplus-enjoyment, that is, a perfectly balanced universe where the object-cause of desire cannot be brought to effect.

17. This is the reason why this pass is always shown in a way that points out its artificial

character (one perceives immediately that it is a studio set, with its entire background – including the 'rancho notorious' in the valley below – painted on a gigantic cloth); the same procedure was used by Hitchcock in his *Marnie*, among others. And do we not encounter the same matrix of a pure fantasy space beyond the frontier in Coppola's *Apocalypse Now*? What this film stages is also a kind of 'voyage beyond the end of the world': the 'end of the world' is clearly represented by the burning bridge on the frontier of Vietnam and Kampuchea, this place of general confusion and dissolution where the distinction between reality and delusion is blurred. However, once we trespass across this frontier and penetrate its beyond, the ferocious violence suddenly gives way to an unnatural calm; we enter the pure fantasy space, the kingdom of Kurtz, the obscene father, the reverse of the 'normal' symbolic Father who constitutes reality.

18. This space is similar to that of the 'transcendental *Schein*' in Kant. Although the Idea of Reason does not belong to the field of reality, of possible experience, it functions as the symbolic closure that totalizes, fills out, its field – if we progress in reality to its utter limit, we suddenly find ourselves 'on the other side', in Ideas to which no reality corresponds.

19. See Jacques Lacan, *Le Seminaire, livre VII: L'ethique de la psychanalyse* (Paris: Editions du Seuil, 1986), chapter XX.

20. Beside the *real* impossibility and the *symbolic* prohibition there is a third, *imaginary*, version the economy of which is psychotic: incest is necessary and unavoidable since every libidinal object is incestuous. An exemplary case of it is the Catharic heresay that prohibits *every* sexual relation, claiming that intercourse with *any* libidinal object, not only with one's parents, is incestuous. As to these three modalities of incest (its impossibility, prohibition, necessity), see Peter Widmer,

'Jenseits des Inzestverbots', *Riss* 2, 4 and 6, Zürich 1986–87.

21. Here we encounter the function of the 'subject supposed to believe': the existing order is legitimized via the fact that any doubt about it would betray the naïve belief of the Other (of the foreign worker who believes in the USSR and who, by means of this belief, confers meaning and consistency upon his life). As to the notion of the 'subject supposed to believe', see Slavoj Žižek, *The Sublime Object of Ideology* (London: Verso, 1989), pp. 185–6.

22. For another reading of this paradox see Žižek, pp. 45–7.

23. See Sigmund Freud, *The Interpretation of Dreams* (Harmondsworth: Penguin 1977), chapter II.

24. Jacques Lacan, *The Seminar of Jacques Lacan, Book II: The Ego in Freud's Theory and in the Techinque of Psychoanalysis* (Cambridge: Cambridge University Press 1988), p. 159.

25. Ibid., p. 154.

26. Ibid., pp. 154–5.

27. Ibid., p. 168.

28. Ibid., p. 161.

29. Michel Foucault, *This Is Not a Pipe* (Berkeley and Los Angeles: University of California Press, 1982).

30. A somewhat homologous effect of the real occurs at the beginning of Sergio Leone's *Once Upon a Time in the West* (1984): a phone rings endlessly; when, finally, a hand picks up the receiver, the phone continues to ring – the first sound belongs to 'reality', whereas the ringing that continues even after the receiver is picked up comes out of the non-specified void of the real. What we have in this scene, of course, is a kind of reflective redoubling of the external stimulus (sound, organic need, etcetera) which triggers the activity of dreaming: one invents a dream integrating this element in order to prolong sleep, yet the content encountered in the dream is so

traumatic that, finally, one escapes into reality and awakens. The ringing of the phone while we are asleep is such a stimulus *par excellence*; its duration even after the source in reality ceases to emit it exemplifies what Lacan calls the *insistence* of the real.

31. The point was made by Joan Copjec, in a paper delivered at the City University of New York; a longer version of that paper is presented in this volume (chapter 6).

8

HOME FIRES BURNING: FAMILY NOIR IN *BLUE VELVET* AND *TERMINATOR 2*

Fred Pfeil

When we think about *film noir* in the present, it is well to remember the categorical instability that has haunted it from the moment French critics coined the term in the late 1940s as a retrospective tag for a number of previously withheld American films which now, upon their foreign release, all looked and felt strikingly similar. Ever since, critics and theorists have been arguing about what *film noir* is, which films the term includes, and what social or psychic processes it engages. Does *film noir* constitute a genre; or a style that can be deployed across generic boundaries; or a historically specific movement within Hollywood cinema? These intrinsic questions and debates have their own momentum and energy, but derive extra charge from an associated set of extrinsic questions regarding *film noir*'s relationships to other, noncinematic social transformations, especially shifts in gender identities and relationships in the USA after World War Two. Did the spider-women of so many *films noirs*, despite their destructiveness, constitute a challenge to the restoration and extension of a patriarchal–capitalist gender economy under whose terms men controlled and ran the public sphere while women, desexualized and maternalized, were relegated to hearth and home? Does the aggressive sexuality, power and plot controlling/generating/deranging force, of, say, a Barbara Stanwyck in *Double Indemnity*, Jane Greer in *Out of the Past*, Gloria Grahame in *The Big Heat*, together with *film noir*'s characteristically deviant visuality – its cramped asymmetrical framings, its expressionistically harsh lighting contrasts and lurid shadows, the whole twisted and uncertain spatiality of it matching the male protagonist's lack of control over the breakneck deviousness of its plot – constitute a real and potentially effective subversion of the dominant order, as Christine Gledhill suggests?[1] Or is it simply, as neoformalist film historian David Bordwell asserts, that 'these films blend causal unity with a new realistic and generic motivation, and the result no more subverts the classical film' – or, we may presume, anything else – 'than crime fiction undercuts the orthodox novel'?[2]

The debate smoulders on unresolved, and perhaps irresolvably, depending as it does on some broader knowledge or agreement as to what indeed constitutes subversive or progressive work within a pre- or non-revolutionary cultural moment and social formation. More directly, the question is: how can any capital-intensive work, such as film, produced for a mass audience be progressive, and what are the signs that it is? How (and how well) would such work *work*? What (and how much) would it *do*? More crudely still, how far can a work go and still be produced and distributed within a system whose various structures are overdetermined by capitalism and patriarchy (not to mention racism and homophobia)? What is the most, and the best, we can demand or expect?

Such messy questions press themselves on us today so insistently that a whole new interdisciplinary proto-discipline, 'cultural studies', has been constituted just to deal with them. Their urgency for us is, after all, inevitably consequent upon the dimming of the revolutionary horizon, and the loss or confusion of revolutionary faith, not only within the socialist left but throughout all the other feminist and 'minority' movements in the seventies and eighties. In the USA the revolution, to the extent that there was one, came from the right – recall 'new right' guru Paul Weyrich's proud proclamation in the wake of the first Reagan election in the early 1980s, 'We are radicals seeking to overthrow the power structure' – against the liberal-corporatist state and the sociopolitical good sense that flowed from and supported it, both of which have been dismantled and rearticulated in quite different ways. Given this combination, then, of disintegration below and regressive hegemonic reintegration from on high, the whole notion of what Gramsci called a 'war of movement', of deep structural and institutional change, has come to seem to many once-insurrectionary spirits to be inconceivably crackpot or even worse, a grisly ruse of the very power (à la Foucault) it pretends to oppose; so that a permanent 'war of position', the ever partial and provisional *détournement* of otherwise intractable institutional arrangements and practices, becomes literally the only game in town.

I describe this situation here not to deplore or criticize it, nor to attempt to resolve the questions of cultural politics that flow from it; it is, for better and for worse, the set of circumstances we in the developed West, and the USA in particular, now inhabit. So it will serve both as the context from which we must think about the meaning and direction of some of the newest mutations in the *noir* sensibility, and, dialectically, as the subject of that sensibility's reflections back upon us. But before turning to consider those mutations, it may be worthwhile to rehearse briefly those aspects of *film noir* conceded to be its constitutive features, even by critics who otherwise disagree over where it belongs and what it means. These aspects typically involve a combination of iconographic, stylistic, narrative and thematic features: iconographically they stretch from the dark city streets and lurid jazzy bars to the privatized, alienated space of the car and the modern urban apartment, and down to the close-up level of the cigarette, drink, swanky dress, trenchcoat and slouch hat; stylistically, from the use of voice-over and flashback to expressionistic lighting and decentred and unstable compositions, often in deep space; narratively, they include a new emphasis on deviant psychological motivation, the deviousness and frustrating confusion of the male protagonist's project or quest, and the outright hostility, suspicion and sexual attraction between the often confused and weary male protagonist and the duplicitous, powerful femme fatale (with a good asexual wife–mother figure optionally dead or waiting in the wings); and thematically, they consist above all in the 'absurd' existential choice of moral behaviour according to one's own individual ethical code, in a hopelessly dark universe in which more consensual authorities are ineffectual, irrelevant, or corrupt.

In Bakhtinian criticism, the concept of the chronotope provides us with a useful tool for synthesizing and mediating all such features into a common image of a given narrative form, its quintessential phenomenal 'feel'. Vivian Sobchak's, 'Lounge Time: Post-war Crises and the Chronotope of Film Noir' usefully reconstructs *film noir's* chronotope:

> The diacritical contrast that structures film noir . . . is between the impersonal, discontinuous rented space of cocktail lounge, nightclub, hotel, and roadside café, on the one hand, and the familiar, unfragmented secure space of domesticity on the other. The noir chronotope has no room for children or for rituals of family continuity: 'no weddings, no births, no natural deaths, no family intimacy and connection can be eventful here.' Even leisure is more suffered than enjoyed in the 'lounge-time' of the shadowed space of film noir. The characters generated by this chronotope are transient, without roots or occupation, in a world where murder is more natural than death. The chronotope of film noir . . . perversely celebrates the repressed hysteria of a postwar cultural moment when domestic

and economic coherence were fractured, spatializing and concretizing a 'freedom' at once attractive, frightening, and ultimately illusory.[3]

If such a 'cultural moment' sounds much like our own seventies and eighties just past, we would none the less do well to resist the urge to invoke the similarity as straightforward explanation for the 'return' of *film noir* during those same years, in such films as *Body Heat* (1981) and the remakes of *Farewell, My Lovely* (1975) and *The Postman Always Rings Twice* (1981). Instead, it is the very notion of 'return' itself that needs to be explored.[4] For whatever *film noir* was in the forties and fifties, it will not be again three decades or more later by dint of straightforward imitation, and not only for the general reason that no such slavish reconstruction could ever escape the fetishizing and ossifying effects of its intention simply to repeat, but because the meanings and effects of the original *films noirs* even today must still be experienced and understood in their relation to a whole system of film production, distribution and consumption – the Hollywood studio system, in effect – which was in its last hour even then and is now gone. As Thomas Schatz has recently reminded us,[5] it was that system that most fully standardized and customized the look, feel and plotlines of film genres (from MGM classics and costume dramas to Warner's gangster pics and Universal's speciality in horror), some of them genres from which *noir* had something to steal (for example, the deep shadows and expressionistic framings of the horror film), but each and all of them together a system of techniques, conventions *and*, not least, audience expectations (for example, the romantic happy ending and/or the satisfying restoration of law and order) that *films noirs* first defined themselves by violating.

Bordwell's contention, quoted above, that these transgressions quickly fall into place as simply a new set of techniques, conventions and routinized audience satisfactions, is still debatable. But the view that the meanings of *film noir* must be worked through in relation to contemporaneous generic productions and the 'classical Hollywood style' in general, I should think, is not. So when the studio system breaks up into the present 'package-unit' system in which individual producers assemble production groups and materials on a film-by-film basis, employing what is left of the studios primarily as a distribution arm, and generic production atomizes too as the specialized constellations of talents and resources once fixed in position to produce it are dispersed, we may expect that the working parts of the *noir* machine of effects and responses will also break apart into so many free agents, capable of being drafted into any number of new, provisional combinatory teams, all according to the same recombinant aesthetic economy which, for example, a decade ago brought us the television series *Hill Street*

Blues out of a directive to its original writers to knock out a combination of a sitcom *Barney Miller* and the action-adventure series *Starsky and Hutch*.[6]

In this newer Hollywood, quintessential site of the intersection between the flexible specialization of post-Fordist production and the free-floating ideologemes-turned-syntax of postmodernism, the transgressive energies and subversive formal practices that first animated and defined *film noir* may indeed be most alive and well where they have migrated from the now-conventionalized site of their first appearance towards some new and even perverse combination with other formal and thematic elements in similar drift from other former film genres. Such, at any rate, is the hypothesis of this chapter, whose specific claim is that *film noir* in particular, homeless now as a genre, none the less currently finds itself most alive where its former elements and energies form part of a new chronotope whose chief difference from that non- or even anti-domestic one outlined by Sobchak for 'classic' *film noir* lies in the extent to which the newer one includes, and indeed is centred on, home and family, even as it decentres and problematizes both. Through a look at two successful recent films, *Blue Velvet* and *Terminator 2*, I mean to show how home and family are being destabilized, *noir*-ized in both. The large differences between these two films, in terms of aesthetic strategies and audiences, only make the similarities of results of each film's processing of *noir* elements that much more striking and significant. Striking in what way? How significant and for whom? Connected to what other transformations and praxes, under way or to come? Those questions will be raised again on the other side of the following readings, forcing us again to hedge and answer them as best we can in the absence of any clear or shared utopian goal.

BLUE VELVET AND THE STRANGELY FAMILIAR

It is too easy to tick off the *noir* elements in David Lynch's art film hit *Blue Velvet* (1986). The investigative male protagonist Jeffrey (Kyle McLachan), caught between danger-ous, dark-haired Dorothy Valens (Isabella Rossellini) and bland, blonde, Sandy (Laura Dern); the far-reaching nature of the evil Jeffrey uncovers and the entanglements of the police themselves in its web; the homoerotic dimension of the relationship between Jeffrey and the film's arch-villain Frank (Dennis Hopper): any college sophomore with an introductory film course can pick out these features, just as anyone with an introductory psychology course can pick up on the oedipal motifs hiding in plain sight, beginning with the collapse of Jeffrey's father and ending with his restoration. Michael Moon, in one of the best commentaries on the film, nicely summarizes the familiar story of what happens in between:

> . . . a young man must negotiate what is prepresented as being the treacherous path between an older, ostensibly exotic, sexually 'perverse' woman and a younger, racially 'whiter', sexual 'normal' one, and he must at the same time and as part of the same process negotiate an even more perilous series of interactions with the older woman's violent and murderous criminal lover and the younger woman's protective police-detective father. This heterosexual plot resolves itself in classic oedipal fashion: the young man, Jeffrey, destroys the demonic criminal 'father' and rival, Frank; rescues the older woman, Dorothy, from Frank's sadistic clutches; and then relinquishes her to her fate and marries the perky young daughter of the good cop.[7]

Blue Velvet (David Lynch, 1986)

Such a blatant evocation, or perhaps more accurately, acting-out, of the standard image repertoires of generic *film noir* and psychoanalytic truism will, it is worth noting, not be obvious to everyone – only to those who, thanks to college or some other equivalent educational circuitry, have the cultural capital to recognize the codes at work. Assuming such an audience, though, the point is to consider such paint-by-number material not as finished product, but as starting point and second-order raw material for the film's subsequent elaborations. If it would be a mistake to accept such generic material at face value, in other words, it would be just as wrong to write it off and look for what else is 'really' going on instead.

Our first job, then, is rather to consider *obviousness* in *Blue Velvet* as a feature in its own right – one with its own multiple, complex effects. But to take this subject up in turn is to notice immediately in just how many ways Lynch 'shoves it in our faces' as well as how many things 'it' in that last phrase comes to be, so often and so many that a certain kind of 'ominous–obvious' may fairly be said to constitute both the film's thematic subject and its formal method alike. An exhaustive reading of *Blue Velvet* along these lines could in fact begin with the film's very first image, the rippling blue velvet against which its opening titles appear, shot in such extreme, quasi-magnified close-up that, as Barbara Creed points out, its smooth, soft surface appears mottled and rough as bark.[8] But I would rather concentrate instead on the images that follow those credits, a sort of music video to the Bobby Vinton oldie of the film's title, falling in between (in both a chronological and a stylistic sense) the credits and the storyline that picks up at its end. Here is a list of the shots that compose the film's dreamy opening montage:

1. Tilt down from perfectly blue sky to red roses in medium close-up against white fence. DISSOLVE to
2. Long shot: fire truck passing by slowly on tree-shaded small-town street, with fireman on it waving in slow motion. DISSOLVE to
3. Yellow tulips against white fence, close-up as at the end of shot 1. DISSOLVE to
4. Long shot, small-town residential street: traffic guard beckoning for schoolchildren to cross, again in slow motion. DISSOLVE to
5. Long shot: white Cape Cod house and yard. CUT to
6. Medium shot: middle-aged man with hose, watering yard. CUT to
7. Long shot, interior: middle-aged woman inside, sitting with cup of coffee on couch, watching television, which displays black-and-white shot of man crossing screen, gun in hand, and from which issues sinister *film noir*ish music. CUT to
8. Close-up of hand holding gun on television screen. CUT to
9. Man with hose, as in shot 6, but now off-centre at screen left.

Actually, the sequence at this point has already begun to speed up somewhat, moving from shots of approximately five seconds apiece (shots 1–4) to an average of three (5–8). From shot 9 on, moreover, the sequence will quicken and warp still further, as an increasingly rapid montage of increasingly close-up shots of kinked hose/sputtering tap/vexed man, joined with a soundtrack in which the diegetic sound of water fizzing under pressure is combined with a gradually rising and apparently nondiegetic buzz or roar, towards the man's collapse, the hose's anarchic rearing upward, a slow-motion shot of a dog drinking from the hose beside the fallen man, the sound of the dog barking, a baby crying, a rushing wind combined with a mechanical rustling noise, as we go down through the lawn in a process shot pretending to be an unbroken zoom-in to a horde of swarming, warring black insects whose organic–mechanical noise-plus-wind now swells up to an overwhelming roar.

What is one to make of such an opening? Given our previous training in how to read a film's spatio-temporally orienting shots and narrative cues, it seems to me that in part we struggle to do the usual with this sequence: to read it narratively, place ourselves in it, 'follow' it out. And, of course, our efforts and presumptions in this regard are not entirely in vain. Okay, we say, it's a small town, and here's a particular family inside it, a dad and mom, and look, something's happening to the dad so things are off-balance now, not right, gee what happens next? But we say this only in part and against a kind of semic counter-logic or inertial drag instigated by the very same shots – at least or especially shots 1–4 and the slow-motion and extreme close-ups that close off the sequence (other such shot combinations will serve as the disjunctive ligatures between one section of the film's narrative and the next) – in the degree to which all these shots overrun their narrative or, in Barthesian terms, proairetic function and force attention on themselves in some purely imagistic way instead, Bobbie Vinton, blue sky, and red roses at one end, roaring wind, mechanical rustling, and ravening black insects on the other.

If, moreover, such a difference from the opening of conventional film falls somewhere short of effecting a total break with the prevailing model of filmic narrative, its relative distance from that model is none the less made all the more apparent by the lurch that follows back toward typicality. Like a second beginning, the shot sequence that follows opens with a set of establishing long shots of the town of Lumberton, simultaneously named as such by the local radio station on the soundtrack, after which we are shown Jeffrey the film's protagonist for the first time, pausing on his way to visit his hospitalized father in order to throw a stone in the field where he will soon find the severed ear of Dorothy Valens's husband and thereby set the film's *noir*ish plot into full motion. So now, in effect, we are invited to take a deep breath, relax, and begin a conventional reading of the film: only once again, not quite. For this sequence will no more settle into assured conventionality than the last completely broke from it. The deejay's radio patter is slightly, well, skewed – 'It's a sunny day,' he chirps, 'so get those chainsaws out' – as, on a visual level, is the sequence of images itself, in which the aforementioned shot of Jeffrey in the field is followed by two brief red-herring long shots of downtown – one of an unknown car pulling onto the town's main street, the other of an unknown man spinning what might be a ring of keys as he stands in front of a darkened store – before the sequence slips back into gear with a close-up of Jeffrey's father in his hospital bed as Jeffrey's visiting presence is announced.

From its outset, then, *Blue Velvet* is characterized by the *partial and irresolute* opposition of two distinct kinds and pleasures of narrative: one characterized by the relative dominance of what, following Barthesian narrative theory, I have called the *semic*, and the other by the equally relative dominance of the establishing, fixing and plotting functions of the *proairetic*. Less pretentiously, of course, we could speak of the predominance of *image* over *storyline*, and avoid French poststructuralist theory altogether, were it not for the real yet perverse relevance of Barthes's terms and the psychopolitical valences attached to them, for this particular film. To discern this relevance, we need only recall, first of all, that within that theory the placing, naming and motivating functions of the proairetic, and its predominance in conventional narrative, are held to be defining symptoms of the constitutive *oedipality* of such narrative energies and desires, or perhaps more precisely of the binding and containment of such desire; just as the atemporal and never-fully-repressible bursts and upwellings of the semic are identified with the carnivalesque freedom of the unregulated, post-, pre-, or even anti-oedipal social and individual body. Then all we have to do is notice how in so far as such definitions and categories do hold water for us, *Blue Velvet* gets them – though once again, only sort of – wrong from the start, observing this oppositional distinction and flouting it at the same time by reversing what one might have thought was their 'natural' order: for what kind of narrative text is it, after all, in which the fall of the father is *preceded* by a sequence of images predominantly semic in nature, but *followed* by one that more or less falls obediently into story-plotting line?

A postmodern text, of course: the kind of postmodern work that, as in Cindy Sherman's first acclaimed photographs, is concerned both to hybridize and hollow out the cliché. For simultaneously hyperrealizing and decentering narrative and cinematic convention is what *Blue Velvet* is about, both its way of doing business and the business itself. Visually, as Laurie Simmons's description of Lynch's style suggests, its techniques and effects are most clearly related to those of pop art, though more that of Rosenquist, say, than of Andy Warhol.[9] Such perfect two-dimensionality – so different from the expressionistically crowded and askew deep spaces of classic *noir* style – simultaneously flattens and perfects all its glazed gaze captures, from roses to ravening insects, soda fountain booth to severed ear, while on the film's soundtrack, the same sense is created and reinforced by Badalamenti's score which, here as in *Twin Peaks*, flaunts its barefaced imitation of *misterioso*-à-la-Hitchcock-composer Bernard Hermann one minute, gushing romantic strings à la Dmitri Tiomkin the next, with some dollops of the kind of insipid finger-popping jazz-blues once written for the Quinn-Martin television detective series, and soundtrack scores of the first living-room *films noirs*, thrown in on the side. Such pre-digested product thus functions as the musical equivalent of the clichéd dialogue of the script and the two-dimensional visuality of the cinematography, each overdetermining the other into an aggregate signal of intentional derivativeness and knowing banality whose obverse or underside is clearly that moment when, aurally and/or visually, that which we take as the *ur*-natural (the clicking and mandibular crunching of the insects, the robin with the worm in its mouth) becomes indistinguishable from sounds of industry, the sight of the obviously animatronic – in short, the synthetic constructions, material and imaginative, of human beings themselves, recognized and felt as such.

In early industrial Britain, Keats invited his readers to the edge of one sublime mode of hyperattention, a falling into the object's depths so intense the viewer's own consciousness is eclipsed ('A drowsy numbness pains/My sense'). In the postmodern, late industrial mode of Lynch's film, however, the gleaming but off-kilter perfection of such recherché surfaces as those we have examined constitutes its very own warp, and the terrified rapture of the romantic swoon away from consciousness is replaced by a queasy awareness of anxious affiliation to and guilty/paranoid complicity with all that we are so familiar with in what we see and hear, as in this scene in which our hero Jeffrey has a talk in the den with Lieutenant Williams, bland-blonde Sandy's father and police detective, consequent to Jeffrey's discovery of the ear:

> WILLIAMS: You've found something that is very interesting to us. Very interesting. I know you must be curious to know more. But I'm afraid I'm going to have to ask you not only not to tell anybody about the case, but not to tell anybody about your find. One day when it's all sewed up, I'll let you know all the details. Right now, though, (*glancing sidelong, sneaking a puff on his cigarette*) I can't.
>
> JEFFREY: I understand. I'm just real curious, like you said.
>
> WILLIAMS: (*slightly smiling*) I was the same way myself when I was your age. That's why I went into this business.
>
> JEFFREY: (*laughs*) Must be great.
>
> WILLIAMS: (*freezes, sours smile*) It's horrible too. I'm sorry Jeffrey; it just has to be that way. Anyway Jeffrey, I know you do understand.

Each sentence, every phase, is 100 per cent B-movie cliché, and delivered as such, with all the wooden earnestness the actors can muster. Yet I hope my transcription also conveys something of the extent to which, even as that dialogue rattles out, Williams's suspiciously askew reactions and expressions move our reactions not so much against the direction of the clichés as athwart them. On the level of the storyline, and given our past experience of both oedipal narrativity in general and *film noir* in particular, they may prompt us to wonder if Father/Detective Williams won't turn out to be one of the bad guys after all; on the level of what we might call the film's enunciation, though, and in light of all else we have seen about this film so far, such a moment is apt to engender a far more fundamental distrust, less the suspicion that we have not got to the bottom of this yet than the full-blown paranoia that there may be no bottom here at all.

So to the closing moments of the film, when Jeffrey and Sandy and their families are both completed and combined around the exemplary centre of their good love, the famous moment when that robin shows up with the worm in its mouth and Jeffrey's Aunt Barbara, looking over his shoulder and munching on a hotdog, says 'I could never do that!' provokes a complicated laugh from the audience. On the one hand, of course, it is about both the ironic relation of the amorally predatory robin to the goopy speech Sandy gave earlier in the film, in which robins figured in a dream she had had as emblems of pure good, and the reinforcing irony of Aunt Barbara's self-righteous disavowal of the very appetitiveness she is displaying by stuffing her mouth. On the other, though, given the bird's obvious artificiality, the music's clichéd goopiness, and the hypercomposed flatness and stiffness of the *mise en scène*, it is also about the anxious and delightful possibility that Aunt Barbara – and Jeffrey and Sandy, for that matter – are robots, too. And of course they are, in the sense that they are constructions of sound and words and light, spaces where Lynch & Company's projections meet our own; and in this sense so are all the characters in every feature film. Yet if every film in the Hollywood tradition invites its audience to recite some version of the Mannoni formula *Je sais bien mais quand même* on its way into and through the story-world it offers, *Blue Velvet* is none the less distinctive for the steady insistence with which it ups the volume on its own multiple, hybridized and hyperrealized elements of *retrouvée*, pushing its audience to acknowledge its own 'I know very well' at least as much as its 'but even so . . . ', and so to taint and complicate a heretofore blissfully irresponsible and safely distanced voyeurism with its own admissions of familiarity as complicity, anxious lack of distance, guilt at home.[10] 'You put your disease inside me!' Dorothy says to Jeffrey and, of him, to everyone around her at one point; and so he/we did; but in another sense, of course, the disease, 'it', was there/here/everywhere all along, and we have 'it' inside us too.

It is this 'it', this recognition and admission of the obvious artifice, that we carry with us alongside and through those obvious elements of *film noir* and of oedipal pyscho-pathology that have themselves elicited so much critical commentary. Some writers have concentrated on Lynch's blending and blurring of genres (MacLachan's Jeffrey as both Philip Marlowe and Dobie Gillis) and generic chronotopes (the smoky nightclub in the small town, the naked 'dark woman' in the family's living room), whilst others home in on the sheer mobility of male-hysterical fantasy in the film: the dangerous, vertiginous, yet perpetual oscillations between sadism and masochism, 'Daddy' and 'Baby', hetero- and homosexual desire, as all these are acted out (in both senses of the term) in the film's excess of primal scenes (Jeffrey with Dorothy, Frank with Dorothy, Jeffrey and Frank with Ben, Jeffrey with Frank). Yet even those who have attempted to consider and synthesize both these manifest topical areas have tended to miss, or at least underestimate, the full measure, meaning and effect of the de-realizing, de-naturalizing formal operations of the film, and the extent to which they power the movement toward what Michael Moon describes as 'the fearful knowledge that what most of us consider our deepest and strongest desires are not our own, that our dreams and fantasies are only copies, audio- and videotapes, of the desires of others and our utterances of them lip-synching of these circulating, endlessly reproduced and reproducible desires' even before the generic mix is evident and the sexual–psychoanalytic heyday/mayhem begins.[11] What fascinates and appalls in *Blue Velvet*, what simultaneously underwrites and undermines the mixed messages of its generic play and desublimated oedipality, is the sense of the fragility of the symbolic, its susceptibility to the metonymic 'disease' of constant slippage that is always already inside it, a *gynesis* of both film and family that irresolves without overthrowing, that keeps home un-natural while forcing us to own up to the familiarity of all that is officially Other and strange, that makes home-making a dislocating experience, from blue-sky beginning (plenitude or emptiness? true blue or fake void?) to blue-sky end.

TERMINATOR 2: ANY WHICH WAY BUT LOOSE

Things are somewhat different in the recent blockbuster sci-fi hit *Terminator 2: Judgment Day* (James Cameron, 1991), if only because investors are unlikely to put up $90 million for a project whose meanings, pleasures and rules of editing derive from the principle of the semiotic erosion of narrative conventions, irresolution as an aesthetic way of life. The overall regime of pleasure in the blockbuster film is, rather, a paradigm of late capitalist consumer production: it must keep us constantly (though *not* continuously) engaged without demanding much attention; knock us out with all the trouble it has gone to just to give us an instant's satisfaction; and not only offer us options but also affirm and even flatter us for whichever ones we pick.

To define blockbusters in terms of such hard-wired business requirements is, however, not to mark the point where analysis of their significance ends, but rather to suggest where it has to begin. For if the blockbuster typically invites us to 'have it either and/or both ways', then both the character of the contradictory options offered and the name and definition of the 'it' can be read as complex signposts showing the way to the mainstream culture's ideological *points de capiton*,[12] the places where collective social desire — for transformation and salvage, revolution and restoration, anarchy and obedience — is simultaneously fastened and split. This, to take up one early example, is the interest of those opening scenes of *Terminator 2* in which the two synthetic creatures from the future first appear in present-day Los Angeles bent on their opposed missions, to protect or kill the boy John Conner, and to this end outfit themselves in the garbs and roles of ordinary mortal men. The T-800, a.k.a. Arnold Schwarzenegger, cyborg simulacrum of Sarah Conner's would-be killer in the first *Terminator* film, arrives in the blue, burnished glory of his hypermuscled nakedness in front of an equally gleaming semi-truck parked across from a biker bar he will soon scope out and bust up, leaving in full regalia, in shades and leathers, and astride a Harley hog, to the heavy-metal strains of George Thorogood and the Destroyers stuttering 'B-b-b-born to be bad'. In the following sequence, however, in which we meet the protean, pro-grammed-to-kill *all*-robot T-1000, we are taken to a desolate patch of no-man's-land underneath a curving span of LA overpass to which a city cop has been called to investigate the strange electrical goings-on accompanying this unit's passage through time and space: whereupon the T-1000, assuming for the moment a proto-hominoid silver shape, sneaks up on the cop from behind, kills him and takes on his steely-eyed Aryan form, complete with uniform, as his central identity for the rest of the film.

In the span of these two brief scenes, entertainment professionals James Cameron *et al.* have already provided us with a wide range and satisfying oscillation of identifica-tions and exclusions, pleasures and disavowals. For starters, there is the linkage and differentiation of Arnold in his *ab ovo* muscle-builder's pose and the parked semi behind him, suggesting as this composite image does both Arnold himself as gleaming machine, icon of burly masculinist culture at its most spectacularly developed pitch, and Arnold as a display item quite out of this dingy quotidian work world altogether. Such ambivalence, together with its options for enjoyment, is then carried right into and through the mayhem at the biker bar that ensues, in which those menacing scumbags are first literally summed up by the T-800's hi-tech apparatus then disarmed and disrobed, resulting in a new version of the composite Arnold image, both 'badder' and 'higher' than the bikers, at one and the same time pure realization of their outlaw nature and antithesis of their downwardly mobile sleaze. And the ambivalence of this newly sublated figure will then be further marked and played out against that constructed in the next sequence around the evil T-1000, which begins in turn by cueing off our conventional identification with the figure of law and order poking around in the dark shadows at the margins of the normatively social, but ends by conflating these two figures – one, a white male LA cop – as formless evil (a particularly pungent if fortuitous manoeuvre, we may note, given national exposure of the racist brutality of Police Chief Gates's Los Angeles Police Department a scant few months before this film's release).

I will return soon to consider further the exact nature and significance of the *agon*, or contest, between this bad-guy-as-good-guy and the good-guy-as-bad. For now, though, let this opening example serve as a demonstration of the play of opposition and symbiosis essential to *Terminator 2*: that is, as a demonstration of processes that combine a fair amount of mobility granted to our various desires and fears with a lack of ambiguity at any given moment as to what we ought to think and feel. One minute the bikers are low-life scum, then Arnold is a biker; one minute the LA cop is bravely doing his duty, the next minute he is a remorseless assassin; yet throughout all these inclusions and exclusions we are never in doubt about which side to be on. The punctual clarity of such a 'preferred investment' strategy, as we might call it, thus stands in marked contrast to the real ambiguities of judgement and feeling that are the warp and woof of classic *film noir*, in the figures of, for example, the morally shady detective and the smart, alluring femme fatale, and is even farther away from the constant sliding and seepage within Lynch's film. In fact, the first thing to observe about most of the features of *film noir* taken up by *Terminator 2* is the degree to which they are, as in *Blue Velvet*, both untrustworthy as straightforward quotation or appropriation yet, paradoxically, all the more significant for that.

Take *Terminator 2*'s narrative strategy, one of the film's several *noir*ish qualities. In classic *film noir*, as we know, the question of who is in control of the film's narration is often central to its meanings and effects.[13] In *films noirs* like *Gilda* or *Out of the Past*, that question is posed by the disjunction between the male protagonist's tightlipped voice-over and the sinister twists of the enacted plot in whose devious turnings the figure of the femme fatale seems to exert a powerful hand. And at first it seems that something of the same, but with a postmodern, postfeminist difference, is true of *Terminator 2* as well. Here, too, the laconic decisiveness of the voice-over contrasts with the narrator's

Terminator 2: Judgment Day (James Cameron, 1991)

Terminator 2: Judgment Day (James Cameron, 1991)

comparative lack of control over the film's action; only here the destination towards which the plot careens is enlarged from individual catastrophe all the way to planetary nuclear holocaust as a result of the entropic drift of masculinist techno-rationality; and the tough-guy narrator is a woman.

On this level, then, *Terminator 2*, like its predecessor, appears to be a sci-fi 'feminist *film noir*' pitting its female heroine Sarah Conner against various individual and collective 'hommes fatales' in a simple yet effective inversion of the old device. Yet while such a conclusion is, I think, not entirely false, even less could it be declared simply true. For one thing, it is obviously *not* Linda Hamilton who is the big star of *Terminator 2*, but Arnold Schwarzenegger; nor is it Sarah Conner who, for all her stirring efforts, is finally able to save the world, if indeed it has been saved, but the proto/semi-male T-800 who supplies the vital edge. For another, and for all the *noir*ish haze and green/blue/black suffused throughout the film, on the level of narrative there is virtually no confusion about what is going on, or how to feel about it. Just as clearly as we know from moment to moment who is good and who is bad, we know Arnold the T-800 protector will rescue boy John from the clutches of the wicked T-1000; and when boy John insists they break into the state hospital for the criminally insane and rescue his mother Sarah, we know they will be able to pull that off as well. When the three of them, plus Dyson the computer scientist, are on their way to the headquarters of Cyberdyne Corporation to destroy those fragments of the first Terminator from the previous *Terminator* film, which, when analysed and understood, will result in the construction of the SkyNet system of 'defence' that will in turn trigger off the holocaust, Sarah's voice-over, atop a night-for-night shot of a dark highway rushing into the headlights and past, intones the *noir*ish message that 'The future, always so clear to me, had been like a dark highway at night. We were in uncharted territory now, making up history as we went along.' By this time, though, such a message comes across as mere atmosphere, the verbal equivalent of the aforementioned laid-on haze, rather than as any real entrance into 'uncharted' territory on the part of a plot in which we know where we are, and where we are headed, each step of the way.

Yet if the relation between narration and enactment in *Terminator 2* is less an innovative extension of *film noir* than first appeared, it is not hard to locate more genuine expressions of a *noir* sensibility in the film's sense of space and time. In terms of space, *Terminator 2* early on takes its leave of the sunstruck residential neighbourhood where John Conner lives with his ineffectual foster parents, and spends the rest of its running time either keeping its distance from or destroying any and all traditional domestic space. And its classic *noir* preference for the bleak sprawl of southern

California freeways, state institutions, research centres, malls and plants over any closed familial enclaves is matched by its implicit flattening of time even across the gap of nuclear apocalypse. The premiss motivating *Terminator 2* – that in the wake of nuclear apocalypse a resistance led by the adult John Conner continues to struggle against the inhuman power of the machine, so that both sides, resistance and power network, send their mechanical minions back in time, one to protect John-the-boy and the other to 'terminate' him – insists on a difference between present and future that the film's depictions erode. Here in the present, official power – whether in the form of the sadistically panoptical mental hospital, the gleaming surfaces and security systems of the soulless corporation, or the massively armed and equipped, anonymous police – already runs rampant; here already, before the bomb falls, the hardy band of guerrilla terrorists resists, the fireballs blossom and the bodies pile up in the perpetual dark night of Hobbesian confrontation between bad anarchy and good.

Terminator 2 thus not only reconstructs the fallen public world and queasy temporality of classic *film noir* but also constructs them together in the form of an apocalypse that has, in effect, already occurred. Like Walter Benjamin's once-scandalous Angel of History, the film's chronotope offers us a perspective from which modernity appears less a 'chain of events' than 'one single catastrophe which keeps piling wreckage upon wreckage, and hurls it in front of [our] feet', a 'storm' that is 'what we call progress'.[14] Yet the very incongruity of such a rhyme between the ruminations of a Marxist–modernist intellectual in Europe at the end of the 1930s and a contemporary Hollywood blockbuster film raises its own set of questions concerning what 'conditions of possibility' must have been met before such a view could become mainstream. What preconditions must be met before a mass audience can find such an anti-progressive perspective pleasurable, can 'want to believe this', as Leo Braudy says of the rise and fall of generic perspectives in general;[15] and what consequences follow from *Terminator 2*'s particular channellings of that desire?

Fredric Jameson suggests that the predominance of dystopic visions in contemporary science fiction signals the general loss of our ability even to conceive of, much less struggle to enact, a utopian social vision, trapped as we are within both an imperialist nation in decline and the overheated 'perpetual present' of postmodernist culture.[16] And much of *Terminator 2*, with its timed bursts of violence merged with state-of-the-art special effects, offers itself up to such an interpretive hypothesis as Exhibit A. (Call to reception theorists: how many in the American audience recognized in the evil cybernetic techno-war depicted in *Terminator 2*'s opening post-apocalyptic sequence an image of a hysterically celebrated Gulf War just past, in which 'our' machines mowed down their human bodies, as the saying goes, 'like fish in a tank'? And what were the effects of this surely unintentional echo?) Yet here again, like a good blockbuster, *Terminator 2* also invites us to critique the violence it presents, and quite explicitly, in Sarah's diatribe to scientist Dyson. 'Men like you built the hydrogen bomb,' she roars. 'Men like you thought it up. . . . You don't know what it's like to *create* something.' It is a speech that might have been drawn from, or at least inspired by, the works of such essentialist critics of male instrumental rationality as Susan Griffin, or such proponents of a maternalist-based women's peace movement as Sarah Ruddick or Helen Caldecott;[17] and it is there for the taking, not instead of but right along with the violence it decries.

The ease with which this moment's feminist critique of Enlightenment takes its place alongside brutal displays of techno-violence, though, should not blind us to its value as a clue to what is deeply and genuinely moving – in both the affective and narrative senses of the word – in *Terminator 2*. After all, the film we have described so far is one in which a fundamentally uneventful frame (the apocalypse that has already occurred) is constructed as backdrop for a plot whose terms and ends (T-800 saves boy; saves Sarah; saves world; destroys evil twin, a.k.a. T-1000) are all pretty much known in advance. If the cybernetic machine that is *Terminator 2* none the less appears at all alive and in motion, its assignment rather involves an extensive renegotiation and reconstruction of the hetero-sex/gender system itself, and that little engine of identity and desire called the nuclear family in particular. And indeed, we have already hinted at one important aspect of that renegotiation in our discussion of the *noir*ish space of action in *Terminator 2*, which gives us the ranch-style home and residential neighbourhood of traditional American domesticity as the place of the *phoney* family (the foster parents of which are promptly dispatched), and the new 'mean streets' of mall and culvert, corporate research centre, freeway and desert, as site of the new true one.

This relocation of the family unit of Mommy/Daddy/Baby to the place where the *noir* hero used to be, out in public and on the run, is likewise braided with a complex transfiguration of all three roles in the family romance, part transforming and part regressive in each case. Most prominently is of course ultra-buff Linda Hamilton's Sarah Conner as fully operational warrior-woman, like Sigourney Weaver's Ripley in Cameron's *Aliens* only more so, phallic mother with a complete set of soldier-of-fortune contacts, cache of weapons and survivalist skills.[18] Conversely, there is 'the Arnold', fresh from *Kindergarten Cop* and therefore all the more available for refunctioning from killing machine to nurturant proto-father who, as Sarah's own voice-over puts it, 'would always be there and would always protect him [i.e., John the son]. Of all the would-be fathers, this machine was the only one that measured up.' And finally, rounding out this new holy family is golden-boy John, who as grown-up rebel leader sends Arnold back to the past to protect his childhood self, but who as a kid must teach both Mom and Dad how and when to cool their jets.

If, as Constance Penley has shown us, the first *Terminator* film posits John Conner as 'the child who orchestrates his own primal scene' to run the energy of 'infantile sexual investigation' into the project of re-marking the difference between the sexes through remaking/displacing it as 'the more remarkable difference between human and other',[19] then in *Terminator 2* he must be both father-to-the-Man and father-to-the-Mom. Arnold must learn from him that 'you can't kill people'; while Sarah must be domesticated away from the Mother-Wolf fury in which she is enmeshed. That in this latter task, as unerringly right-on as young John is, it helps to have a Dad around is perfectly evident in the follow-up to the film's one overtly erotic moment, when having interrupted Mom's commando raid on the Dyson home, John confronts her, now collapsed in a heap and moaning 'I love you, John – I always have.' 'I know', he answers hoarsely, and falls into her embrace. A second later, though, we are all delivered from this hot-and-heavy scene before it goes any farther and shorts out the film, thanks to the presence of Arnold, whose stern let's-get-going glance at John literally pulls the boy out of Sarah's dangerous clutches and allows the action to roll ahead.

But for that matter, it is also clear by the end of the film that for all John's moral sense and Sarah's muscles, they both still need Dad – and a Dad who is not *that* different after all. For in the course of *Terminator 2*'s movement from shopping mall to shop floor, both John and Sarah are demonstrated to be ultimately ineffectual in their struggle against T-1000 and the forthcoming holocaust alike. For all her desire to change the dystopian course of history, and all the paramilitary training, Sarah is unable (too 'womanish'?) to pull the trigger on Dyson: just as, despite the fortitude that enables her to gun down her own T-1000 simulation when it appears,[20] she is incapable of defeating this tireless, emotionless, yet endlessly mutable villain by herself. Could this be because, as the film also shows us through Sarah's own recurrent and prophetic holocaust dream, she herself is after all a split subject only one of whose forms is warrior-like – and that one, compared to the apron-frocked housewife–mother on the other side of the fence, merely a secondary product of, and compensatory defence against, her terrible foreknowledge of the apocalyptic future as the history-that-already-hurts?

At any rate, for whatever reason, deliverance can only come from a real man, that is, from another machine-guy like the T-1000, though one minus the mutable part, and plus a modicum of moral–sentimental sense. 'I know now why you cry,' Arnold the T-800 tells the John-boy in that touching final moment between defeating the T-1000 and lowering himself down into the vat of molten steel that will terminate him too: 'but it's something I can never do.' The moral equivalent of such affective male positioning in the film, is, of course, that grisly motif we are free to enjoy as sadistic joke and/or, God help us even more, take seriously as moral improvement: namely, Arnold's oft-demonstrated commitment to maiming (usually by kneecapping) rather than killing his human opponents, as per the John-boy's moral command.

By such means *Terminator 2* gets it all in its renegotiation of paternal masculinity, offering us Arnold's stunted moral-affective capacities as simultaneously hard-wired limitation (push come to shove, he's still only a machine) and virtuous necessity (what a man's gotta do). And indeed we might as well have come to the same point from the opposite direction; for the converse of all I have been saying is also true, and equally well demonstrated in the final victory over the T-1000, despite its technological superiority to our Arnold. How is it, after all, that Arnold the protector is able to rise from the dead, as it were, even after the T-1000 has driven an iron crowbar straight through his back? Or, perhaps more accurately, how is it that we find ourselves able to *believe* that he does?

This, I think, is how. You will recall that at this moment of greatest extremity, a small red light begins to shine far, far back in his eye – the sign, we are told, that his back-up power is kicking in. What then encourages us to swallow such a manifestly inadequate explanation – after all, there is no sensibly consistent reason why a T-1000 would not know about, or would fail to notice, an earlier model's alternative energy source – is the primary distinction between 800 and 1000, most explicitly rendered in the comparison between Arnold's near-death and the T-1000's dissolution. For the T-1000, the liquid-metal prototype, there is no deep red light to which it can resort, no power back-up to call on when all else fails; there is only an orgiastic extravaganza of special effects, recapitulating with oozy swiftness all the metamorphoses its liquid-metal shape-changing abilities have enabled it to undertake throughout the film. By contrast, then, with this horrific (but spellbinding!) swoon through difference, is it not clear that compared with the T-1000 Arnold, our new man, has a core-self – or, if you will, individual soul – and just enough of one, whereas the T-1000 is merely the embodi-ment of evil dispersion itself, endless semiosis as the highest form of technocratic death-rationality?

If so, in its implication that the capacity, *and just enough of it*, to feel and make moral choices marks our new adult Daddyman out from both inhuman rationality (or is it semiosis?) on one side and the all-too-human (or is it fanaticism?) on the other, *Terminator 2* might plausibly be said to have thrown its family out on the street only to turn it every which way but loose, that is, only to redirect us and it back to the fixed ambiguities of a masculinist humanism whose very vertiginousness is uncannily, and literally, familiar. But then this reconstruction – just at its most triumphantly synthetic moment, too – half dwindles, half mutates into one final set of ambiguous-available options for our attention, anxiety and desire. At the close of the film, is our pathos extended to working-stiff Arnold lowering himself down into the soup, just another self-sacrificing husband and father off to work at the plant, 'just another body doing a job'? Or do we shift our sympathies to the figure of Sarah Conner fiercely holding onto John-boy, and see her instead as that arguably more up-to-date figure of the eighties and nineties: the victimized and abandoned single-mother head of a homeless family?

CONCLUSIONS IN FLUX

> That it 'keeps going on like this' *is* the catastrophe.
> Walter Benjamin [21]

> I'm in the middle of a mystery.
> Jeffrey in *Blue Velvet*

So far, we have looked at the overdetermining yet mutually subverting interplay of formal means foregrounded by *Blue Velvet* as part and parcel of its project to bring the urban spaces and *ur*-narrative of *film noir* into the formerly secure domestic spaces of the small town and the family. We have also examined the narrative–dramatic operations through which *Terminator 2* reconstructs the family even as it moves it out to the mean streets. One film constructed for and consumed primarily by the culturally up-scale, and therefore with a corresponding emphasis on meaning-through-style; the other made for a mass audience and, accordingly, with its meanings and judgements carried largely by its plot. Yet the main burden of this conclusion of sorts must be to consider some of the social meanings, possibilities and effects implicit in the overall project taken up by these films in this particular postgeneric, postmodernist moment: that project, we have been suggesting, is the domestication of *film noir*.

As a kind of side-door entrance into such considerations, it may be worth taking note of a few aspects of our two films unmentioned until now: specifically, those that draw on the economic and racial codes of mainstream, white capitalist culture. The former is most obviously referenced in the very selection of a steel mill as the site of *Terminator 2*'s climactic ending, given the function of steel production in contemporary socio-economic discourse as the paradigmatic icon of the Fordist industrial world which we have now, depending on whom you read, shipped off, frittered away, or even transcended, but in any case lost, in our national economy's shift toward a 'post-Fordist' regime with service rather than manufacturing industries at its core. Yet similar allusions to a vanished or vanishing industrial world can be found throughout *Blue Velvet* as well, from its frequent reminders to us of its small town's extractive-industry base (for example, in the deejay's patter, or the image of the mill yard in which Jeffrey comes to the morning after being assaulted by Frank) to the ominous brick warehouses in which Frank seems both to live and conduct his dirty work, and arguably even to the anachronistic spider mike Dorothy employs in the implausibly located nightclub where she works.

Though the uses to which such imagery is put in each of the two films are multiple and complex, in *Blue Velvet* the evocation of industrial culture is part and parcel of its overall construction of an environment where nature and culture lose their borders, and danger and pleasure coincide; whereas *Terminator 2*'s uncanny yet nostalgically recalled foundry adds an extra measure of weight and yearning to the triumphant restoration and victory of the old male-dominant nuclear family and breadwinner ethic that went along with the socio-economic era just past. More generally still, though, and in keeping with many other contemporary polygeneric films from *Lethal Weapon* to *Batman*, the iconic spaces and imagery of Fordist production and industrial culture in both our films function as a late-twentieth-century equivalent to the feudal mansion in the chronotope of the eighteenth-century Gothic novel: namely, as a *ruin* (though a capitalist one) in which to place the monstrous dangers of the present and/or stage a regressive deliverance from out of the sex/gender system of the past.

I will have more to say elsewhere on the subject of these new capitalist ruins.[22] For now let us turn our attention to the inflections and incitements of racial marking in these films, a practice whose operations paradoxically take on all the more significance in so far as racial discourse and positioning may at first sight appear to play such a small part in our two films' overall schemes, practices and effects. From a normatively 'white' point of view, after all, racial marking would seem to be an issue only at those rare moments when someone 'non-white' shows up on screen, and then only as a question of how that 'non-whiteness' is defined. What such a normative perspective thus typically, indeed systematically, fails to acknowledge is the essentially relational operation of all racial discourse and representation, or in other words the way every construction of a/the racial Other generates by contrast an implicit definition of what it means to be 'the same' – that is, in the present instance, 'white'.

Let us take a quick look back at our two films from this relational perspective, then, to see what implications we find in their nominally innocuous-to-honorific depictions of the 'non-white'. In *Blue Velvet*, there are the two store-uniformed and aproned black clerks who work at Jeffrey's father's hardware store, peripheral even as secondary characters, and seemingly memorable only because of the whimsically transparent little *shtick* they play out in the scant few seconds in which they appear, in which the sighted one uses touch signals to cue the blind one as to price or number of objects, and the blind one pretends he has with magical prescience come up with the number himself. *Terminator 2*, on the other hand, while 'randomizing' race among those cops and hospital attendants destined to be casually crippled or killed, places non-whites in secondary roles of clearly greater significance: Dyson the corporate scientist and his family as African-Americans; Enrique, Sarah's former soldier-of-fortune comrade-in-arms, and his family as Hispanics.

In *Terminator 2*, in fact, the self-approvingly 'nonracist' liberalism we seem to be meant to read off from these last two sets of non-white characters and groups is more or less spelled out within the film. Sarah's musings, quoted above, on how well Arnold the T-800 fills the paternal bill are immediately followed by a softly sunstruck montage of her old Hispanic running buddy's Mommy-Daddy-Baby unit caught unaware in the midst of unselfconscious domestic bliss, the sight of which is then as immediately linked to a recurrence of that dream of nuclear holocaust that separates Sarah from her own apron-frocked domestic self. Likewise, a short while later, Dyson's more up-scale family life is depicted in similarly idyllic and conventional terms, Mom taking care of Baby, Dad smiling over them while hard at work, in the final moment before Sarah's assault. The liberal progressivism of such representations thus announces itself in the contrast between the settled, happy domesticity of the non-white families above (Dyson's) or below (Enrique's) the social level of the aberrant and precarious white one on which we stay focused. We could put the same point less generously but no less accurately by saying that such progressivism is itself little more than a stalking horse for the conservative project that rides in on it, namely, the (re)constitution of the regulative ideal of the old male-dominant, oedipal–nuclear family for whites, coming at them, as it were, from both sides.

Moreover, though *Terminator 2* neither represents nor endorses any non-familial social ideal, it still seems significant that both our non-white *patresfamilias* are associated from the start with contemporary visions of social disorder and mass violence. For many if not most white viewers at least, Sarah's rapid allusion to Enrique's past as a *contra*, combined with his gun-toting first appearance and his family's desert location, will call up a *mélange* of unsorted and uneasy impressions from *Treasure of the Sierra Madre* to the mainstream media's spotty yet hysterical coverage of a decade of messy and unpleasant struggle 'down there', plus attendant anxieties over 'their' illegal entry and peripheral existences 'up here'; the Afro-American Dyson, meanwhile, is straight-forwardly depicted as the author of the technological breakthrough that will eventually give us SkyNet, the fully autonomous, computerized war technology that will soon trigger nuclear holocaust as the first move in its war against humanity itself. One wonders, in fact, how many white viewers recoiled from Sarah's verbal assault on a *black* man as the incarnation of value-free and death-bound masculinist-corporate techno-rationality, and on what level of consciousness they did so, and to what effect: how, detached from its unlikely target, is her didactic essentialist feminism understood? I have no idea, and would not presume to guess. At any rate, though, following this bizarre moment, the film's treatment of Dyson runs once again in familiar ways, towards familiar ends: it rolls out the Möbius-strip time-travel causality of that eighties blockbuster *Back to the Future* in its suggestion that Dyson the black man does not really invent anything[23] (the breakthrough he comes up with turns out to be merely an extrapolation from those remnants of the first Terminator, from the first *Terminator* film, that his corporate employer managed to scoop up); and, as in many other films featuring a once-wayward non-white sidekick, it rehabilitates him Gunga Din style, by including him in the assault on the power with which he has formerly been associated, an assault whose victory is, not accidentally coincident with his self-sacrifice and death.

These regulative procedures by which whiteness learns from and is defined by its Other(s) even as those Others are re-subordinated, stigmatized, and/or punished, are not to be found in *Blue Velvet*, however – or not quite. There another, culturally hipper version of the game of reference and relegation is going on, in which racial difference is placed within quotation marks, and, thus textualized, is both evoked and winked away. So the blackness of the store clerks sits next to the blindness of the one clerk and to the pseudo-magical trick they both like to play, as just so much semic doodling along the margins of this endlessly decentred text in which each element of the normal and conventional is estranged, while each strangeness or Otherness is subjected to a metonymic slippage that renders it both equivalent to every other otherness and empty in itself: blackness = blindness = stupid trick. In the universe constructed by Lynch's postmodern aesthetics, there is no need either to make liberal gestures towards the inclusion of the racial Other, or to discipline and punish that Otherness when it appears. Rather, as the whiff of Amos 'n Andy we can smell around the figures of our two clerks in *Blue Velvet* suggests, and the overtly racist stereotypes (blacks and creoles as figures for a demonically sexualized and violent underworld) in Lynch's more recent film *Wild at Heart* (1990) make abundantly clear, even the most offensive tropes may be called back for a culturally up-scale and predominantly white audience to enjoy under the new postmodern dispensation that such hoary ideologemes are really only to be delected like everything else in the film, including the tropes of 'back home' themselves, as simply so many hyperrealized/evacuated bits of virtually free-floating text.[24]

This examination of both our films' means of (re)producing the locations and distinctive pleasures of whiteness and their regressive deployments of the new ruins of Fordist industrial space this brings us back to the central vortex or stuck place by which we may know contemporary 'family *noir*' when we find it: in the apparent dissolution of the rigid identity/Otherness categories of the symbolic in general, and those of the sex/gender system in particular, into a semic flow or play of boundaries from which, paradoxically, those same categories re-emerge with renewed half-life; and in the astonishingly mobile and contradictory circuitry of desire and anxiety, pleasure and fear, that this process both releases and recontains. *Terminator 2*, as we have seen, plays around with border crossings between male and female, human and machine, the Fordist past and the post-Fordist present, and, for that matter, bio-social predestination ('it's in your nature to destroy yourselves') versus existential possibility ('no fate but what we make'), only to redraw the lines of the old nuclear family system as the last best line of defence against the fluid yet inexorably programmed assaults of the terribly New. Yet this restoration is itself a tenuous and contradictory one, given its figuration through the asexual (or should it be 'safe-sexual'?) coalition of a cyborg Dad and a warrior-woman Mom, half-assisted and half-constructed through the educative and team-building efforts of a child who is thus both effectively as well as literally Father to himself.[25] *Blue Velvet* pulls off what is finally the same denaturalizing/restoring act on a more formal level, by presenting us with a pre-eminently oedipal narrative whose recuperations of patriarchal order are riddled with artifice and suspicion, and eroded by a mode of skewed hyperobservation that simultaneously fills and estranges, exceeds and evacuates the conventional terms in which such narratives used to be couched.

Within contemporary political culture, we know what to call this meltdown and restoration of the categories by which women and non-whites are put back in their place (even *Blue Velvet*'s Dorothy, like *Terminator 2*'s Sarah, is firmly, though hyperbolically, put back in the mother role in that film's closing shots) and white men in theirs, at the same time as the devices of the political rhetoric that does so are brazenly bared, and the very notion of location is smirked away. Its name is Reaganism (or Bushitis, if you like). And certainly, brushed with rather than against the grain, the process by which *Blue Velvet*'s Jeffrey gets to answer girlfriend Sandy's doubt as to whether he's 'a detective or a pervert' by being both, and a good kid besides, is the same as that by which the old actor got to be simultaneously the world's leading authority figure and its largest, most spectacularized airhead. Likewise, our intense enjoyment in *Terminator 2* of the spectacular semiotic mutability of our protean villain, and the stabilizing satisfactions provided by the return of the classically distinct, embodied (if no less synthetically produced) masculinity of our Arnold as Good Old Dependable Dad,[26] rhyme with the joys we have taken over the past four years in the swings from Willie Horton to 'Pineapple Head' Noriega to, in Bush's delivery, 'Sodom' Hussein, together with the pleasures available in the manifestly constructed image of Bush as, like the T-800, another kinder, gentler, ass-kicking guy.

Within cultural theory and practice, feminist critics such as Suzanne Moore and Tania Modleski have been swift to notice and condemn this same process by which the dissolution of the forms and categories of the patriarchal–oedipal–bourgeois symbolic can be taken over by white male theorists and cultural producers, the aptly named 'pimps of postmodernism', to co-opt the pleasures of release and reconstruct new and more mobile means of domination.[27] Yet without disagreeing in any way with these critiques, it remains for us to step beyond or outside them, in accordance with the old Benjaminian dictum that it is pre-eminently the task of the historical materialist to 'brush History' – even, and perhaps especially, that History that is our own present moment – *against* the grain' as well.[28] In other words, we must attempt to read the particular complex of social–psychological needs and desires that gets ventilated and redirected in these films not only as raw material for a new social contract with the same old Powers That Be, but also as a set of contradictory energies which, under the sign of utopia, might be shaped and channelled in progressive directions.

To such a project, this chapter can only contribute a few opening moves. For starters, I would suggest that to take the domestication of *film noir*, or the *noir*ization of domesticity, seriously in this way, reading it against its own tendency, must ultimately require us to refuse the very opposition our two films need to transgress, and transgress in order to demand again. More specifically, we must see that the very comminglings of boundary erosion and restitution, semic swoon and symbolic fixity we have traced in such detail are a sign that these same categories are no longer characterized by their mutually defining opposition but by their dialectical implosion, a revolting-but-conserving action that describes a socio-political impasse, a *sticking* 'point de capiton' whose close kin may be found within contemporary theory.

What I have in mind here are the innumerable, and seemingly intractable, divisions that have appeared over the past decade or so, within and across the domain of what are still called the 'new social movements', between essentialist theory and nationalist political practice on the one hand, and poststructuralist or deconstructive theory and an ever-shifting politics of articulation on the other – not to mention any number of unacknowledged and illicit comminglings of the two.[29] In the first at its most extreme (and, it must be said, caricatured), the unified identity of the oppressed group is seen as both unproblematically given and as inherently superior to that of the equally mono-lithic, uniformly evil oppressor. In the second, that same identity is seen as sheer discursive relationality, merely one false hypostatized stop among others in a chain of social signifiers in constant flux, and therefore open to any and all sorts of 'in-differentiated' deconstruction and rearticulation as we *bricoleurs* of this conjuncture see fit.[30] These two positions, separately and at times in bafflingly contradictory combina-tion, may be said to have virtually covered the field of putatively radical theory in the eighties, or at least those parts of it concerned with race, gender and sexuality within the US and British scenes. Nor is it useful to point out that both positions are quite patently subspecies of ahistorical idealism, as opposed to any properly materialist view: that only sounds like so much cranky lumbering from that old outmoded bully-bore Marxism, trying to push all our struggles into a box labelled Relations of Production, or crush us all flat under its Mode of Production steamroller again.

Though such suspicions have their own historic legitimacy, there is none the less a cost to throwing out the materialist baby with the bathwater; and in the cusp between the eighties and nineties that cost became increasingly manifest as a sacrifice of politics itself. So, for example, Kate Soper among others, writing of the ways both the essentialist and post-structuralist positions within contemporary feminist theory con-duce to conservatisim and/or passivity, points out how 'either difference is essentialized in a way which simply celebrates the "feminine" other of dominant culture without disturbing the hold of the latter; or the critique is taken to a point where the "feminine" and its political and cultural agents in the women's movement and feminist art and literature no longer exist in the sense of having any recognisable common content and set of aspirations'.[31] Either we are right and good already, and our Others are irrevocably wrong and evil; or 'we' are at worst somebody else's dying fiction, at best sheer never-ending flux.

This is not the place to launch a full historical-genetic investigation of the anti-political, anti-institutional tendency within American culture. Yet it seems clear that one effect of the terrible defeats dealt out here throughout the 1980s to every potentially progressive constituency has been to deepen widely held libertarian–individualist suspicions that no structural or institutional transformations for the better are possible, that nothing political can be done. Such an increased and self-confirming hopelessness has, I think, had much to do with the putatively radical theory we have produced over the past decade. What is most absent from the present moment of confusion and dejection all along the left, and most necessary for its redemption, is the confidence that individuals can come together in collective action to transform societies structurally and institutionally for the better. In this respect, the rebelling/conserving schizophrenia of radical theory is at one with the pleasures of the rebelling-but-conserving cinematic texts we have examined: both being not so much about that absence of confidence as presupposing it, and offering us pleasures that can only appear within an asocial kingdom from which such confidence must have been banished a long time ago.

The more general form or methodological implication of this same point might run as follows. If the political events and theoretical critiques of the past decade or so have inoculated us – feminists, people of colour, gays and lesbians, 'post-Marxist' socialists, all of us – against any low-grade Hegelian fever and its chief associated symptom, the chronic assumption of a progressive dialectic chugging away somewhere, *anywhere* in the social universe, they ought not to blind us to the various nonteleological ways in which social desires and social realities continue to work themselves out dialectically – nor to our responsibility to do what we can to make those dialectics utopian again. It is in the service of precisely such insights and responsibilities that *Aufhebung*, that corny old concept of 'cancelled yet preserved in a higher synthesis', must itself be cancelled – as a natural endowment of any group, or tendency of any social force – yet preserved, at least as the possibility that radical practice can connect with socially constructed desire in such a way as to make a difference. Otherwise, whatever the principal locus of its engagement may be, radical social and cultural theory is all too likely to be condemned to an interminable shuttling quite similar to that we have seen in our two films, between the thrilling sublime of one or another form of 'permanent revolution' and the desperate catch-up of attempting to restore and strengthen old identities and game rules feared lost.

Or, to return from the metatheoretical clouds to family *film noir* specifically, it may be that the way to respond to the irresolute resolutions and rebellious conservatism of our films without reproducing their equivalents in theory is to recognize the legitimacy of the needs and desires that underlie the dynamics of the films' operations while refusing their opposed yet commingled terms. Such a utopian reading would then pass through the recognition that even these admittedly corrupt and pernicious cultural productions have both to rest on and run off a widely held consensus that the old nuclear, oedipal, male-dominant, breadwinner-ethic-based family is neither natural nor desirable, and an equally widely held and justifiable anxiety as to the brutal chaos that ensues when the rules of that old system are tattered or in abeyance without any other emerging to take its place: to pass through that recognition and then to take the combination of desire and anxiety it has found *as a resource* for a progressive politics.

In 1983, as the conclusion of her survey of white male revolts against what she dubbed the 'breadwinner ethic' and the oedipal–nuclear families it produced, Barbara Ehrenreich proposed that 'male [white male, that is] culture seems to have abandoned the breadwinner role without overcoming the sexist attitudes that role has perpetuated'.[32] But she went on to suggest that the only way to begin to move beyond this impasse is to struggle for an expanded, democratized, feminist expansion of the welfare state in which women and men alike earn a 'family wage', and in which women are also provided with the 'variety of social supports' necessary for them 'to enter the labor market on an equal footing with men' – including, and especially, 'reliable, high-quality child care'.[33] Her argument is not that such goals, once achieved, would automatically bring an end to sexist oppression, or usher in a feminist utopia; it is simply that without such gains, little new ground for the construction of less oppressive gender roles and relations is likely to open up.

In 1993, of course, after ten more years of repression, rollback and decay, such a programme may seem, like Alec Nove's model of a 'feasible socialism', all the more a combination of the hopelessly insufficient and the wildly utopian. Yet such a hybrid failing, if failing it be, none the less seems to me uniquely exemplary within recent American cultural theory in its insistence on a given set of programmatic political goals; just as that insistence in turn seems infinitely more adequate to the current need to recover the terrain of political agency and possibility than any rehash of the essentialist versus poststructuralist debate. The main point here is that for all the bleakness of the present moment, and indeed precisely because of it, we must none the less learn or relearn to propose *something* more real and more properly political as the outcome of our analyses than the indulgent rages and self-strokings of identity and/or the *jouissance* of poststructuralist free-fall: because the only alternative to such a 'cancelled-yet-preserved' renewal of politics itself is the dubious enjoyment of being permanently stuck, like *Blue Velvet*'s Jeffrey, 'in the middle of a mystery' whose pleasures most of the people we speak for and with can only afford to take in every now and then, when thanks to the magic of movies and political campaigns aimed both high and low, at the theoretically sophisticated and at the masses, the catastrophic 'it goes on like this' is, at no small expense, the subject of a little fun.

NOTES

An earlier and abbreviated version of this chapter appears in electronic-text form in *Postmodern Culture*, vol. 2, no. 3 (May 1992). It is published here in its entirety with special thanks to the Center for the Humanities at Oregon State University for granting the author a research fellowship that allowed him to write it.

1. Gledhill's argument for the subversiveness of the *films noirs* of the forties and fifties may be found in Christine Gledhill, '*Klute* I: A Contemporary Film Noir and Feminist Criticism', in E. Ann Kaplan, ed., *Women in Film Noir* (London: British Film Institute, 1978), pp. 6–21.

2. David Bordwell, Janet Staiger and Kristin Thompson, *The Classical Hollywood Style* (New York: Columbia University Press, 1986), p. 77.

3. Summarized in Robert Stam, *Subversive Pleasures: Bakhtin, Cultural Criticism and Film* (Baltimore: Johns Hopkins University Press, 1989), p. 12. Sobchak's essay is, unfortunately, unpublished to date.

4. Here I feel bound to note that my argument regarding these 'neo-*noirs*' converges with that of Fredric Jameson concerning what he calls 'nostalgia' films of the seventies and eighties, but with a difference: I am less concerned to relate their hollowed-out aesthetic of 'pastiche' to any larger and more global 'cultural logic of Late Capital' than to place that aesthetic within the particular commercial and institutional context in which it acquires its initial sense. See Fredric Jameson, *Postmodernism, or The Cultural Logic of Late Capitalism* (Durham, NC: Duke University Press, 1991), pp. 19–20 and 279–96.

5. Thomas Schatz, *The Genius of the System* (New York: Pantheon, 1988).

6. See Todd Gitlin's account of the rise and fall of *Hill Street Blues*, and his argument that the 'recombinant aesthetics' of television production are the quintessence of late-capitalist cultural production, in his *Inside Prime Time* (New York: Pantheon, 1983), pp. 273–324 and 76–80 respectively.

7. Michael Moon, 'A Small Boy and Others: Sexual Disorientation in Henry James, Kenneth Anger and David Lynch', in Hortense J. Spillers, ed., *Comparative American Identities: Race, Sex and Nationality in the Modern Text* (New York: Routledge, 1991), p. 142. This is the place, moreover, to declare the general debt my reading of *Blue Velvet* owes to Moon's insistent exploration of the film's sexual-discursive 'underside'.

8. Barbara Creed, 'A journey through *Blue Velvet*: Film, Fantasy and the Female Spectator', *New Formations*, 6 (Winter 1988), p. 100.

9. 'Take something comforting, familiar, essentially American,' Simmons writes, 'and turn up the controls, the visual volume. It's overheated technicolor . . . [e]very detail is picture-perfect and it reeks of danger and

failure.' Quoted from the anthology of responses compiled in '(Why) Is David Lynch Important?' *Parkett*, 28 (1991), p. 154.

10. Mannoni's widely cited formula first appears in his *Clefs pour l'Imaginaire, ou L'Autre Scène* (Paris: Editions du Seuil, 1969). For another recent consideration of the relationship of the circuitry of disavowal and enjoyment it describes to postmodernist culture, see Jim Collins, *Uncommon Cultures: Popular Culture and Postmodernism* (New York: Routledge, 1989), p. 110 ff.

11. The full sentence from which this quoted material comes is worth quoting in full for the linkage Moon makes, and claims the film makes, between the film's sadomasochistic homoerotics and the mobile discursivity of the desires it displays: 'When Lynch has Frank mouth the words of the song a second time [Ben having done so, to Frank's anguished pleasure, back at the whorehouse a short time before], this time directly to a Jeffrey whom he has ritually prepared for a beating by "kissing" lipstick onto his mouth and wiping it off with a piece of blue velvet, it is as though Lynch is both daring the viewer to recognize the desire for each other that the two men's newly discovered sadomasochistic bond induces them to feel *and* at the same time to recognize the perhaps more fearful knowledge that what most of us consider our deepest and strongest desires are not our own, that our dreams and fantasies are only copies, audio- and videotapes, of the desires of others and our utterances of them lip-synchings of these circulating, endlessly reproduced and reproducible desires' (Moon, p. 146).

12. Buttoning or quilting points, a concept borrowed here from Lacan via Slavoj Žižek. See especially Žižek's insightful and hilarious essay ' "Che vuoi?" ', in his *The Sublime Object of Ideology* (New York and London: Verso, 1989), pp. 87–129.

13. Not to mention *noir*ish melodramas of the same moment: see Mary Ann Doane's

illuminating discussion of these issues in her *The Desire to Desire: The Woman's Film of the 1940s* (Bloomington: Indiana University Press, 1987).

14. Walter Benjamin, 'Theses on the Philosophy of History', in *Illuminations* (New York: Schocken, 1969), trans. Harry Zohn, pp. 257, 258.

15. See the opening pages of his fine discussion of 'classical' film genres in Leo Braudy, *The World in a Frame: What We See in Films* (Garden City, NY: Doubleday, 1976), pp. 104–24.

16. Fredric Jameson, 'Progress Versus Utopia: Or, Can We Imagine the Future?', *Science Fiction Studies* vol. 9, no. 2 (1982).

17. Susan Griffin, *Woman and Nature: The Roaring Inside Her* (New York: Harper and Row, 1978); Sarah Ruddick, *Maternal Thinking: Toward a Politics of Peace* (New York: Ballantine Books, 1990).

18. The hysterical panic provoked in (some) male quarters by the appearance of Linda Hamilton's ninja warrior in *Terminator 2* and Susan Sarandon and Geena Davis's incarnations as vengeful *bandidas* in *Thelma and Louise* in the same summer of 1991 is a topic worthy of investigation in itself. For a sample, see Joe Urschel's *USA Today* editorial, 'Real Men Forced into the Woods', 26–28 July 1991, which argues, as far as I can tell, half-seriously, that the powerful women characters and male-bashing plots of the two aforementioned movies leave men no choice but to join Robert Bly's mythopoetic 'men's movement' and return to nature! I am grateful to my friend Gray Cassiday for bringing this phenomenon to my attention.

19. Constance Penley, 'Time-Travel, Primal Scene and the Critical Dystopia', in Annette Kuhn, ed., *Alien Zone: Cultural Theory and Contemporary Science Fiction Cinema* (London and New York: Verso, 1990), pp. 121 and 123.

20. Here the comparative term might be Jennifer O'Neal's fatal paralysis at the sight of her cloned self at the climax of *The Stepford Wives* (Bryan Forbes 1975).

21. Quoted, from the notes for the uncompleted *Passagen-Werk*, in Susan Buck-Morss, *The Dialectics of Seeing: Walter Benjamin and the Arcades Project* (Cambridge, MA: MIT Press, 1989), p. 375.

22. See the concluding section of Fred Pfeil, 'From Pillar to Postmodern: Race, Class and Gender in the Male Rampage Film', forthcoming in *Socialist Review* and in my *White Guys: Studies in Postmodern Power, Choice and Change* (forthcoming from Verso, 1993).

23. See Fred Pfeil, 'Plot and Patriarchy in the Age of Reagan: Reading *Back to the Future* and *Brazil*', in *Another Tale to Tell: Politics and Narrative in Postmodern Culture* (London and New York Verso, 1990), especially pp. 235–6.

24. For a prescient early warning of this phenomenon, first spotted in the high-cult realm of the visual arts, see Lucy Lippard, 'Rejecting Retrochic', in *Get the Message? A Decade of Art for Social Change* (New York: E. P. Dutton, 1984), pp. 173–8; and for a recent assessment of its presence and effects in contemporary American popular culture, see Suzanna Danuta Walters, 'Premature Postmortems: "Postfeminism" and Popular Culture', *New Politics*, vol. 3, no. 2 (Winter 1991).

25. See Pfeil, 'Plot and Patriarchy', pp. 227–41.

26. The distinction between the 'classical' and the 'grotesque' body is drawn from Bakhtin and elaborated brilliantly by Peter Stallybrass and Allon White in their *The Politics and Poetics of Transgression* (Ithaca, NY: Cornell University Press, 1986). What seems worth noting here, however, about the figure of 'our Arnold' and perhaps about other contemporary ideal-images of contemporary white straight masculinity, is the degree to which the 'classical' and 'grotesque' seem to be mutually contained and containing within such figures, in a way that seems connected to the broader thematic and political argument I am making here.

27. Tania Modleski, 'The Incredible Shrinking He(r)man: Male Regression, the Male Body, and Film', *Differences* vol. 2, no. 2 (1990), pp. 55–75, and Suzanne Moore, 'Getting a Bit of the Other – the Pimps of Postmodernism', in Rowena Chapman and Jonathan Rutherford, eds., *Male Order: Unwrapping Masculinity* (London: Lawrence and Wishart, 1988), pp. 165–92.

28. Benjamin, p. 257.

29. For some examples of the latter, see my 'No Basta Teorizar: In-Difference to Solidarity in Contemporary Fiction, Theory, and Practice', forthcoming in Inderpal Grewal and Caren Kaplan, eds., *Postmodernism and Transnational Feminist Practices* (Minneapolis: University of Minnesota Press, 1993).

30. Examples of the first are so numerous and easily come by that it would seem pointless, and perhaps even preferentially abusive, to single out a few representative instances here; the *locus classicus* of the second tendency, though, must surely be Ernesto Laclau and Chantal Mouffe, *Hegemony and Socialist Strategy: Towards a Radical Democratic Politics* (New York: Verso, 1985).

31. Kate Soper, 'Feminism, Humanism and Postmodernism', *Radical Philosophy*, 55 (Summer 1990), p. 14.

32. Barbara Ehrenreich, *The Hearts of Men: American Dreams and the Flight from Commitment* (Garden City, New York: Anchor Press/ Doubleday, 1983), p. 182.

33. Ibid., pp. 176–7.

9

NOIR BY *NOIRS*: TOWARD A NEW

REALISM IN BLACK CINEMA

Manthia Diawara

Le film noir est noir pour nous, c'est-à-dire pour le public occidental et américain des années 50.

Raymond Borde and Étienne Chaumeton, *Panorama du film noir américain*

Looking eastward from the towers of Riverside Church, perched among the university buildings on the high banks of the Hudson River, in a valley far below, waves of gray rooftops distort the perspective like the surface of a sea. Below the surface, in the murky waters of fetid tenements, a city of black people who are convulsed in desperate living, like the voracious churning of millions of hungry cannibal fish. Blind mouths eating their own guts. Stick in a hand and draw back a nub. That is Harlem.

Chester Himes, *A Rage in Harlem*

There are two modes of *film noir* criticism: one is formalist, the other is content-based. Feminist criticism, for example, has for the most part emphasized the formal elements of *film noir* – the chiaroscuro lighting, the voice-over narration, the multiple points of view, the convoluted plot, the eroticization of violence, in order to show how these devices of the genre work to stabilize patriarchy, how the genre maintains itself through the production of the femme fatale and the prevention of an emergence of other types of women. Formalist criticism links the epithet *noir* to the grotesque, the sinister, and the image of women as treacherous. Women, bad guys, and detectives are in these films, considered 'black' by virtue of the fact that they occupy indeterminate and monstrous spaces such as whiteness traditionally reserves for blackness in our culture. In *film noir* the opposition between dark and light, underworld and 'above board', good and evil is blurred and it is the collapse of these boundaries that causes the characters to partake of the attributes of blackness. From a formalist perspective, a film is *noir* if it puts into play light and dark in order to exhibit a people who become 'black' because of their 'shady' moral behaviour. Through its focus on formalist devices, feminist criticism exposes *film noir*'s attempt to paint white women 'black' in order to limit or control their independent agency, their self-fashioning.[1]

Marxist criticism also belongs to this first, formalist mode; it equates the *noirification* of film style and characters in the genre with pessimism and the decay of the capitalist system. It is in this sense that, commenting on the *noir* writers of the 1930s and 1940s, Mike Davis states that 'Noir was like a transformational grammar turning each charming ingredient of the boosters' arcadia into a sinister equivalent. Thus, in Horace McCoy's *They Shoot Horses Don't They?* (1935) the marathon dance hall on Ocean Pier became virtually a death camp for the depression's lost souls.'[2] This reading of the *film noir* as a kind of Marxism *manqué* is echoed by Carl Richardson, in an excellent study entitled *Autopsy: An Element of Realism in Film Noir*. For Richardson, too, *film noir* derives its realism from a sense of pessimism, a light cast on the dark background created by the Depression: 'It is traumatic for an individual to lose a set of beliefs. For a world-wide coterie of intellectuals and artists, it is a dark, frustrating process. It is a film noir on a large scale.'[3]

But there is another side to *film noir* criticism, one that is complicated through ethnicity and the present crisis in American cities; it involves the description of such films about black people, or directed by black film-makers. I want to make the argument here that the new black directors appropriate the style of *film noir*, among others, to create the possibility for the emergence of new and urbanized black images on the screen. Whereas the first epigraph, taken from Raymond Borde and Étienne Chaumeton's famous book, describes *film noir* as purely a style that uses the tropes of blackness as metaphors for the white characters' moral transgressions and falls from grace, the second epigraph, from Chester Himes's *A Rage in Harlem*, focuses the *noir* style on black people themselves. For Borde and Chaumeton, *film noir* is black because the characters have lost the privilege of whiteness by pursuing lifestyles that are misogynistic, cowardly, duplicitous, that exhibit themselves in an eroticization of violence. Himes, on the other hand, opposes that which is above – Riverside Church and the buildings of Columbia University – and that which is below – Harlem – to highlight less an aesthetic state of affairs than a way of life that has been imposed on black people through social injustice, and that needs to be exposed to the light. Himes's text is a protest novel which deploys the *noir* style to shed light on the desperate conditions of people who are forced to live below. The novel's grotesque imagery – 'a city of black people who are convulsed in desperate living, like the voracious churning of millions of hungry cannibal fish. Blind mouths eating their own guts' – may be as conventional as any description of violence and pessimism in the *noir* genre, but what is unusual about *A Rage in Harlem* is the way it uses the conventions of the genre to subvert its main tenet: that blackness is a fall from whiteness. For Himes, black people are living in hell and white people in heaven not because the one colour is morally inferior to the other, but because black people are held captive in the valley below the towers of Riverside Church. The *noirs* in Himes's text are black people trapped in the darkness of white captivity, and the light shed on them is meant to render them visible, not white. Himes's text and the recent run of black films that participate in the discourse of *film noir* (*Joe's Bed-Stuy Barbershop: We Cut Head, Deep Cover, One False Move, Juice, Illusion, Chameleon Street*, etcetera) force us to re-examine the genre and its uses by black film-makers. They orient the *noir* style toward a description of a black public sphere and a black way of life.

It is clear therefore that formalist criticism of the *noir* genre runs the risk of reducing *films noirs* by *noirs* to a critique of patriarchy or of capitalism, and thus of minimizing on the one hand the deconstruction of racism in the renewed genre, and on the other hand a delineation of a black way of life in America. I submit that a thematic or content-based criticism of *films noirs* by *noirs* is more appropriate to analyse black rage, class conflict among black people, and the specificity of black culture in the texts. It is misleading, for example, to see black *femme fatales*, neurotic detectives and grotesque bad guys as poor imitations of their white counterparts; these characters may be redeployed in the genre by black film-makers in order to represent such themes as black rage at white America. In a paradoxical sense, the redeployment of *noir* style by black film-makers redeems blackness from its genre definition by recasting the relation between light and dark on the screen as a metaphor for making black people and their cultures visible. In a broader sense, black *film noir* is a light (as in day*light*) cast on black people.

BLACK RAGE AS *FILM NOIR*

Set in Harlem, *A Rage in Harlem* tells the story of the entanglement of Jackson, an honest and 'very religious young man', with underworld characters who stabilize their environment through moral inversions.[4] Jackson's own brother, Goldy, is a stool pigeon who dresses as a Sister of Mercy, speaks in biblical riddles, and sells tickets to heaven in front of a department store to Christians 'full of larceny who fall for that'. Goldy lives with two other men, and 'all three impersonated females and lived by their wits. All three were fat and black, which made it easy' (p. 34). Theirs is a world policed by detectives such as Coffin Ed Johnson and Grave Digger Jones who people in Harlem believe 'would shoot a man stone dead for not standing straight in a line' (p. 44). Grave Digger and Coffin Ed control black people in Harlem by unleashing their rage on them: a rage that seems to consume the detectives themselves, and spills out grotesquely and in a misogynistic manner onto intruders and those Harlemites who step out of line:

> They took their tribute, like all real cops, from the established underworld catering to the essential needs of the people – game-keepers, madams, street walkers, numbers writers, numbers bankers. But they were rough on purse snatchers, muggers, burglars, con men, and all strangers making any racket. (p. 49)

The bad guys in the text are typical *noir* characters. Slim, Hank and Jodie are outsiders in Harlem, small-town thugs from the South; they come north to join their former partner, Imabelle, and decide to set up an investment 'racket' as a way of gaining a share in the underground informal market. Hank throws acid in people's eyes, and Slim is described as 'wearing over his suit a long khaki duster like those worn by mad scientists in low-budget horror motion pictures. The legend U.S. Assayer was embroidered on the chest' (p. 68). Jodie is on 'a kill-crazy edge with that knife' which he never parts with, not even in moments of sexual intimacy:

> Jodie was staring over her head, lost in his music. He ran his left hand slowly back and forth over her crisp brown curls as though he liked the sensation. His right arm rested on his thigh and in his right hand he held the bone-handled switch-blade knife, snapping it open and shut. (p. 145)

Imabelle, the novel's femme fatale, is described as 'a cushioned-lipped, hot-bodied, banana-skin chick with the speckled-brown eyes of a teaser and the high-arched, ball-bearing hips of a natural-born *amante*' (p. 6). Imabelle operates by sending conflicting messages to different characters. A trusted lover in need of Jackson's protection, she is a wife and an accomplice to Slim. Jackson never suspects her even when he finds her with the gang that robbed him. She is able to comfort him with her body language: 'She was looking steadily into Jackson's eyes. Her lips formed the words, "Come on in and kill him, Daddy. I'm all yours." Then she stepped back, making space for him to enter' (p. 68). Yet, to Grave Digger, Imabelle is a very dangerous woman who 'saddled Jackson and Goldy with the body [Slim's] and planned to lam on the first train leaving town. She didn't give a damn what happened to any of them' (p. 156). When Imabelle cuts a man in the face with a knife and tells the police that she has never seen that man before, a bystander quotes:

> Black gal make a freight train jump de track.
> But a yaller gal make a preacher Ball de Jack. (p. 117)

The relations between the characters I have just described in *A Rage in Harlem* echo those of *The Maltese Falcon* and many other *noir* texts in which bad guys come to town in search of a lost object which, however trivial or inauthentic it may be, drives the intrigue and leads the characters to pursue vicious and violent crimes that disturb the harmony of the underworld. The dreamlike manner in which Himes's characters slip in and out of rationality is reminiscent of such hard-boiled detective novels as *Pop. 1080* (Jim Thompson), in which the town sheriff is also a serial killer. Furthermore, Himes's text embodies the key elements of the *film noir* genre as defined by Borde and Chaumeton: 'unstable rapport among the members in a criminal gang . . . dreamlike and erotic relations . . . and manhunts that take place in the most unusual settings'.[5] It is even possible to argue that *A Rage in Harlem* is an exotic book in the manner in which it describes black ways of life in Harlem. The text positions the reader as a *voyeur* in descriptions like this:

> [Billie] was a brown-skinned woman in her middle forties, with a compact husky body filling a red gabardine dress. With a man's haircut and a smooth, thick, silky mustache, her face resembled that of a handsome man. But her body was a cross. The top two buttons of the dress were open, and between her two immense uplifted breasts was a thick growth of satiny black hair. When she talked a diamond flashed between her two front teeth. (p. 142)

Himes's black men masquerade as women, and his women look like men; two men, Jodie and Goldy, bear female names. The narrative is rhythmic and delivered in a black soul style achieved through repetition and the use of compound words.

But more than a replay of a *noir* style, *A Rage in Harlem*, reflects a black way of life in Harlem. As I will show later, Jackson's journey through the underworld is also a journey through class conflicts in Harlem, an odyssey through the clash between the so-called respectable blacks and the low-life blacks, the Christians and those who spend their time in bars. Himes explores the *noir* style as a way of describing black rage at being trapped in these conditions. By black rage, I mean a set of violent and uncontrollable relations in black communities induced by a sense of frustration, confinement and white racism. This rage often takes the form of an eroticized violence by men against women and homosexuals, a savage explosion on the part of some characters against others whom they seek to control, and a perverse mimicry of the status quo through recourse to disfigurement, mutilation, and a grotesque positioning of weaker characters by stronger ones. Black rage, directed mostly toward other members of the black communities, is the subject of such classical novels as *Native Son* (Richard Wright), *If He Hollers, Let Him Go* (Himes) and *A Rage in Harlem*, and films like *Straight out of Brooklyn* (Matty Rich,1991), *Chameleon Street* (Wendell Harris), *Deep Cover* (Bill Duke, 1992), *Boyz N the Hood* (John Singleton, 1991) and the film adaptation of *A Rage in Harlem* (Bill Duke, 1991).

Himes's characters are consumed with a rage that the author variously describes as 'a rage-thickened voice', 'a voice of rage', 'a blind rage', and 'a red raving passion of rage and lust'. But since the male characters cannot contain or control this rage, women, and especially 'high yellow girls', become regular targets of violence in *A Rage in Harlem*. For example, Grave Digger unleashes his rage onto Imabelle with violent slaps to her face and threats of mutilation: 'I'll pistol-whip your face until no man looks at you again' (p. 131). Similarly, Coffin Ed reveals his angry disposition toward Goldy, who masquerades as a woman, in a misogynistic manner: 'And I hate a Goddam female impersonator worse than God hates sin' (p. 52). Later in the text, a 'middle-aged church-going man, good husband and father of three school-aged daughters' enters into a 'red raving passion of rage and lust' when he faces resistance from Imabelle: 'But when he thought about a whore hitting a church man like himself, he became enraged. He closed in and clutched her' (p. 114). In fact, the text blames Imabelle for Jackson's becoming mixed up with underworld characters. For Imabelle's love, Jackson was ready, 'solid ready to cut throats, crack skulls, dodge police, steal hearses, drink muddy water, live in a hollow log, and take any rape-fiend chance to be once more in the arms of his high-yellow heart' (p. 96). Toward the end of the book, Imabelle is blamed again for inciting young black men to crime: 'The Lieutenant looked her over carefully.

"Strictly penitentiary bait," he muttered angrily, thinking, It's these high-yellow bitches like her that cause these black boys to commit so many crimes' (p. 130).

Black rage is also released through songs, dance, prayer and, especially, flailing about in the dark. When Hank throws acid into Coffin Ed's face, Himes reports that the detective 'closed his eyes against the burning pain, but he was so consumed with rage that he began clubbing right and left in the dark with the butt of his pistol' (p. 70). The efforts to escape from the police and the frustration of being confined to darkness lead Jackson, too, to flail about: 'He thrashed and wriggled in a blind panic, like a black Don Quixote fighting two big warehouses singlehanded; he got himself turned sideways, and ran crab-like toward the street' (pp. 74–5). Every time Jackson runs away from the police, he remembers lines from spirituals, blues, and folk songs such as:

> Dis nigger run, he run his best,
> Stuck his head in a Hornet's nest. (p. 74)

People in *A Rage in Harlem* often drive fast, as if they could outrun the situation that oppresses them. During a police chase sequence, Himes poetically describes Jackson's driving: 'He was just running. He clung to the wheel with both hands. His bulging eyes were set in a fixed stare on the narrow strip of wet brick pavement as it curled over the hood like an apple-peeling from a knife blade, as though he were driving underneath it' (pp. 134–5). Jackson's black Cadillac, racing at eighty-five miles an hour through a red light on 116th Street, looked to one cab driver like an 'automobile ghost' (p. 134). This passage echoes Richard Wright's short story 'Eight Men', in which black boys running from the firing range of a white man are compared to black lightning. Speed is an important theme in black rage texts, from Ralph Ellison's *Invisible Man* and Richard Wright's *Native Son*, to *Boyz N the Hood* and *Straight out of Brooklyn*. Like flying in Toni Morrison's 1977 novel *Song of Solomon*, running in these texts is a desperate attempt to leave this world behind and find peace in another. Jackson wants to drive 'that hearse off the edge of the world' (p. 136). Earlier in the text, Himes describes one black man's relation to speed as follows: 'Speed gave him power and made him feel as mighty as Joe Louis. He had his long arms wrapped about the steering wheel and his big foot jammed on the gas, thinking of how he could drive that goddam DeSoto taxicab straight off the mother-raping earth' (p. 15).

Himes's narrative coincides with the best tradition of the *noir* style whenever he focuses on scenes of black dehumanization, and the depiction of the grotesque:

Goldy's scream mingled with the scream of the locomotive as the train thundered past overhead, shaking the entire tenement of the city. Shaking the sleeping black people in their lice-ridden beds. Shaking the ancient bones and the aching muscles and the t.b. lungs and the uneasy foetuses of unwed girls. Shaking plaster from the ceilings, mortar from between the bricks of the building walls. Shaking the rats between the walls, the cockroaches crawling over kitchen sinks and leftover food; shaking the sleeping flies hibernating in lumps like bees behind the casings of the windows. Shaking the fat, blood-filled bedbugs crawling over black skin. Shaking the fleas, making them hop. Shaking the sleeping dogs in their filthy pallets, the sleeping cats, the clogged toilets, loosening the filth.

(p. 105)

People in Himes's Harlem are choked by powerlessness, economic deprivation and captivity. The violence in the text becomes a communicative act which is deployed by frustrated characters, and aimed at people who are perceived as obstacles to freedom and economic empowerment. In the scene where Jodie cuts Goldy's throat, the dehumanization of black people through captivity in Harlem is paralleled to the naturalization of the sound of the train on 125th Street, and an eroticization of the blood which runs out of Goldy's wound 'turned back like bleeding lips': 'The sweet sickish perfume of fresh blood came up from the crap-smelling street, mingled with the foul tenement smell of Harlem' (p. 106). In *A Rage in Harlem*, Himes delineates black rage, ignited and directed toward self-destruction, and fuelling homophobia and misogyny. The train's power, which is conveyed through the loud sound that shakes the tenements, coincides with a devaluation of black life. The train is also powerful because of its mobility; nothing hinders its traversing of Harlem and thus its movement into the white world that connotes power, economic prosperity and freedom. Mobility empowers the train, which shakes those 'small objects' that are trapped between the walls, and lack of mobility constitutes a check on the freedom of black people in Harlem. Compared to the train, which occupies the centre of life at 125th Street, black people look like insects that are unheard and unseen. The author of *A Rage in Harlem* implies that black lives in Harlem are always absorbed and rendered insignificant by distractionary forces deleterious to the community.

The flailing of frustrated characters, the dances in the bar rooms, and the rage unleashed onto weaker characters in *A Rage in Harlem* constitute, for Himes, performative acts that mimic the freedom, the speed and the power of the train. Clearly, Himes's celebration of violence and his association of the affectations of the lawbreakers with a *cool* style in black culture are common in *film noir*, too, where the primary identification lies with neurotic detectives and bad guys. But there is something else at play in the identification with lawbreakers[6] in *A Rage in Harlem*. The rage that Jodie vents against Goldy – 'I bled that mother-raper like a boar-hog' – forms a communicative act that valorizes him in the eyes of the narrator, Hank and himself. Jodie has obtained *Juice*, to put it in the lingo of a recent black film of the same title; he is proud of himself because he feels free; for a moment, he has removed an obstacle out of his way.

The use of mobility as a trope of freedom in *A Rage in Harlem* announces *race* as a modality through which the *noir* element is read in Himes's text. Himes shows that the real power is with the towers of Riverside Church and the university buildings on the high banks of the Hudson River, and the train that shakes everything beneath its path. Black people in their subaltern positions are likened to the 'sleeping dogs', the 'sleeping cats', the 'rats between the walls' and the 'cockroaches crawling over kitchen sinks and leftover food'. It is in this sense that every act of rage in the text is far more than just violence unleashed against one's own community; it also becomes, on the one hand, an expressive act against incarceration in the valley, far below the university buildings, and on the other hand a representation of class conflict within the black public sphere.

RACE AND CLASS IN *A RAGE IN HARLEM*

As we turn now to the question of class conflict in *A Rage in Harlem*, we must first distinguish between some of Himes's depictions of the public spheres – the bars, the churches, the police station, the train station, the barber shops, the bookie joints and the streets – that interpellate black people, and often colonize the black life world.[7] As indicated above, the train is associated with escape and freedom for black people in Harlem. The train station is the scene of contestation and legitimation of identity among blacks of different class origins. Imabelle tries to pass for a lady and to catch the train out to Chicago. But she is identified as a 'whore' by a respectable-looking black man who accuses her of cutting him, and she is taken to the police station. Jackson, too, has his identity compromised at the train station. He is stopped by a 'big fat black man doing the locomotive shuffle diagonally across the street'. The man, called Big Fats, is characterized in the text as a drunk who strolls past the police car, but 'none of them said anything to Big Fats. No need to borrow trouble with an able-bodied colored drunk the size of Big Fats. Especially if his eyes were red. That's the way race riots were started' (p. 121).[8] When Big Fats reaches out to Jackson and states: '"Short-black-and-fat like me. You tell 'em, short and fatty. Can't trust no fat man, can they?"

Jackson threw the arm off angrily and said "Why don't you behave yourself. You're a disgrace to the race" ' (p. 121). Jackson, by rejecting Big Fats, locates his blackness in an ethics of respectability that is class-derived. But a little later, at the station, a porter challenges Jackson's right to belong to a different class of black people by refusing to check his luggage until he displays a ticket. In fact, this scene ends with Jackson lowered from the status of self-proclaimed respectable black man to that of outlaw, like Big Fats.

Himes's point seems to be that black identities are unvarying within public spheres like the train station and the police headquarters in *A Rage in Harlem*. For Himes, when these systems enter in relation with the black life world they reproduce colonialist and repressive structures. Through them, black identities are always interrogated and reduced to stereotypes; they colonize the black life world, permitting only the repro-duction of such black subjects as whores, lawbreakers and falsifiers, who have to be policed. For the black subject, the passage through these institutions constitutes a struggle to conserve his/her identity. Class distinctions between black people seem to make little difference within these public spheres. Most of the scenes at the police station show Imabelle fighting for the right to define herself; but, to the police, the black women they bring to the precinct are all prostitutes: 'A young white cop had arrested a middle-aged drunken colored woman for prostitution. The big rough brown-skinned man dressed in overalls and a leather jacket picked up with her claimed she was his mother and he was just walking her home' (p. 50). Clearly, for Himes, these public spheres do not constitute good life service institutions to the black life world: they obstruct the emergence of different classes among blacks, and the reproduction of modernized black lifestyles.

For Himes, the emergence of black cultural, class and economic aspirations takes place in other public spheres, such as the church, the bar rooms and the informal sectors. It is through his religious identity that Jackson distinguishes himself from his twin brother Goldy, his landlady and others in the text whose behaviour contradicts the Christian way: 'Jackson was glad none of his acquaintances knew he had such a brother as Goldy, a dope fiend crook impersonating a Sister of Mercy' (p. 30).

Unlike the train station and the police precinct, which colonize the black life world in *A Rage in Harlem*, Christianity constitutes its public sphere through the presentation of a way out for black people. For Himes, it is this promise of a good life society to recompense the daily obstacles in Harlem that renders Christianity attractive to the black life world: 'The people of Harlem take their religion seriously. If Goldy had taken off in a flaming chariot and galloped straight to Heaven, they would have believed it – the godly and the sinners alike' (p. 28). Father Divine, to whom the text makes several references, and whom people in Harlem 'believed was God', capitalized on the changing nature of Christianity, which can adapt to different life worlds, to create a black nationalist Church, 'a Peace Heaven', with a black God and a promise of a good life society for black people. Himes uses Father Divine and the signposts of his abandoned buildings in order to allude to black people's vulnerability to religious public spheres, and to signal the failure of these institutions to lead to the creation of better societies for black people in Harlem. Clearly, *A Rage in Harlem* is a materialist text, and Himes is more concerned to expose the hypocrisy of the Christian public sphere, which controls black rage through luring black people with promises of 'tickets to heaven'.

The bar rooms and the informal sectors are the places where material aspirations are often realized. As public spheres, the bar rooms enter into relation with the black life world to produce black culture as a distinct American style. The dances and the songs document the way of being in black America; the way characters dress, walk and talk renders them powerful and 'cool' in the bar rooms:

> A medium-sized, brown-skinned man, dressed in a camel's hair coat, brown beaver hat, hard-finished brown-and-white striped coat, brown suede shoes, brown silk tie decorated with hand-painted yellow horses, wearing a diamond ring on his left ring-finger and a gold signet-ring on his right hand, carrying gloves in his left hand, swinging his right hand free, pushed open the street door and came into the bar fast. He stopped short on seeing the ex-pug grab Jackson by the shoulder. He heard the ex-pug say in a threatening voice, 'Leave me see that mother-rapin' roll.' He noticed the two bartenders close in for action. He saw the whores backing away. He cased the situation instantly. (p. 56)

The 'cool cat' described here is Gus, a lawbreaker associate of Hank and Jodie. To identify with him in this passage is, on the one hand, to reproduce the structure of identification in *films noirs* where we are placed on the side of the bad guys, femmes fatales and neurotic detectives. On the other hand, this identification allows a recognition of the streets and the bar rooms as spheres that generate free spaces within which black people are able to engender themselves. A significant part of black culture is reproduced through these spaces. The reader's identification with Gus, a lawbreaker – the desire to stand in his place, dress like him and walk like him – signifies a revalorization of the lawbreaker as hero in the black community where the black life world is colonized by the police and other institutions. To break the law is to fight one's captivity, and to claim the right to invent oneself. Lawbreakers are usually the first to challenge the status quo and to generate new ways of being that later become styles for the community, symbols of freedom, or elements of black nationalism.

Lawbreakers in *A Rage in Harlem* also produce economic narratives from the informal sector that may be seen as the *Stoff*, that is, the material, of *film noir*. Just as Father Divine's church and other nationalist religious spheres promise a heaven for blacks who are materially disenfranchised, the informal sector provides black people with an opportunity to beat the system that is inhospitable to them. The gold motif in the text (one character is named Goldy; Hank, Slim and Jodie come to Harlem looking for their gold) embodies the wish to remove the obstacles of racism out of black people's way, to get rich quickly and to live free like white people in America. The lawbreakers draw black people into the informal sector by keeping alive the dream of becoming rich promptly, and circumventing the colonizing systems. Himes's bad guys mix the language used by advertising agents on Wall Street with the discourse of black nationalism to sell their fake gold. Gus lures Jackson into his snare by explaining to him that the shares in the gold mine are reserved for 'worthy' coloured people:

> A real eighteen-carat gold mine, Jackson. And the richest mine in this half of the world. A colored man discovered it, and a colored man has formed a corporation to operate it, and they're selling stock just to us colored people like you and me. It's a closed corporation. You can't beat it. (p. 62)

The informal sector, with its vision of black social institutions that will support the reproduction of a black good life society,[9] generates more economic dreams for black people than are workable through public systems controlled by white people. Perhaps this is the reason why, in the Reagan/Bush era in which affirmative action is curtailed and the black life world is recolonized, black film-makers are turning to the structure of *film noir* where lawbreakers are not simply bad guys, and identification with them is possible. Himes's *roman sociologique*, which glances at the black underclass in the 1950s, is, therefore, an interesting paradigm for a re-examination of the new urban black films that deploy the *noir* style to unleash black rage against the colonization of the black life world in the 1980s and 1990s.

NOIRS ON *NOIR* IN THE REAGAN/BUSH ERA

The emergence of black male cinema in the 1980s is linked in part to the development of rap music, which thematizes the culture of black youth in the urban areas. Rap musicians created the condition of possibility for a black good life society where art that describes black rage from a black point of view is commoditized in order to raise black consciousness, and to uplift black music producers in the economic sphere. Rap is the music of identification *par excellence* with the lawbreakers. The new black films use rap musicians (Ice T and Ice Cube) who impersonate lawless men in the narratives and who play rap songs to support the themes of the films and reinforce identification with certain scenes. Crucially, both rap music and the new black films picture black men and women[10] trapped by systems, and the performative acts that enable them to remove obstacles out of their way and to reinvent themselves.

It is in this vein that Himes's representation of black rage and his identification with the structure of the *noir* style become important for the analysis of black films today. The attempts by Himes's characters to remove obstacles, by any means necessary, out of their way coincides with an ideology of black progress and modernism which, if present in a film, reinforce its links with rap music and the new black nationalism, and if absent, associate the film with the conventional *film noir* style. Using Himes's *A Rage in Harlem* as a paradigmatic text for the way in which black artists inter the roots of *noir* struc-

Deep Cover (Bill Duke, 1992)

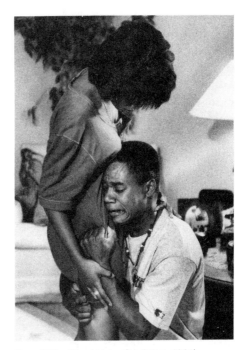

Boyz N the Hood (John Singleton, 1991)

ture in their works, it is possible to distinguish two categories of *films noirs* by *noirs* in the Reagan/Bush era. The conventional category includes films like *A Rage in Harlem, One*

False Move (Carl Franklin, 1992) and, possibly, *New Jack City* (Mario Van Peeble, 1991) which belongs more to the gangster genre than to *film noir*. The realist and black nationalist category includes films like *Joe's Bed-Stuy Barbershop: We Cut Head* and *Malcolm X* (both Spike Lee), *Boyz N the Hood*, *Straight out of Brooklyn*, *Chameleon Street*, *Juice* (Ernest Dickerson, 1992), and *Deep Cover*.

The film *A Rage in Harlem* employs the *noir* genre differently from Himes's text. The film reintroduces the funk associated with Himes's characters in bar rooms and in the streets; but most of the identification with transgressors, which is innovating in Himes's text, is attenuated in the film. Goldy no longer masquerades as a fat black woman going by the name of Sister of Mercy, but instead as a slick Father of Mercy played by Gregory Hines. Himes's famous detectives, Grave Digger and Coffin Ed, are no longer tough and misogynistic cops, but buffoons who always arrive late on the scene of the crime. Crucially, the role of public spheres like the police precinct and the train station are not shown as hindering the development of black subject positions. In the film, Jackson and Imabelle leave Harlem for Mississippi on the train, whereas in the book Imabelle is stopped at the train station. Most of the eroticized violence in the film is directed toward white cops, whilst, in the book Himes emphasizes black on black crime, misogyny and sexism.

The power of the film lies with its rethematization of funk as a black cultural element, its *noir*-like narrative structure, and its characterization of Imabelle, played by Robbin Givens, as a black femme fatale. The scenes of the undertakers' ball and Cathy's saloon are filmed with a particular recourse to funk that reproduces black culture's lawbreaking tradition. I refer here to that heroic and defiant tradition within black culture that dares every form of policing the black body, mind or air. Artistic lawbreaking consists in mimicking through dance, song and storytelling the heroic performances of blacks who resisted the policing of the black life world in America. In the scene of the undertakers' ball, the master of ceremony, with his magic potions and snakes dangling around his neck, is the master of funk. Like the transgressors whose acts he is dramatizing, the master of ceremony must look grotesque and terrifying, and possess the powers of a voodoo priest to be able to exorcize his foes. When he sings, 'I Put a Spell on You', the people who dance to the tune are temporarily empowered like him; their bodies escape the colonization of the Church and other controlling systems. Moreover, they enter into funk, and become emancipated.

Imabelle as the femme fatale (she is a 'killer', she does not get killed at the end), controls the actions of other characters around her. She is always dressed in red, white or blue, except at the end where she wears a black top with a red skirt. She is as tough as any man in the film, but wears a look of sexualized innocence that keeps her in everybody's game. Imabelle changes at the end of the film, presumably leaving the world of crime to live a forever happy life with Jackson in Mississippi.

By allowing his characters to leave Harlem for the South – a temptation that Spike Lee resisted at the end of his film *Joe's Bed-Stuy* – the director of *A Rage in Harlem* opted for a nostalgic ending in which black people are linked to their roots in the South. In *One False Move*, too, the violent crimes in the city are relocated to the South in order to connect them to the unresolved race relations there; and the protagonists are made to revisit the scenes of their 'original sins' before dying. *A Rage in Harlem* rings a conven-

A Rage in Harlem (Bill Duke, 1991)

tional note in its dénouement by restoring Imabelle to a traditional position for women, namely, wife. The film begins with Jackson thanking God 'for not putting obstacles in my way, such as women'. Imabelle's involvement with Jackson, at first, seems like a distraction from Jackson's resolve to save money and be a good Christian. It is interesting that the film is less ambivalent than the book in its treatment of Christianity's guarantee of progress for black people. But as the story unfolds, Imabelle moves from the status of minor distraction to principal player who stands up to Jodie, scares Goldy with her reckless driving, and finally kills Slim. For a while, Imabelle is like the lawbreakers in the book, and the characters in rap songs, who refuse to be colonized by the system in place. She removes every impediment that stands in the way of her goals. The informal sector emancipates her from the traditional roles of mother and domestic worker. But as the point of view shifts again, we come to see Imabelle through Jackson's eyes. Straight out of the romance genre, Jackson is a knight, intoxicated by love, who wants to fight fair and square in the underworld for Imabelle. He throws away his gun, and asks Slim to put down his knife: 'I'll fight for her like a man.' Slim gives the *noir* response to Jackson's chivalry: 'I can't believe you'd say a funky shit like that.' We will remember that in the text Jackson says the opposite: 'I'm not going to fight them fair,' in response to Goldy's warning that 'Those studs is wanted in Mississippi for killing a white man. Those studs is dangerous' (p. 43). Himes's characters, like rap lyricists, believe that a fair fight will not get them far in America.

The point of the film of *A Rage in Harlem* is to create a comic space by mixing the romance and *film noir* genres, by deflating the tough detectives, and by attenuating the scenes that seem out of bounds by the rules of *bienséance* that prevail in Hollywood. But the flight of Jackson and Imabelle to the South signifies surrender to an Afropessimism that views the city as bad and the return to the South as symbol of the repair of the black family, identity and natural life. Jackson turns down his share of the money at the end, and runs after true love. Clearly, this constitutes an anti-materialistic dénouement, which also veers away from the realistic style of Himes's text, rap music, and other new films. By turning to the nostalgic simplicity of the South, the film implies that black rage is a product of the city. Jackson looks to the South as a place to rest his tired feet.

The new black nationalist and realist texts, on the other hand, posit materialist demands that, as I have shown in Himes's text, resist the colonization of the black life world by systems that are controlled by white people, and revalorize the public spheres that emancipate black women and men. Even in *Boys N the Hood*, though the protagonists go South at the end of the film, they go to black institutions where they plan to acquire the knowledge necessary to modernize their communities. The construction of a black community that can emancipate black lives from the ghetto is the goal of many other recent films. In *Deep Cover*, the main character realizes at the end that

> . . . public law in this society has a long history of committing offenses against the African American community, from slavery to Jim Crow and onwards. The very structures erected to acquire liberties and property for African Americans often existed outside of the law. So, for an African American to embrace public law and to further pledge to uphold that law means sacrificing on some level a commitment to a Black nationalist loyalty.[11]

In *Juice*, too, the transformation of the main character at the end of the film constitutes a step toward the emancipation of the community from the ghetto. It was unfortunate that *Juice* and *Straight out of Brooklyn* received little attention during the rise of the new black films. Less glossy than *Boyz N the Hood*, and, unlike Spike Lee's films, less oriented toward cross-over and race relations narratives, *Juice* and *Straight out of Brooklyn* are masterpieces of black realism as *film noir*. *Juice* imitates the realist style in its detailing of the everyday life of four urban black youths. We see them wake up in the morning, get dressed, eat breakfast and leave home. They are ordinary kids who love their parents and the other people in the neighbourhood. But soon the film gets scary as they begin to skip school, shoplift, rob a neighbourhood store and kill the owner. In one of the scenes, arguably the most brilliant among recent film imitations of urban black youth realism, the four boys see on television an eyewitness news report on the death of one of their

Juice (Ernest Dickerson, 1992)

friends, who had just asked them to participate in the robbery that ends his life. As the audience watches the boys watching their friend on television, art and reality become blurred, and the structure of identification reveals that people in the audience, too, may be related to the four boys on the screen. The colonization of the neighbourhood transforms it into a ghetto, and the value of black life decreases. The boys gradually change from innocent children to dangerous criminals who terrorize the neighbourhood. The friendship relations between them become unstable, and they begin to kill one another, until one of them realizes the deleterious effects of this vicious circle and changes. The ending of *Juice*, like that of *Deep Cover*, restores the characters to the community, that is, toward a black good life society. The film constitutes a rite of passage from childhood to adulthood, from chaos to organization, from powerlessness to empowerment.

It is perhaps due to the nationalist dénouements of rap music, of writers such as Toni Cade Bambara, and of recent black films that Malcolm X, the paradigmatic black nationalist figure, is able to make a return as a commodity in the public sphere. It is also remarkable that Spike Lee's 1992 film *Malcolm X* makes recourse to the new black realist style and to *film noir* as a narrative device. Malcolm's transformation in the first part of the film is similar to character changes at the ends of films like *Deep Cover, Do the Right Thing, Joe's Bed-Stuy Barbershop: We Cut Head, Boyz N the Hood, Juice,* etcetera. Through their transformations, these characters acquire a consciousness of the need for blacks to care for blacks, for resistance to colonizing structures, and for a movement towards a good life society founded on an amelioration of existing material conditions.

NOTES

1. See E. Ann Kaplan, ed., *Psychoanalysis and Cinema* (New York: Routledge, 1990). On woman as 'dark continent', a familiar device for linking white women to blackness in order to discipline and punish them, see Ella Shohat, 'Gender and Culture of Empire: Toward a Feminist Ethnography of the Cinema', *Quarterly Review of Film and Video*, vol. 13, nos. 1–3 (1991).

2. Mike Davis, *City of Quartz: Excavating the Future in Los Angeles* (London and New York: Verso, 1990), p. 38.

3. Carl Richardson, *Autopsy: An Element of Realism in Film Noir* (Metuchen: Scarecrow Press, 1992), p. 183.

4. Chester Himes, *A Rage in Harlem* (New York: Vintage Crime/Black Lizard, 1991). All further references to the novel will be to this edition.

5. Raymond Borde and Étienne Chaumeton, *Panorama du film noir américain* (Paris: Les Éditions de Minuit, 1955), p. 46.

6. See Regina Austin, ' "The Black Community", Its Lawbreakers and a Politics of Identification', *Southern California Law Review*, May 1992.

7. See Jürgen Habermas on the colonization of the life world by systems in Jürgen Habermas, *The Theory of Communicative Action, Volume One: Reason and the Rationalization of Society* (New York: Beacon Press, 1984).

8. The Rodney King incident is interesting in the light of the sociology of race relations that Himes provides here. In spite of class differences and the heterogeneity of subject positions, blacks are still interpellated by such events as the Thomas/Hill controversy, the Mike Tyson trial, and the Rodney King trial.

9. On the black good life society, see Manthia Diawara, 'Black Studies, Cultural Studies: Performative Acts', *Afterimage*, October 1992.

10. Whereas the 1980s and 1990s action films are, so far, made by black males, both men and women participate in the production of linear action-oriented rap music. See Tricia Rose, 'Never Trust a Big Butt and a Smile', *Camera Obscura*, no. 23 (May 1991).

11. Jacquie Jones, 'Under the Cover of Blackness', *Black Film Review*, vol. 7, no. 3 (1992), p. 32.

1 0

DEMOCRACY'S TURN: ON

HOMELESS *NOIR*

Dean MacCannell

[A]ny shelter in which may be established a viable, temperate relation of one sex to the other necessitates the intervention . . . of that medium known as the paternal metaphor.

Jacques Lacan, *Seminar XI*

In *film noir*, the proletarian and sub-proletarian areas of American cities are represented as a kind of space where character is tested, a space of intellectual machismo, functioning for the left much as the African jungle functioned for the right as the habitat for a white hero of a certain type. In a 1957 essay, Normal Mailer paints a monochromatic ethos for the existential man of action who 'goes native':

[N]o wonder that in certain cities of America, in New York of course, and New Orleans, in Chicago and San Francisco and Los Angeles, in such American cities as Paris and Mexico, D.F., this particular part of a [immediate post-World War Two, young adult, white male] generation was attracted to what the Negro had to offer. . . . Any Negro who wishes to live must live with danger from his first day, and no experience can ever be casual to him, no Negro can saunter down a street with any real certainty that violence will not visit him on his walk. The cameos of security for the average white: mother and the home, job and the family, are not even a mockery to millions of Negroes; they are impossible. The Negro has

the simplest of alternatives: live a life of constant humility or ever-threatening danger. . . .
Knowing in the cells of his existence that life is war, nothing but war, the Negro (all
exceptions admitted) could rarely afford the sophisticated inhibitions of civilization, so
long as he kept for survival the art of the primitive, he lived in the enormous present. . . .
So there was a new breed of adventurers, urban adventurers who drifted out at night
looking for action with a black man's code to fit their facts. The hipster had absorbed the
existential synapses of the Negro, and for practical purposes could be considered a white
Negro.[1]

Mailer describes or, more precisely, invents a black-and-white image from which he can
derive a new 'feeling' or sensibility adequate as 'motive' (in the literary, psychological
and forensic senses) for his 'new urban adventurers', a sensibility that attained ultimate
expression in the *noir* films of the same period.

What is still lacking, and yet necessary, I will suggest here, is an ideological critique of
the notion of the 'city as jungle' that accompanies this invented sensibility. I will argue
that an unanalysed incorporation of the *noir* version of the city into left political
consciousness disarms the left when it comes to critical examination of contemporary
urban problems, especially homelessness. I will further argue that the homeless can
teach us humility *and* to be better dialectitians when it comes to our criticisms of the
current social order.

FILM NOIR AND THE HOMELESS

Perhaps the best way to characterize *noir* sensibility is as 'false nostalgia' or 'constructed
nostalgia'. What is produced is a sense of loss of something that was never possessed,
something that never was (for example, the 'White Negro'). The stark cinematography
of *film noir* represented the American city not as a place of childhood roots, nor as an
idealized place where we once lived and left, nor as a place to which we desire to return.
That is, the city is not constituted through a simple nostalgic appeal to a universalizable
'past' and a possible utopic future – as in *The Wonder Years*, say. Rather it figures as the
guilty horizon of bourgeois comfort and detachment.

That no one would really want to live in the imagined proletarian and subproletarian
space of *film noir* is precisely the basis for its attraction. It is a space of survival:
demanding, exhausting. Caught in the interior space of *film noir*, a merely ordinary
person would want to flee to the suburbs, to Levittown or Orange County, California.
But as the fantasy frame for a reality that is represented as 'harsh', 'cold' or 'stark', in

the end its 'grittiness' becomes the basis for its deeper appeal to the ego: it presents a version of everyday life in the city that is adequate to the ego's exalted view of itself. Perpetually exposed to imaginary risk and opportunity, the *noir* hero proves himself mentally and physically. The groundless 'nostalgia' these fictions provide historically disconnects us from the real sources of our suffering while catering to our sense of self-importance. As such, these films would be found high on any list of manufactured sensibilities that hold advanced capitalism together on a psychic/cultural plane.

One of the nonreversible changes Reagan and Bush visited on America was the removal of the kind of urban domestic space once inhabited by the poorest of the working poor. During the 1980s, US cities lost more than half of their low-cost housing via condemnation, removal or gentrification, processes driven by changes in tax and building codes aimed precisely at remaking the American urban environment. As the proletarian areas of the city are renovated and removed, they are not replaced by quality (or any) housing for the poor. The corresponding growth is in highly profit-able, architecturally clever southern California style condos priced 'within reach' of couples and families with two white-collar incomes. Gone with low-cost housing are the walk-up, low-rent offices of entrepreneurs content to subsist at a break-even level of profit. Also gone are the cheap but clean hotel rooms rented by the week or month.

Homelessness is the precipitate of these policies which seek to rebuild the American city and in the process remove any architectural traces of the working class. The policy package is part of a larger perverse fantasy of classless capitalism, sometimes called the 'Reagan Revolution', in which Orange-County-style bourgeois utopias are built on social exclusion. The remaining decent low-cost housing is now in the hands of state and local agencies and nonprofit organizations that serve the poor. There is intense inter-agency struggle for administrative control of housing that can be used as temporary shelter for their clients. Among the poor, there is a struggle to qualify to get on the waiting lists for the remaining housing. In the meantime they live in the streets, cars, abandoned warehouses, subways, and in vacant lots.

Following a logic that is something more than historical coincidence, the current Technicolor *film noir* renaissance (*Public Eye, The Two Jakes*, even *Barton Fink*, etcetera) occurs exactly as the interior space of classic (1945–55) *films noirs* is being excised from the American city. All but gone is the kind of hotel room in which Philip Marlowe once regained consciousness – the torn window shade, the single bare lightbulb hanging from a twisted wire, the iron bedstead, the water pitcher and basin used for shaving. There are no longer blocks of poor-but-respectable families living in faded tenements for the hero to wander through, looking for some undefined thing that he will recognize on first sight. There are no more characteristically appropriate offices for the hard-boiled detective; and no more by-the-week rooms for the femme fatale to rent, no questions asked.

Whilst the disappearance of the actual spaces of *film noir* has been highly consequential for those forced into homelessness, it has not presented a problem to the makers of revivalist *films noirs*, who can reconstruct virtual gritty reality in the form of film sets. Now we have a fictional recuperation of the proletarian city just as the actual proletarian space is historically lost. This double movement, to the extent that it shapes the theoretical *un*conscious, stymies understanding of the homeless situation. Who could possibly want to save this abject, filthy, dangerous space, except as a kind of fictional forbidden territory habitable only by heroes, villains and fools? This space was created to serve as a place from which to flee, or to enter only as a matter of courage beyond reason. With jails, asylums, old folks' and foundling homes, charity hospitals and the like, this space defines the imaginary boundaries of urban misery. Yet the fact remains that the abject interior spaces of *film noir*, originally a nostalgic bourgeois phantasm of gamey or 'real' subproletarian existence, could, if preserved, serve as a sheltering haven for the homeless.

THE EXERCISE OF THEORETICAL FREEDOM IN *FILM NOIR*

Film can represent life in such a way as to provide critical distance and insight that might otherwise be lacking in unreflected experience. *Film noir*, from the beginning, was quick to exercise theoretical licence and a certain self-consciousness in this regard, this being one of its defining characteristics. What does it mean for us to continue to dream of an industrial age, a class-based society and the principle of universal inclusion, that is, a society in which the proletariat has a home and a moral voice, and can make a difference?[2] There is a kind of innocent codependence of *film noir* sensibility and Marxist criticism, each providing the images and concepts that the other believes it needs.[3] Mike Davis has argued that the intentional structure of Los Angeles-based *film noir* uses an 'existentialized Marxism' to unmask a 'bright guilty place'; that it insinuates 'contempt for a depraved business culture' and is a 'mirror of capitalism's future'; 'a kind of Marxist *cinema manqué*', a shrewdly oblique strategy for an otherwise subversive realism'.[4] Slavoj Žižek similarly but more broadly argues that *film noir* exposes a symbolic order that is neither neutral nor benign, within which 'an obscene sadistic Other watches over me'.[5] In short, *film noir* affirmed in a popular genre that capitalism is not a fair game and it anticipated the critical insight that patriarchal judgement only pretends to be disinterested, whilst its true aim is to protect the privileges certain members of society enjoy over others.

These are crucial insights, but they no longer depend for their conveyance on a fictional medium with theoretical pretensions. The consequences of the symbolic disturbance highlighted in these films are now directly lived by those evicted from their most characteristic spaces. Still, there are things to be learned from the films. Classic *film noir*, we are repeatedly told, emerged after World War Two, but it eludes historical 'solutions' because it instantly became a crucial component of its own historical context. How could anyone try to grasp the problematic details of Western post-war self-understanding without *film noir*? *Film noir* is our faded old black-and-white family album from this period. Like other albums, it contains a family embarrassment that we would all want to forget, and perhaps some clues about the beginnings of current difficulties.

RITUAL CONSTRAINT IN *FILM NOIR*

Democracy had joined forces with Soviet Marxism to vanquish fascism. But a great deal of blood had been spilled in the process. It was a war of European against European, American against European. Not everyone who fought against fascism was deeply anti-fascist. There was a close family relation between the adversaries, horrendous violence, murder and guilt, and thus a need for a totemic ritual to distribute the guilt and to try to reassure that there would not be a repetition of the violence. Popular cultural entertainments privileged forms that affirmed that the winners were not perfect and the losers not all bad, while searching for a new common enemy. By openly questioning the ultimate 'goodness' of capitalist and democratic values, *film noir* contributed some of the hardest ritual work of expiating guilt for World War Two. The durability of the genre may be tied to its performance of this function. But, as ritual, *film noir* brought up a more complex set of critical problems. Like the mother who favours the bad child ('because no one else will') left *film noir* exhibited a tenderness toward fascism in the pure heart of democracy. One finds in *film noir* an aesthetics of violence and other fascist values on both sides of any moral equation: the 'good guy' is as likely as the bad to resort to intimidation, physical punishment and 'justice' without trial.

Thus *film noir* came to function less as criticism of capitalism and the paternal metaphor and more as an inoculation against them. Identification with *noir* heroes allows viewers to live passively within the order of capitalism while imagining themselves to be opposed to it. The dice are always loaded against the anti-hero of *film noir*. He knows it and persists anyway. He wins a moral victory by fighting corrupt authority to a draw, engaging in some of the same violent practices as employed by authority. One is even happy with a near draw if the hero does not lose too badly, given that the forces against him are massive, even global. The answer to the question of whether or not *film noir* can ever be an incisive critique of capitalism cannot be unambiguous, since it cannot ignore some of these more problematic aspects of the genre.

NOIR'S DARK SECRET – EXCLUSIONARY DEMOCRACY

The still unexamined tension at the heart of *film noir* is that between senile capitalism and democracy. *Film noir*, not necessarily in the mode of full self-consciousness, anticipated the attack by capitalism on democracy that has just begun, producing the homeless as its first casualties. The problem between democracy and capitalism seems to have its origins in an aggressive, pragmatic drive on the part of capitalism to make democracy do its bidding, or to clear it out of the way. After defeating its external enemies, fascism and communism, capitalism entered its 'twilight years'; increasingly it began to turn its fading powers against its own partner, democracy, for harbouring and promoting a historically antiquated, inefficient ideological surplus. From the perspective of mature capitalism, the historical purpose of its partnership with democracy was (1) to break the privilege of aristocratic classes, making way for new entrepreneurial elites, and (2) to win the hearts and minds of socialists and others still tied to noncapitalist modes of production by offering them freedom of speech, choice, etcetera. Once traditional privilege is destroyed, and everyone is involved in the same system of global economic relations, there is no further need for democracy. In fact, in the current historical moment, any openness or broad base of decision-making, any balancing of different interests, any voicing of interests other than those of economic self-interest, is seen as intolerably opposed to the continued development of free-market economies. Only a 'sold out' democracy is acceptable, that is, one that goes through the motions of giving a voice to the people while actually supporting a narrowing of social and economic interests.

Classic *film noir* has an almost fatal fascination for the confrontation between capitalism and democracy, which it witnesses with an implacable numbness. In count-

The Big Clock (John Farrow, 1948)

Monsieur Verdoux (Charlie Chaplin, 1947)

Shadow of a Doubt (Alfred Hitchcock, 1943)

less films, *The Big Clock* (John Farrow, 1948), is only one example, a tainted, slightly compromised, democratic hero battles corpulent and decadent capitalism to a draw, or a near draw. The basic principle that is compromised in these films, and in democracy as it is currently inflected, is inclusion: everyone is supposed to have a 'place' in it; anyone can win; everyone has a voice. But all too often this voice (most notably in the form of the voice-over) is one of bitter compromise. The players in *film noir* usually know they are on the take, living off crumbs thrown to them by their oppressors. Still, they are capable of cynical detachment, even from their own condition, able to see all sides of the situation and their place in it. Only those who actually admire and look up to their oppressors are represented as servile and abject.

LIVING *FILM NOIR* TODAY

Technically, it is not precisely a 'home' that has been denied the 'homeless'. More precisely, it is a 'place', or the right to be included in society, criticism, fiction, policy – a place in the symbolic order. Many of the 'homeless' manage to build architecturally creative homes for themselves from cars and vans, packing crates, parts of freeway overpasses, subway systems, etcetera. A woman I met in Washington, DC, lived in a system of boxes over a heating grate on a crowded sidewalk on Pennsylvania Avenue: she had an easy chair with side tables, a Coleman lantern for reading at night, a portable television which she shared with passers-by, and a large canvas she wrapped herself and her 'stuff' in at night to hold the heat and produce a more-or-less official-appearing and protected stack of boxes. What she lacked was not a home but a proper place, a shelter under the dominion of the paternal metaphor.[6] The societal investment in this kind of place is not to be underestimated. It is also the only kind of location or address that can be used socially to identify her, that would allow others, including her family, but also representatives of the police, Internal Revenue Service, the welfare department, etcetera to find her. In other words, my acquaintance had a home and even neighbours, but her home did not provide her with a social place and so she was excluded from the social order in many other crucial ways: she could not register to vote, apply for work, file a crime report, or any other taken-for-granted right that requires one to give an address.

This problem is distantly prefigured in *film noir* by the pseudo-expulsion of the hero from all 'viable temperate' human relationships. But unlike the homeless, expelled emphatically from the social order, the *film noir* hero always hangs onto hope that even a compromised democracy can continue to have a place for everyone and to guarantee fundamental freedoms. The hero moves through any and every situation liminally as a kind of cipher of the unrealized possibility of the coexistence of democratic openness and capitalistic closure. The hero abjures regular, ordinary, routine, normal, for-profit pursuits, does not have an evident class perspective, operates within the law only when it is convenient for him to do so, and has few institutional attachments or obligations. But he never really gives up his place in the social order. The hero demands a paradoxical combination of rights: to be completely detached from society *and* at the same time to be allowed total access to every part of it. The homeless would see his combination of attachment and detachment as manifestations of good fortune and bad faith. He holds himself external to and above specific class, domestic and institutional relations in order not to be marked by any specificity. He is thus free to enter into everything. If some heavy attempts to block his entry into a club or a back room where a deal is being made, he shoves the guy aside. Philip Marlowe walks freely through the mean streets of the city's underside in one scene and, in the next, strides with the same nonchalance across the oriental carpets of the hot-house billionaire General Stern-wood. In its most positive manifestation, *film noir* affirms the right of Democratic Everyman to go anywhere as a matter of principle. If he encounters a worthy adversary along the way, it can only be himself.

The Ray Milland character in *The Big Clock* knows from the outset that the mysterious murder suspect he is supposed to be tracking down is himself. He attempts to expose the actual murderer while covering his own incriminating trail. His task is made difficult because he is trapped in the headquarters of a giant prototypical global corporation (one that operates in all time zones – hence 'the big clock') and because of the great diversity of the settings through which he has left a trail to be covered. These settings include the highest boardrooms and offices of the corporation, a rustic mountain cabin where he should have been vacationing with his wife, the luxuriously appointed apartment of his boss's murdered mistress, nightclubs and bars at all levels from elegant to seedy, the apartment and studio of a bohemian artist, a children's home, an expensive antique shop, a pawnshop, and finally behind the scenes of industrial technology, inside 'the big clock' itself. The Ray Milland character treats every one of these settings with equally bemused detachment, showing no partiality toward, or greater or lesser comfort in, any of them.[7] It is left to his lackeys to comment on one of the bars to which he has been sent in search of clues: 'It's a very sordid place – disreputable clientele.'

Film noir established democracy's dark side, not as an articulated message but as a critically constructed *mise en scène*. The *noir* hero and contemporary homeless people are in a 'through the looking glass' relation: originally and in the first place, he and they stood outside the capitalist social 'totality', giving us our first glimpse of it as something not neutral, not fully inclusive; he schmoozes and shoves his way back into society, where he exposes its bias and corruption. But the homeless remain on the outside, not just outside some desired part of capitalist society: not outside the middle class yet in the working class, for example. They remain outside everything, outside class itself.

Between *film noir* and the contemporary situation of the homeless there has been an absolute shift in what is commonly and implicitly understood by the term 'society', a shift that remains unremarked by sociology and anthropology. The space of *film noir* was inclusive in ways that corresponded to an earlier theoretical ideal of society as promoted in classical sociological texts. Society contained, or made a place for, all its members from the highest-born to the lowest, from infancy until death and beyond, for the criminal, the infirm and the insane. This universal catalogue of places was also the *mise en scène* of *film noir*. After Goffman and Foucault we were forced to acknowledge that 'having a place' for some also meant bearing a radically stigmatizing label or a damaged identity. But under naïve classical theoretical ground rules, no one could be left out; everyone had to live in society and to remake society together. There was something resembling consensus that whenever the economic terms of universal inclusion became visibly intolerable for large numbers in the 'disadvantaged' classes, wealth should be partly redistributed either via social programmes or, if the other party is in power, through riots and looting. That the poor, the insane or the criminal could simply be turned onto the streets, that the 'legitimate' members of society could retreat into gated and guarded communities, that the poorest of the poor could simply be excluded from 'society' and asked to 'keep moving along', these exclusionary societal 'solutions' were (and continue to be – even as they emerge as historical reality) theoretically unthinkable. The victory of capitalism over other economic forms has been accompanied by a new attitude, a casual indifference toward the socially excluded. Now that capitalism no longer has an audience, the homeless do not necessarily constitute an embarrassment.

MURDER AND THE FAMILY

It is worthwhile to ask from what sort of arrangement the homeless have been excluded? This is the exact point at which *noir* theoretical sensibility most effectively short-circuits history, allowing us to see the future by looking into the past.

A defining characteristic of *film noir* is an insistent nonchalance about murder. It may be committed for a reason, in Slavoj Žižek's words 'vulgar and acquisitive', or it may be committed just to 'provide a corpse'.[8] The hard-boiled detective mouths some truisms about the ultimate cruelty of the act as he sets out to find the killer. His drive is formalistic in ways that go beyond the conventions of the genre. Each step is motivated mainly by professionalism, a need to get the job done, to clear up all the loose ends. He becomes other than professionally involved in the search for the killer only if the suspect also turns out to be his love interest (as it often does), his partner, or himself. Guilt is so diffuse in *film noir*, so much a part of the corrupt background of the action, that the hero can always plausibly muse, 'Who's to say who really did it? Yeah, I know she put in the knife, but was she really the guilty party? Any more than you or me?'

This excessive demand that guilt for murder be shared all around is the opening in *film noir* for the perverse accommodation of capitalism by democracy. It is also the theme that allows *film noir* to examine the dark side of democracy, which is its nearly exclusive right among popular entertainments. The redistribution of guilt that appears thematically in *film noir* can be traced to changes in family structure that came with the simultaneous arrival of modern economic and democratic relations: as wealth is concentrated, in order for the system to continue to function, guilt for social pathology must be distributed among the innocent.[9] Standing in the way of this distribution of guilt is the traditional idea that responsibility for fair judgement is the basis for authority and all other serious concern for justice. Interestingly, we have arrived back on the ground of the old, original 'paternal metaphor'.

The pre-democratic, so-called 'traditional', patriarchal or oedipal family was founded on a murder (the sons murdered their father), and society was reorganized in such a way as to prevent a repetition of the crime. This is accomplished, in part, by rendering paternal authority *figural*. In a metaphoric reprise of the original murder, the real father disappears from the scene to be replaced by the 'father figure'. The sons will never be able to get at him again. The original murder was committed out of jealousy: the primal father monopolized sexual pleasure, keeping all the women to himself. The killing of the totemic father and the institution of universal marriage guaranteed women for every man, but only on condition that no one attempted to become again the totemic father, that is, have all the women. Thus the father figure stands at the head of the incest-free family, the figure of control, including especially self-control, measure, temperateness, restraint. He is also the figure of *loss* of the kind of intense absolute pleasure that might have been enjoyed by the original totemic father who is now dead. '[A]ny shelter in which may be established a viable, temperate relation of one sex to the other necessitates the intervention . . . of that medium known as the paternal *metaphor*.' That is, real relations are of necessity replaced by symbolic relations. The symbolic order governed by the paternal metaphor is an efficient mechanism for the resolution of conflict, the determination of guilt and innocence, and distributive justice. This resolution and determination is the work of the father figure. Once he has renounced his own self-interest and deleted total pleasure from the scene, he can sit in the position of Maxwell's sorting demon, assuring a kind of universal equilibrium. Of course, on occasion the symbolic order comes unglued, the paternal metaphor is kicked aside, there is a return to the real, and traditional family members kill each other. But this is not the kind of murder that is characteristic of *film noir*.

Murder in *films noirs* happens off to the side of traditional family relations and without reason or motive that is commensurate with the crime. Far from being the intended victim of the crime, the father is usually trying to cover up for some member of his family. He hires a detective he believes he can control or manipulate because the detective is reported to have a questionable reputation. The daughter may or may not have committed murder. Perhaps she is being blackmailed for some petty transgression. Whatever happened, the most important thing is to keep it quiet and to set up the detective to take the fall.

We cannot discover the grounds or the motives for these murders by going back to the origins of the family and the lethal conflict that traditional family structure was built upon in such a way as to attempt to hold it down. Rather, it is necessary to go back to the moment that traditional family structure was inserted into generalized democratic arrangements. By now, it is commonplace to engage in 'politically correct' celebration of the 'loss' of paternal authority and the opening of the symbolic order that began with the modern democratic revolutions, or religious right mourning of the same loss and opening. Too little analytical attention has been focused on the possibility that we are not dealing here with a *loss*, however this might be viewed. It takes a certain cold-blooded *film noir* or homeless sensibility at the level of theory to notice, that for all its pathological manifestations, traditional family structure, under democracy, has been replaced by something more pathological still.

This is the side of democracy that is becoming the virtual field of 'hard-boiled' critical theory. Žižek suggests that the introjection of traditional family structure into democracy involved a specific mutation of the father figure. No longer the 'absent father', guarantor of the symbolic order, democracy gave us the *present* father, not symbolic but real; this father is not ignorant but obscene. Juliet Flower MacCannell describes the same transformation in her *Regime of the Brother*:

> Since the Enlightenment 'traditional' society has been supplanted by what Freud calls an 'artificial group' (*die Masse*) making its patriarchal ideals at best a charming fraud, at worst an ideological cover for another kind of exercise of power, the command to conformity. . . . [The leader] is not necessarily Other, in the manner of a father, not an ego-ideal, but an ideal ego . . . [H]e claims no special right, he is not the privileged son and heir, but only one among brothers. As such he acts as the father without being him, and can draw upon reserves of a now simulated affect (paternal love). Retaining the 'name' of the father he embodies a misnomer (or a metaphor), for he is really only first among equals. As mere metaphor he is obliged to exercise the paternal/parental function of 'protecting and saving' – a metaphor incarnate is too weak a figure to sustain real community, embracing diversity. It can only mirror the same. But it is not too weak to found the group as a kind of simulacrum or art form . . . Had it fulfilled all its promises a democracy so founded might have provided a new form of human community, and definitively displaced the Oedipal model and its malevolent clones. It did not. Instead, it retained the Oedipal form, but not its substance (to moderate the ego-centered passions . . .). Under the 'name' of the father another and sadistic Other – unconscious, superego, *It* – has begun its reign of pleasure and terror. The Regime of the Brother begins.[10]

It is here that we find the ground of murder in *film noir*: committed in the name of ideal 'traditional values', including 'traditional family values', it aims not to protect tradition, but to use it as a cover and excuse for evil. Under the guise of the traditional father figure (that is, the figure of denial and lack) a neo-totemic or capitalist father operates who once again thinks he deserves and can have it all, all the pleasure and all the wealth. And 'democracy', in the employ of evil, is used to redistribute the guilt for excess and usurpation to everyone except those actually responsible for the crimes.

In *film noir*, the father is not the intended victim of the crime as the oedipal father was. If a father is implicated, he most likely will have been involved in *arranging* the murder, seemingly out of a sense of duty to his family, to protect the ideal 'image' of his family. He does this not out of concern for his family *per se*, but because his self-representation as a 'traditional father', father of lack and self-denial, is a useful cover for his drive to 'have it all' and his presumptive right to limitless enjoyment. In hard-core *film noir*, this obscene father will not even have to pay for his crime. Murder, at a double remove from the dramatic action, can occur for any reason. Murder is now fully institutionalized as a taken-for-granted event that is not in itself worthy of consideration or concern. All that is important to the action is the preservation of an *image* of ideal bourgeois freedom and respectability. This image is held up as an ultimate ideal, but it is not. It is only the outer wrapping or mask for the free play of the capitalist father who pretends to assume the responsibilities of a patriarch but does not and, in fact, enjoys the privileges of the totemic *père jouissant*. This is what *film noir* is stammering to tell us about ourselves: trying to warn us about the wrong turn that democracy, bent by and acquiescing to capitalism, is about to take.

Two films expose this turn with surgical precision: Charlie Chaplin's *Monsieur Verdoux* (1947) and Alfred Hitchcock's *Shadow of a Doubt* (1943).[11] To do so, they must leave the 'mean streets' of tough-guy *film noir* and enter the bourgeois interior, the home.[12] The central figure in both films is an 'ideal' man, handsome, well-dressed, well-built, intelligent, entertaining, middle-class, and democratic. Juliet MacCannell comments, 'they are perfect men who are also murderers and assassins'. Verdoux's crimes may have originated with a mistake he made concerning 'what his wife wants'. After losing his job as a bank clerk, in order to maintain his crippled wife and son in a domestic setting of complete bourgeois respectability he embarks upon a career of serial bigamy and murder, marrying rich women, killing them and giving his inheritances to his first wife and child. He is throughout the perfect model of the modern man in general in that he can believe absolutely in his own innocence so long as he tells himself that he is doing it 'for the family'. And if there is a whiff of evil here, it is his wife and child who would be at fault, because he is driven to commit his crimes only by his sense of duty toward them. He occupies the middle of the middle, pretending to continue to be a 'man of affairs', to go to work, to 'do his duty', to be perfectly correct in every way. And he is absolutely pitiless toward his victims. Of course, only incidentally – as a kind of by-product of the sense of propriety that causes him to kill – he enjoys wealth, freedom, exotic entertainments, and limitless sexual conquests, all of these being necessary to the performance of his duty toward his wife and child.

Verdoux's piety and pitiless cruelty is matched only by the Joseph Cotten character, 'Uncle Charlie', the 'Merry Widow killer', of Hitchcock's masterpiece. Cotten, on the run, visits his exaggeratedly respectable sister and her family in an overly idealized American small town. The sister's family is made up of her husband and two daughters. The husband is something of a noodle, spending all his time playing a game with a neighbour in which they attempt to outdo each other in pretending to plot perfect murders. The eldest daughter, played by Teresa Wright, is very beautiful and is nicknamed 'Charlie' after her uncle whom she has rarely seen but who has been held up to her all her life as the model of intelligent, attractive manhood. The mother's entire life is based on her admiration for her brother and her fantasies of his travels, his complex and successful business dealings, his famous associates, all of which he charmingly takes for granted, wearing the whole mantle of urbane male perfection as casually as he wears his too-perfectly tailored suits. The rare visit of this important worldly person to the perfect small town is a major civic event and a special evening is planned in his honour. Against the grain of all this, his beautiful niece and namesake comes to suspect that her marvellous uncle is the serial killer described in the radio reports from distant cities. For most of the film, the viewer has no way of knowing whether she is correct in her suspicion, or just overly imaginative, projecting evil onto him to block her incestuous desires. When she first confronts him with her suspicions, he denies his guilt but sides with the killer saying, 'They are fat cows feeding off of excess. They live off the remains of their dead husbands. They don't deserve to live.'

The post-oedipal or *noir* murderer is a capitalist 'angel of death'. The murderer executes those 'guilty' of nothing except a kind of enjoyment that the capitalist would want to monopolize for himself. Monsieur Verdoux and Uncle Charlie pause and notice whenever they find someone enjoying surplus-value, and they kill. The neo-totemic or capitalist murderer is fully repatriated or taken back into the family as the 'uncle', the 'brother', or the 'obscene father', so long as he succeeds in his seemingly effortless appropriation of surplus-value. The family, for its part, necessarily becomes all the more ideal to accommodate the presence of so marvellous a figure.

THE HOMELESS HERO: REAL *NOIR* TODAY

Unfortunately, we are not yet sufficiently aware of what the homeless already know: in today's society, no one is guaranteed sheltering protection simply by virtue of being a normally behaved, reasonably intelligent, educated, moral, productive member of society.[13] Anyone can be cast out. Homelessness is not a matter of character, identity, mental or other competency. It involves budget cutbacks, layoffs, rent deposits. If there can be a lesson for democracy in this negative historical moment, it should be a reminder that no person, group, class or other social segment has any greater social standing than as a model for the others. These are not necessarily models that will be copied or emulated, but always ones that can help to shape knowledge and improve the general conditions of existence either by positive or negative example. The homeless, now on the plane of history, tell the truth that *film noir* tried to anticipate: that the moral formulations of the paternal order are sham.

Statistically, the homeless have been around at least since the beginnings of 'modern rational capitalism', as Weber liked to call it. But before the final victory of capitalism they were called 'drifters', 'bums', 'tramps' and 'winos', never 'homeless'. Within the framework of senile capitalism, the term is assuming heavy imaginary significance. When one utters or hears the word, one is supposed to experience a pleasurable sense of security for having a home. But without a simultaneous hygienic suppression of any capacity for dialectic thought, this word 'homeless' is potentially dangerous in use, in the postmodern community. For it blinds us to the fact that the rights of citizens who still have homes are increasingly infringed upon in subtle and less subtle ways.

The homeless are the expulsed subjectivity of a social form which, by rejecting even one human being, loses all rightful claim to conscience. The homeless are the soul of senile capitalism, set to wandering when it died its first death. They move around in public space, their carts filled with worthless 'belongings', a parody of the other postmodern figure, the yuppie. What they are actually carrying are heavy spiritual and ideological burdens. Within the framework of advanced capitalism, they represent *lack*. It is precisely this crucial lack, this particular lack of a 'home', which invests them with significance as the true precipitate of advanced capitalism. Spiritual homelessness is suffered by every disinherited child of capitalism, but it can never be admitted, not by the ones who have a material home, those whose role it is to humour and coddle their obscene father. Only the actually homeless can tell the truth: that everyone under advanced capitalism is 'excluded but present'. Everyone lives only their relation to production and consumption, trading in their human relationships for 'an immense accumulation of commodities', tied less to each other than to their overflowing shopping carts.

Is it possible to carry this line still further to compare the travels of the homeless to those of the yuppie tourist? No. It is exactly here before the possibility of two forms of nomadism, two different ways of being out of place, that the analogy breaks down, leaving the homeless and the *noir* hero together on one side, and yuppie tourists on the other, providing us with the possibility for a subversive choice in our wandering. The homeless, the *noir* hero and the tourist can all be said to constitute a territory by their movements, following known pathways between points. But the tourist weaves together all the various attractions and sanitized public fixtures worldwide. His movements bind together the high points of global culture as framed by global capitalism. The tourist will set forth on his travels only on the promise that the tour is circular, secure in his belief that he can go home again. The homeless person and the *noir* hero know better. Their movements have nothing to do with the official definition of social spaces. Their movements outside of official pathways are the primary grounds for their existence and they cannot go home by definition. If a homeless person (or a *noir* hero for that matter) stops along the way to watch television in a store window, to piss in the privacy of a stairwell, to sleep next to the hot lights of a billboard, it is because these places have been forgotten, at least temporarily, by the official marking and policing apparatus. They are temporal interstices in advanced capitalism produced by the momentary presence of the excluded. The tourist assumes that everything is owned by someone and identifies with the Owner of Everything, nicely staying between the lines on the officially marked paths that bind Everything together. For the homeless and the *noir* hero, the marked path, the road, the sidewalk, the trail that has been laid down in advance are each only one way of going from place to place, and not necessarily the best way, or the way that will get them to their destination, or the way that offers least resistance. They may even feel the need to stay off the road for purposes of movement. The homeless will use the road for something other than passage. They may harvest it for aluminium cans for example, as the *noir* hero harvests it for false clues that he knows have been laid down by an adversary to trick him, that will eventually lead him to his adversary. They have no use for the proper boundary or the separations and hierarchies encoded in spatial arrangements. There are no internally imposed limits or boundaries around their space that correspond to the territorial markings of private ownership. And for this reason, they know that they can never ultimately hide their feelings in the interior of a personal or private 'subjectivity'. They must hide out in the open, fully exposed.

Their plight in this regard is virtually the opposite of that of the capitalist children who continue to seek shelter in the home of the father, on the condition of not exposing the father for what he has become. This compromised consciousness must wage a constant fight to appear to have a subjective interior, a certain subjective intensity, a history of its own of which it can be proud. Those who have sold out to advanced capitalism for nothing but the appearance of having a home, a place, can no more prove themselves than the homeless can hide themselves. In its very drive to represent itself as being composed of real families and communities, in its make-over that mockingly refers to 'tradition' even after it paints itself up, senile capitalism becomes nameless and placeless. The mind that assumes the burden of guilt for senile capitalism without full compensation becomes disconnected from everything it claims to value. All that is left for it is manic thematization. It engages in a kind of filing frenzy at the level of the total society to produce the appearance that everything has a 'place' and nothing need ever be out of place. Everything is thematized: restaurants have themes, neighbourhoods have themes, streets are named after trees in alphabetical series (Aspen, Beech, Cypress, Dogwood . . .), the town is zoned 'Mediterranean', etcetera.

The only resource that the last capitalist community has to draw upon for its humanity is the homeless. It remains to be seen whether this is democracy's turn. Does capitalism have sufficient character to confront its corruption of democracy, to make its fathers, brothers, sons and uncles responsible for something other than their own limitless enjoyment and accumulation, all carefully hidden behind the pretence of tradition, temperance and self-denial? We will know if it is capable of having a distinctive character, interesting, contradictory and worthy of respect, when it takes the homeless back in, all of them. Otherwise, the homeless will rapidly grow in numbers and consciousness to the point where only the handful of real capitalists are left with a 'place' 'in' 'society'.

NOTES

1. Norman Mailer, 'The White Negro', *Advertisements for Myself* (New York: G.E. Putnam, 1959), pp. 340–41.

2. The question is almost eerie in the context of a policy that favours export of unskilled and semi-skilled work to Third World countries while promoting the collective fantasy that the United States has become a 'consumer society'.

3. This was anticipated in Mailer's final remarks in 'The White Negro': 'It is almost beyond the imagination to conceive of a work in which the drama of human energy is engaged, and a theory of its social currents and dissipations, its imprisonments, expressions, and tragic wastes are fitted into some gigantic synthesis of human action where the body of Marxist thought, and particularly the epic grandeur of *Das Kapital* (that first of the major *psychologies* to approach the mystery of social cruelty so simply and practically as to say that we are a collective body of humans whose life-energy is wasted, displaced and procedurally stolen as it passes from one of us to another) – where particularly the epic grandeur of *Das Kapital* would find its place in an even more God-like view of human justice and injustice' (p. 358).

4. Mike Davis, *City of Quartz* (London: Verso, 1990), pp. 18, 21.

5. Slavoj Žižek, *Enjoy Your Symptom* (London and New York: Routledge, 1992), p. 158.

6. This is not to say that the homeless are not particular about their place 'outside' the symbolic order. Some homeless form temporary communities of eight to twenty individuals who sleep in groups for safety and warmth, sitting – sides touching – with their backs against a buildings and legs extended across the sidewalk. I have observed that once an order in the line-up is established, it mainly holds night after night. Thus, when someone arrives after everyone else has gone to sleep, rather than taking a place at one end of the line, the latecomer will usually go to his or her 'proper place' in the line and demand to be inserted between her established partners. This, of course, causes everyone to have to crowd closer together and shift positions slightly up and down the line; this is usually the occasion for grumbling, but the accommodation is made.

7. This is also the central plot device in the 1970s television series *Charley's Angels*. Charley, the phallic figure par excellence, is never present. He is only a disembodied voice of command. His 'Angels' are his 'stand-in' detectives, attractive young women who do his bidding. They are served by a eunuch, Boswell, and their main characteristic is that they can fit in anywhere. Each week they go underground into no matter what situation: the violent world of drug lords and motorcycle gangs, a formal reception for the state governor, a suburban high school, water skiing with a mobster, rural shacks and urban slums, etcetera. Wherever they go, they are dressed perfectly for the part, their speech and manners so well adapted to the setting that no one would suspect that they are not completely *at home*. To the extent that *Charley's Angels* reproduces this crucial aspect of classic *film noir*, perhaps the series deserves recognition as a derivative, loony genre: 'ditzy *noir*'.

8. Žižek, p. 163.

9. This thesis is fully dependent on theoretical formulations provided by Juliet Flower MacCannell's *The Regime of the Brother: After the Patriarchy* (London and New York: Routledge, 1991) and the work of Slavoj Žižek.

10. Juliet MacCannell, pp. 11–13.

11. In these remarks I rely extensively on Juliet Flower MacCannell's analysis of the two films in 'Fraternité et égalité: pour les femmes dans une culture globale', *Diplômées*, no. 162 (September 1992), pp. 166–75.

12. Žižek suggests that the 'contingent and nomadic framing' of scenes in *film noir* situates it like an Edward Hopper painting to reveal the inside and outside at once. To better understand the opposition *noir*/homeless, it is necessary to sustain examination of the unusual moment in *film noir*, its glimpses into the interior of allegedly normal homes and communities. Methodologically, there is no *noir* device better suited for this purpose than Hitchcock's *Shadow of a Doubt*.

13. In the following paragraphs I return to a problem addressed earlier in *Empty Meeting Grounds: The Tourist Papers* (London and New York: Routledge, 1992), pp. 105–13.

NOTES ON CONTRIBUTORS

.

JANET BERGSTROM is Vice Chair of the Department of Film and Television at UCLA. A founding editor of *Camera Obscura*, she worked with the journal for over fifteen years. The author of a number of articles on Lang, Murnau, and Weimar cinema, she recently curated a retrospective of the films of Asta Nielsen for the Musée d'Orsay in Paris. She is currently working on two projects on French cinema: a monograph on Chantal Ackerman and a study of post-war French *film noir*.

JOAN COPJEC is Director of the Center for the Study of Psychoanalysis and Culture and a professor of English and Comparative Literature at the University at Buffalo. She was until recently Senior Editor of *October*, working with the journal from 1981 to 1992. Her book *Read My Desire: Lacan against the Historicists* is forthcoming from MIT Press.

ELIZABETH COWIE, Senior Lecturer in Film Studies at the University of Kent, Canterbury, was a founding editor of *m/f*, a journal of feminist theory, and is editor, along with Parveen Adams, of *The Woman in Question* (Cambridge, MA: MIT Press/*October* Books and London: Verso, 1990). She has a book forthcoming from Macmillan on film theory, psychoanalysis and feminist critiques.

MANTHIA DIAWARA is Director of Africana Studies at New York University where he is a professor of film and literature. He is the author of many articles on theory and film and his book *African Cinema: Politics and Culture* was recently published by Indiana University Press (1992).

FREDRIC JAMESON is Director of the Center for Critical Theory and Professor of Comparative Literature at Duke University. Among his numerous books, the most recent are *Postmodernism, or The Cultural Logic of Late Capitalism* (London: Verso, 1991) and *The Geopolitical Aesthetic: Cinema and Space in the World System* (Bloomington: Indiana University Press and London: British Film Institute, 1992).

DEAN MACCANNELL is Professor of Community Studies and Development at the University of California, Davis and Adjunct Professor of Sociology and Critical Theory at the University of California, Irvine. He is the author of *The Tourist: A New Theory of the Leisure Class* (New York, Schocken, 1976) and *Empty Meeting Grounds* (New York and London: Routledge, 1992).

FRED PFEIL is the author of *Another Tale to Tell: Politics and Narrative in Postmodern Culture* (London: Verso, 1990) and of *White Guys: Studies in Postmodern Power, Choice and Change*, which is forthcoming from Verso. He is a professor of English at Trinity College, Hartford, Connecticut.

DAVID REID is the editor, most recently, of *Sex, Death, and God in L.A.* (New York: Pantheon, 1992). He is currently completing work on a book about New York City and the American empire from 1945 to 1950, to be titled *The Brazen Age.*

MARC VERNET teaches film at the University of Paris III and at the American Film Program in Paris. Coauthor, along with Jacques Aumont, Alain Bergala and Michel Marie, of *Aesthetics of Film* (Austin: University of Texas, 1992), he has published widely in French and English on film subjects, including several important articles on *film noir*.

JAYNE L. WALKER is the author of *The Making of a Modernist: Gertrude Stein from Three Lives to Tender Buttons* (Amherst: University of Massachusetts Press). She has taught at Cornell and the University of California, Berkeley and teaches currently in the Writing Program at the University of California, Davis.

SLAVOJ ŽIŽEK is a researcher at the Institute of Sociology at the University of Ljubljana. He has published several books in Slovene, French and English including, most recently, *Enjoy Your Symptom: Jacques Lacan In Hollywood and Out* (New York and London: Routledge, 1992) and, as editor, *Everything You Always Wanted to Know About Lacan But Were Afraid to Ask Hitchcock* (London and New York: Verso, 1992).